Caution and Cooperation

NEW STUDIES IN U.S. FOREIGN RELATIONS

Mary Ann Heiss, editor

Caution and Cooperation

The American Civil War
in British-American Relations

Phillip E. Myers

The Kent State University Press
Kent, Ohio

© 2008 by The Kent State University Press, Kent, Ohio 44242

ALL RIGHTS RESERVED

Library of Congress Catalog Card Number 2008001522

ISBN 978-0-87338-945-7

Manufactured in the United States of America

LIBRARY OF CONGRESS CATALOGING-IN-PUBLICATION DATA

Myers, Phillip E.

Caution and cooperation : the American Civil War in British-American relations /
Phillip E. Myers.

p.   cm. — (New studies in U.S. foreign relations)

Includes bibliographical references and index.

ISBN 978-0-87338-945-7 (hardcover : alk. paper) ∞

1. United States—Foreign relations—Great Britain. 2. Great Britain—Foreign relations—
United States. 3. United States—Foreign relations—1861–1865.

4. United States—History—Civil War, 1861–1865—Foreign public opinion, British.

5. Public opinion—Great Britain—History—19th century. I. Title.

E183.8.G7M94 2008

327.73041—dc22   2008001522

British Library Cataloging-in-Publication data are available.

12 11 10 09 08   5 4 3 2 1

To Cathy, Andrew, Sarah, and Sonja

Contents

Acknowledgments

At the University of Iowa long ago, professors Laurence Lafore and Lawrence E. Gelfand, my dissertation advisers, instilled in me not to forsake the challenges of research and writing about international relations in large and British-American relations in the eighteenth and nineteenth centuries specifically. At Western Kentucky University where I work Professors Robert Haynes and Marion Lucas offered helpful comments early in the process. Early in the project, Dr. John Beeler of the University of Alabama generously loaned me microfilm of the Alexander Milne Papers, which he is editing (the first volume is published). I cannot thank him enough. Dr. Duncan Andrew Campbell of the University of Swansea read successive drafts of several chapters and offered encouragement as the project took shape. Terry Manns, my colleague in research administration who is at California State University at Sacramento, dutifully read a draft of this work when it was twice as long, picked out the weakest sections, and said, "I could tell that you were tired when you wrote them." I appreciate his encouragement and collegiality over the years. Selina Langford and Debra Day of Interlibrary Loan and Dr. Brian Coutts and Professor Jack Montgomery of the Western Kentucky University Libraries procured research materials for me throughout the project. I am especially indebted to Dr. Mary Ann Heiss of Kent State University and Dr. Lesley J. Gordon of the University of Akron for their reviews of the manuscript. Finally, I am most appreciative of the guidance and promptness of Joanna Hildebrand Craig, editor-in-chief at Kent State University Press and Mary D. Young, the project editor. It was fitting, but entirely coincidental, that I was sitting in my sixteenth floor hotel room in Québec City looking across at the government buildings and part of the fortress when Joanna's email message came announcing interest in the book. Who could have selected a more reflective place for that moment? I further appreciate the unanimous vote of the Editorial Board of the Press to publish it.

I am grateful to Laurence Clarendon to use information from the Clarendon Papers at the Bodleian Library, Oxford University. The Trustees of the Palmerston Papers at Southampton University and The Crown permitted me to cite from the Palmerston Papers. I am also appreciative of the Syndics of Cambridge University Library, the British National Portrait Gallery, the Library of Congress, and the Naval Historical Foundation to use images in their care.

Last but not least I must acknowledge the patience that my family displayed throughout this decade-long process; and the hours that my wife, Cathy, put into ordering and "brushing up" the images on her computer.

Having said all of this, I accept responsibility for any errors or oversights in this book.

Illustrations

Introduction

Realism and Private Diplomacy

The most earnest task confronting British and American statesmen when the American Civil War broke out in April 1861 was to stave off an international war. Fortunately, the two Anglo-Saxon nations had enjoyed nearly a half-century of peace since 1815, and in 1861 British-American relations were more dependable than at any time since American independence. But they were also ridden with distrust. Neither Britain's shaky Liberal government that was still shy of completing two years in office nor America's new Republican government wanted the American civil conflict to make them enemies. Neither power (nor anyone else) had any idea of the course the Civil War would take, and both decided to adhere to the traditional policies of caution and cooperation.

Despite the desire of both powers for peace, the Civil War seriously threatened relations between the two. Hard-pressed Union leaders believed on scanty evidence that many British upper-, middle-, and working-class subjects were pro-South despite being adamantly opposed to slavery. Ultimately, so Unionists heard, pro-Southerners argued that an independent Confederate state would eventually abolish slavery and become a modern nation. As a result, Unionists' fears that Britain would recognize Confederate independence strained relations.

There were further strains that have caused historians to believe in the possibility of an Anglo-American war during this time period. The Union's aim for self-preservation without announcing that emancipation was a primary war aim until January 1, 1863, made many Britons believe that the Republicans were turning on a poor but proud South in a most imperious manner. When the shooting began, newly elected president Abraham Lincoln announced that his primary war aim was preserving the Union, which was beyond the comprehension of many British subjects and their leaders who had philosophically supported European national independence movements against the conservative powers and now saw a parallel with the South's secession from the Union. Many aristocratic leaders had always believed in the Union's inevitable demise. They now argued that the

1

Union's simplest way out of the sectional crisis was to the let the South have its independence, because they refused to believe that reunification was possible.

Conversely, although the numbers are just as imprecise, the Union had a respectable group of British supporters. Because the British government never detected that public opinion swayed significantly enough to take sides, it remained neutral, just as it had in the recent successful Italian and Greek national unification movements. The scrambled nature of public opinion about the American Civil War buttressed nonintervention and the continuation of peaceful relations.

There were obvious reasons for nonintervention. The traditions of antimartial spirit in Britain and the United States, retrenchment from big military budgets, Anglo-American commercial and financial connections, and self-proclaimed isolation from Europe since 1815 caused a cautious and realistic foreign policy that was the opposite of the punitive realism that was becoming ascendant in Europe. The European balance of power changed with the revivification of France during the 1850s and the early Civil War years. It was further amended with Bismarck's advent in Prussia from 1862 and Prussia's aggressions in Europe during the Civil War. (Prussia was pro-Union.) The upshot was that, as the Civil War grew more protracted, British diplomatic power diminished in Europe and it became more isolated from influencing the conservative powers than at any other time in the century. It could not afford a war with the Union before or after 1861 in the popular, economic, or strategic senses. Realistic British leaders remained aloof from actual or potential conflicts on both sides of the Atlantic Ocean. Any war in which Britain might find itself a combatant threatened to disrupt its unprecedented prosperity and complicate the worsening situations in Europe and in North America. Pinched by the international instability, Britain avoided conflict to develop its free-trade empire and to maintain its traditional isolationist foreign policy that had raised great industrial and imperial wealth at little military cost.

American foreign policy paralleled that of Britain in many ways. The United States followed the British policy of isolation from European affairs and by 1861 was building a transcontinental and global empire by peaceful means. It needed British financial and naval assistance in China and Japan, where antebellum cooperation to gain trading outposts continued through the Civil War and beyond. These complementary foreign policies, commerce, and investments underlined the mutual desire to continue peaceful relations.

Despite the mutual peaceful attitude and the Union's domestic predicament, a haze of uncertainty still surrounds the true course of Anglo-American relations during the Civil War era. It is helpful to examine the chances of war between the two cousins, and a long view is needed to clarify this vital issue. Chapter 1 reviews the trends in relations after 1815 to show the growth of a rapprochement by 1861. Chapter 2 shows how antebellum cooperation remained the strongest trend during the first six months of the conflict, and to tell a longer story, into 1864 because Britain refused to overturn its traditional posture of nonintervention.

Chapter 3 shows how the *Trent* affair of November and December 1861, commonly believed to be the event that brought the Union and Britain closest to war, was less threatening than believed when seen against decisions since 1815 and the dependable methods of cooperative problem solving that had underpinned those decisions. Moreover, the outcomes of the affair are discussed into the first half of 1862 to show how quickly relations returned to peaceful traditions. Within the long span of relations, the *Trent* affair was pivotal because its resolution, through private diplomacy and good sense, released tensions accumulated during the Civil War's first eight months and kept relations on a cooperative track for the rest of the conflict. Neither power wanted to repeat the scare and, in Britain's case, the expense that it caused. Seen in a positive light, the affair proved the peaceful, noninterventionist aims of both governments and cleared the diplomatic system to manage issues. To illustrate this mutual resolve, Chapter 4 discusses examples of cooperation on land and sea during the pivotal year of 1862.

With caution and cooperation predominating early in the conflict, Chapter 5 demonstrates that any war fever that existed on either side of the Atlantic was lanced by the fall of 1862 when the British cabinet's intervention debate reaffirmed cooperation rather than intervention. Chapter 6 shows how Lincoln met his own cabinet crisis during the same time period, as Radical Republicans pressed to harden the war effort and oust Seward, if not Lincoln himself. Like Palmerston, Lincoln had to wend his way out of his own cabinet crisis. Taken together, these two chapters show that pressures on both cabinet and chief executives caused parallel reactions and reinforced cooperation. Somewhat like the military scare the *Trent* affair raised, the rebellion within the Republican Party made both governments realize more than before why it was important to support the other in power to uphold transatlantic peace. The work of Palmerston and Lincoln in maintaining their cabinets made each body more aware of the criticality of supporting the other's staying in power because of the workable mutual relationship that by now had proven worthy of withstanding tensions. The majority of both cabinets refused to consider an international war, and the nucleus of these cabinets remained intact throughout the rest of the Civil War.

With a middle diplomatic and political ground reached by the beginning of 1863, the next six chapters show the improvement of relations through the war's climax in April 1865. Chapters 7 and 8 depict the explicit mutual support in 1863 and 1864. Chapter 9 analyzes the weaknesses of Confederate diplomacy and the impact they had on the easing of British-American tensions while tensions between Britain and the Confederacy increased. Chapter 10 shows how Britain and the United States cooperated to end the slave trade and also maintained commercial partnerships in the Far East. Chapter 11 discloses how quickly the United

States returned to a peacetime military and commerce that depended on good relations with Britain. Chapter 12 shows how diplomacy covered the return to normal relations. I argue that the end of the war was accompanied by a stronger desire for a comprehensive treaty to settle all differences, some of which extended from as far back as the declaration of American independence. Chapter 12 shows that in 1871 the two countries acknowledged the cautious and cooperative relations with the comprehensive Treaty of Washington and the unprecedented international arbitrations that it spawned. Together, Britain and the United States set the precedent for peaceful solutions while Europe dissolved into war.

These events were the culmination of the course that relations had taken after 1815 and demonstrated that the Civil War was not as unique and threatening to relations as historians have believed. I believe there is a strong argument that for these reasons the Civil War was contained by the contingent traditions. The conflict failed to dictate a change, or watershed, in the traditional tendencies of caution and cooperation that had anchored relations in peace. In other words, the consistency of diplomatic management after 1815 was manifested in Civil War diplomacy rather than a new and dangerous track. The fact that the arbitrations of the early 1870s were an example of dispassionate settlement reflects the tone of relations before and during the Civil War. The arbitrations were unique when compared with contemporary European fighting solutions and underlined the British-American desire for peace at all costs.

Chapter 12 concludes by explaining how Britain and the United States stood by each other during the European wars of the 1860s and early 1870s with neither taking advantage of the other's predicament: Britain supported Reconstruction, and the United States made no attempt to embarrass Britain's weak standing in Europe. This kind of mutual support was seen many times prior to the Civil War. For example, wartime disputes were either resolved or held in abeyance along with unresolved antebellum issues until there was a mutual political need for a general settlement. Just as the British had not taken advantage of American prosecution of the Mexican War, neither had the United States taken advantage of Canadian political weaknesses and the British prosecution of the Crimean War. Britain refused to embarrass the United States as American political parties weakened and fell apart under the pressures of the sectional crisis, and the United States refused to embarrass Britain in Europe during and after the Civil War.

Because I argue that the Anglo-American peace set in more deeply than previously as a result of the Civil War, my conclusions differ from existing interpretations. Historians have tended to see Civil War diplomacy constrained by the beginning and end of the military event with little consideration of antebellum or postwar diplomatic contingencies.[1] Yet the Civil War was not a historic watershed or obstacle in relations, because past cooperation held up and grew stronger. Put another way, on the diplomatic level, the Civil War continued decades of private conflict management and resolution. Thus this study looks for the evidence of the growing cooperation not only during the Civil War but from Lee's surrender at Appomattox on 9 April 1865 to the Treaty of Washington of 8 May 1871, where existing studies have fallen short. This observation raises the question that if traditional arguments that the Civil War left Anglo-American relations sour enough to break up, why did relations persist in their usual manner of cautious diplomacy, cooperation, and negotiations during that six-year interim and result in the most comprehensive treaty of the century? And why do studies that do consider the contingencies conclude that the Civil War's end implied dependable relations?[2]

This work's contention that the dependable prewar relationship was briefly interrupted but not permanently disrupted by the Civil War runs contrary to the past three decades of histories written on both sides of the Atlantic that have viewed Civil War diplomacy as self-contained and paid little attention to antebellum or postwar relations. This traditional approach implies that relations were near collapse during the first two years of the war. But, as will be shown, statesmen cooperatively employed past methods to manage disputes from the outset of fighting into the fall of 1862 when chances of British intervention waned in the minds of the British cabinet and Confederate leaders, and British-Union cooperation intensified. Indeed, British interventionists were a distinct minority in cabinet and parliament in the antebellum era and throughout the Civil War. This consistency strengthened after 1865. Moreover, Parliament and the public were never enthused about intervention. Despite their roles as the number two and three ministers, at the critical time from late September through early November 1862, Prime Minister Henry John Temple, third viscount Palmerston, ultimately ignored the interventionist desires of Lord John Russell, the foreign secretary, and chancellor of the exchequer William Ewart Gladstone, the only two important ministerial advocates of intervention. (Even they did not want to upset relations, however, but conceived of an intervention to stop the bloodshed and their fears of an incipient slave insurrection.) Palmerston's adept indifference maintained his relationship with Russell and his leadership of the declining Whig element in the Liberal Party. His letting Russell criticize Gladstone for the latter's famous Newcastle speech of 7 October 1862 declaring that the South had made a nation, broke up the two interventionists and caused both of them to support Palmerston's anti-interventionism. Meanwhile, there was no chance, short of a climactic Confederate military victory, for them to gain adherents. Lee's retreat from Gettysburg and Grant's conquest of Vicksburg in early July 1863 seemed to ensure a Union victory. If Palmerston lost office, Russell and Gladstone knew that they would fall also. Political ambition and intervention were antagonistic.

Moreover, all three of them, especially Palmerston, thought ill of the South as an ally because of slavery. Despite all that historians have correctly written about the prime minister's animosity toward Americans, his method had always been deterrence and indifference, and his refusal to rile the North implied his superior need for peace with the despised "republican mob" to maintain his power. His belief that "Britain had no eternal friends and no eternal enemies but only eternal interests" made him "the great nineteenth-century practitioner of realpolitik." He lived for "expediency rather than principle; and he proved himself capable of having second thoughts on decisions that bore great risk."[3] No better example exists than his refusal to approve of intervention in the fall of 1862.

Indeed, the argument for Anglo-American relations congealing can be seen through Confederate foreign policy. The South gave up on British intervention by late 1862, if not earlier. It was aware that nonintervention was the attitude that pervaded the British cabinet. It was chagrined that Britain recognized the Union blockade of the chief Southern ports before the blockade of those portals was effective. The government in Richmond recognized Russell's cooperation with the Union on the most explosive disputes, and rebel leaders knew that he showed more cooperation than interventionism in 1862. Measured against his refusal to truck with Confederate diplomats, his brief push for intervention in the fall of 1862, and his overall desire for peace with the Union, Russell's behavior makes him a most ironic statesman of the Civil War era.

We must credit President Jefferson Davis and some of his top field commanders, such as Robert E. Lee, with figuring out Russell's ironic stance by the time the war was little more than a year old. The South was aware that in 1862, a transitional year to improved British-Union relations, Britain's policy toward the Civil War merged with Lincoln's steadfast desire for peaceful international affairs. The persistence of the mutual desire to cooperate on the diplomatic high road continued antebellum habits, while the South's inability to muster a cooperative foreign policy with the European powers contributed to its acute isolation in the war's last years.

France was the third power in the nonintervention equation that must be integrated with the story of cooperation. Instead of accomplishing its aim of breaking up British-American relations, France's actions were another significant reason that inspired the two governments to cooperate. France and Britain had been rivals for decades. British leaders feared a surprise cross-channel invasion from the 1840s onward. The specter of another Napoleon at the helm of the French state became reality in 1852 with the accession of Louis Napoleon as Emperor Napoleon III. This imperious ruler soon became the most mistrusted power in Europe. French relations with Britain and the Union faded throughout the Civil War concomitant with the growing bad feeling between Britain and the South and the recuperation of British-Union relations. These developments brought the British and the Union closer for a number of reasons. The opportunistic Napoleon III awkwardly tried to use the Union's distractions to push Britain to recognize the independence of the Confederacy while he established a French monarchy in Mexico. He tried to frighten the British into believing that Union victory meant the subsequent conquest of Canada and Mexico. He played a treacherous game that antagonized all of the players, including his foreign ministers, and his antics in Europe produced similar results until his defeat by Prussia in 1870, the same year that Britain and the United States seriously prepared for comprehensive treaty making. Throughout this period Britain became more defenseless in Europe, and the United States needed British financial assistance and commerce to fund the Civil War debt. By looking at the British-American relationship in this way, one can begin to see that there were many more reasons for caution and cooperation.

Britain's nonintervention ultimately led to a comprehensive treaty with the United States. Perhaps the largest point to be made regarding this issue is the quickness with which the major British-American treaty of the nineteenth century was made after the Civil War ended in 1865. In 1871, they finally resolved longstanding and Civil War disputes. The timing of this negotiation presents a compelling reason for the extension of the antebellum rapprochement into the Civil War and its aftermath. The treaty led to, a year later, an international arbitration that was characterized by mutual accommodation to settle the *Alabama* claims, which was the most potentially destructive dispute that resulted from the Civil War. The Treaty of Washington culminated nearly a century of diplomacy, reinforced the rapprochement, and kept relations on a steady course of friendship and understanding throughout the rest of the century and beyond.

1

The Antebellum Rapprochement

The growth of cooperation between America and Britain after 1815 provides a clearer understanding about the activities and outcomes of the British-American relationship before, during, and after the Civil War. Britain and the United States stopped competing militarily for advantages in North America after 1815, and the absence of military maneuvers and the discovery of using diplomacy to settle disputes enabled relations to grow into a rapprochement from 1815 to 1861.[1] The British and American governments used similar principles of diplomacy because each had much more to lose than to gain from war. They refused to intervene when either got into international trouble, shelved disagreements that they could not resolve, and shrouded their dislike for one another to maintain peace. When they negotiated, they negotiated in private, out of the purview of public opinion. Personal communication was "more significant than official channels. Dispatches, memoranda, and reports undeniably exercised great influence, but personal letters and conversations had an enormous impact. Private correspondence from a friend not only appeared more trustworthy, it had the stamp of candor."[2] The fact that provocative disputes were contained for decades attests to the mutual will not to fight. Repeatedly, diplomacy absolved the cousins of their mutual antagonisms and ensured peaceful settlements. To find the basis of this peaceful diplomacy, one has to dig through the bluster that was often in the news and look precisely at the actions of the governments' views of national self-interest. Older histories support this view: "It may be doubted whether the various questions dealt with and settled between the two great English-speaking nations from the [Rush-Bagot] Treaty of 1817 . . . can be equalled for general sanity and fairness by any similar number of agreements made between any other Powers since history began. Nor, as far as definite acts are concerned, have the relations between any two nations ever been at once so intimate and so free from serious injury to one another."[3]

In *Great Britain and the American Civil War,* Ephraim Douglas Adams advised for this longer view to explain the dynamics that charged relations. Although he hesitated to analyze why peace was the strongest characteristic in relations, he saw the value of the antebellum contingencies in explaining why the Civil War did not shatter relations. He implied that the peaceful destiny of both governments stemmed from cooperation. He did not believe that the Civil War was "an isolated and unique situation, but that the conditions preceding that situation—some of them lying far back in the relations of the two nations—had a vital bearing on British policy and opinion when the crisis arose." Adams noted that "understanding the elements that influenced British perceptions of America during the mid-nineteenth century requires looking back to the end of the 1820s."[4]

The mutual desire for peace stemmed from the foreign policy of both governments resting on the same philosophical structure, what Walter McDougall terms "unilateralism" and "minimalism." Unilateralism meant that both governments eschewed formal alliances. Minimalism meant that each government wanted to gain maximum economic and strategic benefits abroad without aggression and at the lowest cost possible. These two strategies also meant that in the four decades before the Civil War British governments followed a realistic policy toward the United States instead of warring over disputes because the benefits of peace were too great to lose. The United States thought the same way: the rewards of a cooperative relationship were stronger than those of war. By the Compromise of 1846, Britain realized that the balance of power in North America had shifted to the United States, but that it was more important for Britain to surrender this costly stance than contest it. Britain could surrender without loss of honor, and it was hesitant to anger its best trading and investment partner. By the mid-nineteenth century the huge British banking houses led by the Baring brothers, the Rothschilds, and the American George Peabody and Company were at the height of their control over the Atlantic economy. These financiers knew how to build wealth, and the United States was critical in their pursuits. Historian Jay Sexton points out that American foreign indebtedness grew to unprecedented proportions in the twenty-five years before the Civil War. Thus it is no wonder that the Barings and their American agents such as Daniel Webster were forces in maintaining the diplomatic peace, to the extent that "ninety percent of the United States' foreign indebtedness in 1861 was of British origin."[5]

Despite what E. D. Adams wrote about the rapprochement's being detectable from the 1820s, this shift to dependable relations can be detected as early as before the War of 1812. This war was an anomaly in relations, and the British had tried in vain to stop it in June 1812 but were too late. Relations improved after the war, as evidenced by both governments' getting trade back on track, and ambiguous and incomplete agreements became permanent manifestations of the cooperative relationship. Britain needed the United States as an export and investment base, and it needed peace to import American cotton to keep its textile industries booming and to protect its weak North American colonies of Canada and the Maritimes

(Newfoundland, Nova Scotia, New Brunswick, and Prince Edward Island). Bilateral trade was restored by agreement in 1815. Signs of rapprochement continued in 1817 when the Rush-Bagot Agreement demilitarized the Great Lakes to remove that border region from conflict. The agreement stood as the first reciprocal naval disarmament "in the history of international relations." Probably just as important in the antebellum decades was the wide-ranging and practical Convention of 1818 that further eased potential border tensions by demarcating the Canadian-American boundary along the 49th parallel from the Lake of the Woods to the Rockies. It called for joint occupation of the Oregon Territory west of the Rockies to the Pacific, and it was renewed in 1826 and continued until 1846. It also enabled New Englanders to fish in British colonial inshore waters where the best fishing was found; and they could dry and transship their catches from colonial shores. Even before the Convention of 1818, Britain refused to commit resources to the Northwest Coast, an area rich in furs and strategic locations for the Royal Navy to operate and support commercial operations into the Far East. In the decades that followed, conflicts were resolved by the mutual policy of conciliation and cooperation.[6]

These actions show that Anglo-American leaders worked to maximize their commonalities and shelve their differences. Both were each other's best trading and investment partner, experienced industrial growth, and had expansionist goals. Both experienced social dislocations, with immigrants in the United States spilling into the eastern cities and into the farmlands of the Midwest and the far West, and in Britain, with farmhands dislocated into the teeming industrial cities by mechanization and the promise of higher wages. In addition, both governments were extremely suspicious of French pretensions in Europe and abroad. The Anglo-French rivalry remained after 1815, became pronounced by the 1830s, and grew apace over the next two decades. By 1861 the two powers were involved in an intense rivalry capped by the first modern arms race over ironclad ship construction and British fear of a surprise cross-channel invasion by French steam vessels no longer controlled by wind and waves.

Furthermore, at no time throughout the antebellum period could Britain withstand a two-front war against France and the United States. To guard against this eventuality, Britain and the United States advanced transatlantic commerce and popular democracy, both of which strengthened the common bond of democracy. The 1830s brought unprecedented foreign investments into the United States. Few Americans resisted this impetus to support the transportation and industrial revolutions. By 1838, foreigners had invested $110 million in American businesses. The ties between Britain and the United States were strengthened in this way because the huge increases in investments in American development showed that the United States could be trusted in fiscal matters. Baring Brothers spent huge sums on lobbying, propaganda, and its network of American agents, such as Webster, but also on journalists, politicians, and religious leaders.[7]

Other mutually beneficial movements occurred during this time. As the abolitionist movement flowered in the United States and took a strong hold on the Whig and then Republican parties, British antislavery legislation triumphed and the franchise was modestly extended. In the 1840s and 1850s North and Central American boundary settlements succeeded through British and American compromise that enabled the completion of American transcontinental expansion and mutual commerce in Central America. It is unsurprising that British Liberal and Conservative ministries sent leading financiers to Washington to negotiate these treaties partly to deflect the pressure of public opinion.[8] Whether the territory negotiated was north or south of the American borders, the treaties were negotiated privately and quickly out of a desire to maintain calm relations. By the early 1840s both governments were aware that diplomatic disputes were not "in the interests of either British capitalists or their American debtors."[9]

As already suggested, Palmerston was the key player that prevented Britain from going to war to solve the various American problems in the antebellum period. What was it about his career that made his blustering always stop short of war with the United States? From 1807 through 1865, he served as war minister, foreign secretary, home secretary, and prime minister. As a young administrator he learned about the realistic diplomacy that the British foreign secretaries of the day practiced to keep the peace. This realism helped to create the Convention of 1818 that settled boundary and fishery disputes until clearer agreements were possible. Palmerston unsurprisingly pursued a mild American policy during his first tour at the Foreign Office from 1830 to 1841, and President Andrew Jackson and his successors generally reciprocated his work. In 1835, Palmerston wrote that the United States and Britain were "joined by Community of Interests, & by the Bonds of Kindred." Over the next two years he refused to encourage Texas independence or block its entry into the Union. Moreover, he stated, "that as far as our Commercial Interests are concerned we should have no objections to see the whole of Mexico belong to the United States." In 1839, he wrote that "Commercial interests [with the United States] . . . are so Strong . . . that it would require a very extraordinary state of things to bring an actual war." He deepened the friendship with the United States during his last five years as foreign secretary.[10]

In the 1840s, with an even more peaceful foreign secretary, the earl of Aberdeen, Britain privately ceded huge amounts of North American territory to the United States. Secretary of state Daniel Webster and Lord Ashburton, who was a member of the Baring family but had renounced his American investments, negotiated the Maine boundary treaty privately and quickly in Washington in mid-1842. British financiers did not want a war over the disputed boundary. The Rothschild's American agent, August Belmont, wrote to the home office in London that "England, in a war with her largest debtor, the consumer of her manufacturers, has all to lose and nothing to gain." If negotiations were unsuccessful and a battle of national honor ensued, British investments would be completely suspended, trade would be reduced, and a run on banks might occur. Moreover, successful negotiations would increase American security rates on the London Stock Exchange. Webster (also a Baring's agent) and Ashburton both agreed, as Webster remarked, "No difference shall be permitted seriously to endanger the maintenance of peace with England."[11]

Amid these pressures, the Webster-Ashburton negotiations showed that Britain and the United States respected each other's intelligence and power, as they ignored traditional protocols and calmly negotiated a complex treaty concerning twelve thousand square miles bordering Maine, New Hampshire, New York, and Vermont. In what was becoming commonplace in the Anglo-American diplomatic tradition, they ensured that the provisions were not written until after the talks, kept few minutes, and exchanged few notes. The treaty tranquilized the Canadian-American border and provided joint operations against the slave trade (which the United States did not uphold until after the Civil War began). It also ended the illegal operations of groups who resented Britain, such as the Patriot Hunters, a secret society of Canadian rebels and their American supporters who disturbed relations during the Canadian rebellion against the mother country in the late 1830s. The treaty's extradition provisions prohibited flights for safety across the border. Further cooperation came to the chagrin of Maine's leaders, from Webster's ceding territory along the contested Maine and New Brunswick border to Britain. This cession of territory was the only one made in any American treaty. With that treaty American leaders realized that Britain preferred not to fight about remaining territorial disputes to the extent that the treaty did not have to be precise in all respects, another common outcome. For example, Webster dropped demands for reparation for escaped slaves in return for a British pledge not to interfere with American ships brought into British ports that might be commandeered by slaves, as in the *Creole* case. Moreover, both parties expressed regret to each other over the awkwardness created in relations by the *Caroline* and McLeod disputes a few years before that had resulted in the death of an American at the hands of the British. As Jay Sexton writes, this treaty was created because it was at this time (and other times as well) more prudent to cover up the sore spots in relations than to negotiate a substantial treaty that would have proved impossible to accomplish.[12]

The Webster-Ashburton Treaty of 20 August 1842 proved to be a model to use in realizing cooperation over other sore spots in relations. A few years later, as the "Oregon question" began to fester, Boston author and diplomat A. H. Everett wrote President James K. Polk that Britain would "acquiesce" and negotiate an "equitable adjustment." He reminded the president what British leaders had already certified: that trade was the basis for British foreign policy, and trade with the United States was worth more to it than all of its other commercial connections. Everett concluded that the abuse of the United States by the British press should not be perceived as critical to relations because the British government realized the "absolute political necessity, of entertaining friendly intercourse with us."[13]

Polk did not heed Everett's advice, however. The president went the way of the Democrats and blustered for "fifty-four forty or fight," while emitting his famous manifesto that "the only way to treat John Bull was to look him straight in the eye." Secret lobbying by the Barings and Sen. Daniel Webster's call for a compromise border at the 49th parallel gave the president more to think about. Conservative foreign secretary Aberdeen supported this plan, which was published in London journals. Moreover, Britain's practical needs overrode forceful solutions. Both governments wanted to lower tariff barriers to increase the mutual economic benefits. For immediate purposes, Britain could import more staples from the United States to alleviate the plight of the starving Irish in the midst of the potato famine. American leaders were thoughtful about the challenge of funding a war against their largest creditor.[14]

In a fashion reminiscent of the Webster-Ashburton Treaty, the Oregon Treaty of 1846 was negotiated just as rapidly and privately in Washington in June 1846. In terms of the extent of the territorial cession to the United States, it far outdistanced the Webster-Ashburton Treaty. The United States gained more than 500,000 square miles of contested territory in the Pacific Northwest. In support of Everett's prognosis, Palmerston proclaimed "that nothing could be more calamitous to both countries, than a war between Great Britain and the United States." This treaty too was imprecise, with the water boundary along the 49th parallel extending through Puget Sound left unsettled because neither side could agree to lose control of the strategically located Haro Strait and deep water ports of the region that divided the San Juan Islands from Vancouver Island. As the natural boundaries of the United States began to be realized through these treaties, British statesmen and financiers showed that American Manifest Destiny, thought by prideful American leaders and midwestern Democrats to be a predetermined, God-given right and a symbol of national honor worth fighting for, was not as important as expanding finance and maintaining peace. As Jay Sexton points out, "There can be little question that the larger financial and commercial interdependence of Britain and the United States that they embodied connected the two nations to such an extent that leaders on both sides of the Atlantic desired to avoid war at all costs." With the Mexican War brewing and thirty Royal Navy ships dispatched to North American waters as a deterrent to war, Polk opted for compromise over Oregon. As Sexton summarizes, "for the second time in less than five years, cool heads prevailed during a diplomatic crisis."[15]

These cool heads continued to dominate relations with the tensions that the Crimean War of the mid-1850s threatened to unleash in British-American relations. With the British government distracted fighting Russia in the Near East, expansionist America took the opportunity to steal a march on Britain in the Western Hemisphere. Nothing happened as a result, because the expansionist focus of the United States was southward and westward, not northward, and it was blurred beyond achieving its natural frontiers that had been accomplished by the Oregon Treaty of 1846 and the Mexican War. In keeping with its traditional policy of not intervening in European affairs, the United States refused Russia's requests to fit out privateers against the Royal Navy and British and Canadian merchant ships, and Anglo-American commerce continued to flourish. After several years of tragedy on the windswept Crimea, Britain and its ally France won, primarily due to French efforts. The war nearly bankrupted Britain. After the war, amid growing rivalry with France and Russia, Britain exercised more characteristics of unilateralism and minimalism abroad with a foreign policy that continued to emphasize deterrence, nonintervention, and military retrenchment. In addition to cooperation in Central and North America, Britain and the United States collaborated to enhance commercial self-interests in China and Japan.

The Crimean War caused one problem that threatened the British-American rapprochement, but it also showed that no matter how piqued Americans became, like the British, they preferred diplomacy to fighting. In this event, unilateralism and minimalism kept the cousins out of war with each other in 1855–56 during the Crampton affair. John Crampton was the veteran British minister to the United States. He was considered friendly to British-American cooperation and enjoyed a successful diplomatic career. But the huge losses of the British Army in the Crimea brought orders from Whitehall to recruit troops clandestinely in the United States and ship them out through Nova Scotia in violation of the American Foreign Enlistment Act of 1818. Crampton was zealous about establishing a recruitment organization. His recruitment ring was quickly discovered, as was his duplicity. At Prime Minister Palmerston's behest, Foreign Secretary Clarendon, who was "obviously involved in the fiasco up to the hilt," ordered Crampton to cease recruitment in June 1855, but he apparently continued through early August.[16]

Clarendon's cease and desist order was conditioned by British public opinion, which was a growing force in Britain and supported the White House's solution to deflect the situation by recalling Crampton. Sensitive to opinion, Clarendon hastened to recall his minister and express regret to the United States.[17] In November 1855, merchant and manufacturing leaders worried that "unless we bestir ourselves there is no knowing how soon the reckless gambler at the head of affairs [Palmerston] may involve us in senseless quarrels with our Brother across the water." On 2 November Sir George Grey, the home secretary, wrote that "a real quarrel [with the United States] is so unnatural that I trust it will be averted by the good sense . . . of both countries." The liberal Leeds Mercury thought the West Indian fleet was provocative and discouraged the ministry from "considerations which would make hostilities with the United States an evil of the first magnitude." When parliament

returned in February 1856, Radical MP (member of Parliament) John Arthur Roebuck, who had led the committee investigating mismanagement of the Crimean
War, said that war with the United States would be a war "between brethren, the
evils of which would surpass anything that could be imagined. We are the only two
great free nations at the present time." Chancellor of the exchequer William Ewart
Gladstone echoed Roebuck's sentiments on the evening of 4 April, which aroused
an already angry Palmerston. As the session continued, led by Gladstone, the Peelite conservative wing of the Liberal Party supported the Americans, with Sir James
Graham writing to Gladstone on 16 May, "Even if we had a better case, the risk of
War with America is an unpardonable Error."

In this atmosphere, Crampton was dismissed at the end of May 1856, and in
retaliation Palmerston and Clarendon thought about sending American minister
George Mifflin Dallas (who had only arrived) home, but they refrained from revenge because of the opposition of cabinet, Commons, and public opinion. The
liberal middle class believed that American expansion into Central America was
conducive to increasing British commerce and that cooperative relations were
paramount. Palmerston agreed and retreated for the same defensive reason as he
had from opposing the United States over Texas in 1836. Not only did the cabinet
not want trouble with the United States over Crampton, but also on 4 June 1856 Sir
Charles Wood, the first lord of the admiralty, wrote the prime minister that Britain had no interests in Central America and should withdraw peacefully. Russell
told Clarendon that the region was in the U.S. sphere, and "we have no reason to
complain & no business to interfere." Moreover, the moderate Clarendon quit his
hard line and reminded Russell that the British and American naval commanders
cooperated in the Gulf of Mexico to protect their commercial interests and the
territorial settlements.

With these considerations, the usual process of British-American diplomatic
business brought another peaceful conclusion. Palmerston was conciliatory in the
Commons because he wanted to conserve the "many causes of union and so many
mutual interests as between Great Britain and the United States." In this regard,
"Palmerston and Clarendon showed commendable self-restraint."[18] As in the past,
Palmerston repressed his initial bluster. Although infuriated by Washington's behavior, he only pouted and refused to send a replacement to Washington and scoffed at
the American action by elevating Crampton as British ambassador to Spain.

Palmerston was not about to infuriate the United States over such an affair.
There were too many existing issues that required cooperation for the national
self-interests of both countries. Cooperation continued globally from 1857 until
1861 over other potentially divisive issues. A clearer revision of the Clayton-Bulwer
Treaty was concluded. The U.S. Navy assisted the Royal Navy in accessing treaty
ports in China and in opening up Japan to Western commerce. The United States
again refused to take advantage of Britain's woes when the Indian Mutiny rocked

Britain in 1857. In 1858, Britain backed down when the United States government was stirred up by the British capture of slave traders under the American flag. The governments cooperatively shelved the San Juan Water Boundary dispute in Puget Sound in 1859. During the Conservative interlude under Lord Derby, Crampton's replacement, Lord Francis Napier, arrived in Washington in 1858 and fell to work maintaining amicable relations.

As the settlements of these disputes demonstrated, Britain and the United States were in no position militarily to fight in the antebellum period. The Federal army was primarily a weak, unprofessional frontier force of sixteen thousand. The navy consisted of forty wooden ships built primarily for coastal defense. In 1854, Congress quickly stifled attempts by Secretary of War Jefferson Davis to add several new regiments to the army. In both countries the antimartial spirit remained ascendant as it had in Britain for centuries and in the United States since independence. British subjects were uncomfortable with large standing armies despite the assumed French threat. Britain's tragic experience in the Crimea was still fresh in the minds of its subjects. Painfully aware of this experience, strategic planners realized that war takes on its own form no matter how disciplined the state behind it. In executing the Crimean campaign, British leaders had discovered the inadequacies of their war plans, organization, and leadership, as Roebuck's commission reported.[19]

Moreover, war was dangerous to political careers. The war ousted the Aberdeen coalition government and put Palmerston in office as prime minister for the first time to salvage what he could in the Crimea. Yet the aftermath of the Crimean War proved too much for Palmerston, whose patriotism was not convincing enough to move a majority of his cabinet, Parliament, or public opinion to create a superior steam navy to compete with the navy that France was building and to guard against a rumored French invasion. He was further opposed by the queen, both political parties, and the Radical Liberals who represented the industrial interests and a large section of public opinion. Throughout the rest of his political career, Palmerston had to battle retrenchment from military affairs. Both Liberal and Conservative governments existed on small majorities and refused to challenge the electorate and public opinion with military solutions to foreign predicaments. For all of these reasons, nonintervention and military retrenchment peaked by 1861, when Palmerston's second Liberal ministry was two years old.

At the same time, a similar penchant for military retrenchment was evident in the United States. The weak navy is a case in point. Certainly, a threat of war with Britain was not uppermost in the minds of U.S. leaders in 1860 when senators John Sherman and Owen Lovejoy proposed a drastic decrease to the naval appropriations bill that aimed at modernizing a rotting fleet. Lovejoy wanted to liquidate the navy altogether.[20] This retrenchment group had no use for the army and navy amid the growth of production and trade. Rather, Federal policy played on the antimartial spirit of Northern Democrats and conservative Republicans in an attempt to coax the Confederates back into the Union and continued to do so well into the conflict. While President Lincoln struggled to prosecute the war, he could brook no foreign interference and simultaneously had to keep foreign relations serene to prevent intervention. His policy took advantage of the prevailing British-American rapprochement as the conflagration was not enough to overcome unilateralism and minimalism. Despite the challenge of conquering a huge amount of territory and trying to blockade the South's 3,500 miles of coastline, little was done to rejuvenate either service until after Fort Sumter.

Thus, the fate of both countries was tied up in antimilitary tradition. The sweeping revival of British national confidence after the European liberal revolutions of 1848 in France, the German states, Italy, and elsewhere denigrated popular interest in military affairs. In the years before the Crimean War, Britain showed its true national colors of military weakness in imperial and homeland defense. From 1847 to 1852, the attempts of Liberal prime minister Lord John Russell to increase the income tax to keep the forces from reduction did not impress the House of Commons. Russell's proposed tax was abandoned. Public opinion showed up defense advocates Palmerston, Sir John Burgoyne, inspector general of fortifications, and others as "alarmists." People were tired of hearing about invasion scares and national defense weaknesses. In the 1850s Chancellor of the Exchequer Gladstone began his retrenchment agenda with a "military" tax falling most heavily on the middle classes to keep it firmly behind retrenchment. He knew that any increase in military expenditures conditioned the pound's rate and was unpopular. War critics on both sides of the Commons such as David Hume, Richard Cobden, and John Bright and Conservative leader Benjamin Disraeli impugned taxes to increase the military as a "war vote." Thus retrenchment held sway despite the threat that some British leaders felt from France.

This threat was deflected because the Crimean War divulged the lack of military organization and a weak military education system reflected in poor senior military leadership. There was a powerful peace party in the cabinet composed of Gladstone, the Duke of Argyll; Sir George Grey, the second Earl Granville; and secretary of war George Cornewall Lewis. In the face of this strong opposition to boosting armaments, Palmerston lamented that in democratic countries men were prouder of being gentlemen than officers, whereas the opposite was applied to nondemocratic countries. Antimartial traditions made neutrality rather than armed might the cheapest method of self-defense. The neutral, antimartial policy became self-fulfilling. There was, as in the past, no comprehensive reappraisal of foreign policy principles by the cabinet. Left alone, "Palmerston and his colleagues intended to go along much as they had been and for much the same reasons."[21]

Similarly, with the emphasis for resolving disputes on diplomacy, aversion to war was the primary consistency in British and American foreign policy. Diplomacy was the realistic solution for dispute resolution. Protected by ocean barriers,

Britons and Americans habitually distrusted large peacetime standing armies. Large armies were perceived as obstacles to developing democratic societies. In the wrong hands, standing armies could become instruments of despotism. Moreover, they were costly and thought to siphon funds from the development of a diverse industrial base and the public works necessary to sustain industrial expansion. After 1815, Britain underwent four decades of severe defense reductions. Proposals that aimed to increase the British army against France failed. Britain's standing army remained half the size of that of France and Germany and was less than a third of the size of Russia's army.[22] Britain was prepared to fight only limited wars to keep imperial peace. The Royal Navy was to defend against French attack and to maintain imperial sea-lanes.[23]

Like Gladstone and other Liberals, Whigs, and Radicals, Lincoln was never a proponent of warfare. Indeed, his opposition to the Mexican War injured his political career as a young congressman from Illinois in the late 1840s. He helped develop the Republican Party from 1854 on as the true Union party that aimed to block the expansion of slavery. Lincoln's political focus was on internal transportation improvements to raise the status of the common man coupled with sensitivity to the slavery question. Associated with national improvements was his idea that slavery was a moral wrong and an obstacle to a free society. Thus leaders in both Britain and the United States were in no position to solve differences with violence because of their goals of prosperity and moral concern for humankind. With massive social changes afoot in both nations, and the diplomatic traditions in tow, the Anglo-American relationship was being redefined.[24]

There was strong consistency in the lack of fighting spirit in Britain after 1815. In 1821, Castlereagh had become the great conciliator and mover of the British-led European diplomatic system to keep France from again upsetting the balance of power. Twenty-five years later, Conservative foreign secretary Aberdeen believed that the French "go to work in such a roundabout way that it is difficult for them to inspire confidence."[25] Aberdeen worried about "an enormous expense and general distrust," and the Admiralty shared his view. In the 1840s, Prime Minister Sir Robert Peel, mentor to Aberdeen, Gladstone, Lewis, and other luminaries in the Palmerston ministries, opposed excessive defense spending for the same reasons. Peel charted the way by not wanting "any show of preparation which is costly, calculated to excite suspicion and apprehension, and does not really advance us in our object."[26] Seen this way, it is unsurprising that several hallmark treaties were concluded between Britain and the United States in the 1840s and neither government wanted to fight the other during American expansionist wars against Mexico over Texas and to annex the Southwest to complete the boundaries of the republic. The financial houses also played a role in maintaining the peace. When the United States annexed Texas in 1845, for example, the Barings urged Peel's government against resistance to promote good relations with the United States.[27]

After 1846 many British Liberal and Conservative leaders took Peel's conciliatory cue and opposed escalating the arms race with France. Thus, as foreign secretary under Russell from 1846 to 1852, Palmerston was unsuccessful at maintaining
the British military at a high state of readiness despite his persistence. His cabinet
"Memorandum on the Defence of the Country" on 18 December 1846 failed to
receive a majority. Two years later Russell failed to raise taxes to fund improvements. By 1851 British military leaders had assessed national defenses against the
French threat and believed that the situation was desperate. Sir John Burgoyne,
the leading national defense expert, noted the "apathy on the defense question in
the country . . . standing as it does on the brink of a frightful precipice. The mel-
ancholy thing is the indifference of our statesmen to the question." By the early
1850s, despite upsets in Europe, what was thought to be a direct challenge from
France under Napoleon III, and the French and Russian threats to Britain's sphere
of influence in the Middle East, Britain refused to empower its armed forces. If it
refused to equip itself to use force successfully against European threats, it would
probably have taken a severe jolt to get Britain to fight the United States, and
its unpreparedness for the Crimean War has already been discussed. Finally, the
antimilitary lobby was supported by popular hostility to the army. Laborers disliked the army because it kept law and order, innkeepers disliked billeting troops,
and Parliament and the landed classes feared the army as a political force that
answered to the queen and not to Parliament. In 1860, Gladstone disagreed with
Palmerston that a field army was needed to protect London against a French invasion. In 1862, when the fate of the American Union hung in the balance, Disraeli made "bloated armaments" the main charge in his attack on the government
against Derby's "misgivings."[28]

As we are beginning to see, Anglo-American relations were influenced by
the French contingency. Palmerston had been suspicious of France since he had
drilled at Cambridge as a schoolboy to oppose Napoleon's invasion plan in 1806.
In 1809 he entered the central government in the noncabinet post of war minister
in which he served until 1829, and foreign secretary (1831–40). In the latter role
he remained suspicious of French pretensions. As foreign secretary, he began to
use the French threat to embellish his political stature when "he had become the
symbol of Britain's mid-Victorian success."[29]

Palmerston's advocacy of a French threat throughout the antebellum period
was not unsupported by tradition. During his first foreign secretaryship (1830–41),
rival French foreign minister Guizot challenged him in the Mediterranean and
felt that France was pinched between British and European absolutists. Guizot
tried to break the unstable Franco-British cordon from 1830 onward.[30]

Thus, at the same time that diplomats were deterring civil conflict in North
America in the 1840s, Britain needed dependable relations with the United States.
Returning to the Foreign Office in Lord John Russell's Liberal ministry in 1846,

Palmerston could not put himself in a position of weakness, and any anti-American moves were difficult to explain to the public because European rivalries and revolutionary developments were the government's primary focus. Acting within this perspective, Palmerston raised alarms about the French threat to maintain his power. He believed correctly that France wanted to resurrect its Napoleonic hegemony. Franco-British imperial squabbles caused war scares in the 1840s and 1850s. During these two decades Palmerston believed that French hatred made imminent a surprise cross-channel attack by a steam navy because seaborne invasions were no longer dependent on winds and tides. He opted for the deterrent policy he had used in the Oregon dispute that argued that a weak Britain encouraged France, and "to improve our defenses is the best way to prevent it being necessary to employ them."[31] By 1847, even moderate Whigs such as Clarendon, a Palmerston protégé, upheld the foreign secretary's anti-French policy. As the French government fell in 1848 emitting Louis Bonaparte as president, Clarendon wrote on 1 April that the cabinet should arouse the public against France, and Russell warned that France could land forty thousand troops in Britain in a week. By January 1848 the cabinet supported a greater defense effort as relations hinged on the ironclad naval race.[32]

While warning about the probability of a French cross-channel invasion, Palmerston muted chances of a flare-up with the United States. The Anglo-American financial relationship had grown more interdependent with the boom in U.S. bonds overseas beginning in 1848. British capitalists had helped the United States finance the Mexican War even though they opposed American expansion, because, as Jay Sexton explains, expansion strained Anglo-American relations. But the financial interests of the two countries were complementary, and the financial houses of Rothschild, Barings, and Peabody partnered to broker for the United States the $15 million indemnity for the acquisition of Mexican lands ceded as a result of the Mexican War. This financial cooperation continued in the 1850s, especially through investments in state and railroad securities. Moreover, American industrialists used British loans to buy superior British steel.[33]

In 1850, as conditions in France remained unstable, Palmerston continued to contribute to the atmosphere of peaceful relations with the United States when he completed the Clayton-Bulwer Treaty over contested territories in Central America. American westward expansion was coupled with the discovery of gold in California in 1848. These contingencies opened up the need for safer, faster, and less expensive transportation between the coasts. The idea of a transoceanic canal through the isthmus of Central America brought British and American claims to territory into conflict. But again practical needs inspired American secretary of state John Clayton to invite Britain to enter into a joint agreement to build a canal in 1849. In the event, Clayton proclaimed to Sir Henry Bulwer, the British minister with whom he negotiated the treaty bearing their names: "England is the home of my forefathers and the blood of the Anglo-Saxon forms the basis of the population of this country." Clayton was also motivated to desire a partnership in Central America by the need to attract British investments for building a canal and for political stability in the region, which was a precondition to potential investors. Clayton's action represented a growing continuity in Britain's policy of cooperation with the United States. Moreover, a joint isthmian agreement could stabilize the politics of the region to gain investor confidence. Leading American entrepreneurs, such as Cornelius Vanderbilt and William Aspinwall, conveyed to Washington the need for British cooperation, and Clayton informed the British that the United States would cease expansion into Central America if a joint agreement could be made.[34]

In both cases policies were overridden by a material need to quicken transportation time to California that, if nourished, had long-lasting potential for the overseas trade of both parties. For this reason, the United States was ready to tear up an unratified treaty with Nicaragua and to prohibit further expansion into Central America to ensure British investments. This position contradicted the American expansionist tradition, the Monroe Doctrine, British "gunboat diplomacy," and the nationalism of both countries, as Sexton insightfully explains. Just as before, the needs of the moment were satisfied because negotiations were conducted in secret in Washington, even without the full purview of the British and American cabinets. In the interests of flexibility, Clayton and Bulwer followed earlier negotiators when they saw fit to overlook contentious issues having to do with territorial rights to create an agreement. The putative canal and adjacent regions were neutralized from fortifications, colonization, or political control by either party by Article I of the treaty. Article V held that the canal would be forever free and investment capital secure. Although unresolved contentions continued to rankle, the treaty ended future British expansion in Central America just as the Oregon Treaty had done north of the border.[35] Almost sounding like Aberdeen, Palmerston believed the ensuing Clayton-Bulwer Treaty in the spring of 1850 was "a Bond of Harmony between the Two Countries in regard to local Disputes." Finally, the Clayton-Bulwer Treaty threaded through the decade as a symbol of the rapprochement. The treaty demonstrated that the two powers could continue to meet and resolve contentions. Several prominent revisions were made to define respective interests in Central America almost up to the Civil War.

Compromise continued to be British policy as well in the triangular relations with the United States and Canada. In 1849, economically depressed Montreal merchants pressed for annexation to the United States, which was uninterested. In this case, a threat from its own colonists, Britain refused to arm Canada because it wanted Canada to govern itself with its own political and economic self-sufficiencies. In 1853, Russell told American minister Edward Everett that in foreign policy "our two countries should maintain a real Family Compact."

The compact was demonstrated again a year later when Britain sent another aristocratic negotiator, Lord Elgin, the governor general of Canada, to Washington to quickly conclude the unprecedented Reciprocity Treaty of 1854. During this period of confusion and weak leadership in London and Washington, Foreign Secretary Clarendon's suspicions of the United States grew despite his work for the treaty, which was the answer to borrowing time for Canada to become economically self-sufficient. There was a long history that made treaty making auspicious. By the Convention of 1818 Americans could fish for the choicest catches of cod and mackerel within the three-mile limit on specified coasts off of Newfoundland, Nova Scotia, and the Gulf of St. Lawrence. However, as the decades passed, New Englanders began to fish in the contested shore waters of Nova Scotia, Newfoundland, the Gulf of St. Lawrence, and elsewhere to the disdain of the colonists. Trouble arose during the fishing season of 1852, but the American Navy and the Royal Navy patrolled the fisheries amicably and exchanged social visits. The 1854 season promised more trouble, but the two parties continued to cooperate to keep the colonists and the New Englanders from shooting at each other or fighting onshore. British minister to the United States Crampton wrote Clarendon on 6 March 1854, as the season began, that secretary of state William Marcy did not fear a collision even if negotiations failed. He was prepared to cede every point except registry of American vessels in order to make a treaty.[36]

The ensuing treaty not only pacified the fisheries and represented the growth of a British-American rapprochement in the middle of the 1850s but also created an unprecedented customs union in natural products to develop industry and trade along the common boundary. By helping to build a national economy instead of the existing weaker provincial economies, Britain symbolized a long-held desire for the colonies to establish responsible government and economic self-sufficiency. (In the 1850s the United States made no attempt to annex the colonies and would only accept them if they came of their own accord.) In fact, the Reciprocity Treaty of 1854 sent zealous Canadians a warning that British diplomacy rather than war was the principal method to deter Canadian and American fishermen from fighting each other over inshore rights or other border squabbles. Joint naval cooperation continued to keep New Englanders and colonists from conflict in the fisheries. Moreover, American politics of the intensifying sectional struggle between North and South kept even the most ambitious northward expansionists, always a politically weak minority, from lobbying for the annexation of the colonies as free states. Finally, the Reciprocity Treaty illustrated that the United States was interested in acquiring territories south of the border and not to the north, and the treaty quelled the desires of Montreal merchants to be annexed to the United States.[37] It opened free trade in enumerated natural products and allowed free fishing between Canada and the United States for ten years. New Englanders could fish in the most profitable colonial inshore waters and Canadians could fish American waters to the 36th parallel. The treaty assisted Canadian industry and prevented a blowup in the North Atlantic fisheries. Moreover, the treaty strengthened Canadian-American social and economic interdependence at the expense of Britain's trade monopoly with its colonies and "served as evidence to British capitalists of an Anglo-American rapprochement."[38]

The four treaties showed that caution and cooperation were the leading British-American aims. Palmerston could afford to do little else and maintain his power. As prime minister from 1855 to 1858, he ran his government on a "day-to-day, hand-to-mouth, basis." During his later years as prime minister, he defined politics as "largely a matter of getting from Monday to Friday without conspicuous damage."[39] Certainly, these were not the words of an old war minister with a deliberate policy of weakening the United States. Lord Granville, a cabinet conciliator, declared that Palmerston "had no idea of a sound policy" and understood no cabinet office except the Foreign Office. Palmerston did not need policies or reforms because of the unprecedented prosperity. His geniality and realism made him reluctant to change domestic and foreign policy.[40]

Thus, under both Liberals and Conservatives, the cabinet managed matters as they arose and, like Palmerston, did not enjoy facing American problems. Except for his emphasis on naval deterrence, ministers ignored unresolvable problems or created ambiguous agreements. Anna Ramsay argued that except for "Salisbury, Dilke, and possibly Disraeli, no British minister between 1830 and 1890 ever sat down to think out clearly for himself, putting aside tradition and precept, a definite policy in foreign affairs." As the foreign secretary of the leading constitutional nation in Europe, Palmerston talked about upholding democracy abroad and used this patriotic ploy to solidify his popularity. Meanwhile, he followed his mentor George Canning's policy of remaining free from entangling alliances and used his acute sense of public opinion to maintain his prestige.

In his second and last Liberal ministry (1859–65), Palmerston and foreign secretary Lord John Russell formed a cooperative foreign policy team. Whenever possible they preferred to make decisions privately (just as they made treaties) because cabinets were time consuming and their deliberations were made public. This private method turned out to assist British-American relations during times of stress. The outcome of indifference to long-term foreign policy making and reform, owing to political weakness, was a neutral policy toward British politics, Europe, and North America.

Likewise, on the brink of the American Civil War, the Conservative opposition had no method except to refuse to adopt a clear position on any issue while pursuing an inactive foreign policy. Inactivity impacted directly on the nonaggressive policy toward the North during the Civil War. Palmerston had a "truce" with the Conservatives based on nonintervention and reduction of naval armaments, which fit well with retrenchment-minded ministers who were his greatest political worry. This alliance of convenience helped the Liberal Party to maintain control and, guided by Palmerston, to assert its vision of progress conditioned by minimal government and free trade. As Angus Hawkins points out, the 1850s did not witness disillusionment with the principle of party, but there were too many different ideas about party principles for any one party to gain ascendancy without allies from across the political spectrum. In summary, Palmerstonian foreign and domestic policies were based on compromise to maintain the delicate political balances at home and abroad. To think otherwise would, in the words of Paul Kennedy, be "a staggering misreading of British political priorities in the early 1860s."[41]

On the brink of the American struggle, these policies were rendered critical by what was by now the traditional immediacy of the French threat. This threat continued to move Britain to maintain stable relations with the United States as the perceived French menace took on threatening proportions. In contrast to the British and the Americans, Napoleon III continued to increase his army until the Anglo-French crisis, from 1859 to 1861; at that time it numbered about 400,000, which was the largest in Europe.[42] Even Palmerston's retrenchment-minded ministers could not ignore Napoleon's military buildup, and British defense spending grew from about £300,000 in 1858–59 to £325,000 in 1859–60 and to nearly £650,000 in 1860–61. The Royal Commission on National Defenses was paid £950,000 in 1861 and £970,000 in 1863.[43] A volunteer movement was established in 1860–61 to meet the French threat. Most of this increase was directed at Europe rather than North America.

British fear of France grew as the American Republican Party was formed to save the Union and extinguish slavery. The United States was thus distracted from pressing an aggressive foreign policy, which was never a strong point for Washington. The weak midcentury American governments resembled those in Britain. Washington faced growing violence in Kansas and Nebraska, Southern threats of secession, and the general disintegration of American politics during the Democratic administration of James Buchanan who presided with partiality toward the South. His failure to provide a solution to the sectional controversy added fire to it as the Republican Party seized on Democratic weakness with an antislavery policy. If the Republicans could obtain the presidency with a restrictive policy on slavery, leaders like Abraham Lincoln believed, slavery would die.

Lincoln was fortunate that British politics and foreign problems distracted it from taking advantage of the disintegration of the Union even if it had wanted to intervene. Prime Minister Derby's fear of naval inferiority in 1858 gave way a year later to Palmerston's fear of yet another ironclad French invasion. He said that the new French dockyard at Cherbourg was like a "knife pointing at Britain's jugular" and "a great arsenal and excellent harbour directly facing the Channel and the South Coast of England." The fast French fleet could outdistance the British wooden fleet and raid dockyards. In 1860, France was building six seagoing and nine coast-defense ironclad warships, and only a lack of funds prevented more. Palmerston favored a screw liner and armored ship buildup because he believed the French naval expansion was for the English Channel or the Mediterranean, the two quickest ways to weaken Britain and its empire. Britain and France were in the thick of the ironclad buildup amid warnings that Britain was becoming a second-rate naval power. By 1861, Britain had 149 first-class warships, but it only had two ironclads available, the *Warrior,* which was more than twice as large as *La Gloire,* and *Ironside.* In light of the naval race, public apathy, poor home defenses, and only sporadic increases in defense spending, Britain was hard-pressed to prosecute a war anywhere. Naval weakness was one reason the government kept policy making in the *Trent* affair in November and December within the boundaries of traditional private diplomacy to help Lincoln and Seward back away honorably. As long as Gladstone ran the exchequer, lucrative economics prevailed at home aided by fewer taxes that favored the lower classes.[44] Palmerston was a realist and had no reason to shake up international relations.

Deterrence was Britain's best bet. Indeed, it was its only bet. As first lord of the Admiralty, the twelfth Duke of Somerset, and British vice admiral and commander on the North American and West Indies Station, Sir Alexander Milne had demonstrated many times before, and as military historian Russell Weigley points out, "The coming of steam power had destroyed the ability of its [Britain's] best warships to cruise indefinitely in American waters as the blockading squadrons had done in 1812. Even with a major base at Halifax, or possible aid from Confederate ports, the British navy would have found it a precarious venture to try to keep station on the U.S. coast." Weigley continues, "A war with America would have posed the danger of destroying altogether the facade of British military preeminence. . . . Whether feared by the North or hoped for by the South, British intervention in the American Civil War was little more than a chimera."[45]

Other international problems exacerbated Anglo-French relations on the eve of the Civil War and distracted London from understanding the escalating American sectional crisis. Bad feelings erupted over northern Italy where Napoleon III took Nice and Savoy to block Austria. Britain favored a unified Italian republic (Russell wanted to add Rome and Venetia) as a bastion against French or Austrian advances against the European balance of power. In the Middle East, Britain and France supported opposite sides in a religious civil war. Palmerston interpreted plans for a French canal through Egypt as a threat to Britain's commercial lanes in the eastern Mediterranean, India, and the Far East. Personal differences between Palmerston and Napoleon III intensified suspicions. The religious civil war in the Middle East showed their differences. Palmerston wanted the Turkish government to solve the problem rather than the great power congresses favored by Napoleon III, where he thought that he could enhance Bonapartism. The British desired not to provoke Europe as the alliance system crumbled and Napoleon III tried to lead

The HMS *Warrior*, shown in 1860 when it was launched. Weighing 9,200 tons, it was the greatest ironclad steam battleship of the day and was a vivid symbol of the naval arms race with France. Naval Historical Foundation

it. The Middle Eastern rivalry showed how differently Britain and France looked at foreign policy: Britain was beginning to originate a policy of splendid isolation, and France continued to follow the opportunistic motives of Napoleon III.[46]

Beyond the Liberal government's distrust of the French emperor and its desire to push American affairs into the background, British public opinion remained opposed to a conflict. Many realistic leaders of the British middle and upper classes acquiesced to American progress. The London *Times* expressed popular sentiments about the United States. In 1852, it indicated that the "temperate and friendly spirit, which is alone consonant to their close relationship and enormous common interests," guided relations. In 1853, it held, "We have so little desire to check or impede the growth of the United States of America in conformity with those wise principles which were handed down to them by the founders of the Republic that we are satisfied the rapid and successful progress of that country is of essential advantage to ourselves, as Englishmen, and to the general interests of mankind." In 1856, the newspaper noted "a bond of mutual interest, the mainte-nance of which had become a matter for constant concern in the both countries." Moreover, other newspapers and middle society believed that American progress ensured the ascendancy of the Anglo-Saxon race.[47]

A primary obstacle to that ascendancy, and to perfectly dependable relations, was the obliteration of slavery, which the British had outlawed in 1808. Tensions continued because the United States balked when the Royal Navy began stopping its slave ships in 1833, and the United States tried to convince France not to sign a treaty for mutual right of search. American leaders thought that the treaty by Britain with European nations was a pretext for dominating the seas. By 1839, the Yankees were the only hole in Britain's policing of the slave trade. They rejected the Quintuple Treaty of 1841, insisting that the national flag protected ships from foreign searches, and broadcast that it policed its own merchantmen. In 1842, the United States stopped searching its own ships for slave traders. Yet British Lib-eral and Conservative ministries refused to fight the United States over the slave trade. Partly as a result of the treaties between the two powers, relations improved during the 1850s. Moreover, Britain's military had not performed well during the Crimean War despite the fact that it had emerged with victory; the war had also unearthed a crisis of confidence in its military ability and an acute perception of how overextended it was internationally.

Britain knew its limits on the eve of the Civil War, and it followed an isola-tionist doctrine. In 1858, the London *Times* played peacekeeper. The newspaper refused to castigate the United States for ignoring the stop-and-search policy for slave traders off Cuba. In early June, the *Times* remarked that the threat to friendly relations caused by the arrests of slavers carrying the American flag was not worth the risk to peace. As the United States began war measures against Britain, the *Times* expounded that Americans had a perfect right to prevent their ships from being boarded just as the British would be incensed if the American Navy boarded its ships whether they were slavers or not. By late June, Britain had stopped boarding American ships and showed that it had no intention of going to war over the anti–slave trade issue. The ministry and Parliament refused to support such a war, while the evidence shows that the United States was ready to fight.[48] The most effective outcome was the reversal of roles on the high seas on the eve of the Civil War. Usually, Britain was on the offensive at sea, but now the United States had assumed this role. Neutral Britain refused to act because the tables could be turned if Britain became a belligerent.[49]

Finally, strong British humanitarian and financial sentiments reinforced neutrality and peace. British investments in the Northern states continued at high levels. British investors, for instance, manifested antislavery investment tactics by preferring to invest in Northern railroads. Pro-North British leaders such as John Bright and Richard Cobden held a portion of the 66 percent of British stock in the Illinois Central Railroad, and Abraham Lincoln protected the interests of the railroad and its bondholders. Conversely, the one-crop economy of the South was unpopular to investors because of concerns about drought, soil exhaustion, slave insurrections, and the growing chance of a civil war. Moreover, in the 1840s, three Southern states—Mississippi, Arkansas, and Florida—had defaulted on their interest payments and repudiated their debts of $11.5 million owed to British investors. In addition, Jay Sexton writes, "Slavery, in short, made the South an unsafe destination for European capital," and George L. Bernstein points out that, in general, "The Civil War was no different. British attitudes and policies had evolved over the previous twenty years."[50]

Personal exchanges aided the good feelings brought about by cooperation on the large issues. In 1858 good tidings were exchanged between Queen Victoria and President James Buchanan over the newly laid Atlantic cable (which soon broke and was unavailable during the Civil War). With some trepidation, ex-Conservative prime minister Lord Aberdeen, who pursued a conciliatory American policy in the 1840s, wrote that Britain was "in a rapid course of *Americanization.*" Lady Palmerston expressed a similar sentiment to Monckton Milnes, who was pro-American, that "I think we are fast verging into Democracy and Americanism."[51] Relations improved when the prince of Wales visited the United States and Canada in the fall of 1860. He was the first member of the royal family to tour the United States and was greeted with a "tumultuous reception" in New York City. President Buchanan commented on the visit's success, and Queen Victoria deemed it an "important link to cement the two nations of kindred origin and character." The exodus of Southern Democrats from Congress in 1861 assisted the rapprochement because they had been the ones who threatened Britain's interests in Central America and the Caribbean. Since the War of 1812, Northerners had been more pacific than Southerners, who had been chief agitators for the aggressive policy in Texas and Mexico in the 1830s and 1840s and for the filibusters in Cuba and Central America in the 1850s.[52]

The rapprochement of the late 1850s was further validated by Britain's response to the disputed San Juan Island water boundary in Puget Sound in August 1859. This dispute marked the closest that Britain and the United States came to fighting before the Civil War. It included the dynamics of all of the disputes since the 1840s: manifest destiny, filibustering, boundaries, military force, annexation, strategic locations, and the antimartial spirit that pervaded both democracies. The dispute evolved from a practical oversight of the makers of the Oregon Treaty. It was a dispute that Palmerston had ignored to prevent trouble when he returned to the Foreign Office in 1846, soon after the Oregon Treaty was signed. But the filibustering of pro-South Federal officers in Washington Territory reenlivened the dispute. The British were still debating the water boundary with American diplomats as Major Robert Anderson and his small Federal complement surrendered Fort Sumter. But nobody had to surrender in the Pacific Northwest, and traditional private diplomacy overcame yet another misunderstanding.

Since 1846, both governments preferred indifference to settling the water boundary. But as American settlement on the archipelago increased, pressure mounted on the remnants of the British-sponsored Hudson's Bay Company, long the commercial monopoly in the region. In the late 1850s, without authorization from Washington, the government of the newly constituted Washington Territory tried to annex the archipelago. In August 1859, the military governor of the territory, Gen. William S. Harney, sent an unauthorized military contingent with artillery under Capt. George Pickett to the island on the pretext of maintaining peace between the British settlers and the American settlers—one of whom had killed a British pig rooting on his property. This event has gone down in history as the so-called Pig War. The British were about to land marines to contest the occupation when a cease and desist order was received from the British naval commander on station. A Virginian, Pickett might have had the naive idea that an Anglo-American war might keep the Union united and the slavery question forgotten.[53]

The San Juan Island water boundary dispute also symbolized the British-American global cooperation of the 1850s and 1860s. Control of the archipelago meant control of the best harbors in Puget Sound, which had significance for control of the Far Eastern trade. The archipelago blocked the development of Britain's Pacific imperial naval headquarters at Esquimalt at the tip of nearby Vancouver Island, which was obtained in 1846. The British were lukewarm about developing the base because of an indifferent attitude about the Northwest. Yet if the United States controlled the narrow Haro Strait between Vancouver Island and the continent, Esquimalt could easily be threatened. To save geopolitical face, private diplomacy preserved the national honor of both sides and protected the governments from public scrutiny until permanent settlement was possible. In fact,

Parliament was not called back into session in late October 1859 after news of the encounter reached Britain. A debate on San Juan, coupled with the concomitant dispute over the Royal Navy's forcing its way up the Peiho River to extract commercial concessions from the Chinese emperor with the support of the U.S. Navy, and the French rivalry, threatened Palmerston's power.[54]

In other words, San Juan demonstrated that British-Americans followed established methods of settlement through compromise. Gladstone and his colleagues in the retrenchment bloc of the cabinet did not want war because they were not convinced of the superiority of the British case for San Juan. Gladstone refused to believe that the archipelago was worth a fight "even when the interests involved were considerable." Palmerston's usual first impulse to fight was thwarted by Gladstone and Somerset. Sir Edmund Hammond, the permanent undersecretary at the Foreign Office, supported them. Neither thought the distant area was critical to British global security or to the informal empire. Fortunately, British naval commanders on the spot, from the lowest lieutenant to the commanding admiral on station, offered further support. British Royal Navy captains Michael de Courcey and Geoffrey Phipps Hornby refused to land the two thousand marines from their warships to contest the American occupation.[55] These officers acted independently for nonintervention. Their moderation was wise because the American government disavowed General Harney's unauthorized action.

The Admiralty praised Hornby's discretion in the interests of compromise and deterrence. Historian Barry Gough has written that Hornby "rightly held that the British could afford to be forbearing in view of their superior naval strength." Hornby wanted to blame any rupture squarely on the United States just as Lincoln wanted the Confederacy to bear the responsibility for firing the first shots of the Civil War. Along with Adm. R. Lambert Baynes, who became the senior British naval commander soon after Harney's action, the British reasoned that the issue was potentially explosive but doubted that the American occupation jeopardized British lives or Britain's claim to the archipelago.[56]

Washington acted quickly to defuse the situation. Once it learned of Harney's "filibuster," the Federal government dispatched Commanding Gen. Winfield Scott on a peacekeeping mission. After a four-week transcontinental journey, Scott met with Harney and told him that the British were uninterested in forcing the American settlers off San Juan Island. He further told the expansionist general (who had been insubordinate to Scott several times during the Mexican War and was known to be bloodthirsty) that he was reducing the number of troops on the island to keep cordial British-American relations. He ordered Harney to relinquish command and return to St. Louis for reassignment. On 5 November 1859 Scott ordered the withdrawal of all but one company of Federal soldiers and all artillery to the USS *Massachusetts*. The British were pleased with Scott's work. The portly

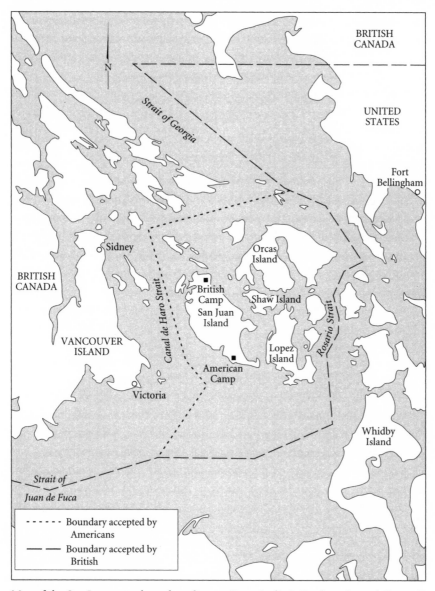

Map of the San Juan water boundary dispute. From Leslie J. Gordon, *General George E. Pickett in Life and Legend.* (Chapel Hill: Univ. of North Carolina Press, 1998)

general reminded Harney that until the ownership of the island was determined, "British subjects have equal rights with American citizens."[57]

Scott's amelioratory statement was accompanied by British Foreign Office complaints that their subjects did not fall under American laws, and he questions why the Department of State had allowed the incident to occur. Yet this contention was not something that the British wanted to fight over. In fact, looking at the academic parts of the squabble enabled both parties to move away from a punitive solution. The Foreign Office wanted to know why Harney had violated the understanding with the Hudson's Bay Company. Scott returned to Washington and wrote that only the "forbearance of the British" stopped escalation. (Harney had refused to go to St. Louis and ordered Pickett back to San Juan on 10 April 1860.) Faced with the embarrassing and mutinous Harney, Scott again recommended that Harney be relieved and recalled. The State Department agreed and informed British minister Lord Lyons that the War Department had revoked Harney's orders to Pickett and enforced Scott's arrangement with the Hudson's Bay Company and the Royal Navy for a joint occupation until the two governments settled. Harney was again relieved of command and ordered to report to the secretary of war.

The dispute was peacefully resolved with Harney's removal, but the boundary commission and diplomats failed to agree on the water boundary. In January 1861, the newly installed secretary of state, William Henry Seward, wanted to settle the dispute as the sectional crisis threatened. On 16 March Lincoln asked the senate if the question should be submitted to arbitration. On 19 March Charles Sumner, a Radical Republican with social connections in British high society and an inveterate abolitionist, recommended arbitration, but Congress delayed until December. In May, Seward warned Russell in a dispatch that Lincoln "only partially softened," and Lyons feared that the joint occupation might cause another incident.[58]

As it turned out, neither government wanted to take advantage of the other's plight. Britain and the United States cooperated to keep the water boundary issue dormant. A friendly joint military occupation was established to shelve the issue until a settlement could be made. The joint occupation consisted of one hundred soldiers each, although half of the American troops were withdrawn when the Civil War erupted.[59] The British garrison was on the north end of the island, and the Americans were encamped on the south end. The joint occupation continued on friendly terms until the Treaty of Washington of 8 May 1871 provided arbitration by the German emperor who found for the United States in 1872. This decision ended the last dispute between the two powers over territorial sovereignty in North America, and it delineated the final boundary line of the continental United States.[60] Instead of exacerbating the problem, diplomacy put it to sleep. The key fact was that the Royal Navy was ordered to back down just like it had been ordered to sail away from an encounter with the United States in Hawaii in 1842 when the Americans had pronounced the Tyler Doctrine to discourage the other powers.[61] Moreover, the Royal Navy was not deployed during the Central American or Canadian disputes in the 1850s. When it came down to it, diplomacy, not military force, was the deterrent as perceived by both sides.

For our purposes, San Juan was important as the last major event that synthesized the character of British-American relations before the Civil War. San Juan showed that diplomatic relations were cooperative and that there was an arsenal of tactful maneuvers that both governments knew well how to use to prevent war. Co-operation over San Juan indicated that part of the fiber of cooperative relations was the increase in power of the noninterventionists in Palmerston's cabinet. It was con-sistent with Britain's nonintervention policy of not wanting to hold or acquire terri-tory at the cost of the United States. In fact, both governments were peaking in their isolationism and minimalism to preserve foreign interests. These were roughly the same lines of policy that formed during Civil War disputes. The outline for the later intervention debate in the British cabinet was drafted with San Juan because the cabinet was nearly unanimously against intervention despite the ascendant British force on station. But as we have seen, deterrence and not combat was the cabinet's tactic. Besides, Palmerston, Russell, Gladstone, and Somerset refused to condone fighting for San Juan. They were supported by George Cornewall Lewis, Argyll, and Granville, the same ministers who refused to support intervention in the Civil War two years later. This group was the heart of the cabinet, and all but Gladstone refused to let Palmerston and Russell break away in 1862 as will be discussed in chapter 5. Somerset spurned Palmerston's urgings to reinforce the squadron around Vancouver Island as the United States had only one small warship there, and he op-posed sending more land forces because of fear of desertion, which was a common practice among British sailors on American shores, and because of the expense. In addition to these considerations, he and his colleagues opposed war.[62]

Thus the track of peace between the United States and Britain was clear before the Civil War. More peace factors existed than war factors. Cooperation was em-bedded in the roots of the relationship. A prewar rapprochement was created from tradition, commerce and investments, antislavery, antimilitarism, Francophobia, and compromise (especially on the British side). Private diplomacy resulted in a number of treaties that reduced territorial tensions. Americans were indebted to British investors for $444 million (up from $110 million in 1838), and the latter's antislavery premonitions and lack of trust in the South caused investors to pre-fer the North. These interdependencies relative to an array of contingencies were housed in the shielding tradition of pacific resolution. These contingencies be-came basic to the interests of both governments to maintain stable relations when the Civil War broke out. Stability was accentuated by British neutrality, coupled with the United States' refusal to allow the Civil War to become an international conflict. The longer the war, the more the British benefited from commerce with the North and the South. The noninterventionist cabinets and public wanted to avoid conflict to live peacefully with both the winner and the loser.[63] The course of British-American relations had not varied during the Civil War just as it had not varied during disputes since 1815. The structure of relations enabled both gov-ernments to continue with antebellum diplomacy.

This review of contingent antebellum events casts doubts on depicting the Civil War as a relational crisis because of the demonstrated success of private diplomatic relations. Antebellum diplomacy shows that Civil War diplomacy cannot be interpreted only within the confines of the event alone. The rapprochement evolved from decades of experiences stemming from foreign and domestic causes that created the reserve to resolve problems peacefully. The compromise settlement over discordant territorial claims in North America in the 1840s and 1850s began Britain's withdrawal from the North American balance of power, thus easing tensions. The 1850s reinforced the predominance of the British-American custom of private talks and fortified the mutual noninterventionist foreign policy.

2

Caution, Cooperation, and Mutual
Understanding, 1860–1864

Before the Civil War, Britain's leaders decided that if the American sectional rivalry turned into a shooting war they would not intervene militarily or diplomatically to mediate the dispute. Palmerston wrote Russell in December 1860 that unless the North was militarily devastated, "Nothing would be more inadvisable than for us to interfere in the Dispute, if it should break out, between any of the States of the union, and the federal government." Continuation of trade with the Union was paramount to maintaining the government. Palmerston listened to powerful merchants and financiers who were understandably worried about what the American war might do to commerce. He did not want to upset his delicate political balance or economic prosperity. Caution was the best policy to maintain commerce and to stay out of potentially embarrassing international situations. Palmerston had Russell notify financial leader Thomas Baring, head of the pro-North British investment firm, that "Lord Palmerston & I think it would be unsafe for us to mediate in American affairs unless we were called upon by both parties to do so—& even then we should be unwilling." Similarly, Russell notified Lord Lyons in Washington, who in turn notified British consuls, not to show any partiality to the Southern states. Moreover, Britain refused to use the Union's distraction in the war to press about the San Juan Island water boundary controversy. In response to Lyons's belief early in 1861 that Seward might try to keep the Union together by raising a foreign threat, Russell replied that Britain would be "forbearing," and he refused to give the seceded states any inclination of Britain's recognizing or encouraging recognition of independence. These movements meant that Britain wanted peaceful relations with the United States from a "consciousness of strength, and not from the timidity of weakness." Throughout 1861 Palmerston "demonstrated admirable restraint in keeping the ministry and the public at bay."[1]

Nevertheless, tensions with the Union occurred between February and June 1861. In February, Russell tried to prevent a blockade of the Southern ports by warning Washington about interfering with British shipping. His warning failed to make the Union understand that the Confederacy was entitled to recognition as a belligerent. His plea made Unionists, trying desperately to prevent secession, mistakenly believe that Britain favored the South. But the blockade was legal only in war, and the Union understandably wanted a favorable state of war. As military historian Russell F. Weigley recently writes, "The United States's objections to British and French recognition of the Confederacy's belligerency [in May and June, respectively] were thus inconsistent and excessive, because the Lincoln administration had to treat the Confederacy as a belligerent and to that extent as a sovereign state."[2] After Fort Sumter fell, Russell hurried to let the Union know that Britain would not challenge the blockade. Thus the queen's neutrality proclamation of 13 May evidenced British neutrality in the Civil War. It was a further attempt to ease tensions, although it infuriated the Union, whose leaders believed it was the first step toward recognizing the South's independence. But that was an erroneous assumption made in the uncertain early war months. The proclamation recognized the South's belligerency because the Federal government could not blockade itself. It also prohibited British subjects from enlisting in foreign armies and navies and from building warships for combatants in Britain.[3]

In reality, the proclamation exuded Britain's caution. It complemented Palmerston's premature recognition of the blockade as effective to further ease tensions. This policy had an immediate impact on Lincoln's cautious foreign affairs, which enabled him to overcome Seward's feeling that Lincoln alone had to stop the war. In the event, the president implemented the blockade without creating friction with Britain. Acting under Lincoln's instructions to avoid "giving any cause of offense or irritation to Great Britain," Seward was being impractical, as Lincoln was quick to see. The South was bent on war unless the Union completely vindicated slavery, which Lincoln was not about to allow until he sensed that public opinion supported this effort. The president's primary purpose at this stage was to preserve the Union. Nevertheless, feeling like "he held the key to all discontent," the new secretary of state tried to forestall the blockade and to maintain stable relations with Britain. Seward told British Minister Lord Lyons on 20 March 1861 that he did not want the blockade established if it compromised British trade. He even mentioned repealing the Morrill Tariff, which had just been ratified by Congress, and which was a stigma to foreign trade. He intimated Union strategy by remarking that he was trying not to anger the South in hopes that the states might return to the Union. He wanted to take Lyons to the president to discuss these points. Nevertheless, Seward lost to the cabinet, and the blockade was set up after war broke out.[4]

Fortunately, Lyons supported the blockade. On 15 April he wrote Russell that a Union blockade under international law was more acceptable than Lincoln's other scenario to "close the ports." If that had occurred, Lyons said, "an immense pressure would be put upon Her Majesty's Government to use all means in their power to open those ports." Moreover, Seward's actions in trying to halt the blockade

William Henry Seward, American secretary of state, 1861–69. Seward's vision of a reunited America and his loyalty to Lincoln caused him to follow a peaceful policy toward Britain throughout the Civil War. Library of Congress

showed that he wanted peace with Britain unless the British recognized Confederate independence, which was negated by the neutrality proclamation. Seward did not mention any plan to fight Britain, and on 10 April he rejected any plan to use San Juan as a reason to cause a war. Instead of trying to pick a fight with Britain, perhaps to reunify the Union, Seward spoke of the common Anglo-American language, customs, and religion that bound the two countries together.[5]

The secretary of state's peaceful gestures negated his "foreign war panacea" bluster, which involved the threats of Spanish and French incursions and pretensions in the Caribbean and in Mexico. But even this tactic was short-lived, because Lincoln denied it and Seward was half hearted about it. At the same time, Britain's neutrality shielded the government and contained the Union's outrage. Meanwhile, neither Union nor British leaders immediately began to resolve neutrality disputes, which might have elevated tensions. This peaceful course was recognized by Southern writers: "Gushingly unhappy as to our family quarrel," diarist Mary Boykin Chesnut wrote on 4 March 1861, Britain refused to oppose the Union's extension of the right to stop vessels bound for neutral ports to search for Confederate contraband. Britain's neutrality "absolved the North of responsibility for any possible future outrages committed against British subjects by the South." Britain assumed the neutral role that the United States had proclaimed during the Canadian Rebellion of 1837. As Mary Chesnut sensed, the proclamation was not intended to show partiality but to recognize that a state of war existed and that the Union and the Confederacy could prosecute the fighting to the greatest extent. As the war continued, Lincoln realized that the proclamation empowered him against blockade-runners. The Supreme Court vindicated Britain's action in 1863 in ruling that the blockade's existence proved that a state of war existed and that a formal proclamation of neutrality was appropriate.[6]

Like Seward, Russell worked to maintain the peace by turning a cold shoulder to Confederate agents in Britain. He countered Confederate sympathizers in the House of Commons by stating "that there should not be among us anything like exultation at their [the North's] discord." He displayed "an icy neutrality" toward supporting a slave state. He twice received Confederate diplomats unofficially to send Lincoln and Seward a message that the ministry refused to recognize Confederate independence. Palmerston supplemented neutrality with his deterrence policy by sending three regiments to Canada aboard the speedy *Great Eastern.* Lincoln seemed not to notice because he had his sights set on resolving the Union's dilemmas. In September 1861, Palmerston wanted to send more troops but was stopped by Colonial Secretary Newcastle, First Lord of the Admiralty Somerset, and Secretary of War Lewis. These ministers were concocting a new imperial strategy that focused on the French rivalry and protecting commercial lanes. The Civil War broke out before this strategy was fully designed.[7]

Britain also refused to use the unsettled San Juan issue to take advantage of the Union's crisis. President Buchanan wanted to settle before leaving office, but politics forbade him from withdrawing the American claim to the Haro Channel that would cede the San Juan Archipelago to the United States. "Old Buck's" desire to settle did not mean that Russell's arbitration draft would fare well in Washington. The arbitrator was to decide the channel through which the boundary would run and have the United States pay the Hudson's Bay Company (HBC) $500,000 to surrender its rights to the part of the archipelago determined to be American territory and in addition to HBC holdings on the mainland. An attempt to push

Lord Richard Bickerton Pemell Lyons, British minister to the United States, 1859–64. Lyons was a reserved, sensible minister who guided Britain through the worst tensions of the Civil War. Library of Congress

through a convention in the last months of Buchanan's administration failed. Throughout the spring and summer Russell probed for possibilities of keeping alive the spirit of settlement in the two governments. Yet to avoid controversy as the Union's crisis deepened, he heeded Lyons's advice and, in league with Seward, suspended negotiations to keep the friendly joint military occupation. It was best to keep the matter a private and cooperative one between the two governments, because the Senate's anti-British mood, fed by Britain's neutrality proclamation, was not conducive to settlement. Lyons again asked Russell for instructions in early November 1861, but the foreign secretary thought it best to delay to keep peaceful relations.[8] Russell proved his respect for the Union's trials by not taking advantage of its poor military showing at Bull Run in July of that year, and afterward, its continuing lack of military leadership and organization.

In proclaiming neutrality and using the troops sent to Canada to neutralize the frontier rather than to threaten the Union, Britain shunned responsibility for subjects committing unneutral acts. The proclamation gave the Union control of captured British blockade-runners because it rejected protection unilaterally to keep peace. Pro-North Liberal MP William E. Forster exclaimed that neutrality deterred Englishmen from helping the South and "is alleged to have credited pro-Union supporters in the cabinet for securing the Proclamation."[9] Along with Forster's point, the premature British recognition of the blockade's effectiveness tempered the good feelings that British recognition of Confederate belligerency created in the South.[10]

Britain's refusal to contest the Union navy's capture of blockade-runners weakened the South's war effort throughout the conflict. David G. Surdam points out:

The blockade raised the cost of shipping such [war] materiel and eroded the Confederacy's ability to purchase war materiel. Second, the blockade raised transportation costs to high enough levels to *preclude* the shipment of many bulky products, especially railroad iron and machinery. Third, the blockade forced Southerners to import goods through less convenient ports; the goods imported via the Rio Grande at Matamoros (formerly spelled Matamoras)/ Brownsville required a lengthy, expensive wagon haul back to central Texas. Fourth, the blockade combined with non-intercourse edicts to severely reduce the imports of Northern and European-produced civilian goods. The reduced flows led to shortages and higher prices and contributed to civilian discontent. Thus, although the blockade failed to "starve" the Confederacy of all necessary war materiel, it may have severely constricted the supply and therefore impeded the Confederacy's war-making efforts. The focus upon imports misses two of the blockade's important achievements: disrupting intraregional trade and denying the Confederacy revenue from exporting raw cotton and other staples.[11]

Always the realist in her agony for the South, Mary Chesnut wrote when the war was barely more than a year old that the blockade-runners "are filling their pockets, and they gird and sneer at the fools who fight."[12]

The blockade-runners were not the only impediment for the South as Britain and the United States cooperated early in the war. In addition to his colleagues, Russell refused to conduct diplomacy with the Confederacy. He believed Lyons's

Lord John Russell, first Earl Russell, British prime minister, 1846–52, and foreign secretary, 1859–65. British National Portrait Gallery

observation that the louder Seward blustered about what he believed to be Britain's favoritism for the South, the less threatening he actually was. Russell responded that "Mr. Seward must not get us into a quarrel. I shall see the Southerners when they come, but not officially, and keep them at a proper distance."[13] Palmerston agreed with Russell's tactic. To remain neutral, the prime minister continued with his usual attitude of ignoring the United States and concentrating on the intensifying European problems. To Palmerston: "The United States had become an unpredictable interloper into the diplomatic scene, one which annoyed him for many reasons, not the least of which was that he knew so little about her." He

William E. Forster, MP, defender of British neutrality and the proponent of the North in the Civil War. British National Portrait Gallery

detested Americans and wanted them to leave him alone diplomatically. This attitude represented an outlook that many other British leaders had long held. So as not to arouse the United States to anger, throughout the Civil War he pursued a public policy of caution and suborned his private predilections for the good of the peace and the continuation of his ministry.[14]

But Palmerston's attitude was especially ironic in respect to the United States, and the irony was conditioned by his astute realism in foreign policy. Despite his detestation of the Yankees, he followed a peaceful policy and refused to take opportunities given to him by the Civil War to weaken the Union. His conflicted state of mind resulted from his perpetual suspicions of the North. But now the South came under his suspicions as well. The two entities gave him a stronger reason to remain neutral from the pervasive confusion and catastrophe. Because Lincoln had not justified the war to exterminate slavery, Palmerston considered that his long-held belief about the self-seeking nature of American politicians had just entered a new phase. Palmerston realized that there could be no measured outcomes in Britain's favor. Political historian E. D. Steele argues, "The second Palmerston government, like the preceding Tory administration, carried appeasement of the United States to lengths scarcely imaginable in the very recent past."[15]

In early May 1861, the prime minister was abrupt about remaining neutral when he met with Confederate envoys. From then on he refused to see them and wrote them to "put in writing any communications they wish to make to him." The Confederates were shocked by this news. William L. Yancey resigned in disgust, sailed home, and told his fire-eater friend Robert Barnwell Rhett that, just as the latter had warned, "I went on a fool's mission." He said that the queen and Prince Albert, the royal consort, supported the North, although he thought "Gladstone we can manage," but the Confederates had no friends in antislavery Europe. Yancey exploded the King Cotton myth by saying that the British refused to raise the blockade to avoid fighting the North. The Southern belief that "an informal embargo on the export of raw cotton from Southern ports would coerce Europeans into intervening in any potential war" was sorely mistaken. The disgruntled Rebel agent realized that European recognition meant the North's defeat.[16]

True to Palmerston's realism, the agents witnessed Russell's allaying misunderstandings about the blockade to protect British interests. Historian Jay Sexton points out that "British shipping and investments in the Northern states, as well as Britain's largest commercial market, would be endangered" by a war with the North. Commerce and finance with the North were more vital to Britain's interests than recognizing the Confederacy merely to ensure cotton shipments and immediate economic benefits for the banks. These two long-term guarantors of British prosperity remained ascendant in British relations with the North to the South's detriment throughout the war and were factors in preventing intervention in the fall of 1862. The North also benefited early in the war from the pro-North stance of the Baring Brothers. In late 1861 the Barings financed Thurlow Weed's propaganda mission to Britain. Weed was Seward's political mentor and manager, and the Barings' funds enabled Weed to dine with British leaders, publish pro-Union messages in newspapers and pamphlets, and purchase arms. Thomas Baring, the head of the firm, supported the Union in Parliament.[17]

Another war-long precedent was set when Russell said that it was "desirable not to open a contentious correspondence [with the United States] on the separate cases in which the legality of the blockade may be disputed." He tried to be proactive to maintain the cooperation of Seward and the Federal government. From May through July 1861, Lord John, who became first Earl of Russell on 31 July, instructed

Henry John Temple, third Viscount Palmerston, British Prime Minister, 1859–65. British National Portrait Gallery

Lyons to research blockade policy to substantiate future claims. He responded to the alleged Union threat to close Southern ports with a measured instruction to Lyons "not to get into a quarrel sooner than we can help, nor at all if we can help it" and to refer difficult cases to the law officers, whom he knew would deliberate over time thus allowing any tempers over one case or another to cool down. He hoped that "if we can tide the summer over without serious hostilities, perhaps the coming autumn may see negotiations between the two combatants." To define the cooperation, Lyons was to convince Seward to approve of the Declaration of Paris of 1856 negotiations. Seward pledged to uphold the last three provisions, which outlawed privateering, protected noncontraband goods on neutral ships, and proclaimed that a blockade had to be effective to be legal. Lyons reported that one promising outcome of these talks was that Seward had suggested privately—outside of the purview of Sumner and the Radical Republicans who wanted to suffocate the South, win the war, and abolish slavery—that the Union government "might even shut its eyes" to Europeans trading with the South if those powers refused to recognize Confederate independence. The secretary of state summarized his cooperative attitude to American minister to Britain Charles Francis Adams on 21 July: "However otherwise I may at times have been understood, it has been an earnest and profound solicitude to avert foreign war that alone has prompted the emphatic and sometimes, perhaps, impassioned remonstrances I have hitherto made against any form or measure of recognition of the insurgents by the government of Great Britain."[18]

The talks failed to accomplish everything that Britain wanted, because Seward could not accept British and French neutrality riders. This was because of the prevailing Union belief that the powers favored the South. Conversely, the British and French feared that the secretary of state used the Declaration of Paris to rope them into supporting the Union, and Seward was suspicious that his signing the declaration might move the Europeans one step closer to recognizing the independence of the Confederacy.[19] But diplomacy remained ongoing: Britain and the Union continued to talk privately about the blockade and other differences. Despite suspicions of each other, relations remained peaceful throughout that first dismal summer and early fall of the war. Although Seward never agreed to the Declaration of Paris formally because neither Britain nor France consented to treat Rebel privateers as pirates, he repaid Russell's cooperation by respecting the declaration throughout the war. From the beginning, therefore, Seward followed the direction of Lincoln's speech of 3 July to remain friendly with Britain and France.[20]

Another example of the mutual understanding was cooperation to allay the potential for war over the hastily approved congressional port-closing act in July 1861. This act enabled the Federals to collect customs duties on shipboard without the formal blockade at penalty of forfeiture of ship and cargo. Seward influenced Lincoln to "say nothing" about actually implementing the act despite pressure from most of the cabinet and the Radical Republicans. He instructed Adams to assure Russell that foreign commerce was safe as long as Union sovereignty was respected. Equally important, Seward read the instructions to Lyons privately to underline his peaceful intent. The Seward-Lyons cooperation was noticeable in July as a result of Seward's leadership. Lyons wrote Russell and Sir Alexander Milne, commander of the North American and West Indies Squadron of the Royal Navy, that the port-closing question was temporarily settled by informal means and that Lincoln was not going to be hasty in issuing the proclamation to close the ports. As a result, Lyons noted that Seward suddenly exuded a "prudent and pacific mood" and that he should monitor and send information home rather than criticize the Union for passing the act. He continued that Seward alone among Lincoln's cabinet members prevented controversy over the port-closing act and might be "opening his eyes to the real dangers of a quarrel with England." Henri Mercier, the French minister in Washington, followed a similar policy, going so far as to write to Milne's counterpart, Admiral Reynaud, not to bring the French fleet to New York or any place in the United States because the sensitive Federals might construe such an event as a show of force. Thus Seward's actions for peace gained British and French cooperation but threatened his own position in the cabinet and drew more disdain from the Radical Republicans.[21] Among cabinet members, Navy Secretary Gideon Welles supported the port-closing act and joined Sumner in believing that Seward was soft on Britain. Welles showed his inexperience at fathoming the form of cooperative diplomacy, and fortunately his perspective on relations with Britain failed to convince Lincoln. The stand that Lincoln and Seward took on the ports question stands out because the British cabinet decided to risk war if it was ever implemented. As a result, Lyons wrote on 5 August, "Things are going smoothly between the U.S. government and my French colleague and me just now. May this happy state of things last."[22]

The Union defeat at Bull Run on 21 July no doubt caused Seward to become more peaceful, but the evidence shows that his cooperation predated that battle. His dispatch to Adams on the day of the battle was pacific. After news of the Union defeat was spread, true to what Lyons wrote in early August, Seward stopped pressing the British to withdraw the neutrality proclamation. He postponed further discussions with Lyons about the closing of Southern ports because the bill was not implemented. Lyons therefore wrote home that despite the pleas of British consuls in the South, the Royal Navy must be kept clear of Southern ports and Britain's neutral outlook must not change.[23]

The peaceful sentiments prevailed in London as well. Upholding an important nexus in traditional diplomacy, Adams told Russell that differences should lie on the table to prevent trouble. Russell agreed as long as the United States persevered in the blockade and did not attempt to close the ports. This neutrality remained even though in October the Union sent a fifteen-thousand-man army to Savannah and Brunswick, Georgia, and Charleston, South Carolina. Lyons restrained the cries of Consul Robert Bunch at Charleston that the Union navy refused to allow British merchantmen to leave Beaufort, South Carolina, because the Admiralty had instructed Milne confidentially not to cause strife in such matters, which favored the Union.[24]

Adams's consistent cooperation with Russell complemented Seward's diplomacy with Lyons. Unlike the Confederate agents, Adams gained British respect early in his tenure. Lyons helped to cement his reputation by describing the new American minister to Britain as an abolitionist who had followed Seward in supporting concessions to the South to prevent war. Adams arrived in London two days after the queen's neutrality proclamation, and his "quiet and unassuming character" helped him to establish amicable relations with Russell. The new minister refused to respond violently despite neutrality being a capital opportunity to register a bitter protest against what seemed to be a pro-South act. From the beginning of their relationship, Russell appeared to be "profoundly civil and disavowed all intention of doing us any harm or the southerners any good, and took amiably a pretty smart hint as to the consequences of pursuing this course." Their first interview was concluded when Russell asked Adams in to lunch "with Mrs R. and all the little Russells." No doubt the two diplomats' demeanors helped in this attempt at civility. Russell and Adams were of the same size and appearance, although Russell was fifteen years Adams's senior. Both were small, bald, smooth shaven, and sported side-whiskers. They were descendants of historic families of nation builders. They were reserved and spoke honestly. With Russell's favor, Adams was deluged with social invitations. His twenty-one-year-old son and secretary, Henry, believed that Russell supported the Union when he ordered British ports closed to armed vessels on each side and helped defeat Confederate independence motions.[25]

Adams's mission coincided with the beginning of the Union blockade. What Stephen R. Wise calls the "first modern blockade" brought mutual cooperation. The danger was that the blockade reversed the two powers' traditional approaches to wartime shipping. As the world's greatest sea power, Britain had been the principal blockading force and seized neutral shipping suspected of carrying contraband. During the Napoleonic era, the British routinely impressed sailors from American neutral ships.

But impressment was not the issue in 1861. The seizure of British vessels presented an even more serious situation. Anticipating the worst, the British reasoned that neutrality might be compromised if the Union seized British blockade-runners. To prevent a clash over seizures, Whitehall employed an inactive policy despite an outcry from the financial community. Taking a longer view than the financiers, the ministry understood that the Union blockade supplied precedents for sea power if Britain got into another war. In other words, the more liberties the Union navy took that did not hurt the ministry, the better those precedents were

Charles Francis Adams, American minister to Britain, 1861–68. Library of Congress

for Britain. Thus, on behalf of neutrality, Palmerston declared the blockade effective before it was, which "flew in the face of all American precedents, all American permanent interests and doctrines of neutral maritime rights."[26]

The Admiralty understood the potential embarrassments and resisted pressures from merchants, shipping interests, and neutral nations to denounce the blockade. Trade was less hampered by an ineffective blockade, so the Admiralty and the royal law officers turned a blind eye. In mid-June 1861, Lyons disclosed that Lincoln's temperament toward foreign powers was "an earnest solicitude to avoid even an appearance of menace or of want of comity towards foreign powers." In August

Russell instructed Lyons to restrict himself to formal protest at seizures, which meant that he was free to use his own judgment. Once these passive measures began, Lincoln instinctively saw that the British were sticking to neutrality and again instructed Seward to cooperate by allowing shipments to "leak" through the blockade while Union forces regained control of chief Southern ports. He promised reparations to the shippers who lost property to Rebel warships. This was a fortunate overture because Britain's leaders were said by American historian John Lothrop Motley in October 1861 to have positive sympathies toward the Union. Motley intimated that he had spoken with Palmerston, Russell, Cobden, Prince Albert, and Queen Victoria, who all expressed "honest sympathy . . . towards us." When Sumner learned of these conversations, he wrote Seward that: "It has made me happy in the assurance that all will go right in England in regard to us." Motley was apparently correct because Britain strictly enforced neutrality as the blockade tightened, showing that its national self-interest surpassed upper- and middle-class consternation for the Union and the South for disrupting commerce. Despite Lyons's suspicions of Seward's cooperation, neutrality became a security layer for the blockade and a cushion against an Anglo-American war.[27]

Britain's refusal to challenge the blockade flew, as usual, in the face of Palmerston's initial bellicosity. And, just as usual, his ministers gave him pause to concoct a pacific solution to protect British property and maintain cabinet unity. This process began when Palmerston informed Somerset on 17 June 1861 that he thought that improved Franco-British relations permitted sending warships from the home fleet to American waters. Yet, just as in the San Juan Island water boundary dispute, Somerset was reluctant to weaken the home fleet because of the expense and the ironclad race with France, the perennial desertions on American shores, and the expense of sending additional coal supplies for Bermuda, Jamaica, and Halifax. "It is therefore to be considered," the First Lord wrote to Palmerston, "whether our naval force on the North America and West Indies Station is not sufficient." In response to continued pressure from Palmerston and Russell, both Somerset and Vice-Admiral Milne advised that reinforcements might needlessly provoke the Union and ultimately compromise neutrality. In July, Palmerston retreated from strengthening deterrence, and very much in character when he had to retreat, smugly wrote Somerset that although the Union navy outnumbered the Royal Navy along the eastern seaboard, "they know we have plenty more here at home."[28]

Palmerston had difficulty in accepting the naval cooperation that continued throughout the Civil War. But it was really no different from the outcomes of his deterrence policy in response to previous North American crises and by now, as understood by his more pacific cabinet members, an essential element in maintaining cooperation. The conciliatory Milne wrote the First Naval Lord on 5 September 1861 that Union warships in the Gulf of Mexico were "very efficient and always on the move and very zealous [in enforcing the blockade]." By 8 November,

Russell admitted the blockade's effectiveness and refused to embarrass Seward on this issue. Unknowingly echoing Lincoln's insight that leaks in the blockade might help British shipping and reduce tensions, the foreign secretary observed that "British interests may profit . . . by the imperfect manner in which the blockade may be maintained and it is questionable how far they would be advanced by the attention of the U.S. Government being called to the ineffectiveness of the block-ade." Lyons wrote Russell that "it is very far from being a mere Paper Blockade. . . . [I]f it were as inefficient as Mr. Jefferson Davis says . . . he would not be so very anxious to get rid of it." Finally, Russell's official acceptance of the blockade was written on 15 February 1862 as a mark of the strengthened cooperation that resulted from the *Trent* affair.[29]

Britain's naval cooperation with the Union was not transitory. Throughout the war the blockade received the cooperation of Milne and his squadron. The Royal Navy and Union squadrons cooperated during the Port Royal expedition from 20 November through 10 December 1861. Admiral Milne was under Lyons's orders to "shadow" the Union navy to protect the lives and property of British subjects who might be caught in the Union offensive against the strategic fort on the South Carolina coast. Flag Officer Samuel F. DuPont, commander of the Union's South Atlantic Blockading Squadron, which was charged with enforcing the blockade from South Carolina to South Florida, cooperated with the British naval mission. (DuPont had grown respectful of Royal Navy officers during a mission carrying the U.S. minister to China to the Far East in 1858.) At their first meeting, DuPont assured Capt. George Hancock, commander of the HMS *Immortalité,* that he un-derstood the necessity of his mission because he had performed similar missions. DuPont offered his personal help to protect British subjects and kept Hancock informed of his next target to facilitate following the expedition. Hancock ex-changed visits with Union naval officers throughout the expedition and wrote of his respect for the professional manner in which the offensive succeeded and of the "gratifying and agreeable" communications with the Federals. The *Trent* affair occurred during this expedition, and Hancock informed Milne that his Union counterparts "readily admit the madness it would be on the part of their Govern-ment to do anything to promote a War with England." Since Canada was unde-fended, the ministry tried to press the United States by reinforcing Milne's squad-ron with more battleships and frigates than Milne could manage if war erupted. But defense of Canada was not the problem on station. The winter weather was hard on British ships shadowing the blockade, and they were useless against the modern batteries of the Union coastal forts. Rather than complain about the obvi-ous, Milne preferred to inform the Admiralty of the cooperation during the Port Royal expedition and stressed how DuPont understood the importance of Han-cock's being along. Lyons was settling into comfortable relations with Seward at the same time, as was Adams with Russell. Lyons wrote to Milne in late September that "things are going on smoothly here," and on 11 November, four days before he received news of the *Trent* affair, the British minister wrote: "I have no immediate apprehensions, certainly none of anything of sudden import." Like Lyons, Milne remained calm during the *Trent* affair, and the Admiralty withdrew the reinforcements when the trouble passed. He retained only his flagship, the *Nile,* and five smaller frigates.[30]

Admiral Milne's recommendations carried weight with the ministry. He "exhibited tact, impartiality, sound judgment, and legal knowledge," and he meant what he said. He refused to provoke the Union over seizures in 1861. In August 1862 he ordered his officers not to challenge aggressive Federal acts outside of British waters. Early in 1863 he withdrew British warships from the Rio Grande. These cooperative acts enabled Milne to make a positive impression on Lincoln, Seward, and even Welles. Lyons wrote that the Federals saw that "the firm but temperate and conciliatory conduct of the Admiral is owing to the maintenance of harmonious relations between the two Countries."[31]

Somerset continued to uphold Milne's position that reinforcements were unneeded and would weaken the English Channel fleet's defensive role directed against France.[32] Furthermore, there was a larger body of support for friendly relations outside of the cabinet. Impatient Englishmen were reminded that Britain was usually the belligerent, and it was to Britain's benefit to have the Union "extend belligerent rights as far as possible at the expense of neutral rights on the sea." To prevent a British-American war, the *Economist* opposed breaking the blockade. The *Times* held that a blockade was always Britain's best weapon and should not be blunted nor the Union criticized for it. The *Times'* argument carried into 1863 when the Union navy in the West Indies and Caribbean began arresting blockade-runners that shipped goods from the Indies into blockaded ports. Still, the *Times* reminded readers that "if the Americans are determined to rivet this patch upon the hard old international law, we of all people in the world are the least interested in opposing the innovation." Russell was tolerant of the Union's actions despite the sensitive situation. He complained officially about several of the arrests but overall believed in eventual American restitution as in the past.[33]

Thus, the blockade-runners failed to compromise British neutrality. First, cotton exports to England increased from 3 million pounds in late 1862 to more than 20 million in 1863. By November 1863 this trade averaged from 6,000 to 7,000 bales a month and climaxed in early 1865. British ships carried more than 300,000 bales of cotton out of Matamoros between 1861 and 1865, and 213,000 reached England. Second, this was a complicated situation because more groups than British shippers gained. Counterparts in New York and other Union ports ran the blockade into Matamoros to increase profits. There were 1.25 million bales of raw cotton exported through the blockade, with twenty percent through Matamoros. Largely because of the complicated situation, blockade vessels were ordered to avoid angering the

British and to allow trade for shippers with permits. The permit policy was fortunate because it extinguished British-American disputes over captured vessels.
Policy makers also comprehended that most of the trade through Matamoros in
early 1863 was conditioned by more than one hundred miles through outlaw-in-
fested, desolate territory. The supplies and munitions that got through contributed
little to the Confederate war effort.[34] Third, the blockade was effective enough to
gain the British and French respect as a deterrent. It reduced raw cotton exports,
"depressed Southern purchasing power from raw cotton exports and raised import
costs, thereby stymieing imports of iron plating and machinery."[35]

In addition to the stronger blockade structure and the growth of the Union navy,
there was no significant disruption of neutrality from seizures of blockade-runners.
The stronger the blockade became, the more cooperative Anglo-American relations
became. By late 1861, the blockade consisted of seventy-nine steam-propelled and
the same number of sailing warships, and the blockading fleet grew to six hundred vessels by 1865. Moreover, the blockade "sharply reduced" Southerners' ability
to buy imports because of the devaluation of cotton and other main exports. The
cash returns for the risk to the runners dwindled as cotton and other staples fell to
one-third of the usual price in Liverpool and London. Specifically, the blockade
decreased imports of consumer goods from the North and Europe into the Confederacy because runners carried small quantities that ensured the highest profit for
the risk rather than sustained the Confederate war effort. Needed military supplies
such as fodder, meat, iron, and munitions were not profit makers like high-quality
alcohol, drugs, silks, and clothing. All that got into Texas from Matamoros, for example, were shoes and blankets. Throughout the South, the most needed materials
were those that the runners could not bring in, such as railroad iron and civilian
goods, which "contributed to the general demoralization of the Confederacy." The
meat situation was "desperate by the end of 1863." In 1864, food and forage shortages
prevented Gen. Robert E. Lee, commander of the Rebel Army of Northern Virginia,
from neutralizing Federal gains. Historian David Surdam concludes that the Union
navy kept the South from putting a fleet afloat and did more to weaken the South
than believed by historians.[36]

All of these shortages occurred at the worst time for the South. Union cam-
paigns in the Shenandoah Valley and other chief agricultural regions made the
Confederacy desperate for overseas sources and for foodstuffs and war supplies
through smuggling from the North. D. P. Crook agrees with Surdam that "the
blockade forced the Confederacy to breathe through a constricted windpipe, and
the effort became more debilitating with time." Although they wrote thirty years
apart, Crook and Surdam agree that the blockade caused unevenness in goods
that were brought into the Confederacy, heightened inflation, discouraged industry, and disclosed commercial scarcities.[37] In the long run, because the South
used the blockade to supplant its poor industrial base, the blockade made the

South dependent on the blockade-runners, and it is difficult to see how long this artificial lifeline could have continued. Overall the blockade favored the Union. By 1 August 1861, as the excitement over the Confederate victory at Manassas (Bull Run) enveloped Richmond, Mary Chesnut saw the larger picture. Ammunition and other military provisions were already in short supply partly because of the blockade. Help from Europe was not forthcoming. She confided glumly to her diary: "England has made it all up with them [the North], or rather she will not break with them."[38]

Mary Chesnut's gloomy prognostication seemed to be reality. British-Union cooperation improved with the capture of New Orleans, the South's primary port, in April 1862, and Memphis, a key commercial city on the Mississippi, shortly thereafter. The fall of New Orleans was particularly important because blockade-running was halted, and the Union navy could undertake blockade duties elsewhere. Moreover, merchants were unable to shift trade to another port. Taking New Orleans and Memphis enabled the Union to tighten the blockade on western rivers and begin taking over the South's cotton economy to further the war effort. Thus Europeans saw clearly for the first time that the South's coercive strategy of embargoing cotton was at fault for declining cotton shipments. This problem was serious for the South, which "underestimated the Europeans' anger at the coercion." This anger was a reason that Britain redoubled its neutrality and let the blockade intensify. The London *Times* recorded as early as 21 October 1861 that "it seems to be quite true that all Cotton exportation has been forbidden by the Confederate Government in order that foreign nations may be forced to take a side in the quarrel. It would ill become England to make herself the tool of such machination [and intervene against the blockade]." Palmerston's mouthpiece, the *Morning Post,* enjoined that the Confederates had banned cotton exports "to coerce England and France into the recognition of their national independence and sovereignty." In December, the British consul at Savannah reinforced the London newspapers when he wrote Russell that the Confederacy enacted a law against shipping cotton abroad. Confederate emissary John Slidell quickly noticed European anger in response to the South's coercion, which also gave the Europeans the idea that the blockade was effective. When the Confederates began to burn cotton in the winter and spring of 1862 to keep it from invading armies, Lyons, Mercier, and newspapers in the North, the South, and England quickly recorded what happened. Russell passed consular reports to the newspapers about the embargo and cotton burning along the Mississippi River and elsewhere. Thus the Confederate embargo helped to defeat possibilities for recognition of independence and raised a furor abroad. Unionists abetted the South's acts through its consuls and agents in Europe, and Seward used the cotton shortage as a vehicle for cooperation with Britain. By August 1861, he was fully behind Lincoln's insight about the benefits of a leaky blockade. He refused to stop the cotton trade through Matamoros and "promoted trade through the lines." The contraband trade between Liverpool and New York with Matamoros grew, rivaling these two greatest British and American ports in cotton commerce.[39]

In this cooperative spirit, even the most sensitive Union seizures of blockade-runners failed to break up relations. Cooperation was challenged at Matamoros when the USS *Portsmouth* arrived to blockade the mouth of the Rio Grande in February 1862. Its captain quickly seized the 1,200-ton British screw steamer *Labuan* as a "legal prize" for using American waters to offload contraband and take on cotton. On 8 May, amid growing complaints of further seizures by British consuls in the Caribbean, Lyons told Seward that he had strong evidence that the *Labuan* was seized in Mexican waters and, with the British protest, should be released by the prize court. On 21 May the judge of the U.S. District Court in New York, who acted on seizures, ruled that the *Labuan* had been illegally seized in neutral waters and ordered that the ship and its cargo be released.[40]

In response, in March 1862, Seward refused to take coercive action with the Union's West Gulf Blockading Squadron and again drew the wrath of Secretary of the Navy Welles and other cabinet members.[41] They believed that the secretary of state was selling out to the British to keep them neutral. Yet Union naval captains who saw the futility of dealing with British and French naval vessels underlined the reasonableness of Seward's cooperation with Whitehall. They faced continuous embarrassment from the powers' warships for searching neutral vessels. For this reason Adm. David G. Farragut, commander of the squadron, recommended termination of search to prevent complications. He averred that it was impossible to prevent illegal trade unless the Union took over Brownsville, Texas, across the Rio Grande from Matamoros, through which goods were dispatched to the Confederacy. Once again Lincoln supported Seward's cooperative policy. With Lincoln's guidance, Welles reviewed Farragut's recommendations and ordered that no vessels were to be seized off the Rio Grande unless they were on their way to a Texas port and only after being warned.[42]

In all future prize cases Seward ordered the release of British merchantmen seized off Matamoros. In 1863, he acted in the case of the *Sir William Peel*, which good evidence showed had been trading with the Confederacy. The *Peel* was seized in June for contraband trade and for potentially being a privateer, as evidence surfaced that Gen. Kirby Smith, Confederate commander of the Western Department, had sent a naval officer to inspect and advise on purchasing it. The *Peel* was taken to the Federal prize court in New Orleans. In December, Lyons protested to Seward that the ship was illegally seized because the arresting naval officer termed "Confederate Cotton" to be contraband. Certainly, with the liberal cotton trade policy, there were no strong grounds for taking possession of the ship. Seward told Lyons three weeks later that the arresting naval officer had been summoned and that he was ready to release the *Peel* outright because he believed that it was seized in Mexican

Abraham Lincoln, president of the United States, 1861–65. Library of Congress

waters. Welles opposed him with the argument that if the vessel was in Mexican waters, only Mexico could claim capture. Lyons refused to ask the Mexican minister to intervene because the minister represented the Juárez government with which Seward wanted to remain on good terms and which was trying to gain assistance from the Union. Seward wanted to release the ship, while Welles remained critical of him for not knowing maritime law and making "any sacrifice of national or individual rights to keep in with England." Once again Seward won a victory for cooperation: in the spring of 1864 the prize court freed the ship with its cargo but ruled against paying damages.[43]

Despite Seward's precautions, seizures at Matamoros grew. But cooperation grew apace. Vessels were charged with contraband trade in American waters but were freed because the Union could not document to prize courts the proof that the suspect vessels were in American waters. Seward had admitted in March 1862, "Our right to blockade the mouth of the Rio Grande, for the purpose of preventing this commerce, may be considered at least questionable." Like Seward, Vice-Admiral Milne did not want to cause difficulties and instructed British merchant ship captains to ensure that they anchored in Mexican waters.[44]

Historians D. P. Crook and David Surdam defended Seward in freeing seized blockade-runners. Crook believes that Seward's cotton policy kept Britain and France divided over intervention. In other words, Britain maintained strict neutrality against Napoleon III's desire to act forcefully against Union–held New Orleans. Surdam agrees that Seward's policy prevented grounds for intervention, although only about fifty thousand cotton bales were exported from 1 September 1861 through 31 September 1862. By 1862 the growing Union army demand for finished British cotton and other goods grew and remained strong throughout the war, another reason for continued British cooperation.[45]

The *Trent* affair proved the reasonableness of Britain's decision not to protest the blockade. The habits formed for ignoring the Confederate emissaries and respecting Union blockading actions helped to defuse the event. James Mason, one of the two Rebel agents taken off the *Trent*, had an unofficial interview with Russell on 10 February 1862. He reported to Richmond that Russell "seemed utterly disinclined to enter into conversation at all as to the policy of his Government, and only said, in substance, they must await events." Mason reported that the Crown had no desire to depart from neutrality. He was miffed because the queen had not commented on the blockade when she opened Parliament. A motion to recognize the South was postponed because the queen was mourning her husband's death. After the *Trent* affair Mason and Slidell sensed a British-American rapprochement.[46]

As his actions with Mason disclosed, Russell determined to resist the Confederate lobby and believed that an expanded blockade protected England's interests. The implication was that if "evident danger" occurred, Britain supported a "paper blockade" to keep peace with the Union.[47] As far as Russell knew, the blockade was effective because the Union said it was. When Mason presented the foreign secretary with a long list of ships, many of which were coastal vessels making several landings, that had breached the blockade in 1861, Lord John responded with the embarrassing question that if so many ships had beaten the blockade, why had so little cotton reached Britain? Mason refused to mention the Confederate cotton embargo because he knew that Russell sensed blackmail, would not bite, and knew anyway that the embargo was the primary reason for reduced cotton shipments.[48]

Bipartisan support also caused Britain's refusal to make the blockade a *casus belli*. The loophole that enabled the consensus was in the Declaration of Paris of 1856 that prohibited ineffective blockades but did not define that term. Ex-Conservative foreign secretary Malmesbury, who summarized this point in the House of Lords in February 1862, did not believe that maritime powers like Britain were party to this restriction. He was correct, because the Union had blockading warships on station; it was not necessary, or possible, Malmesbury argued, to apprehend every suspect runner for the blockade to be effective.

Russell's desire to maintain neutrality by recognizing the blockade was clear in his correspondence with Lyons, Seward, and Adams. Lord John accepted the doctrine of "evident danger," meaning that while the Union navy was on patrol there was danger of blockade-runners being captured as prizes. With British assistance, therefore, the growing effectiveness of the Union blockading force became a symbol of the strengthening war effort. Of further importance was the ministry's rejection of the South's secession as a right.

The Confederate lobby in the House of Commons, led by William H. Gregory, John Arthur Roebuck, and William S. Lindsay, failed to carry the debate that the blockade was ineffective in early March 1862. Gregory's speech on 7 March presented an impressive array of blockade violations, but the government stopped him cold when his vigor for the Confederacy caused him to pronounce that secession was a right and that separation was a fact. Speaking for the government, solicitor-general Roundell Palmer challenged Gregory. Palmer denied that Gregory or anyone could advocate recognition and be impartial. Palmer espoused the government line that recognition had to await events on the battlefield. Gregory depended on the arguments of anti-British continental writers, such as French jurist Laurent-Basile Hautefeuille, that a blockade had to be truly enforced to be effective. In fact, to refute Gregory, Palmer argued that the ministry was trying to obtain freer blockading powers in future wars by supporting the Union blockade and that it was merely following past principles and practices of international law. Palmer argued that Britain was legitimately resisting "new fangled notions and interpretations of international law which might make it impossible for us effectively at some future day to institute any blockade, and so destroy our naval authority—that great arm of our independence and safety." He said that blockades had never been airtight and that the age of faster steamships made enforcement harder than before. Nor, he continued, could Britain dictate to the Union when a blockade was effective or when it was not. For these reasons the government refused to challenge the blockade's legality, make war against the Union over the blockade, and side with a country that was one of the "last strongholds of slavery." Palmer's statement might have been taken "as an official declaration of sympathy for the North as champions of freedom against slavery." Historian Frank Owsley believes this was "a clever stroke meant to prevent Gregory's motion being turned into a party issue; neither the Conservative nor the Liberal Party would be willing to appear as a partisan of slavery."[49]

The one thing that the Confederate lobby tried not to do—tie the blockade debate to independence—was compromised when Scott William John Bentinck, another lobbyist, urged that England recognize the South. He admitted what Gregory and the other lobbyists had avoided presenting the appearance of objectivity by linking the refutation of the blockade to independence.[50] After Bentinck's tactical error, members of Parliament joined Russell in not cooperating with the South's agents. The groundwork was laid for the Commons to dismiss Gregory's arguments; and Russell gained government support in the Lords on 10 March. He argued what he had previously told Mason, that the North was trying its utmost to make the blockade effective, which was demonstrated by decreases in cotton shipments to Europe and failure to ship British and French products into the Confederacy at prewar levels. Russell reemphasized that any interference meant war with the Union, loss of North American trade, and a slave insurrection.

Moreover, other pro-North Liberal MPs such as William E. Forster and Monckton Milnes cited the possibility of war if the blockade was repudiated and the growing unemployment in Lancashire as evidence of the blockade's effectiveness. Forster blocked the Confederate lobby. He believed the Civil War was a fight between slavery and abolition, and he opposed intervention. He believed that democracy was the most stable political system and was better for the people than the Old World autocracies and even British parliamentary democracy, with its limited franchise. The Union represented the true home of democracy and must be supported. He posited what the Confederate agents refused to say and what Russell knew better: that small coastal vessels represented most of the Confederate success at running the blockade as opposed to ships running in from the open sea. The main Southern ports, he continued, were effectively blockaded. He argued that rather than debating how and why the South represented a purer democracy than the North, the lobby's real motivation was the commercial pinch that showed the South's growing desperation. Forster was probably looking at lobbyist William Lindsay, who was Britain's leading shipbuilder, a committed free trader, and, like British merchants, opposed to the high Northern tariffs. Forster believed that both the textile workers and the government united patriotically under the hardships. Leading newspapers in the industrial districts, such as the Manchester *Guardian*, reinforced Forster and Milnes.[51] The Conservative opposition and the few Radicals led by Bright and Cobden, who managed the important swing votes, supported the ministry against the Confederate lobby. Confederate sympathy was confined to a small group of MPs, and Gregory was forced to withdraw his motion to prevent defeat.[52]

On 10 March, Lord Campbell, a leading member of the lobby, attacked the government's position based on information supplied by Henry Hotze of the *Index*, the

Confederate propaganda journal in Britain. Russell rebutted Campbell in a vein similar to Forster. The blockade was effective because Confederate statistics were primarily those of coastal vessels running in and out of coastal waterways. He used Palmer's by now familiar argument that neutrality had to be maintained to prevent the Union from unleashing emancipation and a bloody slave insurrection to destroy the cotton supply altogether. This argument was aimed at the merchant interests, on whom he urged patience to prevent the situation from worsening.[53]

This rejection was the first of several defeats of the Confederate lobby on the blockade question. On 13 March, Charles Francis Adams wrote, "The talk of intervention, only two months ago so loud as to take a semi-official tone, is now out of the minds of everyone. I heard Gregory make his long-expected speech in the House of Commons, and it was listened to as you would listen to a funeral eulogy." Adams recognized the bipartisan, pro-Union strength in the House and wrote: "The blockade is now universally acknowledged to be unobjectionable. Recognition, intervention, is an old song. No one whispers it." Henry Adams wrote his brother, a cavalry captain in the Union army, that "times have so decidedly changed since my last letter to you. . . . The talk of intervention, only two months ago so loud as to take an official tone, is now out of the minds of everyone." The anti-Union London *Times* "ate crow," in James McPherson's terms, in misjudging "the unexpected and astonishing resolution of the North."[54]

Napoleon III's pro-South feelings cooled at the same time. Having failed in the Commons, Lindsay got British ambassador Lord Cowley to schedule a meeting for him with the French emperor, who was trying to hurry up the production of ironclads. Lindsay traveled to Paris in early April 1862 to "break the logjam of war" in order to normalize trade with the South. He told Napoleon what he had not told the Commons: that the time was right for recognition of Confederate independence and breaking the "illegal" blockade. In response, the emperor seemed to agree about the ineffectiveness of the blockade but remarked that Britain had rejected his two initiatives for a joint repudiation of the blockade. He told Lindsay that the British government dealt unfairly with him and that it shared a copy of the notes taken in conference with Flahault, the French ambassador to Britain, Adams, and Seward.[55]

Napoleon asked Lindsay to carry his idea to Cowley for a joint Anglo-French naval expedition to the mouth of the Mississippi to break the blockade and return with the latter's response. When Lindsay told Cowley of the scheme, he was met with Cowley's "very positive and outspoken" reply that Britain refused to act with the French to break the blockade. Cowley recited the ministry's position that it was too early to determine a victor and that the blockade was effective. It appeared that the North was winning, he told the lobbyist, and denied that France had ever asked Britain to end the blockade, which, he added, was thought to be more effective than ever.[56] There appeared to be no gaps in the British party line.

Cowley believed that Lindsay acted on his own initiative. He discussed Lindsay's visit with Foreign Minister Thouvenel, and he asked about the two dispatches that Napoleon said were sent to London requesting that the two powers repudiate the blockade at New Orleans. Thouvenel denied that any dispatches had been sent and said that his position on the blockade was the same as Cowley's—that the time had passed for recognition of the South's independence and that if attempts were made to repudiate the blockade, war with the United States was inevitable. Thouvenel said that he told the emperor and Eugene Rouher, the French minister of commerce, of his sentiments.[57]

Cowley explained to Russell and Palmerston what had transpired with Lindsay, the emperor, and Thouvenel. Like Cowley and Thouvenel, they were distressed by Napoleon's "indirect diplomacy." Standing on official diplomatic behavior, Russell refused to cooperate with Napoleon's attempt to circumvent the situation and refused to see Lindsay. Palmerston was conveniently out of town, thus precluding the lobbyist from delivering Napoleon's message to anyone in power. Russell wrote "sarcastically" that he worked through the accredited ambassadors, Cowley and Flahault, who were equally angry. Lindsay believed the emperor's communication was sound and tried to see Lord John again, but Russell again refused an interview. On 17 April, Lindsay told Napoleon of his suspicion that there was a secret agreement between Russell and Seward not to question the blockade's effectiveness. The emperor was chagrined with Britain for not reciprocating his cooperation with Britain in the *Trent* affair. For his part, Lindsay gave up trying to see Palmerston after writing him a defense of the emperor's plans. The lobby despaired after failing for the third time to arouse intervention. News of the Union navy's conquest of New Orleans reached London on 11 May, which ended the lobby's attempts. Seward's demand to renounce belligerent rights to the South kept London and Paris inactive. The emperor told Cowley: "I quite agree that nothing can be done for the moment but to watch events."[58]

Thus, by May 1862, British-American cooperation was working splendidly and was dictating the posture of France in the Civil War. William Dayton, the American minister to France, wrote Seward that little was being said about "the propriety of an early recognition of the south." The fall of New Orleans caused Henry Adams to find his usually taciturn father dancing across the floor shouting: "We've got New Orleans." Mason wrote Davis that "the fall of New Orleans will certainly exercise a depressing influence here for intervention." Russell replied to Mason's entreaties for recognition that "the capture of New Orleans, the advance of the Federals to Corinth, to Memphis, and the banks of the Mississippi as far as Vicksburg" meant that Britain continued to wait. Mason tried to activate his lobby, but in June Palmerston wrote Foreign Office parliamentary undersecretary A. H. Layard that "this seems to be an odd moment to Chuse for acknowledging the Separate Independence of the South when all the Seaboard, and the principal internal Rivers are in the hands of the North." Adams thought resistance was about to end.[59]

He was premature, however. On 15 June 1862 in the House of Lords the Marquess of Clanricarde tried to revive the debate when he argued that the Declaration of Paris intended that blockades had to be effective to be legal and that the Union blockade was not effective because it was frequently run. Russell countered that the Federals had not ratified the Declaration and that England had blockaded France under similar circumstances. Neutrality was necessary because of the complicated question of Confederate independence. As if to prove that recognition was a long shot, blockade-running into Mobile faltered by September, because all of the river steamers trying to run the cordon were destroyed or captured.[60]

As Mobile demonstrated, the Union navy improved at stopping blockade-runners. Sir Alexander Milne tried to stop blockade-runners from Bermuda, which, along with Nassau and Havana, harbored a Rebel warehouse. He appealed to the Admiralty for legal measures. On 29 November 1862 he brought up Adm. Charles Wilkes, then on blockade duty in the area. Wilkes was hamstrung by Russell's order of 31 January 1862 that enabled blockade-runners to use neutral harbors. Milne wrote, "If we change positions with Admiral Wilkes, I dare say we would feel annoyed to see several steamers full of contraband of war in a harbour of a neutral power ready to break *our* blockade." On 2 August a law was passed by the General Assembly of Bermuda to prohibit exports of military and naval stores with heavy fines; a forfeiture of ships, boats, carriages, or other vehicles, a fine of more than $1,000 for hindering arrest, and prohibition of food exports. The queen approved it on 17 December 1862. Milne thought that this order weakened blockade-running. In May 1864 Welles ordered that when the Federal navy caught foreign seaman aboard neutral ships they were to be immediately released but were to become prisoners of war if they lacked papers, flew the Confederate flag, or were in Confederate service. U.S. citizens were detained if captured on neutral or Rebel ships. If they were passengers they might be released if they swore allegiance. In sum, both navies used good sense with captured seamen. Milne rarely complained because he believed that they had violated the British neutrality proclamation of 1819 that prohibited subjects from assisting either side in a war.[61]

Milne used his strict interpretation of the neutrality proclamation to stop the blockade-runners from using naval repair yards. He began his campaign on 20 August 1863 when he forbade coal or assistance to suspicious vessels in the Bermuda dockyard. In December he discovered that the navy yard had repaired nine blockade-runners; he repeated his order forbidding repairs or coal except for those vessels in distress and required a bonded sponsor to prevent a repaired vessel from trying to run the blockade for three months. The queen's advocate overruled Milne, who wrote the Admiralty, which then contacted Russell. In March 1864, in the best interests of cooperation, Russell instructed the Admiralty that Royal Navy yards were off-limits to blockade-runners because they were reserved for warships.[62]

Fortunately for Franco-American relations, Napoleon III's advisors when the Civil War began were pro-North and opposed intervention. The first crisis that tested the stability of the North's relations with Britain and France was the *Trent* affair, which resulted in a clearing of the air in transatlantic relations to benefit the blockade issue. After helping to resolve the issue peacefully, French foreign minister Thouvenel assured Seward in early February 1862 that France was not leading an attack on the United States. The blockade was safe from that quarter. Apparently, Thouvenel had just treated John Slidell icily during their first interview. Slidell was trying to arouse support to terminate the blockade by arguing that it was ineffective. The French foreign minister asked the same question the British had raised. If the blockade was ineffective why was so little cotton reaching French ports? He trapped Slidell, who could not admit that the real reason was the South's cotton embargo.[63]

The French government continued to support Thouvenel's words to allay Washington's apprehensions. On 12 February Northern newspapers held that Napoleon III's legislative speech offered nothing to the South except "cool neutrality." In a month French government spokesman Adolphe Billault reassured the North in a Senate speech on benevolent neutrality. Napoleon III upheld neutrality to the Chamber of Deputies in mid-February and remarked that "we must limit ourselves to prayers that those dissensions [between North and South] will soon end." The French faced a collapse of domestic industry from lack of cotton and poor harvests. Thouvenel blamed Britain for not helping to mediate the war and for industrial and working-class desperation.[64]

French minister to the United States, Henri Mercier, pressed France's economic and social quandary on extreme abolitionist Sen. Charles Sumner, chair of the Senate Foreign Relations Committee. Sumner had been passed over for secretary of state in favor of Seward and for minister to Britain in favor of Charles Francis Adams, Seward's candidate. Mercier told Sumner that the United States was too great to be treated shabbily by the European powers, and his actions throughout the war seemed to bear his peaceful desires out. He nagged Seward about ending the blockade to reinvigorate commerce and tried unsuccessfully to coordinate a mediated end to the war despite Lyons's disagreement with his actions. Meanwhile, Mercier grew friendlier with Seward, whose resolve not to allow recognition of Confederate independence or intervention on any terms kept Mercier from doing much more than talking about how to end the war. Indeed, Mercier's trip to Richmond in mid-April 1862 to discuss terms on which to end the war was part of Seward's ploy to stop talk of European intervention and to let Richmond know that the Southern states could come back into the Union peacefully.

Despite his uneasiness about French affairs, Thouvenel opposed Mercier's trip. On 1 May he wrote Mercier the sharpest note yet that his unauthorized visit to Richmond had not enhanced the Franco-British entente or advanced intervention. Napoleon flatly denied that he had condoned Mercier's action, and Flahault intimated this position to Russell. Britain had just pulled out of the tripartite alliance in Mexico, and the emperor was worried that Britain might become critical of his adventure. Russell intimated to Flahault that the two powers continued to march together in American affairs,[65] but there is no doubt that France's embarrassment over Mercier's journey placed its diplomacy more clearly on Britain's tail and made it much more sensitive to acting unilaterally. But in the end, Seward neither gained nor lost anything except closer understanding with Lyons, who knew that Seward was anxious to end the war on terms that the South could define as honorable. No such result occurred, however, except that Britain doubted Napoleon's word and grew more distrustful of the emperor. Seward had again succeeded in driving a wedge between Britain and France by giving Mercier a pass to Richmond, which turned out to benefit British-American understanding and was exactly what both parties needed at that time. British newspapers said Mercier's trip was premature. Palmerston said that the emperor, whom he dubbed the "spider of the Tuileries," was merely spinning more webs.[66]

As French foreign policy became murkier with opportunism that could change from moment to moment, British-American relations became clearer and more dependable. Palmerston summarized support for the Union blockade to the queen on 7 March 1862 while it still leaked badly. He wrote that to intervene against the blockade meant war with the United States and "would be a departure from principles, which if Great Britain was a belligerent she would be obliged stoutly to maintain and act upon." Palmerston and Russell knew that Britain could use the blockade to advantage in similar circumstances. Lyons indicated that the Southern cause was going poorly because they had "fought badly" in recent battles. He questioned if Richmond could hold out much longer. Russell concurred that Confederate defeats at Yorktown, New Orleans, and Corinth "seem to portend the conquest of the South. We have now to see therefore whether a few leaders, or the population entertain these sentiments of alienation & abhorrence [toward the North]." To Seward's joy, French policy was exactly in this frame of mind.[67]

3

The *Trent* Affair and Its Aftermath

in the Rapprochement

With the cooperation that had been achieved over the first spring, summer, and fall of the Civil War, the South was not in the fine position that many in Richmond believed. British-American relations had emerged after the first six months of the conflict with the antebellum sentiments of cooperation intact. These past influences and the mutual desire for peace prevented the *Trent* affair from breaching the rapprochement, and the same spirit infected the relationship after the affair. A recent historian writes that the affair was a "watershed in Anglo-American relations during the war and there was a distinct difference between British attitudes towards the Union before the incident and afterwards."[1]

Another study argues that Seward's cooperation was again demonstrated to untangle the *Trent* affair. Early in the affair at a party at the Portuguese legation, a haggard Seward, perhaps suffering from the effects of too much brandy, threatened through his cigar smoke: "We will wrap the whole world in flames." British war correspondent William Howard Russell was standing nearby and was visibly shaken until another guest told him, "That's all bugaboo talk. When Seward talks that way, he means to break down. He is most dangerous and obstinate when he pretends to agree a good deal with you." What he was trying to do was to seize on the *Trent* affair to warn the British not to recognize or help Richmond.[2]

Moreover, because of the earlier cooperation, the *Trent* affair was managed with usual diplomatic practices. Although one cannot argue that the affair's settlement was determined the minute that it occurred, it was not a watershed event, because of the dependability of diplomatic practices in the relationship and the pronounced temperament of cooperation afterward. All of the players used traditional diplomacy, and the affair was quickly settled.

It took only two months to resolve the affair because the need for cooperation was shared. Like the respective governments, very few British subjects wanted a war with the North because imperial France was the primary threat facing Britain and its empire in 1861. Moreover, there were few anti-North speeches in Parliament during the affair. Despite the North's celebrations at a time when a success in the war was badly needed, there was little saber rattling in Britain. As Duncan Andrew Campbell recently concluded by quoting the January 1862 *Wesleyan Methodist Magazine* just after the affair was resolved, "If there be a war-party in this country, eager for conflict, it must be very fractional and insignificant."[3]

The *Trent* affair thus cannot be seen within the event itself. The antebellum diplomacy of caution and cooperation, concocted within the mutual desire not to cause an international war, makes any other but a peaceful solution difficult to calculate. To date, the affair has been seen too separate from the general flow of antebellum and Civil War diplomacy, which has led to the affair being interpreted more as a prognosticator of conflict rather than as another example of the peaceful structure underpinning relations. To produce any other but peaceful outcomes would have represented a shattering break with the past and upset the trend line in relations as they had evolved throughout the century.

The urgent Union need for loans is another factor that has gone unconsidered in explaining why the *Trent* affair was resolved quickly and peacefully. Jay Sexton's work sheds new light on the resolution of the affair. The event occurred when the Union needed British loans to finance the war effort against the South. The Barings and other British banking houses refused to issue loans as long as a British-Union war seemed inevitable due to the *Trent* affair. The bankers made it clear that their British nationalism was stronger than their desire to make a profit. Knowing this, a Wall Street broker told secretary of the treasury Salmon P. Chase to resolve the matter because another war meant economic ruin. Chase's colleague Atty. Gen. Edward Bates felt the same. His conservative instincts caused him to state that "war with England is to abandon all hope of suppressing the rebellion . . . our trade would be utterly ruined and our treasury bankrupt." Fortunately, Chase agreed with the financial community and his cabinet colleague.[4]

Palmerston and Lincoln promoted a peaceful settlement at the end of December 1861, with Seward's apology to Britain and the freeing of the Confederate prisoners who had been taken off the British mail packet *Trent* without Federal authorization on 8 November 1861 by Union navy captain Charles Wilkes. Wilkes's blatant defiance of international maritime law was not enough to infuriate the British to implement war plans. These plans were too ambitious to be successful, especially in an age when Britain eschewed military encounters. As in the past, future disputes were dealt with cooperatively to avoid repeating the *Trent* affair's ensuing two months of private and public consternation. Lincoln's policy allowed Britain to remain neutral. British thoughts of retribution quickly faded when it was discovered that Lincoln and Seward were working to redress the grievance Wilkes had caused. Not only was his action checked, but also his second round of harassment of British vessels in the West Indies in 1863 (when he was supposed to be on blockade duty off South Carolina) was handled by Britain and the United

States in a coordinated and cooperative manner. The *Trent* affair enabled British leaders to understand that the United States refused to divert the Civil War into an international war against a foreign power to reunite the Union. The British no longer feared that Canada was a Union target because the Americans had made no effort to prosecute military preparations against Canada in the affair. Finally, the affair redoubled the desire of the British not to intervene. While the press and numerous private individuals worked to maintain peaceful relations, Russell supported Palmerston's opposition to war by writing on 16 December, "I do not think the country would approve of an immediate declaration of war."[5]

Robin Winks's remark that "actually the affair of the *Trent* was a popular, but not necessarily a diplomatic, crisis" portrays it within the cooperative relations that grew throughout 1861, improved in 1862, and evolved in 1863 and thereafter. Most recently, he has been followed by Campbell's interpretation that even the public outcry in Britain "was far more moderate than the irrational explosion of anti-Union sentiment that historians have often portrayed." Campbell finds that on 17 November, when news of the affair reached England, there was only one "true anti-Union meeting" and that was in Liverpool, the hotbed of Confederate sympathy. Leading Confederate sympathizer James Spence organized this meeting, and the London papers scorned it. Nor were there other meetings in Britain that first week after learning about the affair. The press preached calm and noted the public's moderation. Campbell believes that E. D. Adams in his study published in 1925 exaggerated the bellicosity of the British press and relied too heavily on the opinion of the Adams family and Americans visiting England. Historians have not surmounted Adams's interpretation. Charles Francis Adams was dealing with an outraged Palmerston early in the affair because he had promised Palmerston safety for British ships. Campbell further argues that the oft-quoted statement that "999 men out of every thousand" wanted war immediately was a quip by an American visitor and was never repeated by a British spokesman as representative of public opinion. Campbell sees the same attitude in Union newspapers. Anger over the neutrality proclamation had escalated since the previous May, but there were no war cries, and despite what earlier historians have written, there was no jingoistic press. Moreover, despite historians' claims, the British press did not universally accept the idea that Seward authorized the seizures.[6]

Nevertheless, historians have consistently interpreted the *Trent* affair as bringing Britain and the United States closer to war than any event during the Civil War, if the not the entire nineteenth century. In 1974 D. P. Crook argued that the hard feelings it left conditioned interventionist movements in Britain and France in 1862.[7] Just a few years after Crook's work, and more in line with my argument, David Krein wrote that because of the *Trent* affair "if Britain were to become involved in the American struggle it was unlikely that the North would provide the provocation."[8] Recent interpretations, such as Reginald Stuart's 1987 study of Canadian-

American industry along the border, and the workable nature of the relationship before, during, and after the Civil War refute Crook's argument. Writing in 1999, Paul Scherer sees Russell's Civil War diplomacy as a peaceful brake on Palmerston in the *Trent* affair and afterward.[9] In 2000, Russell F. Weigley reinterpreted the *Trent* incident as less provocative than historians have believed.[10] Finally, Duncan Campbell's most recent argument speaks to the *Trent* affair as other than a crisis and more of another indication that publics, presses, and governments did not want war and worked privately and efficiently to settle the matter.

The facts seem to best fit the recent interpretations. Palmerston and Lincoln were both sensitive to public opinion and used their perspectives about its tendencies to strengthen their positions. In this event, neither leader succumbed to the initial popular furor. For his part, Seward was thoroughly under Lincoln's guidance in foreign affairs and did not resort to Machiavellian trickery to rally public opinion against a common enemy in an attempt to bring the South back into the Union to fight Britain. He had changed a great deal since his early war days of single-handedly trying to bring the Confederacy back into the Union. In fact, at the end of October he fired Henry Sanford, aggressive head of the Union spy ring in Europe, for planning to run aground a contraband-carrying British ship in the Thames as it departed. It was then supposed to be seized by the Union warship *James Adger*. If the plot had succeeded, relations between the two countries would have been strained. Sanford's removal for threatening British neutrality on 6 November, just before the *Trent* affair, meant that Union spying in Britain would be less aggressive to avoid exciting the British government by ignoring its neutrality.[11]

Palmerston's attitude complemented Seward's will to cooperate with Britain. During the *Trent* affair, after a flurry of expected outbursts, Palmerston instead helped the Union save face, and Lincoln joined in allowing Seward and Russell to diffuse the affair. The prime minister conferred with the cabinet, and as a result, on 30 November, Russell wrote Lyons, "Bearing in mind the friendly relations which have long subsisted between Great Britain and the United States we are willing to believe that the United States naval officer who committed this aggression was not acting in compliance with any authority from his Government, or that if he conceived himself to be so authorized, he greatly misunderstood the instructions which he had received."[12]

The outcome of the *Trent* affair built upon Seward's cooperation from June through November 1861 and Russell's desire to maintain strict neutrality. During that time, Seward became Lincoln's obedient secretary of state and followed orders against a foreign war. Seward communicated well with Lyons and the other ministers in Washington, and he refused to become upset over the tripartite alliance of France, Spain, and Britain to intervene in Mexico on 31 October just before Wilkes's nefarious action. For his part, Russell's failure to sway Palmerston in the first intervention debate the month before the affair helped to allay emotions. So did the

Federal naval victories at Port Hatteras, North Carolina, and Port Royal, South Carolina. These victories gave the British hope for the resumption of cotton commerce, which they believed was the result of the South's cotton embargo blackmail attempt to force Britain and France to recognize the Confederacy's independence. Moreover, Seward informed Russell that Wilkes's action of taking Confederate commissioners off the *Trent* while letting the vessel continue on was unauthorized and that he was "disposed to confer and act with earnestness" to defuse the affair. He inserted in Lincoln's annual message to Congress, which remained silent about the affair, that the United States intended to "commit no belligerent act not founded in strict right, as sanctioned by public law."[13] His utterances implied that shipboard commanders could not decide what was and was not contraband. International maritime law held that the entire prize, including crews and passengers, had to be determined in prize court.

The short-lived war cries were diffused by the longstanding realism of both governments. Since the 1830s, Palmerston had employed a deterrence policy. He continued to use that policy in late 1861. If the United States did not apologize and surrender the Confederates, Palmerston would resort to his most effective strategy of economic warfare. Correspondingly, the United States had never taken advantage of Britain's military weakness along the Canadian frontier because in reality there was no threat. The United States spent $8.25 million between 1815 and 1829 on coastal defenses, but the Royal Navy could still shell major coastal cities. Washington could not afford enough men for both the forts and a ground attack on Canada. Nor were Britain's defensive measures any better. For example, its thirty-year fortress project on Narragansett Bay ordered in 1821 was "utterly useless" and a "massive investment in naval weakness." Its 468 guns were never mounted, and the required garrison of 2,400 men was never sent. In reality there was nothing to protect as Canadian-American commerce and tourism blossomed. Moreover, in 1861 Palmerston was tied up with the peak of the Anglo-French naval arms race and was suspicious of Napoleon III's Mexican adventure, which escalated his long-term fear of imperial France in general.[14]

Indeed, the *Trent* affair was quickly resolved, unlike earlier disputes, such as the *Caroline* incident in the late 1830s, which involved a British-Canadian incursion against American "Patriots" who supported Canadian rebels, the on-the-spot decision that the *Caroline* was an anti-British vessel, and the burning of the boat. Whereas the *Caroline* dispute made relations uneasy for three years because Palmerston stalled to resolve the issue, the *Trent* affair was settled in an astoundingly short period considering the time it took to send transatlantic messages. In fact, it only took one British message to enable the Americans to reach agreement on freeing the Confederate prisoners. However, if the Atlantic Telegraph had not been broken in 1858, it might have been a vehicle for Seward to rapidly alert the British that Wilkes's actions were unauthorized and arrest the affair before the end of November. As it was, delays allowed tempers to rise and then to cool. The absence of the telegraph helped cooperation continue because it allowed reconsideration of initial passions and the establishment of workable plans for settlement. Diplomacy would not have been facilitated by the telegraph.[15]

Time benefited Seward's hope for the cabinet to support his desire to settle peacefully. His position should not have taken close observers by surprise. From the previous June through October he refused to approve any form of foreign intervention "from any, even the most friendly quarter." He responded that Napoleon III's mediation attempt was appreciated but could never be accepted. Moreover, he wrote that "the integrity of any nation is lost, and its fate becomes doubtful, whenever strange hands . . . are employed to perform the proper functions of the people, established by the organic laws of the state." Seward's hard line aimed to prevent war rather than cause it. He received help from British newspapers to maintain Britain's neutrality. On 30 October the London *Times* upheld neutrality with the statement "We can well afford to wait and see this contest brought to a close." Nor was the Southern cotton embargo enough to put Britain over the edge. The *Economist* echoed: "The recognition of the South by all the powers in the world would not affect the blockade one iota." Recognition would be a "distinct and indefensible act of hostility towards the North." Knowing of Seward's no-toleration policy on recognition and the blockade, the journal emphasized that "to insist upon the United States ceasing the blockade would be neither more nor less than to declare war against them." Indeed, British merchants did not want the blockade disrupted because they blamed the South for the cotton shortage. For these reasons, the *Economist* wanted Britain to quietly accept a fair proposal for mediation of the *Trent* affair. Memories of the Crimea lingered, and the journal did not want Britain to drift into another war. The *Spectator* held that strict neutrality must be maintained, but out of its sympathy for the North it demanded that the South's independence never be recognized. The newspaper cautioned: "That English action should help to make a slave empire possible is almost unbearable." The *Saturday Review* argued similarly against quarreling and that conciliation was the way out. The *Times* wanted nothing done "without full consideration of all the bearings of the case."[16] This temperament was reinforced by the *British Quarterly Review* on 7 December. That periodical found the idea of war with America "unnatural and revolting." The *Illustrated London News* stated that despite the acclaim that Wilkes received, there was no evidence that he acted under official orders, and allowance should be made for the problems Lincoln faced. Britain should "make any sacrifice of feeling, not inconsistent with national honour, in order to avert a war with their American kin." *Fraser's Magazine* also opposed aggression because the North had not acted perfidiously and did not want a war with Britain. Moreover, *Fraser's* reminded its readers that Britain did not want the affair to result in warfare because that might mean becoming an unwilling ally of the "slaveowners, whose crimes we have been the loudest to denounce."[17]

Moreover, neither British political party used the emotions the affair stirred up for political gain. In the Commons, opposition leader Disraeli spoke unreservedly to give Wilkes's actions a "generous interpretation" and "liberal construction." In the House of Lords, Conservative Party leader Lord Derby said that American friendship was paramount. The Liberal ministry was even more direct. All fourteen cabinet members softened Russell's initial draft dispatch that threatened war if the Rebels were not returned and an apology not made. Clarendon was not in the cabinet but indicated how cooperative the dispatch became by complaining that "his [Russell's] replies to Seward were too humble."

Whether it was too humble or not for Clarendon made little difference. Russell's proposal moved the resolution forward because it offered the U.S. government a way out of the affair. In addition to Russell's handiwork, the proposal has a coincidental and critical history that upholds cooperation both governments wanted so badly. Queen Victoria's beloved husband, Prince Albert, was dying from typhoid fever, but he too believed that Wilkes acted without authority, and for this reason he provided a "face-saving retreat" for Russell and Seward on 30 November. Albert's revision of Russell's strongly worded proposal upheld the royal belief that peace overrode the dispute, and it belied his distrust of Napoleon III, whom he feared was capable of taking advantage of any scrape that Britain contracted. The prince's revision relieved Gladstone and Granville, and it was endorsed by Palmerston, who "was not spoiling for a fight," contrary to the popular belief. Lady Cowley, wife of the British ambassador to France, purposely told American minister to France William Dayton of the prince's work. She was a close friend of the queen who obviously used this backdoor to show her desire for peace. Dayton passed this tempering intelligence to Seward.[18]

Russell's resulting official dispatch did not accuse the North of being responsible for Wilkes's blunder, assumed he acted without orders, and requested the "restoration of the unfortunate passengers and a suitable apology." To maintain good feelings, Russell secretly instructed Lyons to apprise Seward of these terms before formally presenting the document to deprive the dispatch of any "aggressive or minatory character." Lord John opined to Somerset on 28 December that he would "rejoice" if the Americans released the envoys. In addition, the government's support did not raise a dispute between Crown and Parliament.[19]

All was not smooth politically in Washington. The *Trent* affair occurred when Lincoln was beginning to experience the wrath of Radical Republicans for not quickly defeating the South and abolishing slavery. Thus Charles Sumner, who chaired the Senate Foreign Relations Committee, Secretary of the Treasury Salmon P. Chase, and conservative Post. Gen. Montgomery Blair urged the president to free the Confederates to avoid war with Britain and to hurriedly get on with quashing the rebellion that was literally at their doorstep. At the critical cabinet meeting on Christmas Day, 1861, Chase argued that Wilkes violated the law of

Charles Sumner, Radical Republican senator from Massachusetts and powerful chairman of the Senate Committee on Foreign Affairs during and after the Civil War. Library of Congress

nations, that Britain had the right to ask for an American disavowal, and that the prisoners should be released. And, although Wilkes should be commended for his motives, "The Technical right is undoubtedly with England," as the Confederates could not be taken from the *Trent* unless the entire vessel was seized. The issue had to be settled to quiet the public and prosecute the Civil War.[20]

Despite the support of Sumner and Chase, the *Trent* affair's stresses widened the split in the Republican ranks, which pushed Lincoln to settle to avoid political embarrassments. The "self-styled Radicals," or "Jacobins," as David Donald calls them, were critical of Lincoln and his cabinet and wanted an all-out offensive war to end slavery and confiscate Southern property to make sure the Southern planters could never rise again. On the conservative end was a less clearly defined group that did not want to destroy Southern property. What made matters worse for Lincoln was that neither faction accepted his strong executive powers to develop a winning war effort. To do that Lincoln needed support from the Democrats, other Republicans, Border State leaders, and Northerners, westerners, and easterners.

Most congressmen were of little help to the president either. They were indifferent to him after patronage was distributed, and they had little else to gain. They opposed his statement that he had no policy, and Chase called this no-policy position an "idiotic notion." The statement made the Radicals believe that Lincoln lacked principles and leadership to defeat the South. As Donald points out, the fault was not all theirs. They were direct and overbearing, but Lincoln was "often evasive and elusive." He kept his plans to himself, which infuriated the self-important Radicals. More than that, Lincoln acted with an "intellectual arrogance and unconscious assumption of superiority" that deeply offended these extremists.[21]

Thus, the *Trent* affair collided with this troubling political background and was a further reason for Lincoln's decision to keep the peace with Britain by agreeing to a settlement. Of extreme importance was Seward's work to overcome the Radicals, which improved his relations with Russell and Lyons and helped keep the president in charge of the war effort. Russell accepted Seward's reply releasing the Confederates but did not agree that Mason and Slidell and their dispatches on board the *Trent* were contraband. But an understanding developed. The British now found Seward "peaceful and without any animosity toward England in contrast to his early hostile attitude of April and May 1861."

Of more importance on the American side, but still of significance for the uniformity of policy making, Seward stole a march on Sumner. Sumner worked for peace, with the ulterior motive of being considered by his friends in Washington and London as the Union's premiere foreign policy expert. After the affair was settled, his Senate speech on 9 January 1862 was perceived by British and American leaders as unnecessary. But his quest for power was greater than his common sense, and he was within his rights. He said he spoke to enhance the peace, to advocate a recodification of maritime law, and to arouse "the patriotism and self-respect of my own countrymen by associating the surrender [of the Confederate emissaries] with American principles." Sumner's rhetoric was icily received in England. The London *Times* attacked him for rebuking England. William Vernon Harcourt (Historicus), who had connections in Palmerston's ministry as a noninterventionist, condemned Sumner also. Henry Reeve, Sumner's British friend, emphasized that the senator's criticism of British impressment was a moot point because, after the War of 1812, impressment was a dead issue. The usually friendly Duke of Argyll was equally critical. He told Charles Francis Adams that he disagreed with Sumner's interpretation of international law and that England could resume impressment arguments without any inconsistency with its action in the *Trent* affair.[22]

Sumner was wrong in speaking out because the mutual cautious policy had already settled the affair. Sumner's criticism of Russell was unnecessary. Indeed, it might have threatened the settlement at a time when Russell's closer relations with Adams caused William L. Yancey to accuse the foreign secretary of "truckling to the arrogant demand of Mr. Seward that England should forego her international privilege of hearing the case of a belligerent power."[23] These criticisms caused Russell to redouble his neutrality, and he refused to receive Mason officially. Moreover, the detractors were unnerved when they discovered that the diplomats settled privately without awaiting public support on either side of the Atlantic.[24]

In the midst of the crisis, the hard-pressed Lincoln avowed that "one war at a time" was enough and that Palmerston's temporary warlike actions were the stuff of his usual bluff. Lincoln bore no hard feelings toward Palmerston; and when the prime minister found that even bluff was unnecessary to remain in power, he lost interest. (He boasted early in the affair that he had never gotten England into a war.) His actions showed that neutrality was more important than seizing on the affair as an excuse to fight the Yankees.[25] By that time Congress, Parliament, and politicians in the North and Britain strongly supported the settlement.[26]

The settlement was tied to Wilkes's rather unsavory character and reputation. He had been in the navy since 1818 and was best known for his four-year exploring expedition of the Pacific Ocean from 1838 to 1842. After his voyage he was court-martialed for mistreating his crew, and he was relegated to shore duty. Wilkes was "tactless and a martinet." But he was intensely patriotic and ambitious, and he had a strong sense of duty, except that he thought that American national self-interest was his self-interest. Whenever he was insubordinate he felt discriminated against whether he brooked naval regulations or not, which he did regularly. These traits caused him to break international law to stop the *Trent* in the Old Bahamas Channel some three hundred miles north-northeast of Havana, seize Mason and Slidell, and let the *Trent* steam on to Britain.[27] Wilkes historian Nathaniel Philbrick calls this action "a brazen and illegal grab for celebrity." He took the Rebels to Hampton Roads where he was ordered to carry them to prison at Fort Warren in Boston Harbor. Atty. Gen. Edward Bates summarized Wilkes's reputation after the Christmas Day cabinet agreement to settle: "Capt Wilkes did not bring in the *Trent,* the Steamer for adjudication, so that the matter might be judged by a prize court, and not the Capt. on his quarter deck."[28]

Russell and Seward were reticent in contrast to Wilkes's brashness. Russell did not use the blockade or the Mexican expedition against the North. Seward was at first elated at Wilkes's action, but he quieted down when Gen. George B. McClellan told him that Wilkes's act might lead to war. He did not write to Adams until 30 November, when he commented that Wilkes had acted alone.[29]

Lincoln was also at first elated by Wilkes's action and did not believe that it contained any possibility of war with Britain. The president realized that the captain had abjured international law and that Mason and Slidell were "white elephants," a feeling that the British reciprocated. He worried that the United States had to uphold the rights of neutrals to conduct their shipping freely and wrote, "We fought Great Britain [in the War of 1812] for insisting . . . on the right to do precisely what Captain Wilkes has done. If Great Britain shall now protest against the act, and demand their release, we must give them up, [and] apologize for the act as a violation of our doctrines."[30]

Fortunately, then, British-American policies were parallel, as both wanted to resolve the affair without controversy. Lincoln was "instinctively for peace," Sumner explained to Cobden after seeing Lincoln "daily & most intimately ever since the *Trent* question has been under discussion." Lincoln took Lyons's advice and refused to discuss the affair until he heard from Russell. He told Canadian minister of finance, Alexander Galt, that he did not want a quarrel with England and that he had no hostile designs on Canada. When Galt asked him about the *Trent* affair, Lincoln replied, "Oh, that'll be got along with." Lincoln and Lyons remained aloof. The president kept the matter out of the Senate and the cabinet until the moment of decision on 25 December. War plans were not discussed to invade Canada or to attack the British fleet. Lyons took his own advice and was not seen from the time that he learned of the captures until he presented Seward with Russell's proposal for Seward to surrender the prisoners and apologize in a friendly and private manner. After agreeing to Russell's terms, Sumner told Lincoln that the president should strive "to drive out from the British Govt. their distrust of his Administration & to plant confidence instead." The president told Sumner that he wanted to see Lyons "that [wrote Sumner] he might hear from my lips how much I desire Peace. If we could talk together he would believe me."[31]

Despite his suspicions, Palmerston wanted French support to resolve the *Trent* affair peacefully. Napoleon cooperated because the French people were pro-North, and he was therefore incapable of acting opportunistically to use the affair to weaken both Britain and the North.[32] The depressed French textile workers were upset by the lack of raw materials owing to the blockade but nevertheless wanted strict neutrality. Unemployed workers rioted in Lyons because of the lack of raw materials and food. The British were content to let Napoleon speak for an outraged Europe against the Union, which strengthened Russell's proposal for the release of the Confederate prisoners and an apology. Free of complications from the emperor, Palmerston readily accepted Seward's note that the prisoners would be surrendered. Adams wrote that if Napoleon had not supported Palmerston, Lincoln might have made a stronger argument against England.[33]

Caution and cooperation prevailed. Full of these thoughts, Palmerston swayed the cabinet against a war that he believed was hopeless. Russell agreed and said that the North was going to win the Civil War, weaken France in Mexico, and show Napoleon III that he could not depend on Britain's support in Europe unless he cooperated. Lyons supported caution, which, for the first time in British-American relations in the Civil War, aligned British and Union policy with Lyons and Adams as mediums. During this affair, the British minister began to see that Seward paled at the thought of conflict, and they agreed that dependable relations outranked the British-French entente.

Lyons's revised perspective left Britain and the United States with a greater need to continue the rapprochement because there were no other powers that they either could (or wanted to) depend on. On 30 December, before Seward released the prisoners, Palmerston feared a French campaign with the help of Italian allies against Austria and another against Prussia on the Rhine.[34] Moreover, he worried that Napoleon III would create greater anxieties for Britain by inciting a Polish insurrection against Russia, especially if there was a British-American war. Russell asked Cowley for a memorandum on Napoleon's position to allay the prime minister's concerns, and the British ambassador quickly quelled these fears. Yet Palmerston's concern about France in Europe, and France's threat to Britain's shores, triggered his desire for peace with the United States.[35]

A final possible situation caused by Wilkes's actions would have been if the British had wanted to use the *Trent* affair as an excuse to recognize an independent Confederacy—in that case, they would have missed several chances to commandeer public rage and French support to justify that recognition. But Whitehall never came close to this scenario. First, the cabinet wanted no war with anyone at or since that time. Second, the tripartite alliance in Mexico reflected the larger antagonisms among Britain, France, and Spain. Third, the powers had to commit military and naval resources to Mexico. They could not stretch them to fight the United States. Britain had too many naval vessels committed to the expedition against Vera Cruz, where the alliance had landed its forces, to redirect them against New York or Boston. Farther afield, the Royal Navy in the Pacific was no larger than the American navy. It is not surprising, then, that the settlement was received in Britain with relief. Triumphant emotions were discouraged and so was any "lionisation" of Mason and Slidell.[36]

At the same time, Confederate diplomacy assisted in keeping Britain and France neutral. William L. Yancey, who had done more than anyone else for secession, was the first Confederate emissary to Britain. First, he repelled Russell by unilaterally and arrogantly demanding that Britain recognize Confederate independence over the *Trent* incident. This demand embarrassed the small Confederate lobby in Parliament when the ministry refused to move the issue. Therefore Confederate diplomacy consisted of only an "impassioned plea" to free Mason and Slidell.[37] Second, Yancy did not emphasize the blockade's ineffectiveness to achieve a strong British response to the *Trent* affair. He knew better, as the cabinet had long since recognized its effectiveness to avert a clash even though it remained ineffective, though more efficient. Third, Jefferson Davis refused the advice that the emissaries should appeal with promises to obtain recognition of independence. Instead, he instructed Yancy to appeal for slavery, to pronounce that Confederate cotton was worth $600 million to Britain, and to close with "the British ministry will comprehend fully the condition to which the British realm would be reduced if the supply of our staple should suddenly fail or even be considerably diminished."[38] Fourth, Russell published Yancey's plea for independence, providing Unionists in the Commons with ammunition for the upcoming blockade debate raised by the *Trent* affair.[39] "You must not build up your hopes on peace on account of the United States going to war with England," Robert E. Lee wrote his wife on Christmas Day, foreseeing that "we must make up our minds to fight our battles and win our independence alone. No one will help us."[40]

Public opinion in the North seemed to sense Lee's feeling. Except for a brief time in early December, there was Northern sympathy for a peaceful solution. Most New York newspapers supported peace. The Anglophobic *New York Herald* even averred that an apology might be expedient. Several weeks after the incident, when uncertainties developed about the legalities of Wilkes's action, newspapers called for release of Mason and Slidell without waiting to hear from London. The *New York Tribune* wanted Britain to demand the prisoners' surrender to demonstrate a liberal interpretation of neutral rights. On 24 November, the *New York Times* said that there were no precedents for Wilkes's act, noted that the Union navy was unprepared to fight the Royal Navy, and believed that Mason and Slidell posed no threat to the war effort. *New York Daily Tribune* editor Horace Greeley advocated that Lincoln surrender the prisoners to establish a precedent against capturing belligerent agents on neutral ships. Canadian, Central American, and West Indian rage over Wilkes's act sobered the London *Times* before it surrendered to the public outcry after a week of urging calm.[41]

Northern political and legal leaders echoed the press. James Buchanan wanted the prisoners surrendered. Millard Fillmore wrote to Lincoln on 16 December that war was unwise because it would destroy the "last hope" of reunification with the South that the government had by now discounted. He warned the president about the "double calamities of civil and foreign war at the same time, which will utterly exhaust our resources, and may practically change the form of our government and compel us in the end to submit to a dishonorable peace."[42] Former cabinet members Thomas J. Ewing, Lewis Cass, and Robert Walker said that national self-interest dictated the surrender of the prisoners to avoid war. Just before Christmas, members of the Boston bar said that Britain had the right to demand the prisoners' return to avoid European disdain.[43]

However, desperation pervaded Americans in London who had no idea of the conciliation at home when they read the mixed reviews of the affair in the London newspapers.[44] The *Times* did not believe that the Americans wanted war, cautioned against resentment, and appealed to Federal reason. The popular press warned against revenge. In scores of emotional diatribes against the "unruly" mob believed to rule the Union, writers did not say that England should declare war. They said that England was ready with its navy and recently trained militia (aimed at France) to raise the blockade and obtain cotton in a short war. "There was more talk of what war would be like rather than whether it would come." The voice of reason came from the pro-North Radical *Bradford Review:* Wilkes was legally wrong, but the United States needed time to admit Wilkes's error without causing his government to lose honor.[45] Finally, public derision in the United States, Britain, and Canada failed to dictate a punitive foreign policy. Throughout the Civil War, the battles, rather than heady questions of international maritime law, excited the sustained interest of the voting and nonvoting public.[46]

Moreover, the affair's settlement surpassed the prejudices of even the most learned British intellectuals. At one point Gladstone's close friend, the eminent historian and pro-Confederate Lord Acton, advocated war. In an essay in the *Rambler* in 1861, Acton stated that the Civil War resulted from the North's "absolutism," which he believed was intolerant of what he called natural diversities in society. Acton reflected the upper-class view that the North's fight was immoral because central power should not be used to overwhelm individual liberties and local government.[47] Acton seemed to overlook or did not know about Davis's centralizing tendencies as the war continued, and he may have been misguided on the subject of the Civil War.

Cabinet members and opposition leaders were less prejudiced. On first learning of the seizures, Lord Stanley of Adderley termed the incident "an ill-advised proceeding of the U. States government, which *might* [Adderley's emphasis] involve important consequences" and thought it might "possibly require a Cabinet" but did not know if it was urgent enough for him to stay in London. Argyll termed it a "wretched piece of American folly." Conservative leader Gathorne Hardy, whose brother was among the British regulars hastily sent to Canada, believed that Britain's military preparations were "then considered almost unavoidable." He wrote that Prince Albert had saved Britain from a "calamity," but "war may be upon us, and I see little hope that we can avoid it."[48] The skillful war minister George Cornewall Lewis, "the coolest of all men," did not believe that Seward intended war. At the cabinet meeting on Saturday, 30 November, Lewis expressed his belief that even though Seward might have wanted to capture the Confederates, neither Lincoln nor any of his secretaries had instructed Wilkes or anyone else to do so.[49]

A formidable intellectual and cabinet member, Gladstone argued the same tolerant line. He wrote Argyll, who was not at the cabinet, that he "urged that we should hear what the Americans had to say before withdrawing Lyons. . . . But this view did not prevail." Instead, the cabinet decided that Russell should draft two dispatches for Lyons to present to Seward, which, Gladstone reported to Argyll,

Sir George Cornewall Lewis, secretary of war, 1859–63, ardent noninterventionist. National Portrait Gallery

were "softened and abridged."[50] As we have seen, the dispatches called for release of the prisoners and an apology for insulting the British flag. Gladstone and his wife were dining with the queen and the prince on 30 November when Prince Albert excused himself to tone down the dispatches. Gladstone thought Russell's terms were too strict, and he persuaded the cabinet to adopt the prince's less caustically worded dispatch.[51]

Palmerston was not an intellectual, but his more than sixty years of political experience at the center had taught him common sense. He therefore agreed with

William Ewart Gladstone, chancellor of the exchequer, 1859–66; prime minister, 1868–74. British National Portrait Gallery

the Prince Consort's memorandum and instructed Russell to include the language in his dispatch to Lyons. Lyons was instructed to meet privately with Seward, refer to the "friendly relations which have long subsisted between Great Britain and the United States," and say that Britain was "willing to believe" that Wilkes had either acted without authority or misunderstood his orders. He was to ask Seward to free the prisoners and submit an apology in seven days or leave for Canada. At his first meeting with Seward, Lyons was not to take the dispatch with him and to "abstain from anything like a menace." The main objective of that meeting was to demand the release of the prisoners. Once this was done, Britain wanted a quiet apology through Adams to save Lincoln and Seward from criticism. Nothing was said about reparations. Lyons cooperated with Seward's request for four days before official delivery to let public anger subside and to allow Seward to research the case and write a justification for releasing the prisoners. During this period, Mercier privately went to the State Department on 21 December to tell Seward that Napoleon III opposed war but that, if war occurred, the United States could not expect French support. Like Russell, Seward knew that a British-American war would free the emperor in Europe and Mexico.[52]

Further cooperation occurred when Seward requested privately to see the memorandum two days before Lyons was to present it officially because everything, the secretary said, depended on how it was worded to save embarrassment. Lyons had no sooner returned to the British legation than Seward appeared saying that the dispatch was "courteous and friendly, and not dictatorial or menacing." Lincoln's cabinet could consider the memorandum on its own merits with no "complicating, supercilious or threatening attitude on the British side."[53]

Once Seward accepted Russell's memorandum and freed the prisoners, the affair passed into history. Public rage rapidly ebbed on both sides and enabled a return to domestic affairs. The crisis caused falling prices in Britain, but once it was resolved the market soon recovered. Seward's cooperation erased the arguments of London and European gossips that he wanted war because the Union could not defeat the Confederacy. Since before the outbreak of the Civil War, Lyons's inability to trust Seward contributed to the rumors and the ministry's war preparations. Even Lewis believed war was imminent, as did Lord Stanley of Alderley. Edward Cardwell, chancellor of the duchy of Lancaster, wrote Undersecretary of War Lord de Grey, "I quite share your feeling that we must prepare for war," and was convinced that the Americans had gone far beyond international maritime law, making an ultimatum and war perhaps inevitable. Argyll showed that he embraced Lyons's private letters that called Seward's character into question when he said that he wanted Seward to quit this absurd position that was doing him no good.[54]

Letters and conversations with Americans in Europe helped to allay anxieties. In October 1861 Seward asked Thurlow Weed, his political mentor and a leading Republican journalist, to go to Britain to espouse the Northern cause and upend Confederate propaganda. Weed was widely accepted by British dignitaries. The coincidence that he was in London paid large dividends after news broke of Wilkes's seizures. Weed quickly stressed that Seward had no intention of war. On 4 December, Weed wrote Lincoln that the queen opted for war, if necessary, with "much regret" and was trying to stem the tide. He wrote that a "Member of the Government" told him the same thing. Convinced that the Union had to back down, Weed advised Lincoln to disavow Wilkes for unauthorized action, surrender the prisoners, and satisfy England with an apology. Otherwise they courted a war because British rage showed no signs of abating. The tall, graying newspaperman and political power broker met with Russell privately at Pembroke Lodge, Russell's estate in London, on 6 December. In an hour of conversation before lunch, Russell intimated that the affair could be ended if the prisoners were surrendered. After lunch Russell excused himself, and Lady Russell, after a brief private talk with her husband, took Weed's arm to show him the grounds. As they paused, Lady Russell turned to her guest as if seized with an idea. "Ladies, you know, are not supposed to have knowledge of public affairs. But we have eyes and ears, and sometimes use them. In these troubles about the taking of some men from under the protection of our flag, it may be some encouragement to you to know that the Queen . . . is deeply anxious for an amicable settlement." She intimated that the queen sympathized with the Union and fondly remembered how well her son, the Prince of Wales, was treated during his visit to America the year before and that she was now trying to prevent a war. Weed responded with a courteous bow, and they began to walk back in silence, and Weed remembered how Russell had spoken with his wife before the tour and that she had delivered his message as if directly from her husband. Weed left convinced that the ministry wanted a peaceful settlement.[55]

At this time, in the midst of the worst emotions in both countries, there was good evidence of a thaw in relations as evidenced by Lady Russell's private conversation with Weed. Prince Albert's death on 14 December put another damper on war. People could not ignore the sacrifice he made in writing the memorandum urging a peaceful settlement while desperately ill. Relations between the two countries began to improve, and the grieving, weakened queen refused to hear of war talk.[56] Retired general Winfield Scott, just arrived in Europe, wrote a letter to Paris newspapers that Wilkes's act was not ordered or condoned by the Union government.[57] Furthermore, the English atmosphere was changed by peaceful elements from a number of discordant interests. The extreme Tories opposed war because they did not want Palmerston's power expanded and the Manchester merchants aroused. John Bright and Richard Cobden, two erstwhile defenders of the North, influenced the ministry's deliberations. On 4 December, Bright appealed for peace, and letters from Bright and Cobden to Sumner influenced Lincoln as he wrote his draft reply to Lyons. Cobden did not believe that Palmerston wanted war.[58]

The thaw in Britain was matched in Washington. Lincoln was never vindictive. On 10 December he told his confidant from Illinois, Sen. Orville Hickman Browning, that because he feared trouble with Britain he had written Lyons a draft note that adopted Bright's advice for an international arbitration and lasting maritime rules to prevent future incidents. Then Lincoln opted for Seward's timelier solution at the cabinet on 25 December.[59]

Like Lincoln, the British could not ignore Bright because people remembered his predictions about the Crimean War. In addition to leavening Palmerston's attitude, Cobden wrote and spoke well for peace. Yet of more importance than these two individuals, the Peace Society and the Quakers drew on Bright and Cobden to counsel arbitration and wrote to the Christian churches urging them to support arbitration. The working classes heard pleas for peace from church organizations. The pacifists' work caused Britons to think about peace, and war thus became unpopular. Palmerston reflected on a half-century of political trends and said that, in the end, England tended to follow these nonconformists whom he knew represented a growing political force that he could not ignore. He knew that for the past decade 40 percent of the churchgoers in England and 75 percent in Wales attended nonconformist churches. On 17 December, a general meeting of dissenting ministers urged Russell to keep the peace. These activities caused British popular rage to subside by the third week of December.[60]

For all of these reasons, and despite cabinet support for military preparations, Palmerston had no desire to use the *Trent* affair as a pretext for any type of intervention. But his characteristic early rage caused him to act the part of a popular leader who represented a nation wronged by an upstart republic led by an unknown country bumpkin. In this atmosphere, the British began military preparations in earnest, and Palmerston slapped an embargo on large shipments of saltpeter to the North for making gunpowder. But his suggestion to prohibit export of all war materiel was rejected at the cabinet's first meeting about the affair.[61] These disagreements illustrated that the ministry toed a fine line. If it was pacific outwardly against the initial popular outcry, the ministry could be brought down, so delicately balanced was its majority in the Commons. Thus, outwardly, the cabinet appeared to opt for force, but internally ministers, led by Palmerston himself, wanted a peaceful settlement.[62]

Indeed, the cabinet worried over war preparations. First Lord of the Admiralty Somerset did not believe that Canada could be defended and that the costs of reconquest after a Federal invasion were absurd. Somerset said that instead they needed to consider a cheaper naval war to avoid parliamentary debate about funding a large land army. He envisioned a blockading force of sixty warships shutting down trade with Northern ports. He was far off the mark in not appreciating the distance between Portland, Maine, and Port Royal, South Carolina. But the cabinet had to placate the public, and Lewis, who did not believe war would occur, nevertheless supported Palmerston by recommending thirty thousand rifles, an infantry regiment, an artillery battery, and officers to be hastily dispatched to Canada to be followed by three regiments and more artillery.[63]

The ultimatum demanding the release of the prisoners and an apology was on the way to Seward when Russell persuaded Palmerston to agree that Lewis and Somerset be advised on military preparations by a cabinet committee and the

Duke of Cambridge, the commander in chief. The special cabinet war council met on 9 December. It included Palmerston, who presided, Lewis, Somerset, Newcastle, Cambridge, and Russell. The ministers learned that the military wanted to ship five thousand additional troops and munitions to fortify Quebec and Montreal and assemble a gunboat fleet to control the Great Lakes. They decided to increase the British North Atlantic fleet of thirty warships so that if war began they could raid Union shipping, break the blockade, and impose a counterblockade. The queen approved these preparations while privately agreeing with Palmerston, Lewis, Gladstone, Somerset, and others that war should not occur.[64]

Under the ministry's leadership, the entire British nation geared for war. Even the *Times* printed the rumor that Seward wanted to stop the Civil War and then redirect the North and South against Britain by invading Canada. Three Liberals in the cabinet, Charles P. Villiers, Gladstone, and Thomas Milner Gibson, all supported war preparations. Only Bright, who was not in the cabinet, trusted the United States until proof was received that Seward had ordered the rebuff to the British flag on the high seas and the incarceration of the Confederate emissaries. Casting aside any idea of a pacific solution, Villiers wrote Bright that he had heard on 3 December that Adams "is packing it up."[65] On 2 December, Benjamin Moran, the assistant secretary at the American legation in London, observed that Adams was "gloomy" but said nothing about leaving the legation. Moran wrote that the *Times* "is filled with such slatternly abuse of us and ours, that it is fair to conclude that all the Fishwifes of Billingsgate have been transferred to Printing House Square to fill the ears of the writers there with their choicest phraseology." On 10 December, Moran visited with Sir John Harding, the queen's counsel. Harding was friendly but "grave" and believed that what the British government "objected to was the failure of Capt. Wilkes to take the vessel [the *Trent*] in. It would not do for Naval officers to constitute themselves captors & judges at the same time."[66]

In these circumstances, the French could support the North and risk war with Britain over a principle of international law that they had always agreed on, and on which they could not trust the Americans to support. As previously suggested, Napoleon wanted a British-American war because it would present him with opportunities in Europe and Mexico. He could not act unilaterally, and Foreign Minister Thouvenel realized immediately on hearing of the seizures that the British ultimatum negated mediation. Russell read the draft ultimatum to French ambassador Flahault on 29 November, and the French took England's side. The self-interested emperor thought that a British-American war would raise the blockade and give the French cotton. In Paris, Lord Cowley was convinced that the French hated the English but hated the North more for blockading cotton and threatening neutral rights. Cowley said that Napoleon III tried to maximize the situation out of self-interest, and Russell scrawled on the back of Cowley's letter that he had been sick of French intrigues since the end of the Crimean War. "The crusty old earl of Clarendon" knew the emperor well and intimated to Cowley that Napoleon would "like to take this occasion to make us feel that he is necessary to us and to avenge his griefs against us by causing us to eat dirt or go to war with the North with France against us or in a state of doubtful and ill-humoured neutrality."[67]

Clarendon overlooked Foreign Minister Thouvenel, who was pro-North and collaborated for peace with American minister William L. Dayton. Thouvenel's position was fortunate because, although Lincoln had never wanted war, it was difficult for him to back down. Seward had waited patiently for the president's second thoughts, and Dayton's report helped. Henri Mercier received Thouvenel's missive siding with the British position during Lincoln's Christmas Day cabinet meeting, and Frederick Seward, the secretary of state's son and assistant secretary, hurried it to the White House. French support for the British position helped Seward (who had been waiting for this private message) convince Lincoln and his cabinet colleagues to uphold republican freedom and release the prisoners. Not to accept the British terms would injure Northern commerce and the war effort, might cause secession to win out, would destroy Union shipping, and would bankrupt the Treasury.[68]

Overall, Atty. Gen. Edward Bates summed up Seward's work: "We *must* not have war with England." That said, Lincoln remarked to Seward after the cabinet meeting that in playing devil's advocate with himself, as he often did, he could not draft a personally satisfactory solution that proved the correctness of Seward's decision.[69]

Palmerston's deterrence also had an impact. Two weeks of hearing about the British cabinet's military preparations caused Lincoln to retreat because his position was legally untenable. After his death, his unsent draft reply to Lyons, influenced by Bright and Cobden, surfaced. (Lincoln wrote many such papers and tucked them away in his desk.) It stated that his government had "intended no affront to the British flag or to the British nation." The president wrote that Wilkes acted without orders and that the squabble could be arbitrated if other means of resolution could not be found. If arbitration failed, the United States would make reparation as a precedent for resolving similar cases.[70] As Frederick Seward wrote, "Fortunately for the Union it had a President . . . who combined a logical intellect with an unselfish heart." Both governments realized that there was no time for arbitration. They had to jointly return relations to an even keel because of the Civil War and the situation with France. Seward therefore acted quickly to release the prisoners on 1 January 1862, and a wave of relief swept over both countries and the Canadians. Frederick Seward noted that the American people showed "sterling good sense," and those who disagreed with the decision were lost in the return of public confidence in the immediate decline in gold premiums and the rise of badly needed army volunteers. The younger Seward remarked that the release of Mason and Slidell caused Britain to now admit (albeit in a roundabout way) the doctrine of free ships for which the War of 1812 was fought.[71]

Both nations quickly considered the Confederate agents to be outcasts. Frederick's father knew that the idea of waiting on an arbitration might spawn domestic forays by "disloyalists," such as the Hunter's Lodges headquartered in Buffalo, which were led by Irish revolutionaries who had supported the Canadian rebellion against Britain in 1837 and whose Anglophobia had kept them organized. If such an attack occurred, the Royal Navy might view it as a prelude to a larger strike, and war might occur anyway. Fortunately, however, public morale soared and overwhelmed any violent reaction that Lincoln's cabinet feared. Seward was curiously enough backed by the London *Times,* which criticized Mason and Slidell as "habitual haters and revilers" of Britain and as "the most worthless booty" one could receive, continuing, "We should have done just as much to rescue two of their own negroes." The *Times* asked subjects not to welcome them, and the two men were ignored when they arrived in London. Nor did the rancor end there. An English worker convention labeled the Confederate emissaries "sworn enemies . . . of the working classes of all countries." They had cost the British government $20 million, and the exchequer was sick of them. When they arrived, the *Times* remarked, "We sincerely hope that our countrymen will not give these fellows anything in the shape of an ovation. The civility that is due to a foe in distress is all that they can claim. The only reason for their presence in London is to draw us into their own quarrel. The British public has no prejudice in favor of slavery, which these gentlemen represent. . . . They are personally nothing to us." Similarly, *Punch* and most other British papers said that subjects should not act haughty about Lincoln and Seward's volte-face because they might think that British sympathies lay with the South.

Seward contributed to the general relief. As he had done when governor of New York during the *Caroline* affair, he showed his desire not to support threats to the border, this time by the Irish revolutionaries, when he allowed the British regiments to travel through American territory because ice blocked the St. Lawrence Seaway. He believed that these regiments could block an invasion of Canada by the Hunter's Lodges. He also worked with Lyons to get Mason and Slidell quietly and safely away. As planned, the envoys quietly boarded a British sloop of war, the *Rinaldo,* at Provincetown on the northern tip of Cape Cod where they had been transported from Fort Warren in Boston Harbor. With the envoys on their way, Lincoln joined Seward, Chase, and Sumner at a dinner party at war secretary Cameron's. Seward said that he had released the Confederates with a clear conscience. In response, Sumner recalled that the president had then said, "He covets kindly relations with all the world, especially England."[72]

Throughout the *Trent* affair Canadian leaders had been on edge but had not shown the retrenchment-minded Gladstonians ample proof of financial reconstruction to merit assistance with fortifications and railroad building to safeguard the common border with the Federals. The private diplomacy surrounding the *Trent* affair kept Whitehall from feeling desperation that Canada might be lost unless defenses were modernized. The British cabinet dispute over the railway and defense issues continued irregularly during the war with no consensus. The Gladstonians managed an imperial defense conference meeting in London in April 1865, as the war ended, and remained resolute that Canada had to lead itself into nationhood through finance and a trained militia to provide for its own security. Certainly, neither the *Trent* affair nor the Civil War forced Britain to make Canada a powerful colonial bastion. Instead, the opposite occurred, with Gladstone's ascendant principle that the Canadians had to prove they could build a nation without much British aid. Certainly, here is another indication that the *Trent* affair was transitory, an aberration, and something that neither Britain nor the United States wanted to happen in the first place and did not want to happen again.

This is to say that if Britain had wanted to embarrass the Union in its time of weakness, a better opportunity than the *Trent* affair could not have presented itself, but Britain had no practical reason for breaching neutrality. The Yankees did not threaten Canada, and it was highly questionable that the Army of the Potomac could threaten the Rebels because Lincoln could not get its commanding officer, Gen. George B. McClellan, to move south against Richmond. Moreover, Lyons informed Milne throughout the spring of the impending Federal victories, including the opening for commerce at Beaufort and Port Royal, South Carolina, and wrote that Union victory was near. Russell seemed to have gleaned this feeling from his minister's private letters. Lyons's changed attitude, which was conditioned by the *Trent* affair, fits Weigley's statement that "happily defined, the *Trent* crisis nevertheless was not so dangerous as both the American and British bluster made it appear." As the history of relations evidenced, Britain refused to fight over "one incident of honor in which the issues were obscured by the technicalities of international law. Britain had too much to lose in such a war." It needed Northern commerce, peace for British North America, and focus on France and Europe. Warren Spencer supports Weigley, writing that "from the very beginning and especially after the settlement of the *Trent* affair there was little chance of British intervention in the war." This analysis is strengthened by David Krein's remark that after the affair the North and Britain refused to provoke each other. Adams was overjoyed to receive the telegram of 8 January 1862 that the prisoners were going to be released. "This lifted a load of lead from our hearts, and Mr. & Mrs. Adams heartily congratulated each other," Moran wrote. The next day he observed that "the peace news" was received with "unfeigned joy" everywhere except at the offices of the *Times*, which had finally supported the South and had sensationalized the affair to increase subscriptions. When the news of the prisoners' release was announced in London theaters, "the audiences rose like one & cheered tremendously." Church bells rang.[73]

Palmerston came out of the affair looking very good indeed politically, which is what he wanted to do above all, while his painful gout continued to plague him. Tooting his own horn to look good in public opinion, Palmerston lauded Newcastle, Russell, Lewis, and Somerset of the special cabinet War Committee. He went on privately, "If we had not shewn that we were ready to fight, that low-minded fellow Seward would not have eat [*sic*] the leek as he has done."[74] He "demonstrated that Anglo-American diplomacy could still function under the most inauspicious circumstances." Russell perceived that the Americans liked "to draw in their horns and be disagreeable at the same time."[75]

Lincoln emerged from the affair with higher esteem from Britain and Europe. The resolution of the *Trent* affair enhanced the North's standing abroad because, as Sexton remarks, it had "backed down to Britain and abided by international law." It no longer seemed to the European powers as "the wild government committed to simultaneously waging war against the South and Britain that it appeared to be a few months earlier." (Even that feeling was an overreaction by Britain and Europe.) Seward's conciliatory and cooperative policy in the affair and Weed's diplomacy with leading British statesmen such as Russell and financiers such as George Peabody, an American expatriate banker, upheld the Union cause. Peabody financed public works to house the poor of London corresponded to attempts by Confederate lobbyists to achieve recognition of independence in Parliament. Peabody's humanitarian program cast a dark shadow on the lobbyists' efforts on behalf of a slavocracy (he told Palmerston of his belief that the South was resurrecting the slave trade) and showed the benefits of Anglo-American cooperation in peace. For his charitable efforts, the queen awarded Peabody the Freedom of the City of London.[76] In fact, in consideration of the large number of governmental and private peace workers on both sides of the Atlantic, and the cooperation that they wrought, it is arguable that the overall significance of the *Trent* affair was a confirmation of dependable relations that were strong enough to resist the pushes and pulls on the relationship for the rest of the Civil War.

Of perhaps almost equal importance was the fact that the Confederacy was humbled by the *Trent* affair. From his London cockpit at the American legation, Benjamin Moran noted, "The *Times*, now that Mason & Slidell have been released and public opinion is against them, is mauling those rogues unmercifully today." On 2 March 1862, several months after the affair ended, Russell wrote Lyons that the event never became a party issue: "There is no longer any excitement here upon the question of America. I fear Europe is going to supplant the affairs of America as an exciting topic." Sizing up the London atmosphere, Henry Adams wrote, "The *Trent* affair passed like a snow storm," and "the British Ministry felt a little ashamed of itself, as well it might, and disposed to wait before moving again." Russell had a favorable perspective because he felt that England antagonized the Federals more than was intended by the neutrality proclamation, but he had to satiate public opinion with minimum demands. He told Adams that after Seward released the Confederates he "had no expectation of seeing the Confederate commissioners any more." Slidell seemed to anticipate the foreign secretary's coldness at the time of his release. He believed that being set free ended the chances of the affair causing a British-American war and foreign intervention. For these reasons, Slidell had refused to budge from Fort Warren in Boston Harbor but was removed under threat of force. Finally, Russell cooperated by maintaining the language of strict neutrality by terming Mason and Slidell "enemies of the United States at war with its Government." Perhaps sensing, as Slidell seemed to, that the South was the real loser in the affair, in Columbia, South Carolina, the perceptive Southern diarist Mary Boykin Chesnut continued her gloomy new year's attitude that "Lord Lyons has gone against us. Lord Derby and Louis Napoleon are silent in our hour of direst need. People call me Cassandra, for I cry that outside hope is quenched. From the outside, no help indeed cometh to this beleaguered land."[77]

As the war hit home for the first time, inflation besieged the South. Mary Chesnut recorded the Yankee military victories that Lyons believed promised to end the war. She wrote that Union military power grew in the eastern and western theaters, and "England's eye is scornful and scoffing as she turns it on our miseries."[78]

4

Averting Crisis in 1862

Despite the foreign policy breakthroughs, in 1861 and 1862 Unionists remained perplexed with British neutrality, recognition of Confederate belligerency, blockade running, and the British-built Confederate raiders destroying Northern merchant ships all over the world. Yet cooperation persisted beneath these outward alarms. It is this undertone that historians have missed in analyzing relations in 1862. Building on the good feelings that resulted from the joint resolution of the *Trent* affair and earlier conundrums, relations pivoted away from prospects of international war. The cooperation between Britain and the Union that followed the *Trent* affair, which was also an outcome of previous cooperative efforts, continued through the so-called British intervention debate in the summer and fall. Cooperation took many forms such as Britain's capture of the Confederate raider *Florida,* the conciliatory attitude of both Britain and the Union toward seizures in the Gulf of Mexico, the reluctance of the Admiralty to use force in response to the seizures, the Union's giving up the *Labuan,* and other examples. Instead, similar to the outcomes of the *Trent* affair, it was the Union rather than the Confederacy that profited from the cooperation in 1862, and in December both the Union and British governments expressed relief that the other was still in power. Furthermore, the British government continued to oppose the Confederate lobby successfully, and by a large majority, while Palmerston's cabinet nearly unanimously refused to intervene. On the American side, Lincoln's party survived the fall elections, and his statesmanship kept his cabinet together after an abortive attempt by the Radical Republicans to oust Seward and control foreign policy in December. The Radicals' beliefs that Seward was being soft on Britain and not prosecuting the war hard enough in hopes that the South might rejoin the Union, and their beliefs that Britain should have directly supported the Union, would no doubt have disrupted cooperative relations. Fortunately, Lincoln's leadership averted this prospect, and the end of 1862 witnessed another victory over crisis as had occurred at the end of 1861.

But the settlement of the *Trent* affair added to dependable relations and clarified the weakness of Confederate diplomacy. The British reception of the Confederate emissaries was as frigid as the several thousand miles of ocean they had
traversed from Cape Cod to Liverpool. An icy Russell received James Mason who
had forwarded statistics attempting to show the blockade's ineffectiveness. Russell
remained steadfast for neutrality and the blockade when he said that he found
the information interesting, but he did not encourage more of related information and referred in his conversation to "the so-called Confederate states." Then
he refused to accept the Rebel's credentials "since our relations are unofficial." On
hearing that, Mason lost his temper and left, and the foreign secretary did not
encourage him to return. The firebrand was breaking under the same humiliating
treatment that Yancey had received. "On the whole," Mason reported to Richmond, "it was manifest enough that his [Russell's] personal sympathies were not
with us," that inaction was the British policy, and that Parliament could not be
made to budge for the South. Adams heard of the episode and noted that Mason
was the Union's greatest asset in Europe.

Nor was there any chance for France to force Britain into an American war.
Slidell failed to arouse Napoleon III, who was compromised by shaky finances,
rising unemployment, and an upswing in the North's military fortunes. These fortunes were enhanced by more than 1 million British- and European-made small
arms that were needed in the first two years of the war while Northern industry
converted to wartime manufacturing. As Jay Sexton observes, there was a "pre-
clusive" angle in these sales. Every weapon that the North bought could not be
purchased by the South.[1] Slidell was notified that France refused to act unless England acted first and echoed Mason's advice that the time was inappropriate for
recognition. Napoleon's submission to British policy was disclosed in his speech
on 27 January 1862, which Thouvenel prompted. The speech failed to denounce the
blockade and upheld neutrality.

European intervention was also checked by Union military victories along the
eastern seaboard and the West during the winter and spring of 1862. In the western
theater, the fall of Forts Donelson and Henry in February, Braxton Bragg's concomitant retreat from Kentucky, and Ambrose Burnside's conquest of the Inland Sea on
the North Carolina coast caused Slidell to write that recognition had experienced a
severe setback in Europe. The London *Times* echoed Palmerston's cautious policy
and upheld Slidell's verdict by writing that "the war would have to settle itself instead
of being trodden out by our feet." Against these odds, Slidell tired from Napoleon's
"slippery courtesies." In May, the fall of Memphis and New Orleans and the shelling of Richmond's defenses added to European indifference. Britain followed Gen.
George B. McClellan's Peninsula campaign to take Richmond, as attested by the
visit of the *Rinaldo*'s Captain Hewitt to pay his respects to Seward, Welles, and their
entourage, who were then on a weeklong observation trip.[2]

British-Union cooperation made even more progress when Henry Hotze, the chief Confederate propagandist in Europe, sent gloomy messages to Richmond. By March 1862 Hotze wrote that he and his associates "had been too rapid in [their] conclusions and too sanguine in [their] expectations as regards the policy of Europe, and especially England." He blamed Southerners and Southern sympathizers who refused to understand the European powers' hesitation. Hotze felt that the British were frightened by the *Trent* affair, which underlined their dread of war. In his mind, the affair caused the South "incalculable injury." He noted that both British political parties adhered to neutrality so that the "American Question" was not a party issue. Yet he found only two powerful men "who are our announced enemies." The first was Russell because he "had lately made himself the apologist of the Federal government," and the second was Bright because he "represents or leads no party but himself." Hotze also mentioned Thurlow Weed's work to chastise the Confederacy. He agreed with Mason that the government and Parliament remained passive about the blockade, which he was trying to have declared ineffective by the Confederate lobby, and about recognition of independence, which had less of a chance of being considered.[3]

Certainly, Palmerston's financial leader opted for caution to avoid running up defense expenditures. On 30 January, Gladstone's evening was "disturbed" after he heard of Lewis's announcement of increased military estimates. The retrenchment-minded chancellor quickly responded, "I see nothing to justify any augmentation of force whatever, & even something that might recommend reduction." As he had done during the San Juan Island water boundary incident, Gladstone retreated to retrenchment with Somerset's support. Just as they had refused to increase British seapower in the Pacific Northwest, the duke had not commissioned ships or hired sailors destined for other stations. He sent coal shipments to bases in the West Indies. He wrote Palmerston, "Except for the transports we have incurred no expense for warlike preparations."[4]

Britain was not going on a permanent war footing to aid Canada or the Confederacy or to create a punitive naval infrastructure off of the east coast to prepare to leap into a war with the Union. As Sir John Wheeler-Bennett pointed out, "The peaceful solution of the *Trent* affair . . . spelled disaster for the Confederacy." To complement Gladstone and Somerset's peaceful designs, Russell continued his anti-South posture by ignoring a letter that Davis wrote to Queen Victoria describing Mason's abilities and empowering him to negotiate. Mason believed quite correctly that, now supported by Napoleon III's speech, Russell endorsed the Union blockade as effective.[5]

There was thus no one of consequence to criticize the ministry's growing "policy of abstention" or downright indifference, as Frank Merli suggests, and the private desire to maintain harmony with the Union. This policy was furthered by Seward's reassurance as early as 23 January 1862 that American resentment at the

British-built Confederate raiders would not result in "a policy of unreasonable and litigious exactions upon the British government" during or after the Civil War. Claims for damages would be based on just solutions. He realized "how hard it is for a state to retrace an erroneous course so long as it can be followed without immediate peril." In light of Seward's understanding, on 1 March 1862, Russell wrote that relations were "into a very smooth groove" and that Britain's challenge lay in Northern Italy where it distrusted the territorial pretensions of France and Austria. Further proof of cooperation developed when the United States gave up the British steamer *Labuan* captured as a blockade-runner off Matamoros, across the Rio Grande from Brownsville, Texas, and a hot spot for Confederate contraband trade. Russell took the law officers' verdict that Britain not use force unless the seizures were "flagrant" violations of the neutral waters of Mexico by U.S. cruisers. Such violations were made difficult when "Seward promised Russell that such an occurrence [as the *Labuan*] would not happen again." Russell instructed the Admiralty to notify Rear Adm. Sir Alexander Milne, commander of the North American and West Indies Squadron, of Seward's promise. In addition, Lyons wrote Milne that Seward informed him on 13 March that orders had been issued not to repeat seizures "under circumstances similar to the *Labuan*." Moreover, he mentioned to Seward privately that to ensure peace Britain was sending ships to Matamoros and suggested that Seward do likewise to promote cordiality between the two squadrons. He closed on the positive note: "There are other matters being discussed but nothing likely to cause excitement, or go beyond the ordinary diplomatic sparring; so far as I see at present." Despite Lyons's attitude, Russell was unsure that Seward's cooperation was permanent. He wrote to the Admiralty that the naval force off Mexico should make certain that the Americans be restrained from making such "flagrant" arrests in neutral waters again.[6]

Lyons modified Russell's skepticism about Seward. Cordial relations continued in the Gulf of Mexico. On 3 June Seward told Lyons to assure Russell and Milne that the U.S. government "deeply regretted any instances [of seizures] which might have occurred of irregularity and harshness, and that orders had been sent to exercise the right of search with the utmost courtesy and consideration in the future." The secretary of state reminded Lyons that the opening of the New Orleans and other ports in late April eased neutral trade.[7]

The worsening Confederate situation in Britain in the spring of 1862 strengthened cooperation. The Conservatives again refused to stir up opposition against the Union in the House of Commons because there was no nucleus within the electorate for support. They were as relieved as the Liberals at the calm state of British-American relations. Both parties were aided by the mild winter, which decreased the workers' suffering. Cotton speculators held their stocks for a price rise and therefore did not want to break the blockade. Holders of American railroad and other securities might lose property in case of a war. The *Times* captured the moment in terms no doubt crafted by Palmerston himself: "We have waited so long [to intervene] that we can well afford to wait a little longer."[8]

Moreover, the Confederate lobby suffered a further blow when the ministry won the debate in the House of Commons that the Union blockade was effective. In the early February debate over the effectiveness of the blockade, Mason's argument to Russell that the blockade was ineffective owing to the frequency with which it was run momentarily held center stage. The report was based on data supplied by British consul Robert Bunch in Charleston and by Mason himself. In the debate, Conservative leader Lord Derby "hinted broadly at an attack on the Federal blockade," but his words failed to arouse his followers. Benjamin Disraeli, the Conservative leader in the Commons, was "almost cordial to the Unionists." In the Lords, Russell argued for continued neutrality because he thought the Civil War would end in a few months. The Confederate lobby persisted, and on the night of 7 March 1862 the ministry won an easy victory for continued neutrality. Liberal MP William E. Forster and the ministry's solicitor general, Roundell Palmer, countered arguments by lobbyists William H. Gregory and William S. Lindsay that the blockade was ineffective. Palmer said that Mason's statistics had to be port by port instead of along the entire coast, which counted runners' often multiple stops once they got inside the blockade, or even if they were coastal ships that never ran the cordon in the first place. Forster was so convincing that Benjamin Moran, who was present, wrote that "Gladstone turned round to catch every word, Palmerston looked up inquiringly, Milner Gibson seemed convinced." Moreover, Forster and Palmer showed that the statistics were only from 3 May through 31 October 1861, and not up-to-date as Mason had intimated to Russell. Forster reiterated that Mason's statistics were based on small coastal steamers that did not come in from the open sea. Further measures of the blockade's effectiveness were the rising cotton and salt prices. In addition, Forster said that the ministry could either continue peace through neutrality or try to shatter the blockade and ally with the slaveholding South. News of Forster's speech brought members back, "and cheers were strong." Confederate sympathizers and the press sat with their mouths agape against their convictions. According to Moran, "in ten minutes it was clear Forster had killed Gregory, his motion and the blockade." Russell had already issued a parliamentary paper showing factually that the blockade was effective. Except for his inquiring look at Forster perhaps, "Lord Palmerston," wrote the *Spectator,* "slept through the evening with a tranquillity known to him only when he is going to win." Henry Adams was also in the galleries and wrote that after Forster spoke, Gregory's speech sounded like a "funeral eulogy." The House accepted the blockade as effective, and Gregory withdrew the motion. This pro-Union ministerial victory was punctuated by Mason's indiscretion in the south gallery when Lindsay criticized Seward. Mason's thoughtless cheer resounded through the chamber, badly embarrassing him. Moran believed that he should have been expelled. The *Times* termed the blockade "perfect" again. Thus ended the first important Commons debate on the Civil War—much in the Union's favor.[9]

Clearly, the *Trent* affair and its wake had eased Anglo-American tensions and reinforced cooperation if only because both powers had little other choice, especially regarding the spread of the fighting from Virginia and North and South Carolina to the Mississippi. Russell warned the Lords on 10 March that interference with the blockade would mean war, an emancipation proclamation, and perhaps a slave insurrection. On 4 April, Adams wrote that his duties were "almost in a state of profound calm." As if to support Adams, Lyons informed Milne that the Union seizures of British merchantmen suspected of carrying contraband in the Gulf of Mexico were not serious despite the "alarming" number of complaints, and Seward soon saw to it that even these seizures were stopped with the navy's blessing. Nevertheless, he wrote, British merchant captains must understand that they had to submit to search. They should not give the Union navy a pretext to use force by "resisting and protesting." As a further mark of cooperation, Lyons explained to Milne that "I am ordered not to enter into controversies on blockade cases (when it can be avoided) until the Law Officers of the Crown have been consulted, and instructions sent to me from home." Moreover, Lyons deliberately withheld the seizures' costs and damages from Seward "to keep good relations with the U.S." Finally, Mason conceded that the South had lost the blockade debate and that intervention had taken a backseat.[10]

The demonstrated cooperation over the blockade and the seizures weakened Palmerston's argument for sending more British regulars to Canada or providing funds for fortifications. His deterrence policy rested. On 10 April, the cabinet voted on a Canadian proposal about whether or not to fund the intercolonial railway to improve defense and commerce. Gladstone, Granville, Lewis, Wood, Gibson, Argyll, and Russell opposed the proposal. Palmerston, Somerset, Grey, Cardwell, Newcastle, Westbury, Stanley, and Villiers voted for it, a majority of one. There was no consensus to strengthen Canada.[11] Left to their own devices, the Canadians failed to vote finances on the railroad or defense. Because of this impasse, the British refused to vote greater sums for Canada that signaled the absence of Northern military threat. This vote withheld a source of greater pressure on relations.

Britain needed Union cooperation because its primary foreign concern was still France. The Anglo-French rivalry worsened during the first half of 1862. Britain's inability to have a standing army that was competitive by European standards forced it to continue the entente with France. Britain depended on the French army to enforce its goals in Europe. But the naval rivalry was endemic. On 31 March 1862 Russell wrote Palmerston, "I hope you will stir up the slow & steady Admiralty to some vigour about iron Ships. The French have long been before us, & in six months or more the United States will be far ahead of us unless our builders in the Navy Dept exert themselves." Gladstone continued to speak against military spending, and Palmerston rebuked him, "Even a large yearly expenditure for the army and navy is an economical insurance against Napoleon." Throughout the spring and summer, the prime minister berated Gladstone about military spending reductions. On 23 May, Palmerston defended the military estimates by comparing British strength with that of France. Despite the fact that the *Monitor-Merrimac* battle off Hampton Roads in early March 1862 showed that ironclads could "pass through the heaviest fire from a fort," the House of Commons voted to stop ironclad construction at Spithead.[12] On Palmerston's cue, the *Times* stated that the Royal Navy was obsolete and that wooden ships should be converted to ironclads immediately. Some of British opinion registered the small size and the success of the *Monitor* and supported construction of expensive armored warships.[13]

The retrenchment bloc was reinforced by a larger portion of public opinion, which remained indifferent to defense spending. Public disinterest congealed with cautious government spending and foreign policy. Despite the French threat, ministers refused to make defense an issue that might arouse the people and did not want to commit funds to either Europe or North America.[14] Beyond that rivalry was the inability of either Britain or the United States to risk an international war. On 11 August 1862, Anglophobic navy secretary Gideon Welles confided to his diary, "We are not, it is true, in condition for war with Great Britain . . . , but England is in scarcely a better condition for a war with us."[15]

Indeed, Seward's cooperation continued to develop. He overcame his hatred of the British, dating back to the *Caroline* affair and at the time of McLeod's trial in 1841 when he had been governor of New York.[16] The bloody war and Lincoln's leadership had sobered him. By July 1862 he had been conciliatory toward Britain for more than a year and guarded against any of his countrymen causing foreign complications. An incident precipitated by the Federals during the British intervention debate might have caused the cabinet to support Russell and Gladstone, and the practical arguments of Granville, Lewis, and Clarendon may have been compromised. During the summer of 1862 Seward warned Lincoln to throttle his emancipation program until a major military victory occurred and to ease British fears of a slave insurrection. Then he quelled Federal military commanders who forced British subjects to swear allegiance. At the suggestion of Russell and Cobden, he tried to facilitate cotton shipments to British manufacturers from Southern ports held by the North. These actions persuaded even the pro-South British chargé d'affaires William Stuart that the Confederacy was primarily responsible for interruptions to the cotton supply. Later in the summer, Seward asked Secretary of the Navy Welles to alert naval commanders not to seize foreign ships within the waters of friendly nations unless a careful search revealed the presence of contraband or a mission to blockaded ports. Nor should he allow the navy to tamper with mails that bore official seals on vessels that were seized.[17]

Yet Seward could not control events in Britain having to do with the Confederate navy. Union emotions about British neutrality intensified after July 1862 when
Russell failed to stop the Lairds of Liverpool from building Confederate warships
and fitting though not arming them for war, as arming the ships in British waters
violated the Foreign Enlistment Act. The ministry and Adams observed the construction through a network of spies. When Adams got Russell to detain the *Oreto*
in the spring, British courts ruled that because it was unarmed it did not violate
the Foreign Enlistment Act. This verdict allowed the vessel to sail to neutral waters,
raise the Confederate flag as the *Florida,* take on armaments, and go on to capture
thirty-eight Northern merchantmen over the next two years. The second suspect
vessel was the No. 290, later to be named the *Alabama.* The Americans' detention
documentation, after being validated as condemnatory by a reputable law officer,
failed to reach Russell, who then acted with expedition, but not in time to prevent
the No. 290 with a British crew, from beating the foreign secretary's detention order
by a matter of hours on 29 July. The Americans' incriminating documents were
then found in the ailing law officer John Harding's briefcase. After these two episodes, Russell was determined to uphold neutrality in case the tables should ever
be turned. He was angry at being tricked over the *Alabama,* and he refused to let
subsequent Confederate raiders leave British ports. The Barings and other subjects,
seeing the harm that could come to seafaring Britain if it were ever in the Union's
maritime shoes, supported him.[18]

Adams believed that Russell did all that he could to stop the *Alabama* from
escaping. Privately, Lord John "recognized the laxness of British officials and tried
to rectify the mistake." Most of the cabinet concurred. Cobden wrote to Sumner
that Russell had been tricked. Yet after the *Alabama* had escaped, British and
American diplomats "kept cool heads and proceeded in a judicious manner with
fortitude, if not perfect rectitude."[19]

The *Alabama* burned or bonded sixty-four Northern ships before being sunk
by the USS *Kearsarge* off Cherbourg in June 1864. The *Alabama* and several other
raiders destroyed so many ships that hundreds of American merchantmen were
transferred primarily to British or Canadian flags to avoid rising insurance rates
and being burned at sea. These were tense days for Russell, because it was not in
Britain's best interests to build warships for belligerents.[20] Two other Confederate
raiders built in Britain followed, although their damage to Northern shipping fell
far short of the *Alabama*'s.[21]

The *Alabama* and Laird rams disputes from mid-1862 through the fall of 1863
caused Britain to want closer relations with the United States to prevent the *Alabama*
from being fitted out in Northern ports in a future conflict in which the United
States was a neutral. For instance, American merchants in the Far East might accept
letters of marque from the Japanese government to prey on British shipping.[22]

The CSS *Alabama*, 1862–64. In her brief life she captured or burned sixty-three Union merchant ships and one U.S. Navy vessel. The Naval Historical Foundation

The stage was set for a possible debacle because the United States refused to discuss British attempts to create a common Foreign Enlistment Act. The Americans responded by saying that their laws were sufficient, Roundell Palmer recalled as the Civil War closed. He believed that England's law was no more deficient than that of the United States.[23] Wilbur D. Jones writes, "It is to Britain's credit that she brought up this subject at all, and she might fairly have expected that, once she did, the United States would agree to make the laws of the two nations identical."[24]

Russell refused to let the escapes rest. In June, a month before the *Alabama* escaped, he ordered the *Florida* seized at Nassau to test the Foreign Enlistment Act. Nassau had drawn the ire of Secretary of the Navy Welles: it was the center of blockade-running and the perfect place to outfit or resupply the Confederate raiders.[25] At Nassau, the *Nashville* visited the *Florida,* and, although unarmed, its crewman complained that the ship's destination was changed. It was released by the attorney general of the Bahamas for lack of evidence to detain it. He seized the ship again in July. Within a month of the *Alabama*'s escape, Russell reported the seizure to Adams.[26]

The *Alabama*'s escape posed a crisis for the first time since the *Trent* incident. The British had followed a central trait of Anglo-American relations; indifference to a situation until a crisis developed. After the *Trent* affair, Palmerston and Russell concentrated on Europe. In March 1862, Russell informed Lyons that "there is no longer any excitement here upon the question of America." Indeed, except for Russell, Somerset, and Newcastle, who had heard about the *Florida,* no leading ministers were concerned about Confederate shipbuilding until the *Florida* and the *Alabama* controversies. Gladstone, for instance, was worried about his high budget, which was bringing criticism from his Radical friends whose support he needed for the political coalition he was building within the Liberal Party. Palmerston was busy with the Schleswig-Holstein question and worried about the French occupation of Rome.[27]

Seward did not take firm action against the British for letting the *Alabama* escape. Welles prepared to receive the "usual torrents of abuse" from Seward's passivity but decided not to separate warships from the blockade to chase the "wolf."[28]

The fact that the raiders failed to help the South did not ease British-American tensions. Americans were not placated when world opinion reacted unfavorably to the image of unarmed merchant ships burning on the high seas. British businessmen and pro-North Radicals got the ministry to detain the raiders being constructed to avoid retributive American privateering. For much the same reason, and because of investments in the United States, British insurers and commercial agents had pressed the government to prohibit Confederate shipbuilding in the spring of 1862. Much of the European business community turned against the Confederacy as the depredations mounted.

The leader of Confederate shipbuilding in Europe was also aware of the negative outcomes of the cruisers' depredations. Having been in Britain since early 1862, before the first raiders were built, the astute Confederate purchasing agent, James Bulloch, recommended unsuccessfully to Confederate navy secretary Stephen Mallory that these activities be curtailed immediately because of the moral damage they caused. Bulloch recommended building ships only for defense.[29]

Rebuffed by Mallory, Bulloch toiled loyally to build raiders while he continued to recommend abandonment of what he believed to be a lost cause. He was a vivid example of the divisions that pervaded the Confederacy that Weigley describes in *The Great Civil War,* and as one of the chief reasons for the Confederacy's demise. In sum, the Confederate government depended on a short-term policy of quick fixes and was never able to breed true nationalism or nationhood in the South or gain the respect of the European powers. A fervent disunity prevailed between Southern state governments and Richmond the longer the war continued. The Confederate army's fragmentation and disputes among leading commanders accompanied this disunity. The flames were fed by President Davis's inability to get along with his cabinet members, generals (except Lee, whose patience was tried), and key political leaders. Davis was uncomfortable with criticism, and he refused to delegate to his cabinet offices, especially the War Department. He was intolerant of opposing ideas. Word traveled as early as June 1861 that Davis's failure was a "foregone conclusion." The more he was criticized, the more dictatorial he became. Anti-Davis feelings spread quickly inside and outside of the Confederate Congress. By early 1862 a prominent politician wrote that Davis should be impeached and that his only salvation was lack of confidence in Vice President Alexander Stephens, who had quarreled with Davis and returned to Georgia. When he returned to Richmond in August 1862, Davis and his secretaries snubbed him. By 1862 Davis's active-negative leadership style "had become a critical problem that seriously affected his usefulness."[30]

Davis's pride helped keep the raiders on the high seas and helped to wreck his chances for foreign recognition of Confederate independence. But the Confederacy had no other naval weapons that could successfully combat the Union navy, and so the raiders' depredations continued. Even the Southern naval leaders disliked the raiders. Minor powers were unfriendly, and the South never tried to build warships in such ports.

In this way, a sense of global morality checked Confederate naval endeavors, kept the Civil War from intensifying on the high seas, and contributed to the continuance of the peace. It was best, ironically, to concentrate Confederate ship construction in Britain and France alone, because these operations fell under the neutrality laws if proper proof of their warlike nature could be ascertained by spies under the control of American consuls and the British ministry. The Confederacy gave away the strengths that it wanted to gain from the raiders by constructing the cruisers in Britain. But world opinion presented no other option.[31]

Russell was determined to halt Confederate shipbuilding in defiance of the outdated and ambiguous Foreign Enlistment Act. He responded to Adams's vigorous protests on 4 September 1862 about the British failure to detain the raiders. He regretted the escape and explained that the law officers recommended detention of the *Alabama* based on its intended use and warlike structure. In fact, this exchange of notes and parliamentary opposition to the raiders destroyed the Confederate shipbuilding program.

5

Dissolving Intervention in 1862

Good feelings following the *Trent* settlement, and cooperation in the first half of 1862 gave way to Federal military defeats in the summer of 1862. These defeats led Russell and Gladstone to consider intervention for humanitarian and other reasons.[1] Palmerston was initially interested, but large forces debunked the idea as the months passed. The tradition of isolation in British foreign policy in North America went back to the post–Napoleonic era when the two powers preferred to negotiate rather than intervene against each other. Britain had repeatedly shown that it did not want to fight in North America. It knew that the United States viewed intervention even for humanitarian purposes as a pro-South act and would retaliate. For that reason, Britain could not intervene unilaterally, and it needed France and Russia for support, which would not de-escalate tensions with the Union. The United States had made clear that intervention under any terms was unthinkable. Frank Merli recalls David Paul Crook's point, made in the 1970s, that the establishment of an "independent nation in America never impinged on a vital British interest."[2]

Traditional suspicions in British-French relations stymied joint intervention, and Russia was friendly toward the United States primarily to split Britain and France. The two western European powers opposed Russia's attempts to subdue the Poles and the czar's attempts to expand into central Asia. Finally, beginning in late September, once they found out about Russell's plan, the quantified arguments against intervention by British statesmen far outweighed the qualitative arguments of Russell and Gladstone. Despite the Civil War, they wrote, British manufacturing and commerce continued to boom, public opinion was uninterested in intervention because there was prosperity at home, Palmerston's majority was shaky, sources of cotton were available elsewhere, there were no overt acts of rebellion by the cotton workers, and there was no treasury to prosecute a foreign war. Britain's policy should be one of watchful waiting, so Palmerston concluded, and this instinct satisfied his cabinet. To Palmerston, watchful waiting meant that he was past the dispute and was content to let the Civil War grind on to its natural

outcome. Meanwhile, popular contentment at home and his unparalleled popularity remained uppermost.

While Palmerston worked his way through the dispute, Russell's fear of a slave
insurrection peaked in August 1862, and Seward could not get Lincoln's cabinet to
approve Russell's plan for buying cotton directly from the planters in states under
Union control, despite Seward's promises that a solution was near. Russell refused
to consider the plan further on 23 October, the same day as his informal cabinet
met to consider intervention (discussed later in this chapter).[3] There were more
emotional reasons for intervening, along with wanting to stop the carnage and
free themselves from the daily tensions that the Civil War brought to relations.
Nevertheless, the diplomacy of caution and realism as to outcomes overcame the
qualified reasons that were used to justify the intervention debate.

So why was intervention considered at all? Perhaps the most general reason is
that the war had driven Russell to the depths of his political and diplomatic talents
with its fits and starts. He was tired of it despite his commendable prosecution
of diplomacy with the United States. Several bits of information came to him in
July, August, and September that caused him to focus on intervention. Russell was
informed by Stuart of Seward's belief stated on 21 July that a servile insurrection
would occur within six months to complement the pro-Unionism of that party in
the South.[4] Fearing an unprecedented slaughter of innocent people and not being
able to forecast the future, a stolid Russell began to think that enough was enough,
that there was going to be no end to the bloodshed, and that something had to be
done from the outside. A few days later, on the morning of 29 July, the *Alabama*
escaped from Birkenhead and, once armed in the Azores, quickly began decimat-
ing the Union merchant marine on the world's oceans. Under American pressure
since 22 June to stop the ship from being completed, Russell had tried to secure
evidence to detain the No. 290. Thomas Dudley, the American consul at Liverpool,
was reticent at getting sound evidence to the British government in a timely manner. Russell and the government acted with the utmost efficiency to detain the
vessel. He and Palmerston certainly did not connive to help the ship escape from
Birkenhead.[5] This tension was great in itself because it had ramifications for British
commerce if Britain ever got into another war. It went along with the already-exist-
ing tensions created by Union seizures of British merchant ships.

In late August the massive Union defeat amid unprecedented slaughter at the
Second Battle of Bull Run quickened Russell's resolve to plan a peaceful intervention. Then the bloodiest single day's battle in American history at Antietam Creek
on 17 September and the retreat of Lee's badly depleted army the next day deprived the Confederacy of the victory it desperately needed to convince the world
that it could defend itself as an independent nation. Palmerston now had second
thoughts that the South could win the war. But Antietam gave Russell the idea
that the carnage would continue for quite some time. Then, Lincoln's preliminary

emancipation proclamation on 22 September made Russell believe that intervention had to be achieved or there would be no end to the fighting.

Nevertheless, the concerns of Russell, Palmerston, and Gladstone were insufficient to move the cabinet to intervene. Factors considered before and after the intervention debate indicate that intervention, as an instrument of Palmerston's foreign policy, was moot by the fall of 1862. Palmerston toyed with intervention, but his characteristic caution enabled him to survive the debate because his thinking was with public opinion, which was quite content with isolationism and prosperity. For all practical purposes, Palmerston put the debate to rest in November. A month later Lincoln survived a Radical Republican attempt to purge his cabinet. The survival of both cabinets was critical to maintaining the cooperative relationship.

The survival of the British cabinet, as tied to the intervention dilemma, must be seen against the ministry's progress on the matter up to the fall of 1862. From February through May 1861 Palmerston and Russell informed Lyons of their aversion to war and resolved not to give the North any reason to fight. They understood that Seward blustered for political purposes and ignored his outbursts. In September and October of 1861, Palmerston choked Russell's first plan to intervene despite the Union's refusing Britain's invitation to join the powers in Mexico, an intervention about which Palmerston and Russell were extremely dubious. Yet they intervened with a token force to monitor events and recoup the losses of British subjects. This intervention was not an anti-Union act. The Union concentrated on the Civil War and had not intervened against Spanish incursions in Santo Domingo and had refused to try to regain the South with an invasion of Canada.

In the meantime, Charles Francis Adams gained the goodwill of the Palmerston ministry in late 1861 with assurances that his government was not about to try Britain's patience by threatening Canada. Adams's task was difficult when compared to pro-South support in Britain. He argued that reunion was necessary to keep North and South from becoming two jealous states constantly eyeing each other.[6]

Adams gained Russell's respect during 1862. He knew that Palmerston could not take strong action because a loss in foreign affairs might topple his government, which hinged on a slim majority. For this reason, Palmerston refused to intervene with Napoleon III out of distrust for the opportunistic emperor. The prime minister feared that Napoleon might pull out and leave Britain fighting the United States alone to establish a freer hand in Europe. Moreover, by 1862 Napoleon's designs on establishing a puppet state in Mexico became clearer to Whitehall and increased distrust of the emperor. Russell reaffirmed British neutrality and said that intervention had to be in consort with France and Russia. The latter power could wield the balance. But this was wishful thinking. He knew that the time was not right because there was not a British intervention tradition, a European intervention consensus, or strong public support.[7]

Finally, the traditional realism of the British cabinet stymied intervention.[8] By the late summer of 1862 Whitehall would go to war only in the case of the occupation of the Scheldt Estuary across the English Channel or a French invasion attempt. Indeed, Palmerston's nonintervention had prevailed before the Civil War, and the statements he and his ministers had made since 1861 underlined that fact. Kenneth Bourne writes, "Palmerston could never really convince himself that the possible benefits of intervention were worth the risks involved."[9] Since the first year of the Civil War, most British and Canadian newspapers thought that the United States should remain fragmented. Much of the aristocracy and the middle class believed that the South rightfully resisted aggression and was destined to win and that Britain should not interfere. The newspapers and the ministry failed to understand the dynamics, which prevented a workable intervention plan with clear outcomes. Nevertheless, pro-South sympathizers attempted to draw a parallel with the American colonists' fight in the War of Independence for what they thought was an inherent right. The privileged few in Britain felt that the North could never defeat a vast region of 9 million people. The elite were not strong enough to determine policy, however. Thus Palmerston opened and closed the year 1862 opposed to intervention.

The lack of demand for intervention in Britain, let alone from the European powers, hurt its prospects of moderating the Civil War. This debate progressed through several stages, with each successive stage weakening the cause.

Stage one consisted of the reasons that made intervention seem necessary to its advocates, Palmerston, Russell, and Gladstone. First, Union military fortunes sank with McClellan's retreat from the outskirts of Richmond in July and the Union defeat at the Second Battle of Bull Run at the end of August. Second, it appeared to the foreign secretary and the chancellor that the war was reaching unprecedented proportions in carnage and escalating unemployment in the British and French textile districts. Third, Union seizures of British ships and the depredations of the *Alabama* both increased and created new tensions surrounding the neutrality that Russell had tried so hard to uphold. Palmerston, Russell, and Gladstone considered how Britain could stop the bloodshed until the prime minister learned of the Confederate retreat from Antietam.

Antietam initiated the second stage of the debate. In this stage Palmerston listened to the realistic advice of a wider circle led by Granville and Cornewall Lewis. Granville came out against intervention in late September in a long and elegantly argued memorandum to the prime minister. Gladstone's ill-reasoned and ill-timed pro-South speech on 7 October helped to turn cabinet members against intervention and brought Gladstone under scrutiny for misinterpreting foreign policy. Gladstone spoke out of turn, and Palmerston thought that his chancellor was "too eager to press the weight of international moral authority on Washington which

he had been ready to impose on Vienna [in 1860]." A week later, Minister of War
Lewis complemented Granville's memo and successfully countered Gladstone's
unauthorized public utterances. Palmerston remained aloof throughout October
and in early November disclaimed intervention. From then on intervention was a
dead cabinet issue. Lady Palmerston capped her husband's opposition to intervention and eased British-American tensions by inviting Charles Francis Adams and
his wife to her famous parties again.[10]

Indeed, Palmerston's consideration of intervention was something of a quirk.
His actions prior to the intervention debate negated the chance that he would condone intervention, which would threaten to bring him into alliance with the South.
Palmerston could not surmount his antislavery instincts to chance a war that might
strengthen slavery. By the Battle of Antietam he (and Russell) had already degraded
the South's diplomacy. In July, he easily defeated the small Confederate lobby in
the House of Commons by stating that meddling meant a Britain-Union war. He
reminded the House of the benefits of nonintervention by calling attention to the
South's uncertain national aspirations. He wanted a free hand "to determine what to
do and when," which in reality meant that he did not have to act unless some powerful political force emerged. That was not likely to happen in the extremely balanced Parliament. The Confederate cause was hampered in late July as Confederate
sympathizers cheered the escape of the *Alabama* and reveled at the ineffectiveness
of the Union blockade. Palmerston and Russell were embarrassed and miffed by
this breach of neutrality and moved to stop Confederate shipbuilding, which, along
with the cotton embargo, backfired on Confederate diplomacy.[11]

Palmerston grappled with the fact that, if a case for intervention could be justified, the North would perceive it as a pro-South act to go along with its perception of the "premature" recognition of Confederate belligerency and neutrality. In
a move that was consistent with the private nature of British-American relations
when something had to be done to forestall rising tensions, he thought about approaching the Federal government rather than unilaterally recognizing the South's
independence. Moreover, Britain's motives for intervention were not aimed at
weakening the North. Russell and Gladstone wanted to stop the bloodshed and a
potential slave revolt.[12] For these reasons Lord Russell's intervention plan aimed at
suspending the fighting "in the most friendly and conciliatory of terms." Moreover,
French and Russian support was missing during the cabinet meeting in October.

A further dimension that made the British intervention debate consistent with
antebellum policy can be shown from outcomes on the Civil War battlefields in the
first half of 1862. These victories changed England's sentiments toward the North
by March when Moran wrote that once Nashville fell, the Confederacy started
to become alienated on British soil. Moran believed that the change was proof
that "John Bull always goes with the winners."[13] British pro-North sentiments
expanded with Union victories along the eastern seaboard and in Kentucky and

Tennessee. From February through April, Gen. Ambrose E. Burnside captured every North Carolina port except Wilmington. During the late summer, Confederate general Braxton Bragg invaded Kentucky to regain lost Rebel ground. But his mental energy outdistanced his tactics, and he failed to take Louisville. Union general Don Carlos Buell marched from Nashville to Louisville, organized his forces, and forced Bragg back to Knoxville and Chattanooga.

On 17 September the fortunes of war reverted back to the Union when Lee was forced to retreat from Antietam. Yet this slaughter fortified the desires of Russell and Gladstone. At Antietam Creek, McClellan had superior numbers but as usual believed that Lee outnumbered him at least two to one. His inability to order timely movements enabled Lee to repel Federal advances at a cost of 6,300 to 6,500 Union and Confederate soldiers dead or mortally wounded, with combined casualties of the twelve-hour battle totaling 22,219. One-fourth of the Union troops committed were killed or wounded, and nearly a third of the Confederate combatants met the same fate; this battle saw more American soldiers dead in a single day than in all other nineteenth-century American wars combined, as James M. McPherson reminds us. Despite his untimely and uncoordinated prosecution of the battle in which he committed only a third of his available forces, at the end of the day, McClellan held the initiative. The Rebels still held the town of Sharpsburg above the creek with only a mauled army and stragglers to commit the next day while McClellan had fresh divisions. Particularly severe were the losses to Lee's officer corps. McPherson points out that 118 of 218 of Lee's top commanders were killed or wounded during the battle. Most of the wounded returned, but Lee was forced from the offensive until the following May.[14] The mauling would have been worse had McClellan pursued Lee as Lincoln begged him to do. Michael C. C. Adams writes, "In a year of slow generals he [McClellan] was the slowest and he let Lee get away."[15]

Despite McClellan's caution, the British saw Antietam as giving the military edge to the North. Antietam and the president's preliminary emancipation proclamation of 22 September strengthened Palmerston's pragmatic policy of "watchful waiting."[16] Finally, had the British ministry been pro-South, it could have interpreted Antietam as a draw, thus giving the South more credit than it was due. Yet Palmerston was far from risking this position and interpreted Antietam as a Rebel defeat that turned the course of the war in favor of the North.

Furthermore, Palmerston needed good relations with the North. British shipping was vulnerable, and Gladstone and Russell feared a Union military threat to Canada. Moreover, the cabinet tabled a voting reform bill under Conservative criticism. Russell feared a domestic revolt more than a war with the United States, and he kept on with intervention plans, worrying that "a clash with the great northern democracy or indeed pay for an enlarged army and navy" might arouse the workers.[17]

Russell was trying to placate many interests to save the ministry with its slim majority; and he tried to hide his ambivalence behind his interventionist argument. His real uncertainty about intervention was evident when he instructed Lyons to ask Seward if secession was owing to a few conspirators and if the majority of the people in the country were still Unionist.[18] In early August he insulted Mason for asserting that "twelve million" Southerners maintained independence for eighteenth months and that the majority of intelligent Europeans believed that the Union was lost. In response, Russell quoted Seward that fewer than 5 million whites were Rebels and not the 12 million Mason believed, that many Southerners were restored to the Union, and that the South's restoration was not the impossibility that Mason assumed. In quoting Seward's argument, the diminutive foreign secretary called Mason a liar. He answered pro-Confederate questions for the second time in two months in the Lords and said that Britain remained neutral and had no notice from France requesting a joint intervention.[19] Thus Russell's intervention plan did not favor the South, unless Slidell's idea that the British were waiting for the war to weaken the North is accepted.[20]

Lord John's ambivalence was reflected in the different perspectives among influential Liberals, Conservatives, and Radicals. The queen opposed intervention.[21] In the cabinet, Liberals Argyll and Somerset, and Radicals Villiers and Milner Gibson, supported the North. Derby, Disraeli, and the Conservative opposition opposed intervention. But the outcomes of the military contest were unclear, and only Radicals John Bright and Richard Cobden believed in Northern victory.[22]

Notwithstanding McClellan's embarrassing failure at midyear, 1862 was the year that threatened the high tide of Confederate military feats.[23] Bipartisan support was won for the Union effort throughout the North. By 22 August, Secretary of the Navy Welles wrote, "There is a wonderful and increasing enthusiasm and determination to put down this Rebellion and sustain the integrity of the Union. It is confined to no class or party or description: rich and poor, the educated and ignorant, the gentle and refined as well as the stout, coarse, and athletic, the Democrats generally as well as the Republicans, are offering themselves in the country."[24]

On the British side, Russell's communications to Mason and the government's defeat of the Confederate lobby showed that the ministry lost the little appreciation it ever had for the South's government. By the time British consul Robert Bunch at Charleston wrote Russell that Judah Benjamin's appointment as Confederate secretary of state was "an unfortunate one," Russell had already denounced Mason.[25] The more Davis shuffled cabinet ministers, the more British disrespect for the government in Richmond grew. It also helps explain why Lyons and Seward concocted the Anti-Slave Trade Treaty in March 1862.[26] Getting U.S. support for the suppression of the slave trade was a long-term British objective that further helps to explain why Britain approved this treaty. Common interests such as these grew between Washington and London while the South failed to gain European support with its "King Cotton" embargo.[27]

After Antietam sobered him, Palmerston had little to lose in halfheartedly encouraging Russell to poll the cabinet about whether or not to intervene, while he remained indifferent. Finally, Russell and Gladstone demonstrated that they were not convinced about their desire for intervention, and the latter acted like a private subject rather than the third most powerful cabinet minister. Had there been unity about intervention or serious interest in the debate, the chancellor probably would not have been touring the North Country to speak to the workers and their managers. Instead he would have been in London finding the funds to support the war that Seward had made inevitable with Britain or any other power that intervened. But Palmerston was far from ordering such planning.

At a time when the prime minister was exceedingly cautious about the intervention question, Gladstone's extraministerial actions constituted a major reason why the cabinet dissolved intervention. His overriding quest was for domestic and foreign order. He advocated national self-determination, and he believed that states born this way added to world order. This is why three years before he had banded with Palmerston and Russell in support of Italian independence and had hesitated to recommend that the Ionian Islands should go to Greece. (Despite their support, Britain had not intervened.) In the Ionian situation, Gladstone had recommended further study, which is what he should have done in this case.

But with Gladstone there was always a twist. The year before, on 16 August 1861, he criticized Bright's idea that the Civil War strengthened democracy in the "New World" because Gladstone did not believe that democracy could be imposed by military force. He believed that the war was "doing immense mischief, to all popular and liberal principles whatever." He believed that Lincoln, like past American presidents, did not have to worry about public opinion and could end the war. Here he underestimated the democratic resolve of Lincoln and the American people and showed poor understanding of Union war aims.

Nor does his private correspondence with Russell indicate that he was unabashedly pro-South. He was repelled by slavery because of his strong religious scruples. Even so, Gladstone felt that the preliminary emancipation proclamation was a desperate political act. His energetic and original mind caused him to share this failing with "almost all of his contemporaries," Peter Parish believes. Parish speculates that another reason why Gladstone missed the social nature of the North's struggle was because he was preoccupied with political, administrative, and financial reform priorities. In that regard, Gladstone told Russell in late August 1862 that everyone believed the South was going to win except the North. Thus, "It is our absolute duty to recognise . . . that Southern independence is established." Furthermore, if commerce was not normalized, the Lancashire textile workers might revolt. (They seemed to forget about the docility of the British working class.) In this respect, they wanted to end the war for national self-interest.[28] In sum, Gladstone and Russell saw their initiative as an act of reconciliation with the North similar to their proclamation of neutrality and support for the blockade.[29]

Gladstone suggested intervention after the South's victories over the summer of 1862. He wrote Argyll that he thought Antietam kept the war in balance and had sobered the Confederacy. "I am not sorry for the apparent ill success of the Confederates as invaders. They might have become intoxicated, & entangled, by good Fortune." On 22 September (even before his speech of 7 October), he believed that the growing plight of the Lancashire workers "is a trifle in the eye of humanity, compared to the wholesale slaughter that is going on, . . . since it has long been (I think) clear enough that Secession is virtually an established fact & that Jeff. Davis & his comrades have made a nation." Yet on 24 September, before learning of Antietam, Palmerston's opinion differed from that of Gladstone. He wanted to join France and Russia to propose mediation, which he thought had a small chance of being accepted by the North. He said that private discussions were being held with France, and he stressed that the cabinet had yet to approve an active policy. Being careful, Palmerston stated that both sides had to accept the offer, and he told Gladstone to wait. If the North refused, Southern independence could be acknowledged.[30]

Palmerston was less eager, but Russell wanted to proceed despite the uncertainties. On 26 September, Russell titillated Gladstone with his plan, about which he had privately consulted Palmerston and which Palmerston had intimated to Gladstone. Russell's mediation offer was designed to prevent the Rebels from thinking that mediation was a pro-South move. Nevertheless, the offer included asking the North to concede Southern independence. But ambivalence remained. Russell explained to Gladstone that they should not "have a Cabinet upon this, unless France thought the opportunity favourable, & this was previously ascertained." He wrote Cowley that Britain, France, and Russia should offer mediation. He continued that Palmerston refused to support the plan, which he otherwise agreed with (according to Russell) until, as Palmerston put it, "we see a little more into the results of the Southern invasion of Pennsylvania [Maryland]."[31]

Palmerston was cautious because Antietam and the preliminary emancipation proclamation shook him with fears of a slave revolt as Lincoln's generals freed slaves in territory held by the Union army, and which Britons believed that Lincoln had proclaimed from desperation as it did not free slaves anywhere else. They did not see the proclamation as a primary addition to Lincoln's war aims but as a sign of weakness. Nevertheless, Palmerston parted company with intervention, and without his support Russell's and Gladstone's plan had little chance.[32]

Gladstone's travels in the north of England caused him to lose touch with the "cabinet sentiment from mid-September to early October."[33] He had received conflicting views from his superiors. The prime minister disclosed his traditional discomfort about deciding on American affairs.[34] He also knew something of the Union's resolve. In August 1862, Sumner wrote Argyll of the North's dedication to victory, and his letters were passed among the ministers.[35]

Palmerston's reluctance also stemmed from fear that if intervention failed, the other powers might try to exact retribution while leaving Britain to fight the North. Then, too, Palmerston's advisors opposed Russell's plan. Argyll dismissed Russell's concerns about a slave revolt, feared a war—or at least alienating the North if Britain intervened—and believed that emancipation discouraged Britain's involvement with the Confederacy.[36]

Although not in the cabinet, Clarendon was privy to the secrets, listened to Palmerston, and supported Argyll. Lewis and Lord de Grey at the War Office, Colonial Secretary Newcastle, Lord President Granville, Home Secretary Sir George Grey, Charles. P. Villiers (Poor Law Board), and Thomas Milner Gibson (Board of Trade) informed Russell of their opposition. The queen, who was still in mourning, did not want a cabinet crisis. The cynical Clarendon agreed with Palmerston that "I hate the Confederates almost as much as the Federals but I hope for success and the consequent prolongation of the war because it is only the complete exhaustion of both parties that will prevent their uniting against us." Permanent Foreign Office Undersecretary Hammond believed that attrition was beginning and agreed that nothing should be done. The more the North and the South fought "the less likely will they be to court a quarrel with us or to prove formidable antagonists if they do so." The *Times* and other journals opposed war with the North, even with European support.[37]

When Palmerston and Russell apprised Granville of the mediation plan, he quickly "put his foot flatly down upon any intervention in America." Granville's arguments to Russell on 27 September, before the news of Antietam, were more pragmatic than Clarendon's outburst. The upshot of his thinking was that if Britain recognized the South, if the North proceeded to win more victories, and if the war continued for some time, Britain would most certainly drift into war with the North. Although he thought that the British people disliked the North, sympathized with the South, and needed cotton, England "must not meddle." Like Hammond and Argyll, he balked at mediation because neither the North nor the South had requested it. Granville drew a negative picture of the repercussions: escalation of the blockade and less raw cotton for the Lancashire mill owners when cotton was needed for the first time in the war. Rather than depend on the South, Granville advised that Britain should procure cotton from India and Egypt. He worried that English opinion was "opposed to . . . the South and North on the subject of slavery" and that mediation depended on the untrustworthy Napoleon's support. Moreover, Granville stated that Parliament, the press, and the public opposed intervention. Both North and South would take advantage of a mediated armistice with the edge to the North.

George William Frederick Villiers, fourth Earl of Clarendon, British foreign secretary, 1853–58, 1865–66, and 1868–70, a respected influence in Europe and chief advocate of caution and cooperation with the United States. British National Portrait Gallery

"In that case," Granville continued, "we should appear dupes, we should give false hopes as to the supply of cotton, and destroy the stimulus, which although painful at the moment, is likely to be so beneficial for the future, and by giving us supplies from our own possessions and other parts of the world."[38]

Granville wrote with the confidence of a cabinet leader and businessman with parliamentary and public support. He argued that Confederate independence increased prospects of a British-American war and freed Napoleon III's movements in Europe and the Western Hemisphere. Then Britain might face the North's retaliation and a stab in the back by Napoleon. Granville reckoned that only the combatants understood why they fought and that foreigners could not offer acceptable terms. Who knows but that the North might be close to success, Granville asked. It was "premature" to act in a situation where Britain and the other powers were not invited. He reflected that only Palmerston, Russell, Gladstone, and maybe Newcastle favored intervention. "It appears to me a great mistake."[39]

Granville's memorandum increased Palmerston's doubts. For the prime minister was the key to the debate and the real "danger to Union interests." He remained strictly neutral, although bobbing up and down with Confederate defeat and victory "like the human cork that he was," Owsley writes. On 1 October Granville heard of Lee's retreat and informed Lord Stanley of Alderley that intervention "was a great mistake."[40] Finally, Stanley agreed with Granville that Parliament, the press, and the people wanted to maintain neutrality.[41]

The Confederacy was also bobbing up and down on intervention, and the British retreat was just as critical as that of General Lee. Lee's retreat was bitter for the Confederates, as hopes for victory had been high. Two days before the news reached London, the third Earl of Shaftesbury, Palmerston's son-in-law, informed Mason and Slidell that "a British-French offer of mediation and recognition 'is very close at hand.'" Then news of the retreat stunned the South's British friends. Confederate secretary of state Benjamin wrote that the Confederate lobby "express[es] as much chagrin as if they themselves had been defeated." Jefferson Davis was depressed because Lee had made his maximum effort. The loss, combined with Braxton Bragg's defeat in Kentucky, meant that Davis had a difficult rebuilding job while the North was "just beginning to put forth his might." General James Longstreet, Lee's chief corps commander, wrote twenty years later, "At Sharpsburg [Antietam] was sprung the keystone of the arch upon which the Confederate cause rested."[42]

The London *Times* buttressed McPherson's argument (along with that of Owsley and others) that Antietam had turned the tide on intervention. No doubt embarrassed and certainly stunned, it termed Lee's campaign "a failure," which other British newspapers echoed. Adams reflected Longstreet's point when he enjoined that Antietam resurrected Federal credibility. He joyfully believed that most Britons had expected the Confederates to capture Washington. But Lee's retreat into Virginia has caused "less and less . . . to be thought of mediation and intervention."[43]

Granville George Leveson-Gower, second Earl Granville, Gladstone's colonial secretary, 1868–70; foreign secretary under Gladstone, 1870–74, 1880–85. British National Portrait Gallery

McPherson writes that Palmerston quit intervention by stating that mediation could only be revived if the South won a victory of the magnitude that it had just lost. In that regard, Palmerston wrote Russell on 2 October that a new picture now emerged that looked different from what he had perceived over the past ten days. The "whole matter" of intervention was now "full of difficulty." "By 22 October, it *was* clear to Palmerston that Confederate defeats had ended any chance of successful mediation." Palmerston concluded with his often-quoted line: "I am therefore inclined to change the opinion I wrote you when the Confederates seemed to be carrying all before them, and I am [convinced] . . . that we must continue merely to be lookers-on till the war shall have taken a more decided turn." Antietam was indeed, as Owsley writes, "the deathblow of Confederate recognition" by Britain.[44]

Nor was a majority cabinet vote for intervention clear even if Lee had won, because Russell and Gladstone had failed to enlist cabinet allies. Palmerston's decision broke the triad that might have influenced other cabinet members. Antietam, in D. P. Crook's words, "eroded the unity of the triumvirate, by making Palmerston lukewarm" to intervention, and it "seriously weakened the legal (and hence moral) basis for recognition, a component of Russell's original project."[45]

Despite strong contrary advice and mixed feelings about Antietam, Gladstone and Russell refused to stop. But they split by early October, and Russell, without French or Russian support, found himself alone as he had before. Gladstone remained with intervention because of his desire to stop the bloodshed and because he could not understand why the North refused to accept Confederate independence. In May 1861 he had written, "I think the whole notion of 20 million of Republicans making war upon 10 millions, to compel them irrespective of all differences . . . to continue in free voluntary & equal union with them, which taints and infects their very freedom, [is] one of the most strange paradoxes, and one of the most lamentable pictures that has lately been presented to the eye of humanity."[46]

Gladstone was capable of embracing new courses of political action when charged with emotion. He was being mentioned as the next Liberal Party leader, a role he denied at the time, but which he was no doubt flattered about and for which he was making preparations. His leaning toward intervention did not come about suddenly. He rehearsed his thinking about the war when he presented an hour speech to the Association of Lancashire and Cheshire Mechanics' Institutes on the cotton situation at the Manchester Free Trade Hall on 23 April 1862 before a large, cordial audience. He spoke of the need for welfare for the textile workers more than for the sanctity of the Union. He did not speak as an enemy of the North. He believed that the Union could not be reunited even if the South was subdued. The war was between slavery and freedom, which could not be forced on any people with the sword. Many Americans interpreted the speech as a strong sign of Britain's anti-Unionism and thought he presaged intervention.[47]

In July, with cotton supplies nearly spent, Gladstone, like Russell, was concerned about rioting unless worker distress was relieved. He wrote a long memorandum to Palmerston urging a mediation plan. In the cabinet he urged the prime minister and foreign secretary to adopt intervention. In September, he wrote Argyll: "it is our absolute duty to recognise . . . that Southern independence is established, i.e. that the South cannot be conquered."[48]

Furthermore, Gladstone could not understand Lincoln's struggle to preserve the Union partly because the hard-pressed president had not clarified his slavery policy. Gladstone believed wrongly that Lincoln's cause lacked a higher meaning other than reclaiming the South by force, and he wrote privately that the South was "earnest and united and had earned its independence." But Lyons argued otherwise while in England on leave, and he consistently opposed intervention. The cabinet upheld Lyons's position on 2 August. Nevertheless, by September Gladstone was convinced of the necessity for Southern independence.[49]

In early October Gladstone made a "triumphal procession" through the Tyneside industrial region while unaware that Palmerston opposed intervention. Thousands feted him, and he probably forgot his subservient position in London. He was, after all, trying to increase his political power among the workers and the Radical leaders, and he succeeded because he reciprocated their spirit. He was making a rapid transition from Peelite conservatism to a liberal-radical political position, and he was excited that he had discovered an ability to move huge popular audiences. He may have felt that he could do something that the Conservative and Liberal leaders had not achieved, which was to gain the support of the masses. Since the Civil War was the greatest topic of the day, he was swayed by the prospects of a new political future.[50]

But Gladstone could not escape being identified with the ministry, which he should have remembered. His audiences believed that he spoke of Palmerston's plans for further relief action. He thought Confederate independence was essential to that plan. He thought that he was making a preliminary announcement of the cabinet's position to recognize the South "to a crowded & enthusiastic dinner of near 500" at Newcastle on 7 October 1862. As Allan Nevins writes, "This unwarranted statement, coming from a powerful minister, gave many Britons an impression that the government was about to act." Gladstone averred that the South had "made a nation." His humanitarianism contributed to what Nevins calls his "complex emotions."

In making this famous statement, Gladstone was moved by what he had heard in July from a cousin, Scots fusilier lieutenant colonel Edward Neville. Neville had spent three months with McClellan's Army of the Potomac on the Virginia peninsula. Gladstone read Neville's letter to the cabinet and sent it to the Duke of Cambridge, the commander in chief. Neville's account covered "the grave events on the Chickahominy" and the sufferings and desertions of the bluecoat soldiers against the background of their despondency about retreating when only five miles from Richmond. McClellan's loss of nerve gave the Confederacy renewed hope for British recognition. The South's hopes improved with victories in the Shenandoah Valley and the Second Battle of Bull Run in July and August. But Gladstone was unmoved by this temporary Confederate exuberance less than by Neville's descriptions of the bloodshed and suffering. Gladstone believed that he spoke as the North's friend when he advised it to quit its stubborn attitude against stopping the war. Despite the best of intentions, he was out of touch with Union policy and British policy and embarrassed himself and Palmerston's opposition to intervention.[51]

The speech showed him as an enigma in quest of a solution to a war that he improperly understood from the perspective of either side. Early in the war he had said that England should "stand off in perfectly even-handed non-intervention." But by the end of 1861 he began to see a long war ahead and to think about "the still remote, but ugly question" of intervention to stop the bloodshed and assure cotton supplies. As the war continued he praised the "exemplary forbearance" of the cotton workers but feared upheaval. He had a further motive, which showed his confusion. He complained to Cobden that the war was causing "a *factious* sympathy with the South and slavery such as that which the misconduct of Russia begot among us in favour of Turkey and Islam."[52] Meanwhile, he sympathized with American democracy, and he was unhappy with the upper classes and his colleagues who expressed glee over the North's predicament. These sympathies overshadowed his distaste for the North's high tariffs and Seward's unyielding diplomacy. He was willing to intervene because, unlike Granville, he did not believe that the North would fight.

Nor was Gladstone afraid of the North's growth, and he certainly did not want to disrupt relations. During the *Trent* debate he was "deeply convinced it was for *our* interest that the old Union should continue." Even during his Newcastle speech he uttered warm feelings for the North: "They are our kin. They were . . . our customers, and we hope they will be our customers again." And he denied that his government had "any interest in the disruption of the Union." What moved Gladstone was his overriding penchant for national self-determination and thus political order, in this case Southern independence. He was moved to maintain Southern institutions threatened by "the monolithic and centralizing tendencies of a wartime democracy." He opposed slavery but thought that the abolitionists were weak and that slavery would die a more natural death. He was preoccupied with the opinions of his friend Lord Acton and another contemporary, Walter Bagehot (the editor of the *Economist,* Palmerston admirer, and opponent of democracy) that the Union should not be maintained by war.[53]

But for immediate purposes Gladstone's speech threatened his political career. He had the reputation as the most brilliant and fractious minister, a political Janus. During the last years of the war Gladstone moved away from the Confederacy to the Radical position for reform, and he embraced slavery as the key issue. But as Union military victories mounted and emancipation joined with reunification as Union aims, he changed to Bright's pro-North position.[54]

Thus, from this perspective of Gladstone's past, present, and future statements, Gladstone plunged when he should not have, and in a way he represented the nationalistic bravado of the Palmerston of old. Gladstone broke convention by leaking the intervention proceedings, which the cabinet found unacceptable. Convention barred ministers from entering into the realms of their colleagues, and Gladstone had crossed from treasury matters into foreign policy. It is not surprising that with Palmerston's approval a chagrined Russell scolded Gladstone for transgressing "the latitude which all speakers must be allowed when you said that Jeff. Davis had made a nation." Palmerston believed that "Gladstone was not far wrong in pronouncing by anticipation of the National Independence of the South" but went on that Gladstone "should Steer clear of the Future unless authorized by his Colleagues." The *Saturday Review* held that Gladstone spoke out of turn in "an after-dinner speech to the citizens of a second-rate borough." It was an "extraordinary indiscretion," the paper continued, because the government declined to recognize the South.[55]

Despite the prime minister's softer criticism, Gladstone did not intentionally voice an anti-Palmerstonian policy for the first time. Indeed, he had used "the South has made a nation" just a few weeks earlier in a letter to Arthur Gordon and the previous May in Newcastle. In this way, Gladstone was only saying what he had repeated several times since the Civil War began. At the same time, however, Palmerston had informed Gladstone on 24 September that there was no cabinet consensus for intervention, that he was having second thoughts, and that military events would determine Britain's policy.

Behind Palmerston's position were the nonintervention feelings of the British people and his traditional concern about France. Napoleon III had been cool to British intervention entreaties because he was shaking up his cabinet by dismissing Thouvenel for opposing an aggressive Italian policy. Yet Cowley reported to Russell on 3 October that the emperor was "very anxious to recognize the South, though determined to take no step without us." Cowley heard that Napoleon was telling Southerners that Britain was at fault for nonrecognition. Furthermore, a correspondent reminded Gladstone on 11 October that "popular opinion" did not support his Newcastle view. In this ticklish state, Palmerston meant to end intervention. A further irony in Palmerston's standing fast was that he gave Gladstone the stability that intervention might have threatened. For a British-American war meant a decline in revenue and the defeat of the ministry. Realizing the consequences of his speech, Gladstone observed the strictest caution for the rest of the war and indeed spoke publicly about it one more time only. He admitted that he made a mistake "of incredible grossness, . . . [The Newcastle speech] illustrates vividly that incapacity which mind so long retained, and perhaps still exhibits, and incapacity of viewing subjects all round, in their extraneous as well as in their internal properties, and thereby of knowing when to be silent and when to speak." In early 1863 his review of the Emancipation Proclamation enabled him to understand how unwelcome intervention was to the Union. On 30 June he spoke in the House of Commons for strict neutrality and nonintervention as the national policy against the Confederate lobby. By then the Emancipation Proclamation had changed British opinion to "flow more strongly for the North." Over the next year he continued to reflect regretfully about his shortness of his vision at Newcastle. On 4 February 1864 he wrote Sumner that the war had surpassed the phase when European opinion could alter its course if it ever could have.[56]

Not only had Gladstone's slip helped put the anti-interventionist majority on solid ground, but also it had helped to show up Russell's ambivalence. On 9 October, just two days after Gladstone's speech, Lord John did not think that the North was ready for mediation based on separation and Britain's continued neutrality, but "it would be a fair and defensible course, leaving it open to us to hasten or defer recognition if the proposal is declined. Lord Lyons might carry it over [to Washington] on the 25th."[57] To further illustrate his vacillation, Russell reassured Adams on 17 October that Palmerston and the cabinet regretted the speech, that Gladstone was trying to correct it, and that Britain's neutrality was unchanged.[58] Adams believed that Gladstone expressed a personal view and wisely delayed seeing Russell until he discovered if the speech summarized the cabinet position. The British anti-interventionist press panned the speech, and Adams did not feel that he lacked British support.[59]

To further oppose intervention, Gladstone's speech elicited a decisive counterblast from minister of war George Cornewall Lewis, whose logic and sincerity made him one of the "best-trusted members of the House." He was heartened by Russell's failed cabinet memo on 13 October that may have tried to exploit Gladstone's blunder to rally support but did not define how an armistice might be implemented.[60] Lewis's Hereford speech on 14 October and his countermemo to Russell further neutralized Gladstone's speech and was the "first shot in a high level controversy which effectively killed the chance of an interventionist decision being made at the cabinet projected for 23 October." Lewis spoke realistically for national self-interest through the continuation of the cautious policy. A relieved Adams now understood that there was no decision about intervention. He recorded in his diary on 16 October that Gladstone had "overshot the mark" but feared that the danger of intervention might persist because Russell could send Lyons back to Washington to propitiate his plan.[61]

But Russell's plan for Lyons failed when the realism of Granville and now Lewis, rather than Gladstone's idealism, gained general support. Lewis's speech was timely because cotton prices declined and the angry London commercial classes opposed recognition of the Confederacy because of the cotton embargo. A report from the United States underlined Lewis's point that if the war was stopped immediately cotton shipments would not increase, and the western states were unsympathetic to a negotiated peace and wanted to continue the war. In light of these sentiments, Russell's feeling that Lewis's speech was "imprudent" had little bearing on public opinion. His argument to Palmerston that Lewis should not have publicized "a line of policy not agreed upon by his colleagues" fell on deaf ears.[62]

Like Gladstone, Lewis acted without prompting from Palmerston or the cabinet. The pro-Rebel *Liverpool Courier* suspected Palmerston of encouraging Lewis to set one cabinet member against another. Although this was a favorite Palmerstonian ploy to maintain personal control, there is no evidence of Palmerston's duplicity. Instead, powerful ministers were coming at Russell individually. Like Granville, Lewis opposed a British-American war. He reminded the cabinet that Seward made this prospect abundantly clear. To Americans like Seward, he said, Britain had done enough to favor the South. He countered Gladstone by remarking that the Confederates had not established a clear claim to independence because of battlefield failures. He struck a national chord when he stated that the Confederates were not interested in recognition on any accepted principles of international law. Lewis was particularly sharp not to offer mediation "to heated and violent partisans." Moreover, "an armistice could not be equal in effect on North and South, but must give the Confederacy an advantage [here he disagreed with Granville]." He observed, "Determination on both sides was rocklike, and the North would be heatedly against compromise; that Washington would be sure to show its resentment in a fashion that might lead to hostilities; and that even if the North acceded, Britain and Europe would be utterly helpless in offering advice on boundaries, the slavery question, and other intricate matters."

In the wake of Lewis's speech, and coupled with Granville's arguments and Gladstone's mistake the entire cabinet—except for Russell, Gladstone, and Lord Chancellor Westbury—opposed intervention. Adams wrote years later that the fifteen-to-three vote against intervention was an action to punish Gladstone. Whatever the ministry's intent, the government rightly believed that the British people and the Americans opposed intervention. Home secretary Sir George Grey wrote in support of nonintervention on 27 October after the informal cabinet four days before that had drowned Russell's mediation plan. Russell, he argued, had no evidence that mediation was efficacious. Russia might not join Britain and France. In fact, Grey worried that Russia might inform the United States to strain British-American relations. Moreover, there was a general feeling among ministers that the workers were pro-North and needed the flow of corn and flour from the North. By 28 October, only Russell and Gladstone supported intervention.[63]

The intervention movement dissolved in a larger sense because, as Granville suspected, neither British nor American party politics supported it. To strengthen his nonintervention position, the week before the cabinet projected for 23 October, Palmerston sent Clarendon to see Derby. He found the opposition leader agreeing with Lewis that recognition of the South was the same as precipitating war with the North. In addition, Disraeli criticized Gladstone for suggesting support for the Confederacy; and Parliament clearly debunked intervention. Derby's opposition was the critical factor sealing the fate of the interventionist plan. Thinking realistically like Granville and Lewis, he believed that intervention would fail to improve Southern cotton shipments to the weavers in Lancashire, where he was the largest landowner. Moreover, he did not believe that a mutually acceptable armistice was possible. For these reasons, Derby and his Conservative lieutenants practiced a hands-off policy. Derby believed Conservative support for intervention weakened his chances of reelection on the platform of enlarging the franchise.⁶⁴

Palmerston's realism was further confirmed when word came from the British legation in Washington "to wait." This message was more pronounced because chargé d'affaires William Stuart, tending to affairs while Lyons was in England, was pro-South. Stuart evidenced that ambivalence reigned in British ranks on both sides of the Atlantic. Russell intimated Stuart's advice to Palmerston, which confirmed his decision.⁶⁵ On 22 October the prime minister wrote to Lord Russell that he agreed with Lewis and had decided that the ministry would be "lookers-on till the war shall have taken a more decided turn." Russell's informal cabinet on 23 October, with Palmerston absent, extinguished the debate. Vastly outnumbered and fearing public pressure on the ministry, Russell again hastened to assure Adams of strict neutrality. On hearing this verdict, Clarendon congratulated Lewis for his Hereford speech and for his cabinet memorandum's success in "smashing" Russell's proposal. Always fearful of the worst while exuding complete disbelief at the Union's resolve, Clarendon wrote Lewis on 24 October that Britain needed to be prepared if the Federal government appealed to the British or French in Washington with its own intervention proposal. The ex-foreign secretary believed that neither power should accept a Federal proposal for help without the other. Clarendon believed that the Confederacy's independence was a fait accompli but that Britain should not provoke the North. Along with the resolution of Palmerston and Derby, Clarendon's sentiments probably ended any chance of a formal cabinet meeting to consider intervention. By this point Clarendon believed that Russell kept up his stand on intervention out of vanity.

Clarendon's comment about Russell's vanity perhaps had more than a modicum of truth to it. But fortunately, had Napoleon been eager for intervention, chances are that he would have made his strong support known by this time. The emperor's vanity seemed to have been reduced by Britain's determination not to intervene. Moreover, he was thinking more about Europe as the root of his grand design. By the time Britain decided against intervention, the emperor had reformed his cabinet to be more aggressive in Europe. Edouard Drouyn de Lhuys replaced pro-North foreign secretary Thouvenel. But the veteran Drouyn de Lhuys had similar sensibilities to his predecessor and told British ambassador Cowley that he was inclined to wait on intervention. On 29 October, just two days before Napoleon made his intervention offer, Cowley intimated to Russell that Drouyn de Lhuys had little enthusiasm for doing the emperor's bidding about mediation. A short time later Parliamentary undersecretary of state for foreign affairs A. H. Layard informed Russell that the emperor did not place much importance in the offer but believed that he was posturing on behalf of humanity. Thus all of Napoleon's actions were seen for what they were, and Gladstone was the only cabinet member who supported Napoleon's proposal.⁶⁶

Amid the justifiable British suspicions, Britain, France, and Russia headed Napoleon III's plan to concert for a six-month armistice and a suspension of the blockade. With both British parties opposed, Russell refused the proposal on 31 October. Palmerston was unimpressed with the French initiative and wrote Russell halfheartedly that the cabinet should discuss it on 11 November. Palmerston was aware of the growing strength of the Northern Peace Democrats and decided to wait until after the congressional elections to reassess the situation. But he did not seem to be swayed by Stuart's dispatch of 7 November that the Democrats' victories "are considered to constitute a political revolution" that would obliterate the Radical Republicans' desires to prosecute the war more boldly "by spreading terror across the country."[67]

In fact, Napoleon's tardy offer of support for mediation, stating the same reasons that Russell had laid down in his memorandum of 13 October, decreased the pressure on Britain and caused the Yankees to turn revengeful eyes on France, as the emperor had informed the press of his offer to enhance his public standing.[68] Criticism of the emperor's offer was partly written by William Vernon Harcourt, Lewis's stepson-in-law and was followed up by Harcourt's series of letters to the Times under the pseudonym "Historicus." He upheld Lincoln's view that a rebellion was treason and avoided intervention to preserve England's honor. An armistice was "childish in the extreme," while neutrality protected England until the South became a separate state. Lewis implied (against Gladstone's argument) that to become a legitimate state, a political entity must have more than the trappings of statehood. It had to show the strength to both become and remain a state.[69]

Palmerston made his resolve known on 10 November in a speech at the Guildhall. The Morning Post and the Times lauded his statement that the time was not right to intervene. On 12 November the cabinet again rejected intervention for the record after two days of discussion, with Lewis leading the cabinet opposition. The cabinet considered the matter without emotion and purely within the boundaries of British self-interest. The majority concluded with Palmerston that intervention had few advantages and was risky. The final cabinet decision was therefore foregone. Palmerston saw no advantages in trying to propose mediation. Thus Russell wrote to Cowley in Paris on 13 November that intervention based on friendly and conciliatory mediation was a spent issue. The war seemed to be too much balanced for either combatant to accept it. Russell made a strong point about the absence of support from Russia.[70]

Lyons's messages to Russell from Washington on his return there on 12 November show that he had already made Russell aware of his feelings during their talks in England. No doubt the British minister had detected Russell's vacillation about intervention, and back in Washington his private letters and dispatches emphasized a confidence that there was not a right time for intervention. First, Lyons saw Mercier and downplayed the count's desire for intervention because it would "intimidate" the United States. Second, his messages to Russell explained that times would not be right because the Union would become angry at an intervention proposal whether they were winning or losing on the battlefield. Thus Lyons could not fathom why Mercier thought the times were right for a proposal. The British minister explained that the violent nature of the fighting and the violent party fight over abolition and the course of the war, along with an aggressive Congress, might cause a mediation offer to become a powder keg. Third, Lyons reminded the foreign secretary that he had mentioned to him at Woburn that the Duke of Newcastle believed that the "lower Canadians" would object to mediation because the offer would make it seem that France was taking the lead in American affairs. Fourth, Lyons advised that as a result of the elections just held, the new Congress of 4 March 1863 would have a Democratic majority. The Democrats were less violent for abolition and the war than the Republicans and might be more reasonable about an offer. Fifth, to illustrate another way that the Union was insecure and would not look kindly on mediation, Lyons turned to the military outlook for the North. Here he explained that he did not believe that the Union's grand strategy to take Galveston, Mobile, Charleston, and Savannah and advance again on Richmond was going to be successful despite Seward's assurances to the contrary.[71]

To illustrate his principal arguments, Lyons voiced his opinion that the Union government would consider an offer of mediation an "inconvenience" and that it would leave Seward "evasive and temporizing." It could only increase distrust. Lyons believed that the suspension of the blockade, which mediation would imply, was the "critical point," because "the North will feel that to give up that is to give up the war for ever; and the South must be hard pressed before it accepts an armistice allowing the blockade to subsist." Lyons refuted Mercier's position that mediation would be popular to the American people. To back up his argument, he enclosed a number of New York newspaper articles about the French proposal. His number 467 of 28 November was written on the same day that he explained that the telegraph made the French proposal known to the newspapers and the public. Lyons added that the American press knew that Britain had declined the proposal. When Mercier got the dispatch he told Lyons that he was going to visit Seward. After he saw the secretary of state he intimated to Lyons that Seward "betrayed some emotion, but he had said no more than that for the next six months a truce would be quite impossible." Lyons was careful to point out that the papers represented different shades of the political spectrum, from Democratic (the *New York Herald* and the *New York World*) to support for the administration (the *New York Times*) to abolitionists (the *New York Tribune*). Like Seward, every article repudiated the French proposal. The "unanimity of the Press on the present occasion shows at least that this is not a time at which public opinion would force the acceptance of foreign mediation upon a reluctant cabinet," concluded Lyons. The sensitive situation can be seen when Seward told Lyons on 2 December that the

French proposal had enabled him to perceive that the European powers had been talking about American affairs "among themselves without taking the Cabinet of Washington into their counsels." But because Seward was not cognizant of these discussions, he could not give an opinion, nor would he have done so even had an intervention proposal been made. Neither would an opinion be expressed if any of the powers wanted to advance one now. At Seward's suggestion, Lyons repeated this conversation to Mercier. There is no doubt that Seward was upset at discovering the European powers' intervention discussion and that once again Lincoln soothed his secretary's temper. The president regarded the proposal as a misguided urge by the powers to counsel the North and the South at a time when such counsel was distrusted. Seward was difficult to placate even by the president. He complained that the French proposal gave the South new hope and prolonged the war, and he repeated his warning to France (which would get to England) that intervention under any guise was intolerable. Conversely, despite his ire about the intervention news, Seward remained outwardly conciliatory and told Lyons that he was pleased with Stuart's conduct of affairs while Lyons was on leave. One imagines that Lyons believed that Seward was losing influence with the president, cabinet, and public opinion.[72]

Lyons's view that intervention should be dissolved was reinforced by his discussion in early December with Baron Stoeckl, the Russian minister to the United States. In their discussion on 6 December, Stoeckl produced Russian foreign minister Prince Alexander Gorchakov's answer to the French proposal to recommend an armistice. He told Lyons that he had also received a private note from his superior saying that he was to exercise his own judgment if France renewed its proposal. He was authorized to officially support it if he thought it was desirable. Stoeckl, however, supported Lyons's view that an armistice was unfeasible for many of the same reasons cited by Lyons: The Union promised to strike an offensive soon, the Radical Republicans who wanted the war prosecuted even more fiercely controlled the cabinet and Congress, and the new Congress of 4 March 1863 would no longer be friendly to Lincoln. In that regard, Stoeckl thought it was impossible to perceive how that might change the president's outlook on the war and the prospects of intervention. Unless the Union won smashing military victories the European powers should wait until March to again propose mediation if they thought the times were right. Stoeckl's idea had been nourished during a recent trip to New York when Democratic leaders spoke "cautiously" for intervention but would welcome it when they controlled the administration. Democrats as a body desired peace with or without reunion. The Russian minister said that his country's position was very different from that of England and France. Humanitarianism, the minister said, actuated Russia and friendship, while the Western powers had huge material interests at stake. Stoeckl also said that Seward had told him many times before news of the French proposal reached the United

States that he had no fear of intervention because he had information that England and France would not agree on the matter in the final analysis.[73]

Palmerston did not wait on Russell, Lyons, or anyone else to inform Europe about the decision not to intervene. On 18 November he wrote King Leopold of Belgium, who was pro-South and supported intervention, about why the cabinet refused. His comments amounted to what he believed was the North's new military strength: "If we had thought that such a communication as he [Napoleon III] proposed could have done any good, and was not on the contrary, likely to do mischief," the proposal might have been adopted. Perhaps "some months ago . . . we thought an opportunity for making some communication was approaching. The Confederates were gaining ground North of Washington, and events seemed to be in their favor. *But the tide of war changed its course and the opportunity did not arrive.*" The prime minister's decision showed no sympathy for either warring side, and he demonstrated "that famous ability to go to the heart of a problem." He appreciated probably more than his colleagues, and certainly more than Russell and Gladstone, "that between recognizing the Confederacy and breaking the blockade there was a distance 'as wide as the distance, which separates peace from war.'" Palmerston's words were final. A chagrined Gladstone wrote his wife after the cabinet met on 12 November that "Lord R[ussell] rather turned tail, i.e. he gave way without resolutely fighting out his battle."[74]

Meanwhile, the historic cooperative spirit of Anglo-American relations kept proving its strength. One piece of evidence is the Magee affair. The British consul at Mobile, James Magee, tried to assist the Confederacy by facilitating the shipment of £40,000 in specie to pay British investors' interest for purchasing Alabama state bonds. The specie was to be loaded on the HMS *Vesuvius,* which the Union navy allowed through the blockade to dock at Mobile. Lyons was back in Washington, relieved at not having to deliver Russell's mediation offer to Seward, when he heard about this breach of neutrality, and he feared Seward's reaction at this sensitive time. After the *Vesuvius* steamed for England, Lyons wrote Russell of the breach. Coming at a time when the *Alabama* was at the peak of its depredations, Lyons informed Russell who immediately dismissed Magee and ordered the Admiralty to prohibit any further pro-South action. He notified Adams of what had transpired and what he had done. Adams was again delighted. Benjamin Moran looked up from his candlelit desk in the dreary basement of the American Legation in London and exclaimed to his diary that "this is the first time during the war that malpractices of British officers have been condemned by the Gov't here. I hope it is the beginning of decent behavior in such matters."[75]

Cooperation continued also in cutting off Confederate diplomacy. Mason could "see and hear nothing from the British Government officially or unofficially." He had mixed feelings because Russell had shunned him so long. In July he wrote Benjamin that his mission was a failure, and in September the stubborn Davis ordered him to await events. On 1 October Mason was "cheered and elated" by news of Lee's invasion and wrote, "Recognition is not far off." Upon the news of Lee's retreat, these hopes were dashed, and he felt "that I should terminate the mission here."[76]

Finally, even Davis submitted to the reality of British cooperation with the North. In a speech in Mississippi in December he counseled the Confederacy to "put not your trust in princes . . . this war is ours; we must fight it out ourselves." The British message was so strong that Davis's erstwhile enemy, Confederate vice president Alexander Stephens, supported Davis's surmise. Stephens believed that, despite the jealousy of England and France for growing Federal power, they were opposed to slavery, and therefore he had "never looked to foreign intervention or recognition." On 1 September, Stephens wrote that Davis should recall Mason and the other commissioners. Throughout the rest of the winter and during the spring and summer of 1863 leading Confederates and the Confederate Congress supported letting go of any dependence on the European powers. To the Southerners, Britain had acquiesced in the blockade, had shown such "unusual forbearance in the face of repeated northern violations of neutral rights that she in a negative sense had violated neutrality," and had encouraged the North to continue the war by withholding recognition.[77]

Southerners were in for a further shock. Lincoln's preliminary emancipation proclamation of 22 September was another action that eventually favored British-American cooperation and helped to dissolve the intervention question. McPherson provides a clear insight into how the proclamation stymied the Confederates in Britain and won closer cooperation with the North in the midst of the intervention debate. On 14 October Seward was warned by American minister Dayton from Paris to expect the proclamation to set off a new round of criticism of the North by Confederate sympathizers in Britain and France. Even some Liberals, McPherson tells us, believed that the proclamation was less a genuine antislavery act than a "cynical attempt to deflect European opinion or as a desperate effort to encourage a slave insurrection." They wanted to know why Lincoln failed to announce that the proclamation applied only to states where he had no political power and why it exempted the Northern states where he did have power. William Stuart wrote similarly that he thought the proclamation was "cold, vindictive and entirely political." Russell was critical of Lincoln for not acting decisively against slavery, and he believed that the pronouncement encouraged "acts of plunder, of incendiarism, and of revenge."[78]

These initial attempts to see the preliminary proclamation as stemming from Federal weakness went awry. Pro-Unionists helped to defuse the criticisms by "the ghouls of the English press." As John Stuart Mill put it: "The proclamation has only increased the venom of those who after taunting you for so long with caring nothing for abolition, now reproach you for your abolitionism as the worst of your crimes." Mill believed that these "wretched effusions" came from disheartened conservatives who hated American democracy and could no longer criticize the North for not fighting to end slavery.[79] The British people quickly spoke out through their newspapers. On 6 October, the *London Morning Star* pronounced that the proclamation was "a gigantic stride in the paths of Christian and civilized progress—the turning point in the history of the American commonwealth—an act only second in courage and probable results to the Declaration of Independence." A month later, pro-Unionists advertised the proclamation's merits at meetings and through petitions. The proclamation "confounded European cynics" who believed that Lincoln lacked the courage for this decisive step. On the contrary, the practical Lincoln stated that emancipation was "an act of justice" to enhance Federal military power and to keep the slaves from rising on their own.[80]

The Emancipation Proclamation of 1 January 1863 tightened the grip of nonintervention and fortified neutrality. It represented a new and understandable war aim. Henry Adams wrote on 23 January that "the Emancipation Proclamation has done more for us here than all our former victories and all our diplomacy. It is creating an almost convulsive reaction in our favor all over this country." He wrote of the British acceptance of Americans as special and not as foreigners and that "in fact we are now one of the known and acknowledged units of the London and English world, and . . . the majority of people receive us much as they would Englishmen, and seem to consider us as such." Richard Cobden wrote of the largest mass meeting, which was held in London's Exeter Hall on 30 January, to adopt a petition in support of emancipation, that "[it] has had a powerful effect on our newspapers and politicians. It has closed the mouths of those who have been advocating the side of the South. Recognition of the South, by England, whilst it bases itself on Negro slavery, is an impossibility." Cobden was cheered knowing that the Exeter meeting was strongly representative of the middle class whose representatives acknowledged that the war was now for "Emancipation and Union." Moreover, the first Union relief ships arrived with food for the unemployed Lancashire cotton operatives.[81]

Lincoln's humanitarian gesture occurred as the convergence of views against a British-American war spread to the British people. The workers' support drew a rousing response for peace from the president in late January 1863. Palmerston had been right. Intervention was too much to expect and was a threat to his politics with British public opinion. He recognized that Emancipation compromised those in Britain who clung to the idea of intervention.

Palmerston was no doubt also influenced to dissolve intervention by European events, which paralleled those in the United States and Britain. The American minister to the Netherlands believed that "the anti-slavery position of the government is at length giving us a substantial foothold in European circles. Everyone can understand the significance of a war where emancipation is written on one banner and slavery on the other."[82] In the wake of the Emancipation Proclamation, Napoleon III continued to think about intervening unilaterally, but he knew to do that without the Royal Navy was foolish. By June 1863, neither the French minister to England nor Russell could recall having received a notice from Napoleon that he was interested in intervention. Even if they had wanted to, the English could not now try to rescue the Confederacy, as voters and workers would accuse the government of rescuing slavery. Emancipation extinguished the Union's exaggerated fears of intervention.[83]

The British saw that order occurred rather than the feared slave revolt following the proclamation. Lincoln was firmly in control. Thousands of contraband and free blacks were organized into some 120 infantry regiments and more support units, eventually numbering more than 186,000, with some 134,000 from the slave states. Thus the revolution was manifested in emancipation and the spirit of the Union army. Soldiers became emancipators for human freedom. They were unaccustomed to this revolutionary role, but they eventually took pride in overcoming the horrors of slavery that they could not ignore as they marched through the South.

Moreover, these developments meshed with the lack of veracity in the British aristocracy's support for the South, according to Confederate agent Matthew Fontaine Maury, who doubted intervention. In early 1863, he wrote that the British upper classes were mostly abolitionists and that the South had few British friends because "many of our friends here have mistaken British admiration of Southern 'pluck' and newspaper spite at Yankee insolence as Southern sympathy. No such thing. There is no love for the South here. In its American policy the British Government fairly represents the people." Maury believed that "there is no hope for recognition here, therefore I say withdraw Mason." Maury was right. The London Times remarked that it had been folly for the Confederacy to seek recognition "before it had won it." The Confederate government had long resented the cool treatment its emissaries received from the British ministry, and by the fall of 1863 it clearly had lost patience and turned its attentions to France.[84] By that time the question of intervention had been practically resolved, and turning to France was also a lost cause because Napoleon would do nothing without Britain. British-American cooperation was clarifying itself through cautious and cooperative diplomacy and the foibles of Confederate strategy on land and at sea.

6

Lincoln's Cabinet Crisis of December 1862

in the Rapprochement

The tensions surrounding Lincoln's government and Congress were probably greater than those that caused the British to consider intervention in the fall of 1862. Just as the idea of intervention had grown up in British inner circles in the summer of 1862, the leaders of the Union government and Congress were becoming prostrated by the war's unbelievable demands at the same time. McClellan's defeat on the Virginia Peninsula in July, the widespread disappointment about his failure to take Richmond once he all but had it in his grasp, Seward's cooperating with the British to get them more cotton through conquered ports, the beginning of the *Alabama*'s depredations, Lincoln's go-slow policy toward emancipation, and the pressure to escalate the draft all congealed to cause bewilderment among the nation's leaders.[1] The weak Republican showing in the fall elections was a final straw that seemed to cast severe doubts on the administration's ability to run the war, let alone win it. On the one hand, the British knew as little about the cabal to oust Seward and rule Lincoln's war policy by a handful of Radical and Moderate Republicans as the Union government knew about the intervention debate.

On the other hand, and just as unclear, was the knowledge of a few that Lincoln's leadership grew stronger and more decisive while statesmen believed all was beginning to crumble around him. His sense of duty made him courageous, although "less thrusting and pugnacious than rocklike, an enduring courage that threw back the endless schemers about him as Maine granite with sullen roar throws back the Atlantic surf." His courage enabled him to stick to his foreign policy plan of 1861 to avoid a foreign war. His first annual message recognized the danger of a "factious domestic" party gaining control and arousing foreign intervention. In his second annual address he told Congress that relations with foreign powers were "less gratifying" than usual in order to send the message that the Europeans had better not intervene in any respects.[2] This message, however, did not soothe the feelings of politicians who wanted something done quickly to stem the tide of Confederate battlefield victories and, for those who were more radical, to emancipate the slaves.

Thus, by the fall of 1862, like Palmerston, Lincoln had his own cabinet crisis building up. The angry Radical Republicans were more desperate than Russell and Gladstone, because the Radicals believed that they were witnessing a war that was not being prosecuted with enough fervor. In the November by-elections, they were desperate over the Democratic victories that had bred a peace movement. If Lincoln buckled and one of these groups became ascendant, the international realism of both the British and American governments, the source of their cooperation, might be threatened. By the time Lincoln's cabinet crisis erupted in December, and largely unbeknownst to him, failure of presidential nerve might have reignited the fires of intervention just as realistically as battlefield victory or defeat could have. During the fall and early winter of 1862, as in Britain, internal politics maintained British-American peace, and Palmerston and Lincoln provided the essential leadership.

Most immediately Lincoln had to suffer the Radicals. Even the foreign diplomats in Washington reflected the Radicals' sense of desperation. At the British legation, William Stuart questioned Russell in July whether the North had the human or material resources to continue the war under what he thought was a weak officer corps. Stuart continued that he thought it doubtful that Lincoln could raise 300,000 more volunteers called for on 5 August. He informed Russell, "In my opinion the present calls are beyond the strength of the nation."[3] On 1 December 1862, Stoeckl wanted to talk to Lincoln about conciliation with the South. "I would have done it," he wrote, "except for the fact that it would have served no good purpose. Mr. Lincoln is President in name only. The demagogues [Radical Republicans] surrounding him control him." Lyons agreed. They referred to the animosities of the lameduck Congress. Many Republicans were defeated in the elections and blamed the administration. Defeated Radicals said Lincoln moved too slowly against slavery. Border State Conservatives and their brethren from southern Illinois, Indiana, and Ohio blamed their defeats on the president's preliminary emancipation policy. Both factions believed that Lincoln converted the war into a dictatorship against slavery by suppression of free speech, press censorship, and arrest of political dissidents. Radical Republican House leader Thaddeus Stevens expressed the opinion that Lincoln had engaged in "flagrant usurpations, deserving the condemnation of the community" and insisted that the president treat the South like a conquered province. No longer doubting Seward's sincerity for peace, Lyons feared that if the Radical Republicans succeeded they might resort to a foreign war to strengthen their power over the president. In response to these barbs the president uttered: "If there is a worse place than Hell, I am in it."[4]

Seward was the target of the dissident Republicans' attempt to reorganize the administration with or without the president. Indeed, fully aware of their differ-

ences and ambitions for the presidency, Seward had threatened to resign soon after being appointed when he learned of Radical Salmon P. Chase's selection as secretary of the treasury. Yet, by inauguration day when Lincoln had not responded,
Seward decided to stay, writing that he "did not dare to go home or to England [as
United States minister], and leave the country to chance." By this he meant leaving the country to Abraham Lincoln.[5] But as we have seen, he soon changed his
mind about the president.

Seward bore the brunt of the Radicals' criticism for the military failures, his
conciliatory British policy, and the Democratic victories that had seemingly compromised Union efforts throughout 1862. His critics had a point about the lack
of cabinet unity. There the rift was between Seward, a moderate Republican, and
Chase, who with Stevens and the other "Jacobins" wanted the war to be about
freeing the slaves and weakening the Southern states for all time. With this rivalry
and others, Lincoln's cabinet was split and brooding from the beginning. Lincoln tolerated the internal rivalries as a "creative friction," to use David Donald's
words. He left his ministers alone to run their departments, generally supported
Seward's desire to use the others for his purposes, and understood that the differences among his ministers were not ideological but personal. They stemmed
from trying to obtain "the esteem and affections of the President," as Donald puts
it. Dealing with those vying for his attention was something that this man of immense personal magnetism had lived with all of his life, and he had learned how
to handle prideful men.

Nevertheless, it seemed at times that President Lincoln was the only person of
note who favored Seward. In the fall of 1862, when opposition to Seward was peaking, the two were together nearly every day. Welles thought that their relationship
was so close that Seward treated Lincoln complacently, and Welles further believed
that Lincoln was reluctant to discuss affairs until he had consulted Seward. For this
reason, cabinet members felt ignored by Seward when he began missing meetings
in early September, which was taken as a sign of his confidence that he was Lincoln's
primary counselor. By now Chase did everything he could to stir them up against
Seward. A New York delegation that hated their ex-governor came to Washington
and spread more bad feelings against him. Nevertheless, Lincoln's confidence in him
never wavered. One reason he missed cabinet meetings was to stay business because
of his reputation as Lincoln's second. Without him there, the cabinet secretaries
were reluctant to discuss and decide on matters. Seward was thus able to act alone
on many foreign policy issues in the interests of British-American peace, much as
Palmerston did. At least this was the opinion of Welles, who did not like Seward.
This problem strengthened Seward's detractors. In addition, Lincoln himself came
in for plenty of criticism. In fact, on 10 September the president told the anti-Seward
committee from New York (concocted by Chase) that Seward's removal "would destroy the government."[6]

Lincoln and Seward had much in common—from poor grooming to fondness for animals. Both had a keen sense of humor that they enjoyed sharing with each other. Both got along well with difficult people and knew how to keep their enemies close. They both achieved their goals by conciliation at home and abroad rather than trying to stamp out their critics. The usually imperturbable president admired Seward's lack of vindictiveness toward his many detractors. Moreover, both were astute judges of human nature, although in this Lincoln was superior. They were both able to understand why people acted and with these insights were able to forgive. (Seward asked Chase to dinner when the cabinet crisis was over in late December.) Both were naturally conservative and possessed uncommon finesse and timing. Both knew what they were doing, and, more importantly, excelled in working alone, outside of the insecure cliques and place seekers. Finally, both wanted to emancipate the slaves although they believed them to be socially inferior. Yet they believed that they should be free to pursue their lives through their liberties, and they supported black suffrage. But Seward did not want to force Southern whites to give blacks the vote, and it was his alleged softness on the South that drew so much distrust. Lincoln agreed with Seward, however, and slowly came to believe that educated blacks and those who fought in the Union army should vote. The Jacobins fumed that Lincoln and Seward both believed that the blacks' place was secondary to the restoration of the white man's Union.[7]

Seward, like Russell, tried to maintain power by not disclosing all he knew about matters to his colleagues and only confided in Lincoln. There was animosity between Seward and the cabinet secretaries because of his impetuous desire to run things early in the administration and his working with the Rebels to avoid war until Sumter. Lincoln consistently reinforced Seward's reputation as his second, and this status placed him on the wrong foot with his fellow secretaries, especially those like Chase who were vain, inexperienced in their offices, and prone to jealousy. Although Seward was clearly under Lincoln's thumb, the New Yorker had not won the trust of Chase and other cabinet members. He wanted to keep his hands on the pulse of the government because he believed in the course he and the president were taking. There were certainly private criticisms, such as those in the long passage in Welles's *Diary* on the eve of Antietam that calls attention to Seward's impetuosity.[8] They believed that Seward had overacted in cooperating with Britain.

Welles had mixed feelings about Seward. On 20 September 1862, he was upset with Seward's conciliatory British policy. The Confederate raider *Florida* ran the blockade with British colors flying, and the American naval commander was lackadaisical about stopping the vessel. Yet Welles wanted Seward to remain because if Lincoln ever accepted Seward's resignation the Radical Republicans might cause the rest of the government to perish.[9]

Senator Charles Sumner of Massachusetts, chairman of the Senate Foreign Relations Committee, probably the most powerful of the extremists who despised Seward and criticized the president, was losing his grip on reality as 1862 began. None of the Radical Republicans got along with each other in their individual pursuits of power, including Sumner himself. In fact, the Radicals were more divided than Lincoln's cabinet. Their extreme speeches and writings made them seem like desperate men to Lincoln. The inner circle of Lincoln's administration, except for Chase and Sumner, shunned all of them. This reality caused Sumner and Chase to play a double game. They relished trying to advise Lincoln to whittle away at Seward's credibility while they plotted with other Radicals to unseat the secretary of state.

Furthermore, Stoeckl and Lyons overstated the Radicals' power. None of the leading Radicals—Sumner, Chase, Ben Wade, Zachariah Chandler, or Elihu Washburn—had much impact on the Thirty-seventh Congress that assembled in January 1862. Yet Wade chaired and Chandler was a member of the congressional Committee on the Conduct of the War, where they showed their ignorance of military leadership and tactics by regularly trying to cashier Union generals. They wanted frontal assaults, thought West Pointers were soft on the South, and questioned Lincoln's military appointments. Unlike the president, they refused to learn about military strategy or the new technology that made war deadlier. Chandler showed the committee's penchant for volunteer generals over West Pointers during the *Trent* affair when he remarked, "If England wants war we are ready and anxious."[10] But a cross section of the Radicals wanted Seward out. The moderate Republican senator James W. Grimes of Iowa was as extreme as the Radical core in wanting Seward fired but thought that Sumner "originates no measures but simply makes two or three rather sophomorical set speeches."

Many believed that Sumner and Chase had only one primary aim beyond winning the war, and that was the presidency. Sumner was milder about his presidential aspirations than the energetic Chase. Charles Francis Adams, a fellow Bostonian, who with Sumner had broken with the Whigs to form the Free Soil Party in the 1840s, knew Sumner well enough to describe his disabling faults. Sumner was an idealistic, rhetorical agitator who cared little about what others thought when he attacked them. He was a victim of his vanity (like Seward, Chase, and others with high responsibilities, including Union military leaders) who made opponents instead of friends, despite his virtues of abolitionism and good government. He was not thought of as a lawmaker or a policy maker. Indeed, he was severely caned at his Senate desk by Representative Preston Brooks of South Carolina for, in Brooks's words, impugning the character of Brooks's relative, Senator Andrew Butler, in a "florid, polished and vitriolic" speech against slavery. Sumner, in severe psychosomatic shock, refused to return to the Senate for more than two years after his 22 May 1856 beating. David Donald believes that after the caning Sumner was unable to learn anything from anyone and began to see himself as a martyr. Henry Adams wrote that Sumner's mind "had reached the calm of water which receives and reflects images without absorbing them; it contains nothing but itself."[11] Watching the growing sectional tensions from London, George Cornewall Lewis believed that the assault on Sumner was "the first blow in a civil war." Writing in early 1864, Welles believed that Sumner was "theoretical rather than practical," "egotistical," and "susceptible to flattery from any quarter. There is want of breadth, enlarged comprehension, in his statesmanship." Welles believed that Sumner's "convictions or opinions are weak and change without hesitation if deemed expedient or if his party can be benefited."[12]

Despite his weaknesses, Sumner stood in high esteem with the British and early in the war was not Anglophobic unlike the other Radicals. British ministers read his letters and speeches, seemed to admire him, and took him at his word when he criticized Seward in his letters as the unstable one. He thought that he knew more about foreign relations than Seward and Lincoln and that he should be president, secretary of state, and minister to Britain. Yet over the next two years Sumner lost his integrity with the British as Seward's star rose. The British saw through Sumner's debunking and came to view Seward as an asset.

In this respect, Sumner made it difficult for the British to understand the Union government. In the midst of the British cabinet's nonintervention debate in October, Sumner was provoked at Seward's inability to get an abolitionist Republican governor elected in New York. This latest objection was added to their disagreement over how (in Sumner's estimation) Seward had handled the secession crisis by trying to placate the South and for his being soft toward the foreign powers. Not only did Sumner request Seward's ouster in Boston antislavery newspapers, but also he wrote Bright on 28 October and 18 November that Seward had "neither wisdom or courage," and unless Seward was ousted, the Union was headed for "gloom and tragedy." Sumner blamed Seward's refusal to support direct emancipation as the cause for the Republican loss of identity that led to the Democratic victories. Moreover, the weakness of the Union's generals caused Sumner to write Bright to send "an Englishman who will handle . . . two hundred thousand men." The Union's terrible failure at Fredericksburg on 13 December ignited the Radicals to action. The cabinet crisis escalated, and the nation cried out its discontent. Michael C. C. Adams believes that "Lincoln was never more hated in the North in the weeks after Fredericksburg. As a war leader he appeared hopeless. The rebellion seemed stronger than ever. 'Lincoln compares to Jeff Davis, as a wheel-barrow to a steam engine!' commented a leading Democrat. The President was despised in the Army of the Potomac especially. The soldiers' faith in McClellan as the only man equal to the rebels seemed confirmed by Burnside's defeat." Sumner's knowledge (from Bright) of the British cabinet crisis, the British-built Confederate raiders' depredations against Union shipping, and Gladstone's ill-timed speech all added to his onslaught against Seward.[13]

In the days following Fredericksburg, the Radical Republicans stepped up their arguments for a harsh policy toward Britain and France and annihilation of the South. They worried that in the wake of military defeat Lincoln might not issue the Emancipation Proclamation on 1 January 1863. They were repelled by the defeat of another drive on Richmond and by the stalemate in the western theater. These setbacks led the staunchest antislavery and self-seeking senators, including Chase, to request Seward's resignation.

When the Senate adjourned for Christmas, the Radicals caucused on 16 December to plot how to save the nation. All of the bad feelings the Radicals had for Seward for more than a year came to a head. Vice President Hannibal Hamlin wrote to his wife that Seward "has been regarded as a millstone around the Administration."[14] The thirty-seven senators who caucused inveighed against Seward as the reason for the Union's darkest hour because he was said to be half-hearted and compromising. Allan Nevins writes, "All were convinced that he was the nation's evil genius." The caucus castigated Seward for blocking the "vigorous prosecution of the war," for constantly advocating a patched-up peace, and for overruling the demands of the cabinet secretaries upon the president, who was criticized for toadying to Seward. Privately urged on by Chase, the Radicals followed Maine's William Pitt Fessenden, the powerful chairman of the Senate Committee on Finance and leader of the Senate. He believed the words of Chase and Secretary of War Edwin M. Stanton (who also had presidential ambitions) that Seward had cabinet privileges that threatened the nation.[15] Grimes called Lincoln a "tow string" president, who could survive only "with strong, sturdy rods in the shape of cabinet ministers." The respected Jacob Collamer of Vermont supported Fessenden's opening remarks to the caucus about the imminent national destruction unless Seward was ousted. Wade proposed that the entire Senate visit with the president and demand Seward's removal. Grimes feared offending the president and the country and proposed that Senator Anthony present a resolution of lack of confidence in Seward when the Senate reconvened.[16] Browning called for unity to conquer the Rebels "or they would us," and he did not know of any evidence to prove that Seward was disloyal. If there was evidence, Browning did not think that a resolution to the president to remove Seward was appropriate. In a few minutes calmer minds prevailed to avert a destructive battle with the chief executive when Browning, Preston King, and others opposed Grimes's proposal. Several agreed with Browning for a deputation to inform the president about Seward and concerns about the war effort.[17]

The caucus reconvened the next day, and Chase's extremists tried to pass a resolution that Lincoln himself resign. Illinoisans Lyman Trumbull and Browning jumped to the president's defense. Many others argued that a weak cabinet, with the exception of Chase, and weaker generals spoke for a cabinet reorganization. The caucus resolved to reorganize the cabinet to remove Seward and to inform Lincoln of their opinions. All of the thirty-two senators present agreed to this resolution but Preston King. To make certain that the Radicals dominated the reorganized cabinet, the White House deputation included seven Radicals—Wade, Trumbull,

Howard, Fessenden, Sumner (who made the resolution to visit Lincoln), Grimes, and Pomeroy—and two moderates, Collamer and Harris. Grimes tried to pass a lack of confidence in the Seward resolution, but it was dropped after others said it was too drastic.[18]

Browning's account of his informal meeting with the president upstairs at the White House on 18 December found Lincoln about to give up. He told his old friend, "Since I heard last night of the proceedings of the caucus I have been more distressed than by any event of my life." This was his remark after Browning told him not to quit. To do so "would bring upon us certain and inevitable ruin." Lincoln answered: "We are now on the brink of destruction. It appears to me the Almighty is against us, and I can hardly see a ray of hope." Browning told him, "Be firm and we will yet save the Country. Do not be driven from your post." Lincoln retorted that he could not understand "why will men believe a lie, an absurd lie [about Seward's authority], that could not impose upon a child, and cling to it and repeat it in defiance of evidence to the contrary."[19] In this sense, as Bruce Tap points out, "it was a Republican plea for fervor and energy in conducting the war, a plea to which few party members objected."[20]

After the caucus on 17 December, Preston King told Seward of the plot. Seward and his son, Frederick, who was assistant secretary of state, immediately resigned, because the secretary of state refused to put the president in a false position. King and Frederick promptly carried the resignations to Lincoln who was astounded and asked King for an explanation. King briefed him on the intent of the caucus. That same evening Lincoln went to Seward's house to persuade him to withdraw his resignation, but the morose secretary said he was relieved to be free of official duties. Lincoln responded: "Ah, yes, Governor, that will do very well for you, but I am like the starling in Sterne's story, 'I can't get out.'"[21]

That evening, Lincoln met with the disgruntled senators for three hours and heard them out. They said Seward had not moved the cabinet to direct a vigorous war effort. Sumner reviewed Seward's recently published diplomatic dispatches, which the senator said had subjected Seward to embarrassment at home and abroad. Seward had written other letters that raised questions about his dependability. They continued that better generals were needed who understood the purposes of the war. Wade bluntly remarked that the president had appointed too many top officers "who were unsympathetic to the Republican war goals."[22] Furthermore, the delegation wanted the president to govern through a "cabinet council agreeing with him in political theory and general policy, and that all important public measures and appointments should be the result of their combined wisdom and deliberation." This request was a jab at the president's coalition cabinet, implicating that it was disunified. The delegation asked Lincoln to change his cabinet to create a new unity, and they wanted the Senate to approve the changes before it could meet. They wanted a cabinet congenial to Chase.

Salmon P. Chase, ardent abolitionist, secretary of the treasury in Lincoln's cabinet; Lincoln's chief rival for power but a strong leader at the Treasury. Library of Congress

Lincoln was equal to the occasion. He responded that he had no recollection of Seward's offensive dispatches. He understood over the course of this conversation that Chase was behind much of the delegation's presumed strength. He saw that Chase had turned the senators against Seward and Stanton to gain power over the cabinet and ultimately over the White House. He felt that the meeting revealed how to solve the problem. Thus he let the extremists talk, while, as Nevins points out, "he coldly studied them."[23] Lincoln felt that he knew how to divide the caucus committee and strengthen the cabinet at the same time. He was somewhat in agreement with the committee that he had not used his cabinet enough.

He had these thoughts when he assembled the cabinet on 19 December, which preceded a larger meeting with both the cabinet and the caucus committee that he had met with the day before. All of the cabinet members attended except Seward. Lincoln asked the cabinet to keep his remarks confidential and then explained to them about his meeting with the committee and of Seward's resignation. He told the cabinet that the committee was not bad tempered or bent on ousting the entire cabinet but that the committee blamed Seward for hesitating about prosecuting the war. They believed that Seward caused the Union's failures by modifying the president's behavior for the worst. Lincoln said that he had defended the cabinet's loyalty and explained to the committee that the situation was not as desperate as they believed. He then proposed that the cabinet and the committee meet with him that evening. His goal was to shatter the committee by forcing Chase to show his true colors. Neither Chase nor Bates liked the joint meeting idea, but Welles and Montgomery Blair were strongly in favor, and the cabinet acquiesced. Like the president, Welles and Blair were curious to study Chase, who said that he knew nothing about the plot when forced to choose between his double-dealing and the truth. They were not alone, because those in the know believed that Chase had blown up the balloon from the start to take Seward's place as Lincoln's chief secretary. Lincoln wanted to break up the cabal and maintain control of the war while making modifications that impressed him.[24]

That evening the caucus delegation arrived at Lincoln's office for the joint meeting. Nevins aptly reports, "He did not make the mistake of having the cabinet with him when the committee arrived." Lincoln asked them to meet with the cabinet "for a free discussion," and the delegation agreed. He then invited in his secretaries except for the absent Seward. (Wade was not there either, and Chandler was at Fredericksburg with members of the Committee on the Conduct of the War.)[25]

Before the delegation and the cabinet occurred "one of the most momentous meetings in the nation's history." Lincoln quickly asked the cabinet members to confirm that they had supported his emergency changes in military command and to attest to whether they lacked knowledge of any policy once it was determined. He called upon the cabinet to say whether there had been any lack of cabinet consideration or unity, and he looked pointedly at Chase. Chase was "horribly embarrassed . . . in an equivocal position; he had to make good his accusations to the radicals, or his loyalty to his chief." He either had to break openly with the president or admit to his charges about Seward and the war effort. He said that he generally supported Lincoln's decisions, and the cabinet's role in making them, and did not leave enough room for the other senators to back Lincoln into a corner. Chase compromised himself by saying that he had gone along with the cabinet on all issues, and he thus, with all eyes on him, refused to speak against Seward to escape making his personal ambitions transparent, which, in fact, he was doing without seeming to realize it. Lincoln's joint meeting shattered the backstairs politicians who had tried to weaken the executive power.[26]

Lincoln watched the Radicals implode. Fessenden was irritated by Chase's attempt to dodge the situation and assured the cabinet that the caucus committee had no intention of dictating to the chief executive but only wanted to offer friendly advice. Fessenden stated that the caucus believed that Lincoln and Seward made too many decisions out of cabinet but disagreed when Collamer stressed the combined wisdom of the secretaries. Then Sumner, Grimes, and Trumbull maligned Seward. Welles was shocked when Sumner revealed Seward's letters advising Lincoln to delay emancipation to prevent a slave revolt. At the end of the session Lincoln asked if the senators still wanted Seward removed. The Radical response was split with Grimes, Trumbull, Sumner, and Pomeroy saying yes, and Fessenden, Collamer, and Howard abstaining. Harris said that Seward was important to maintain the party in New York State. When the meeting ended at 1 A.M., Lincoln remained resolute in private conversations with some of the senators.[27]

Lincoln's open-minded tactic controlled Chase. The caucus was surprised that cabinet members were united on the war and consulted regularly by the president.[28] Fessenden bristled at Chase's hypocrisy, and Stanton distrusted Chase for lying about how the cabinet interacted. During a sleepless night, Chase realized that he was perceived as duplicitous but did not want to leave the cabinet. On 20 December he went to Lincoln with his resignation. "Where is it," Lincoln demanded. "I brought it with me," Chase responded. "I wrote it this morning." "Let me have it," Lincoln ordered and snatched it, remarking that "This cuts the Gordian knot. I can dispose of this subject now. I see my way clear." Lincoln also told Chase to remain in Washington. Moreover, he told Stanton, also present to resign, to return to the War Department. Lincoln now held the resignations of Seward and Chase, and the solution, in his own hands.[29]

In contemplating the situation, Lincoln knew that outside of the Radical minority most Republicans preferred to cooperate, and many wanted to advance his policies. On the same day that the president took Chase's resignation letter, a new congressman, Thomas T. Davis of New York, summarized what would happen if Lincoln did not maintain control over the Radical minority. Davis wrote from the Willard Hotel that Sumner and his cohorts could not be brought into the cabinet, that the conservative Republicans would be "annihilated," and that Radicalism and Democracy would struggle for power that might end in a military coup. Seward had to remain to keep a balanced government against the Radicals. The president's actions showed that he agreed. Given the times, the party was unified except, as it appeared to Lincoln, the few Radicals at the head of the caucus. What escaped Sumner was the growing moderation of Fessenden, Trumbull, Grimes, and Howard who hesitated to join the Radicals as openly as they did in the caucus. Lincoln told John Hay, his private secretary, that had he given in, the cabinet "would all have slumped over one way and we should have been left with a scanty handful of supporters."[30]

The Radicals unwittingly did his bidding, and Seward gladly remained as the president's closest advisor. On 21 December Seward wrote the president, "I have cheerfully resumed the functions of this Department in obedience to your command." Throughout the rest of the war, the chief political split was between Republicans and Democrats and not between the chief executive and his party.[31] On 1 January 1863, the Emancipation Proclamation demonstrated Lincoln's ability to weather his worst intraparty controversy. A historian writes that Lincoln "handled and moved men *remotely* as we do pieces on a chessboard."[32]

His detractors in the Republican and Democratic parties during the next two years helped to sustain the British-American peace. They did not make Britain's alleged support for the Confederacy a party issue. They criticized Lincoln for many things, but they never brought Britain directly into the mix. So little did Palmerston want to disrupt the peace that he refused to take advantage of the intraparty rivalries from the beginning of the Lincoln administration to the cabinet crisis. Thus the crisis remained an internal event. Given the point that the Civil War had reached, the cabinet crisis may have been more threatening than the *Trent* affair. The *Trent* was resolved exactly a year earlier because of Lincoln's ability to hold his cabinet together to exercise sound judgment. A year later the animosity of the Radicals and cabinet opposition to Lincoln threatened to upset the cabinet. Had that happened, 1863 might have begun much differently for British-American relations than had 1862 when there had been a new sense of cooperation. British neutrality was particularly helpful during the cabinet crisis. Palmerston's refusal to seriously consider intervention after learning of the Union defeat at Fredericksburg fewer than three months after Antietam is further evidence that intervention was dead, except in the minds of a few Liberal idealists, such as Russell and Gladstone who had not the power to gain adherents.

Lincoln's stake in the outcome of the cabinet crisis was the same as the British stake because neither wanted to lose Seward. Lyons and Russell were pleased that Lincoln defended Seward, and Lincoln appeared more courageous to them. On 19 December, Lyons heard of the cabinet crisis and wrote privately to Russell that he feared a war if Lincoln accepted Seward's resignation and joined the Radicals. "Unless the Radicals can do something *grand* their doom will be certain—this may make them more desperate."[33]

Lyons's fears about the Radicals were allayed when Seward told him on 21 December that the cabinet was intact even though Chase had not withdrawn his resignation. Lyons saw what Lincoln was trying to prevent: "The whole affair seems very foolish as a party move, for it must weaken and discredit both the Cabinet and the President himself, and the possession of the Executive power is becoming more than ever important to the Republicans." Lyons continued: "I shall be sorry if it ends in the removal of Mr. Seward. We are much more likely to have a man less disposed to keep the peace than a man more disposed to do so. I should hardly have said this two years ago." Russell not only embraced Lyons's recommendation but he also rejected another French initiative to mediate after Paris learned by 30 December of the North's defeat at Fredericksburg. Russell wrote Lyons on 3 January 1863, "I see Seward stays in. I am very glad of it." E. D. Adams believes that at this point there were "no open sores in the British relations with America."[34]

Thus, like the *Trent* affair of the previous December, Lincoln's cabinet crisis ended on a stronger British-American cooperative resolve. The cabinet crisis illustrates that the worst trouble of the Civil War was, as Lincoln had said long before, within the United States itself and not with the international community. By the end of 1862 the British-American peace was stronger than at any time since the beginning of the Civil War, despite the lethargic war effort.

Both governments were sidetracked with cabinet crises of their own that reverberated against going to war. A different kind of intervention threatened Lincoln's cabinet than the threatening prospects confronting Palmerston's cabinet the month before. For Lincoln, it was a radical "war clique" that threatened to shatter his cabinet. For Palmerston, it was a conservative "peace clique" led by Russell and Gladstone. In both instances the moderate Republicans and the moderate Liberals emerged successful.

Moreover, Lincoln and Palmerston pursued entirely different methods to end their respective crises. On the one hand, Lincoln took direct control of the Chase-Seward situation after some hours of self-doubt and ingeniously won the day while learning to use the talents and weaknesses of his secretaries. Palmerston, on the other hand, employed indifference to defeat intervention. He did not attend the cabinet meeting on 23 October where George Cornewall Lewis, with massive support both in and outside of the cabinet, won the intervention debate. But Palmerston and Lincoln used the same method of solving their respective cabinet crises by remaining private until the precise moment of intervention. Lincoln did his own work, and Palmerston let others do his for him. Their communications remained private to ensure their aloofness until action became necessary.

Lincoln and Palmerston relied on their wits to restrain headstrong ministers. Neither became upset visibly unless we count Lincoln's anger at Chase when he grabbed the latter's resignation to demonstrate his disgust. After that, writes David Donald, "Chase was almost as remote from making political decisions as he was removed from the planning of strategy."[35] In a larger sense, then, both Lincoln's and Palmerston's internal problems prevented a break. Both cabinets remained intact. Unlike the previous year, Palmerston did nothing to increase British military strength during the intervention crisis. Nor did he take advantage of what he could have surmised to be the impending fall of Lincoln's government, coupled with the Union defeats from Fredericksburg through the next spring. The prime minister did not reinforce Canada as he had done in the *Trent* affair.

Military shows of strength were no longer needed to soothe relations. Relations improved during the rest of the Civil War despite disagreements. "Now I can ride," Lincoln told a senator as he held both resignations, meaning that if Seward went, Chase went. "I have got a pumpkin in each end of my bag," he finished. And he told someone else: "Now I have the biggest half of the hog. I shall accept neither resignation."[36]

Lincoln defeated the Radical minority at its own game, but he did not gloat. Chase learned to hold his tongue and became friendlier to the president, although their relations were never close. Yet Chase's financial acumen was magnificent, and Lincoln needed him. While Chase plotted with a dwindling following, Seward also learned circumspection: "He had accepted Lincoln's leadership in foreign affairs so completely that he once called himself Abe's little clerk."[37]

The successful conclusion to the cabinet crisis left Lincoln dominant, and he preferred "variety and balance to strict unity." In a larger sense, the Emancipation Proclamation and the military draft showed that Lincoln cared little about what the Radicals had tried to do to him. He realized that he needed a strong army to strengthen domestic politics, make emancipation a reality, and keep foreign nations from intervention. Slowly during 1863, emancipation invoked a new spirit of fighting for freedom into the growing Union ranks. Emancipation was a "masterful war blow, and an epochal step in the history of the nation."[38]

It changed the British attitude toward the Union cause, because now Britons could grasp that Lincoln had struck out on the clear course that "made compromise with the rebels impossible."[39] As Howard Jones puts this transformation, "During the hundred-day period following the president's preliminary announcement of emancipation [22 September 1862], British indignation steadily gave way to the realization that the Confederacy's defeat necessarily meant the ultimate death of slavery." This transformation in British opinion gained force as the cabinet crises hit both governments, so that from January to March 1863 British support for emancipation "virtually muted the Southern sympathizers in England." Lincoln was quick to support this change in British opinion. He responded to a congratulatory address from Manchester workers on 19 January. He invoked perpetual peace and what he perceived as a change in British sentiments in favor of the North.[40] Thus British popular support became stronger in the Union's worst military and political hour when Britain could have preyed on the Union. But such was not Palmerston's way.

Lincoln exited the cabinet crisis true to his word that each of his departmental secretaries should "run his own machine." The cabinet was full of the most capable secretaries available. The conservative attorney general Edward Bates, Seward, Chase, Stanton at the War Department, and Welles carved distinguished records before leaving office. Except for Chase, all of these men were loyal to Lincoln and unified behind the war effort despite their petty jealousies. Remembering the cabinet crisis, and of all people, Chase was angry that there was so little unity of action despite his rarely attending cabinets after the crisis. Even after the crisis, Lincoln refused to treat the cabinet as a principal policy-making entity. Chase told friends that "the President limits his participation in the conduct of affairs very much to the War Department. His authority is . . . respectfully recognized by all; Mr. Seward . . . generally reads to him the dispatches sent to our foreign ministers, and he appoints such officers as he thinks fit. But there is almost never any consultation on matters of importance, so that what are called Cabinet Meetings have fallen pretty much into disuse."[41]

The Lincoln and Palmerston cabinets began to resemble each other in their policies. Neither wanted a foreign war. Gladstone and Lewis, like Chase and Stanton, were anxious to succeed their master. Gladstone and Chase, the most ambitious ministers, embarrassed themselves. The chief executives propelled their ministers and prevailed in decision making. These similar experiences stopped war talk in both cabinets. Domestic politics were more important than risking political careers in an international war. Thus the outcomes of the cabinet crises on both sides of the Atlantic helped preserve the rapprochement.

7

Mutual Support in 1863

On 8 December 1863, a year after Lincoln had expressed his desire to maintain peaceful foreign relations in his second annual message to Congress, the weary president presented his third annual message. Disputes with Britain remained, but relations had settled into a steady cooperative give-and-take instead of a communications breakdown that could have led to trouble. Lincoln's address looked back over the year and aimed at putting British-American relations on a sounder footing. He reported, "We remain in peace and friendship with foreign powers, . . . Her Majesty's Government . . . have exercised their authority to prevent the departure of new hostile expeditions [Confederate raiders and rams] from British ports," and so had Napoleon III. Questions about blockade-running and "other belligerent operations, between the government and several of the maritime powers," were discussed and "accommodated in a spirit of frankness, justice, and mutual good will." The decisions of the Union prize courts, he added, "have commanded the respect and confidence of maritime powers." Moreover, he mentioned that the supplemental treaty with Britain of 17 February 1863 to end the African slave trade was destined to terminate that "inhuman and odious traffic." As another measure of dependable relations with Britain and France, Lincoln mentioned the successful conclusion on 11 June in Paris of an international postal convention after talks that Post. Gen. Montgomery Blair had initiated the month before. Its principles facilitated postal intercourse, formed the basis of future postal conventions, and began a system of uniform international charges at reduced postage rates.[1] Even the critical Sumner seemed pleased at the tone of foreign relations. He wrote to John Bright, "There is also the assurance for the present that your Govt. does not mean to make war upon us. This adds to our tranquility."[2]

These events summarize the broadening cooperation that had occurred in 1863. The last thing that Lincoln and Palmerston wanted was war. Probably the best example of Lincoln's pacific attitude came after the midyear victories at Gettysburg and Vicksburg. These successes put the president "in fine whack," according to John

Hay, his private secretary. He did not try to take advantage of the victories to press Britain to repent for "helping" the South by remaining neutral and recognizing the South's belligerency. Indeed, Lincoln told Hay on 6 August that there was no possibility of a war with Britain. He remained focused on preserving the Union, extinguishing secessionist sentiments, and liberating the slaves and the Southern people. Unlike the Radicals, even in this year of unprecedented military fury (46,000 were killed and wounded at Gettysburg alone), he did not wish to humiliate the South or establish a repressive truce.[3] Indeed, the war's atrocities were having a "hallowing" effect on the president, and he mentioned this feeling in his Gettysburg Address on 19 November. In addition, on the same day as his Annual Message, he congratulated Gen. Ulysses S. Grant for winning at Chattanooga and Lookout Mountain and opening the road for Union forces to invade the Deep South.[4]

Union fears of foreign intervention seemed to collapse with Lincoln's temperament and his penchant for cooperation. The same can be said of Palmerston and the majority of his cabinet. Howard Jones suggests that intervention lived on in Russell's mind, primarily for humanitarian reasons, into 1863, but it gathered no new converts. Palmerston's opposition denied Russell from rallying support, and there is no evidence that they quarreled about intervention. Moreover, Palmerston's noninterventionism indicated that he never was interested in prosecuting a war against the Union. Intervention was unpopular in England, but war (with anyone) was more unpopular. In this, as in most other senses, Palmerston understood the public better than any British leader, and he wrote: "They who in quarrels interpose, oft must wipe a bloody nose."[5] Seen this way, Palmerston's and Lincoln's opposition to intervention throughout the war was more decisive than were battles, despite the fact that there were many opportunities for either government to pick a fight in 1863 and 1864. As Duncan Campbell points out, the war's victor hung in the balance until after Lincoln's successful election to a second term in November 1864.[6]

Despite the continued Rebel threat to the Union, Palmerston's steadfast commitment to nonintervention can be seen in his parliamentary work during 1863. Some intervention rumbling continued, but the ministry was unworried by the pro-South opposition. When Parliament convened in February 1863 both houses remained opposed to intervention. On 5 February, Derby told the Lords that he approved of Russell's retreat and that recognition violated neutrality and was "useless" unless Britain was prepared to fight. William H. Gregory, the Confederate lobby leader, advised Mason not to act because the House of Commons opposed intervention. Gregory concluded, "If I saw the slightest chance of a motion being received with any favor I would not let it go into other hands, but I find the most influential men of all parties opposed to it." On 14 February, Russell wrote Lyons that there was no use to offer good offices until both sides got tired of fighting.[7] In March, the foreign secretary held that Northern victory was possible, that recognition of the Confederacy was a dead issue, and that "I shd like anything better than being obliged to take the part of the Confederates." In the House of Lords, Derby and even Confederate sympathizers, who believed an affirmative vote would not result, postponed Lord Campbell's motion to recognize Confederate independence for three weeks. On 23 March, when the motion was discussed, Russell replied that Britain remained neutral and that the future depended on battles. Campbell's motion did not reach a vote.[8]

The parliamentary plight of the Confederacy worsened after that. On 27 March, the Confederate lobby disclosed its desperation to no avail. Laird said to a round of cheers that he would build many *Alabama*s if that is what it took to free the South from Northern tyranny. In response, Palmerston defended his government's actions, and Russell told Adams that the escapes of the *Florida* and the *Alabama* were travesties. Public opinion and leading journals supported strict neutrality even before receiving word of the midsummer Federal battlefield victories.[9]

In mid-1863 the Liberals again defeated the Confederate lobby. On 30 June, Roebuck failed to receive approval of a petition for negotiations with the powers to recognize the Confederacy. The reasons for his failure were evident. He had little influence on the parties, and he was isolated from his pro-North Radical "colleagues" such as Bright and Cobden. John Slidell saw no chance for Roebuck's motion. Napoleon III told him that arousing the United States would jeopardize the French Mexican campaign and commerce. He dashed Slidell's proposal to act jointly with the European powers by saying that the Union navy was too strong. England had to join France to ensure naval superiority, and the emperor always refused to move without England.[10]

Of equal importance to dashing Confederate hopes was Roebuck's "diplomacy," which circumvented the political system. Members of Parliament resented his meeting with Napoleon. Robert Montague, who was pro-South, desired strict neutrality and motioned against recognition because, as Frank Owsley writes, "any form of action would change England's neutral position . . . [and] would be equivalent to war in which England would be greatly hurt."[11] Gladstone still believed in Confederate victory but had not pressed after his failed campaign the previous fall.[12] On track with the ministry, Forster argued to maintain neutrality to save Canada and wheat shipments. Nor was Roebuck correct that Napoleon III alerted his ambassador to jointly intervene. Parliamentary undersecretary Austen H. Layard and home secretary Sir George Grey exclaimed that there had been no communications from the emperor since the previous 10 November. Bright castigated Napoleon's chameleon-like interventionism: "The more I study this war, the more I conclude that it is improbable that in the future the United States will be broken into separate republics." The debate was suspended until 2 July, but Roebuck was either a liar or Napoleon's dupe. On 13 July Palmerston told the Commons that Roebuck's unofficial diplomacy led nowhere. Dayton wrote cogently to Seward that Roebuck's "was the most futile and abortive attempt to help on the recognition of the South that men in prominent positions ever made." Roebuck realized his errors of judgment, and a year later he acknowledged Palmerston's superior wisdom in not acting toward both America and the German invasion of Denmark. In Paris, Foreign Minister Drouyn de Lhuys repeated that Confederate lobbyists had received nothing official from Napoleon except the armistice proposal of the previous November.[13]

If there were still doubters in Britain, the union victories at Gettysburg and Vicksburg in early July ruined all hope for foreign intervention. Of the meaning of these victories, James Morton Callahan wrote, "By August, it became evident that what nature and man's genius had bound together could not be separated by the storms of a single generation. Peoples might come and pass away but the Mississippi would roll on through a united country." The coup de grace came on 10 August when Russell replied to Mason that he refused to change his position on the blockade.[14] On 20 July the London *Star* expressed "deep, devout, and grateful joy" at the victories. The *Daily News* thought that Vicksburg had broken the Confederacy and was more important than Gettysburg. The Confederate cotton loan plummeted. The widespread feeling in the North and Europe was that the Confederacy's days were numbered. Catching this possibility, the London papers criticized Russell's partisanship for the United States. They said that he "licked the feet of Adams and bit every one else who ventured within the length of his chain—while rifles and Irishmen were sent to New York in shiploads with impunity." The *Herald* inquired: "How much dirt is this nation to eat in order to escape the bugbear of an American war?"[15]

The *Herald*'s nationalistic verve failed to catch the British popular spirit for peace. The Conservatives remained quiescent and thus consistent with their support for nonintervention. Even before party leaders received news of the Union's victories, on 9 July Lord Stanley reported on the Conservative Party's continued support for nonintervention. At a meeting called by his father with "ten or eleven present," all but one opposed recognition of the South. They discussed whether a mediation offer ought to be recommended but adopted silence to conserve their strength. The majority thought that a mediation argument "may even be treated as an insult," and no conclusion was reached.[16]

Napoleon III saw no hope of the Conservatives' returning to power and changing to intervention. His Majesty told Slidell that "the Tories are very good friends of mine when in a minority, but their tone changes very much when they get into power." The emperor's distrust of Britain was worse than that. French foreign minister Drouyn de Lhuys believed that if another intervention proposal was made to London, Russell might tell Seward as he had done twice before. France might get into a war with the Union, or so Slidell informed Confederate secretary of state Judah P. Benjamin on 21 June. French policy remained one of strict neutrality, and Drouyn de Lhuys opposed the emperor's intervention in Mexico as had his predecessor Thouvenel.[17]

Before his removal the previous fall, Thouvenel's opposition probably swayed the emperor from advancing the matter but so did the latter's knowledge that he was getting ahead of himself in taking on too much. Eager to seize any opportunity, the emperor wanted the Confederacy to shield his actions in Mexico against Union expansion.[18] The French despot was distracted with his opportunist policy in Italy, and Palmerston feared that he might send French troops to the left bank of the Rhine, an irritating action that he often used to bargain for British support in Europe. Thus the British expected the worst not from the United States but from France while Franco-American relations deteriorated over the knowledge of the emperor's Mexican intervention document the previous fall and his incursions into Mexico.

Looking back on the intervention period, it was well that Britain retreated "from intervention and recognition, and never again came so close. Northern voters chastised but did not overthrow the Republican Party, which forged ahead with its program to preserve the Union and give it a new birth of freedom as Lincoln pronounced. Here indeed was a pivotal moment."[19] By implication, Palmerston's actions caused the South to realize the antislavery wrath of the British people. His statements in the Commons and Russell's cooperation with Seward throughout 1863 were indications of their desire to maintain stable relations by, indirectly at least, supporting the North and, by implication, casting aspersions on the South's integrity.

Britain's cooperation was reciprocated. Throughout 1863, Seward cooperated with Britain's nonintervention policy by keeping the Radical Republicans at bay. He blocked the Radicals over an issue that aroused Britain's jingoistic pride just as the *Trent* affair had. In April, the secretary of state appalled Radical Republican leaders Sumner and Chase by readily complying with Lyons's request to forward captured unopened British mails from the prize ship *Peterhoff* to London in return for taking the ship as a prize. The British government did not contest this action.

In the event, the secretary of state had received word of the British blockade-runner's eventual voyage in late November 1862 when the American consul in London, Freeman H. Morse, obtained a copy of a private letter from the shippers to potential investors. The letter announced that the twelve-hundred-ton screw-propeller steamer had already run the Charleston blockade and returned to England with a valuable cargo of cotton. This time the *Peterhoff*'s voyage was to Matamoros, Mexico, across the mouth of the Rio Grande from Brownsville, Texas, and a favorite neutral port for contraband. (Pre–Civil War American interpretation of international law maintained that suspected vessels could not be seized if traveling between neutral ports.) Seward quickly placed the *Peterhoff* on the Union blacklist, which signaled the navy to watch for it.[20]

The *Peterhoff* left London on 5 January 1863, and the seizure occurred on 25 February. To avoid a clash, Somerset ordered Milne not to attempt to recapture British vessels taken as prizes by the Union navy. Britain was to stay strictly within the law, "even where officers of the Federal Govt may misapply the powers of the law."[21] Yet, true to form, Acting Rear Adm. Charles Wilkes, to whom Sec. of the Navy Gideon Welles had been forced to give the command of the Caribbean Union flotilla, ordered the seizure of the *Peterhoff* by the USS *Vanderbilt* five miles off St. Thomas. Welles had sent Wilkes to look for the Confederate raiders *Florida* and *Alabama*, but the rogue captain spent most of his time searching for blockade–runners and violating the neutrality of ports. The latter action brought protests from Spain, France, Denmark, Mexico, and Britain. Wilkes seems to have been consumed with greed, Nathaniel Philbrick believes, because captured blockade-runners earned prize money for the captors. Ostensibly, however, Wilkes thought that because the *Peterhoff* was bound for Matamoros it was carrying Confederate contraband despite steaming between neutral ports. But this time Wilkes followed procedures and took his prize to New York where the United States asserted the international legal doctrine of continuous voyage, arguing that the cargo of gray blankets, boots, medicines, spades, horseshoes, artillery harnesses, and other military equipment was for the Confederate army.[22]

The anger of the British people about the *Peterhoff* coincided with frustration over Wilkes's harassment of blockade-runners in port to prevent them from reaching open sea. He believed that the blockade was an anachronism in the age of steam. "The breaking up of the contraband trade is more readily accomplished by intimidation and the fear of loss of vessels and cargoes from the apparent and not real difficulties that blockade runners have to encounter," he later explained.

But Wilkes temporarily triumphed again because both governments had their hands full. Lincoln searched for a combative field general to produce victories partly to assuage the Radicals. In late June, the Conservatives challenged Palmerston's foreign policy in the House of Commons. The ministry barely escaped censure by a vote of 313 to 295. Russell passively warned Seward that "lawless adventurers intent only on plunder" with British shipping caused a difficult situation that the Foreign Office might not be able to manage.[23] He implied that he needed all of the help that Seward could give to him to save the British government.

Against this background of helplessness in Europe and appeasement of the United States, the parliamentary debate over the seizures lasted for several weeks. Seymour Fitzgerald argued in the Commons that the North was trying to close the Matamoros trade to the British. The *Times* said that the North was using the blockade and Britain's neutrality to take over the world's carrying trade. The *Economist* argued that the *Peterhoff* case was a more blatant transgression of international law than had been the *Trent* affair.[24]

Wilkes's intimidation tactics also brought reports that Colonial Secretary Newcastle said had "gone near the wind" as far as possible without raising a war cry. The law officers opined that Wilkes's conduct "called for very strong remonstrances," and Lyons was instructed to complain to Seward. But the British minister did not pursue Wilkes's question. Lyons reasoned to Rear Admiral Milne,

whose cooperation with the Federal blockading force had won him a year's extension in command, that "there was so much going backwards and forwards, and so
many messages by word of mouth, that for my part I have never been able clearly
to make out the right of the matter." Lyons refrained from pressing the complaints
of colonial officials. He seemed to agree with Wilkes that the colonials deserved
to be intimidated for constantly breaching neutrality. He wrote that the Bahami-
ans pushed blockade-running "to the extreme limit." Left with little other choice
because of Britain's international weakness and Palmerston's illness, and the Conservatives' constant search for a cause to overthrow the Liberals, Russell agreed to a
"vigilant look out against vessels notoriously intending to break the blockade."[25]

Cooperation ensued between Seward and Lyons to untangle the *Peterhoff* affair. When Lyons discovered the seizure of royal mail from the *Peterhoff*, he asked
Seward to return it immediately. Seward considered interference with a friendly
government's mail more serious than confiscating contraband runners. He urged
Welles to release the mail, but Welles stated that mail was not covered by international law and should not be returned pending evidence. But, in the best
interests of Anglo-American cooperation, Lincoln sustained Seward. Welles was
instructed to forward the *Peterhoff*'s mails as a concession but not as a right.[26]
Much relieved at this gesture, Russell refused to make the case an issue and upheld neutrality by saying that the United States was the only judge of whether a
captured vessel should be under suspicion. Lyons also noted that to minimize
the possibility of an international incident Seward stopped the firing of live shot
across the bows of suspected British blockade-runners instead of the customary
blank gun. Milne was "glad to find by Mr. Seward's reply . . . that the [U. S.] Govt
has taken a reasonable view of my communication. I endeavored to point out the
impropriety of the act and to show that the British complaint was not made in
any factious or unfriendly spirit, and this has evidently had a good effect from the
tone of Mr. Seward's communication to Lord Lyons." On 25 April, Somerset wrote
to Milne, "We have as yet however no ground for believing that the Govt of N.
America wishes for a quarrel with this country."[27]

Like the friendly aftermath of the *Trent* affair, tensions continued to ease. On
30 April, Russell announced that the *Peterhoff* remained a captive but that Seward
had forwarded the mailbags. Seward's act further reduced tensions upon the British government. Relations were further eased when the Supreme Court decided
that the blockade was invalid in the Mexican sector of the Rio Grande and that
the trade from London to Matamoros with the intent to supply Texas was not
unlawful, although contraband was liable to condemnation.[28] With this decision,
on 6 May, the release of the *Peterhoff* and the *Dolphin,* another captured runner,
was imminent. This Union act caused Milne to inform Somerset the vessels were
released because the grounds upon which they were seized were "beyond the control of the belligerents." He wondered to what extent he should interfere: "And

prevent even by force the detention of such vessels by [the] U.S., but it might raise the question of interference with the legal Belligerent rights of search, whereas a Court of Justice will settle the question by Argument as to the Legality of the Detention and if illegally detained the amount of damage therefore considered it to be more prudent to abstain from interference unless I receive instruction from Home as my doing so might cause further complications on a question which has heretofore been one of considerable difficulty with the U. States."[29]

The Confederates could not help but notice British-Union cooperation over the most sensitive of all the potential areas for conflict—the high seas. Mason noted the cooperative tone of Milne, Somerset, and Russell in favor of the Union. He observed that the British avoided collision with the Yankees and yielded everything. He commented on the good relations between Russell and Adams. Russell demonstrated Mason's comment on 18 May in the House of Lords when the foreign secretary declined the marquis of Clanricarde's recommendation to send a squadron to the Gulf of Mexico, denied Clanricarde's charges that Britain ignored international law to cooperate with the Americans, and said that the American judges had always been just and respectful in their decisions concerning seizures. Lord Russell referred to Clanricarde's speech as a "desultory lecture on international law" and said that it was understandable for the United States to suspect vessels bound for Nassau. He noted the exultation of owners and captains of successful British blockade-runners, but he had no sympathy (consistent with his original opinion at the time of the neutrality proclamation) for owners of captured runners' complaints to the Foreign Office.[30] Milne continued to write about the favorable relations between British and American officers. He expressed to Lyons that although Wilkes had seized the *Peterhoff* and *Dolphin* illegally, there was much "frankness and good feeling and attention, and I am exceedingly glad to be able to say so."[31]

Indeed, the *Peterhoff* verdict was a fair one. Inspection by Union officials and testimony by a crew member revealed that the *Peterhoff*'s cargo was indeed intended for the Confederacy and was to be landed at Brownsville. Part of the cargo was declared contraband and was retained by the Union per the verdict of the District Prize Court of the Southern District of New York on 31 July 1863. In return for Seward's private and arbitrary cooperation to return the letters unopened (the matter had not been considered in Lincoln's cabinet, but only by the president), British compliance with the *Peterhoff* decision enabled the Union to extend the doctrine of continuous voyage to include reexport of contraband. Thus a vessel was no longer safe from seizure if it was traveling between neutral ports. The Northern courts upheld that a person "cannot do indirectly what he is forbidden to do directly." This decision meant that docking at an intermediate port, such as at Nassau, did not break a continuous voyage or make the shipment legal. A vessel could be seized anywhere and anytime during the voyage no matter how many neutral stops it made en route to its final destination. Moreover, the decision included that mere suspicion of contraband made vessels liable for seizure. These judgments eased tensions on the high seas because no longer did the port question seem to matter much as an argument to combat a seizure. With Britain's cooperation, the Union had tightened the system around the blockade-runners, and neutrality took on a more decisive tone in the Union's favor. The Union finally understood that it had been prematurely hard on British neutrality. For its part, Britain found itself in the same position as the United States had been at the beginning of the War of 1812 and benefited from the Union prize court's decisions in the long run.[32]

While the prize court was deciding on the seizures, the actions of Parliament continued to emphasize mutual support. In June, British cooperation continued when the pro-South Lord Clanricarde moved that the House of Lords disclose Milne's reports about Union seizures, but Russell and Somerset blocked the motion. Somerset said that Union blockade ships took no chances in letting blockade-runners breach the cordon, just as Britain had acted during its blockades. But in those days the British had committed breaches of neutrality, and the Americans, he said, apologized when they did the same. To raise a discussion of the seizures was "bygone" and to no purpose with the "thoroughly good understanding" about the arrests. Somerset stated that Wilkes was getting along with the British naval officers according to Milne's letters and that the British blockade-runners carried on a "fraudulent trade in direct defiance of Her Majesty's Proclamation."[33]

In turn, Russell defied the law officers by continuing to bar runners from using Bermuda dockyards for repairs. These strategic dockyards were used only for repairing British warships.[34] Russell refused to press continuous voyage related to contraband beyond discussions between Lyons and Seward. He reiterated that the decisions of the American prize courts were fair and that the courts remained independent. Palmerston expressed his appreciation for the Union prize courts' work and how the Federals had refused to sway their decisions.[35]

Seward cooperated even though he knew that his political enemies, led by Sumner and Chase, would attack him. The return of the *Peterhoff*'s mails ignited Sumner's and Welles's bitter argument with Seward that international law required that the mail be turned over to the prize court. Lincoln denied their case that Seward acted against the "best American and British precedents of international law." Lincoln said that "his object was to 'keep the peace,' for we could not afford to take upon ourselves a war with England and France, which was threatened if we stopped their mails." Despite Lincoln's support for Seward for the second time in just a few months, Sumner and his clique lamented, in Sumner's words, "The country is in much more danger from W.H.S. than from Jeff. Davis." But, as so often was the case throughout this period, Sumner's words failed to have an impact on Lincoln. The president's trust in Seward stemmed from their mutual caution in foreign policy, and the president kept the matter out of the cabinet to protect Seward. On 28 April, Welles recorded a conversation between Sumner and Lincoln about the matter in which Sumner indicated his desire to stay out of war with Britain. Welles reported that Sumner had told him, "The President is horrified, or appeared to be, with the idea of a war with England, which he assumed depended on this [*Peterhoff*] question. He was confident we should have war with England if we presumed to open their mail bags, or break their seals or locks." Welles wrote that Lincoln continued by saying, "They [the British] would not submit to it, and we were in no condition to plunge into a foreign war on a subject of little importance in comparison with the terrible consequences which must follow our act." Sumner further intimated to Welles that he could not convince Lincoln to stand up to the British on the mails question. Lincoln was showing his larger view of the stakes of foreign policy, which occluded becoming emotional over seizures whether they dealt with mail or not. Sumner's dissatisfaction with the administration's policy forced him into a contradiction. He wanted peace with England, but he tried to convince Lincoln not to back down and to keep the British mail. From here on, the Radical leader carried less significance as Anglo-American cooperation gained weight, and the more dissatisfied Sumner became, the more he compromised his politics.[36]

Unlike the Radical Republicans, foreign ministers in Washington supported Seward. On 5 May 1863, French minister Henri Mercier commented favorably to Drouyn de Lhuys. On 10 May, Lyons went "farther with Mr. Seward about Admiral Wilkes . . . than I had before ventured to do, and he had just been to tell me that Admiral Wilkes is off to the Pacific." Upon hearing this Lyons was "particularly anxious that it should not appear that I had anything to do with this" and hoped that this "is a sign that other conciliatory acts, not words merely, will follow." Next day Lyons wrote Russell that he had two aims, "which I have been most anxious to obtain at once." One was getting Wilkes away from blockade duty to stop him from causing more incidents that might threaten relations, and the other was the withdrawal of Wilkes's naval squadron from St. Thomas altogether. Ex-foreign secretary Clarendon surmised that Lincoln would not invade Canada because "the Confederates will walk into Washington and we shall sweep away their blockade and help ourselves to cotton. . . . I don't think that war is probable though of course peace stands on a slender thread when such a ruffian as Wilks [*sic*] may any day render a further maintenance of peace impossible."[37] Cobden told Adams that Palmerston opposed war, which "would shiver this ministry to atoms in an instant."[38]

Welles disagreed with Seward on the *Peterhoff*'s mails but not with Wilkes's transfer. On 12 May, Seward read Welles a confidential dispatch from Russell threatening difficulties. Backed by Argyll, Russell, and American financier John M. Forbes, who was in England to stop Confederate shipbuilding, Seward asked for Wilkes's transfer. Forbes's confidential letter quoted Cobden's desire for the transfer, and Welles read it to Lincoln, while Sumner read him Argyll's letter advising transfer. In June, Welles transferred Wilkes to the Pacific to placate Russell. Wilkes's career ended in court-martial in March 1864 for protesting his transfer.[39]

Britain had performed a similar act that could have earned a Union protest and led to trouble earlier in the year. Whitehall quickly repudiated the hotheaded commander George W. Watson of the HMS *Peterel* for fraternizing with Confederates when Watson accepted an invitation from Gen. Roswell S. Ripley to witness an attempt to destroy Union blockade ships at Charleston on 30 January 1863. In the ensuing battle, Confederate rams damaged several warships, and Watson reported the lifting of the blockade of Charleston harbor and approved Consul Bunch's request to inform Lyons. On 10 February, Union naval commanders off Charleston signed a statement condemning Watson's erroneous report, which neither Lyons nor Milne had approved, and Union newspapers castigated Watson and Bunch on 14 February. Seward asked Lyons to remove the *Peterel* from Charleston, and the British complied. For his part, Milne severely reprimanded Watson for "indiscretion in mixing himself up so conspicuously and unnecessarily with Confederate authorities." Milne wrote Somerset on 20 March: "Commander Watson is not a wise man and I am now sending him to Barbados to cruize, as I cannot trust him either at Nassau or on the American coast." Milne ordered Watson's replacement not to show favoritism to either side. The *Peterel* affair was the only time that Seward criticized a British naval officer and asked Lyons to remove a British warship. If Lyons and Milne had not censured Watson, Lincoln might have closed American ports, hindering Milne's ability to maintain neutrality and monitor movements that might have occurred against British possessions.[40]

As seen in his cautious directives to Milne, Lyons's role was critical in this year of transition to dependable relations. He had not raised a stir during the battle between Welles and Seward over the *Peterhoff*'s seizure because he understood Washington politics and, most importantly, that Seward needed support. He wrote Russell on 5 May that he was keeping the "door open for spontaneous acting on their part to the last moment, and have abstained from making anything like a demand or even an embarrassing observation." He described the quarrel between Seward and Welles, seeing the situation clearly that even though Welles, Sumner, and the Radicals were friends of England and peace, they could not resist attacking Seward, "although they are at the same time increasing the exasperation against England." They accused Lyons of "having made the most violent and arrogant demands about the *Peterhoff*." Lyons was angry about being castigated because of what he had said about the United States that was published in Blue Books, so that "everybody is furious with England and with everybody and everything English." Lyons felt that Seward was upset because he did not want the foreign ministers in Washington to write anything about the government except what he wanted. Most of the cabinet opposed Seward, and Britain needed to see the *Peterhoff* crisis through. Seward, he believed, would "stop the vexatious proceedings against our merchant ships." Yet Lyons worried that Seward could not overcome Welles.[41]

In response to this embarrassing infighting regarding the *Peterhoff* affair, Russell took Lyons's advice to be cautious. The foreign secretary refused to intervene for the claimants because the verdict was in keeping with British prize court judgments.[42] Russell wrote the English owners of one of the seized vessels that he had to grant the Yankees rights that Britain used as a belligerent in previous conflicts. He instructed Lyons, "May both nations cool down from this insane fury [over the seizures] before it is too late!" and he instructed Lyons to convey the same message to Lincoln and Seward. Somerset helped when he wrote Milne, "The irritation on the part of the Federals on account of the *Alabama* and probably also of the numerous deceits which have been practised upon them by the assumption of the British flag renders Lord Russell anxious that you should still continue in a central position from which you may be able to watch and to advise on the innumerable questions which arise and which cannot be forseen."[43]

Milne consistently reinforced Lyons's caution and obediently implemented Somerset's instructions. His conciliatory attitude was instrumental in the eye of the potential storms swirling around the blockade. The Admiralty supported his work, and the Foreign Office prompted Lyons's conciliatory recommendations in the seizure controversy. Admiralty instructions in February 1864 again illustrated its peaceful attitude. Milne was ordered to be "extremely careful to maintain on all occasions a perfect neutrality." His subordinates were in no way to give "countenance to vessels under the British Flag which may be employed in a manner inconsistent with the Neutrality which Her Majesty has enjoined all Her Subjects to maintain during the Contest." Difficulties should be referred to Whitehall. Conflict with the United States was to be avoided "at all costs."[44]

There were further ramifications of the *Peterhoff* incident, but these were managed in good turn. The *Peterhoff*'s capture caused Lloyd's of London to refuse insurance to ships bound for Matamoros. Not to be outdone, in May 1863, American shippers asked Adams to certify through Lloyd's that their cargoes for Mexico to use against the French were neutral and could be safely insured. Adams acceded to the emotions over neutral rights and contraband shipments between neutral ports. Not thinking that the Union's neutrality toward Napoleon's Mexican venture might be compromised, he wrote a letter of clearance to Adm. S. F. Du Pont, the commander of the Union's South Atlantic Blockading Squadron. He added unnecessary remarks about the shipment of contraband's being "fraudulent and dishonest enterprises" to contrast it with the shipments he authorized as legal. Lloyd's was angered by the note and dispatched a copy to the London *Times,* which published it. The *Times* accused Adams of running his own prize court and prematurely judging cargoes. British merchants protested that they were becoming supplicants to Adams for "licenses" to legitimately ship their goods abroad. The British were insulted following the *Peterhoff* incident, which was still pending in the New York courts. The *New*

York Times informed the London *Times* that it should pick on its own bootleggers who were profiting mightily. Members of Parliament attacked the United States. Clanricarde, speaking before Wilkes was transferred, said, "Commodore Wilkes might set a broom at the mast head . . . and proclaim that he had swept British ships and British trade away from the coast." Russell was pressed by Lloyd's and the shippers and wrote that Adams's letter was "very extraordinary" and "most unwarrantable" and that it was inconceivable for a diplomat to commit such an act.[45]

England and France formally protested. Lyons said that Adams interfered with England's legitimate commerce, because vessels without a certificate from Adams were at risk. Drouyn de Lhuys remarked that Adams seemed to take pleasure in vessels carrying goods to harm French soldiers. To defuse the matter, Seward disavowed Adams's letter and apologized to Britain and France. Adams believed the apology was a national disgrace in his only serious imprudence of his otherwise successful mission.[46]

Yet Adams's blunder failed to cause a British-American dispute. Understanding the cooperation of Lincoln and Seward privately from Lyons, Russell sought no revenge for Adams's breach of protocol, as evidenced by his continuing to ignore Confederate diplomats and, at summer's end, assuming arbitrary powers for the first time in the Civil War in refusing to let any more Confederate warships, such as the Laird rams, escape. Shortly thereafter, on 30 September, Confederate secretary of state Judah C. Benjamin angrily instructed Mason to leave London and join Slidell in Paris. In the midst of this cooperation, Russell wrote Lord Cowley, his ambassador to France, that he "hardly expect[ed] war with the U.S." He wrote home secretary Sir George Grey, whose cooperation he needed to seize the rams, in a similar vein that "if one ironclad ram may go from Liverpool to break the blockade . . . why not ten or twenty? And what is that but war? If ten line of battle ships had gone from New York to break the blockade of Brest during the late [Napoleonic] war, do you think we should have borne it? 'Do unto others as you wish that others should do unto you,' is a good rule among nations as well as among men."

Grey's undersecretary, Henry A. Bruce, reported from the Home Office on 8 October that he had been "running backwards and forwards between the Foreign Office and the Admiralty, about the seizure of the steam racers [Laird rams] . . . (one of which is expected to make this night an attempt at escape), and have not five minutes left." Russell said the same in Scotland. William Vernon Harcourt wrote to Lady Russell that the speech was of "immense service to Europe and America." Troublemakers were being transferred from the center of activity—Wilkes and Watson because of the trouble they caused—and Mason because of the trouble he was unable to cause. British-American relations benefited in either case.[47]

A new irony emerged to facilitate relations. Since Lincoln's artful victory over the Radical Republicans the previous December, Sumner was perplexed with both Seward and Russell. What added fuel to Sumner's ire was Lincoln's work on behalf of peaceful relations with Britain over the spring and summer of 1863. Not only had his decisiveness kept the *Peterhoff* incident from becoming inflamed, but also the president rejected a privateering bill despite the ravages of the *Alabama* and the potential threat of the Laird rams. The mere threat of a privateering bill had caused Russell to seize the rams in early September as a matter of policy to "prevent a great scandal [with the United States]." On 25 July Lincoln instructed Welles to call off the navy in the West Indies from blockading neutral vessels in port and seizing them on departure. Welles was likewise ordered not to detain crews "or any other subject of a neutral power" as prisoners of war except those that needed to be witnesses at prize courts. Lincoln made clear that these orders were "for the purpose of keeping the peace, in spite of such collisions." He remarked that he could make these orders because he was ultimately responsible for relations with foreign powers. He summarized in the best interests of cooperation, "What I propose is in strict accordance with international law, and is therefore unobjectionable, while, if it do no other good, it will contribute to sustain a considerable portion of the present British ministry in their places, who, if displaced, are sure to be replaced by others more unfavorable to us."[48]

As if to consummate his growing relations with Lyons and the chiefs of the diplomatic legations in Washington, Seward planned to take his counterparts on a train trip to his home state of New York to show off the industry that was winning the war in August 1863. Sumner's jealousy was aroused when he learned of Seward's political maneuver. Upon receiving his invitation, Lyons wrote Russell that "Mr. Seward had made such a point of my going with him, that it has been impossible to get off without telling him plainly that I did not choose to travel with him." Lyons went because Seward "deserves some consideration from us, for if we managed to keep the peace at all without him, we should not manage to avoid a succession of critical questions."[49] After witnessing the burgeoning industry and agriculture of the state, Lyons, Mercier, and Stoeckl probably left the tour convinced of Northern victory.[50]

Meanwhile, Sumner seethed in Washington. He was upset with Lincoln's peace work, disapproved of Seward's returning the *Peterhoff*'s mails, and believed that Seward should be more aggressive in stopping Confederate shipbuilding in Britain.[51] He exploded in a four-hour speech at the Cooper Union in New York City on 10 September and unwittingly contributed to more cautious and cooperative British-American relations, despite his intent to disclose Britain's alleged support for the Confederacy and Seward's conciliatory British policy. He composed the speech on "Our Foreign Relations" to vent at Seward and Russell. The speech was ill timed for Sumner's interests, as it coincided with news of Russell's seizure of the Laird rams. Nevertheless, Sumner believed that it was his duty to instruct the people in case war occurred with Britain; and he tried to aim the oration at Americans and not at the British. If this was his goal, he failed, to the benefit of Anglo-America relations.

The senator tried to salvage his prestige and acted entirely alone. In inveigh-
ing against Seward and Russell, and not Napoleon III, the real nemesis, Sumner
unwittingly decreased his impact on policy, and he enabled the British to see that
American cries for revenge for Britain's neutrality mostly surrounded him and a
small group of extremists. In the speech, Sumner indicted Britain's alleged transgressions against the Union. He cited the Proclamation of Neutrality and what he
believed was British high-handedness in the *Trent* affair. He chastised Seward's
power and ranted about British protests against the blockade and Russell's irritating official diplomatic correspondence defending neutrality. He noted the "unneutral" speeches of Russell and Gladstone in October 1862 and Britain's recognition of Confederate belligerency as a violation of international law. He chided the
British for encouraging slavery by not siding with the Union, ignoring maritime
law, and sending raiders against the Union navy and merchant marine. He accused the British of "flagrant oblivion of history and duty."[52]

Sumner's oration backfired on him and eased British-American relations. On 23
September, Seward wrote to Adams that the speech had redoubled Lincoln's efforts
for peaceful relations and instructed Adams to inform Russell that the United States
"will hereafter hold itself obliged, with even more care than heretofore, to endeavor
to conduct its intercourse with Great Britain in such a manner [that] the civil war . .
. when it comes to an end, leaves to neither nation any permanent cause for discontent." Although he had been skeptical about Britain up to this time and somewhat
sided with Sumner in that attitude, Welles wrote Lincoln on 30 September of his
acknowledgment of the president's "strong desire to conciliate Great Britain and to
make all reasonable concessions to preserve friendly relations with her."[53]

Lyons added credence to the American position. In November he wrote a confidential dispatch to Russell warning about the Union's military superiority over
Britain, which was the reverse of how the two countries stood when the Civil War
began. His trip through New York State, which was thriving on the war, caused
him to conclude that "the United States could now without difficulty send an army
exceeding in number by five to one any force which Great Britain would be likely to
place there [in Canada]."[54]

Hearing all of this from Adams and Lyons, Russell supported Seward against
Sumner's charges: "The Government of America discusses these matters very
fairly with the English Government. Sometimes we think them quite in the wrong;
sometimes they say we are quite in the wrong; but we discuss them fairly, and with
regard to the Secretary of State I see no complaint to make." Two months later
Adams wrote, "The absurd prejudices against our administration, with which I
had first to contend, are now nearly gone. Mr. Seward is no longer regarded as the
bet[e] noir, intending all sorts of shocking insults to the British lion."[55]

Another outcome of the hapless Sumner's speech was that newspapers quit
supporting Sumner when they heard that Russell detained the Laird rams. A fur-

ther irony was that Gladstone had by now come around to support the Union, and he joined his fellow ministers in urging that Sumner's rhetoric be ignored in the interest of British-American cooperation.[56]

No doubt reeling against being panned from all quarters that counted, Sumner became outcast and revengeful. This was unfortunate, because Lincoln valued his advice and welcomed him to the White House, where he was a favorite of Mary Lincoln. Moreover, Lincoln realized that Sumner was the most informed American about what the British leaders thought. But in this instance, as in others before and after the Cooper Union speech, Sumner failed to separate his political arrogance from the cause of British-American peace that he otherwise beheld as sacred in his foreign policy philosophy. The senator spoke as if he had never corresponded with British leaders or embraced their peaceful desires. He was overcome with fear that, despite his fame, politics had no place for him unless he created a new and extreme platform without thinking about how his strong words would influence the powers that be. Instead of ousting Seward, Sumner alienated himself from Lincoln's inner circle. Instead of selflessly using his considerable abilities to help Lincoln, he acted as an individual for the rest of the Civil War. Many questioned his credibility, and soon after the war his cries for annexation of Canada for the depredations of the Confederate raiders fell on deaf ears. "There seems to be rather a better feeling towards England, and perhaps Mr. Sumner and his radical friends will find their virulent attack upon us to have been a mistake," Lyons informed Russell privately on 6 November. The usually withdrawn British minister poured good feeling into relations when he continued, "I am disappointed and disgusted with Mr. Sumner's own conduct—and the more so as he is necessary to use to carry the Hudson's Bay Treaty [to create a joint commission to review the claims of the company's subsidiary, the Puget Sound Company, from lands ceded by the Oregon Treaty] through the Senate, and generally to manage matters affecting us (such as indemnities to owners of wrongfully seized Ships) which may come before the Senate." From then on, Lincoln and Seward took more control of foreign affairs, and Sumner's Foreign Relations Committee only had a "few important topics to consider."[57]

Further cooperation occurred in mid-1863 when Lyons and Seward agreed upon a treaty that had been in the making since the Oregon Treaty of 1846. That treaty neglected to compensate the Hudson's Bay Company (HBC) and its subsidiary, the Puget Sound Agricultural Company (PSAC), for trade losses when the Americans took over the region. Negotiations continued into the 1850s, but an amount could not be agreed on, with sums mentioned from $1.5 million down to $300,000. The United States was trying to prolong the issue for land prices to fall in order to decrease the payment. The latter figure was the U.S. offer when the Civil War broke out. In 1860, Russell had wanted to settle at $500,000 because he feared that Seward would lower the amount once he became secretary of state.[58]

In an early indication of Britain's desire for a comprehensive treaty, Russell wanted to tie the HBC-PSAC treaty to a treaty over the San Juan Island water boundary question in March 1861. Lincoln sent the message for the Senate to approve a treaty between the United States and Britain through foreign arbitration of the water boundary by determining which line was meant by the Treaty of 1846—the Haro Strait, between the San Juan Archipelago and Vancouver's Island, or the Rosario Strait east of the archipelago—and to consider the HBC-PSAC compensation proposal at the $300,000 mark that Buchanan had proposed. However, the Senate was not interested, and it remained angry at Britain's apparent support of the Confederacy. Sumner had just taken over the Senate Foreign Relations Committee and dutifully sent the Senate the proposal to pay a lump sum or establish a commission to determine the sum and to approve Switzerland to arbitrate the San Juan question. This is how matters stood when Fort Sumter was fired upon, and the Senate postponed the matter until 2 December 1861.[59]

From 1861 to 1863, pressure on Russell from the HBC-PSAC continued to mount as HBC officials continuously reported transgressions by American settlers. The tense status of British-American relations throughout the rest of 1861, capped by the *Trent* affair, negated treaty making. As relations calmed down in the spring of 1862, Russell asked Lyons to broach the matter with Seward once again. Lyons, however, failed to see an opening, and the matter again rested until February 1863. In the interim, Lyons saw the necessity for Seward and Sumner to unite over the HBC claims south of the 49th parallel. In February 1863 Russell asked Lyons to reach a settlement on the HBC-PSAC rights. Fortunately, Seward wanted to settle to ease some of the Anglophobia and the Radical Republican stress on him that resulted from the depredations of the *Alabama*. He did not want seething issues to remain unsettled. In response to Lyons's note that the HBC-PSAC issue should be quickly settled separately from the San Juan water boundary issue, Seward wrote that he doubted that the Senate would approve any treaty with a stated amount of payment. Russell agreed with the separation and to work on just the HBC-PSAC treaty.[60]

As happened so many times in 1863 all over the spectrum of relations, the two parties were cooperative. Seward offered to settle, and Lyons "jumped at the chance for he thought years would pass before another opportunity came for settlement as advantageous to the company." He had "grown both to like and esteem this complex individual."

As in June 1846, Britain and the United States moved to settle a major dispute. Lyons's treaty draft drew only minor revisions from Seward, who wanted the king of Italy to arbitrate how much the United States should pay to Britain. Lyons believed that the treaty could not be improved and signed the treaty with Seward on 1 July. The convention established a joint commission to determine the value of the rights of the HBC and PSAC. Lincoln sent the treaty to the Senate, which approved it in 1864. In 1865 the joint commissioners started their deliberations and eventually agreed to pay $450,000 to the HBC and $200,000 to the PSAC.[61]

In his annual message to Congress on 8 December 1863, Lincoln showed his awareness and support of the cooperation that had occurred in so many areas of the British-American relationship in 1863. He emphasized peace with foreign powers, which raised Russell's hopes of a settlement. He spoke of "the effort of disloyal citizens of the United States to involve us in foreign war, to aid an inexcusable insurrection," and he added that these efforts "have been unavailing." After discouraging Anglophobia as detrimental to winning the Civil War, he made a number of comments that were friendly to Britain to disclose his cooperative foreign policy. He spoke of his pleasure at Russell's seizure of the Laird rams and of Russell's public speech making the announcement. Lincoln believed that Napoleon III "promptly vindicated the neutrality which he proclaimed at the beginning of the contest." He echoed Russell that blockade questions, neutral rights, and other issues were managed "in a spirit of frankness, justice, and mutual good will."[62]

But Lincoln's words about the French emperor belied what he knew was going on. In actuality, the French incursions in Mexico offered a further rallying point for Anglo-American relations in 1863 and for the rest of the Civil War. A few weeks after the annual message, Seward confidentially told Welles that he had read Lyons a dispatch on Mexican affairs, which was critical of France and which he had sent to the American minister to Mexico, Thomas Corwin. Palmerston and Russell understood Seward's feelings because they also believed that Napoleon was overextended in Mexico and was less threatening in Europe. Since the Confederate defeats in July, Seward had evinced stronger opposition to the French. During the fall, Napoleon III was disturbed on hearing that the United States might support the Mexican republican government, which it recognized, after defeating the South. Seward's game of creating uncertainty was a primary reason that the emperor never recognized Confederate independence and ultimately withdrew military support for Maximilian after the Civil War. The official belief of the Lincoln administration was that Napoleon wanted a British-American war to free him in Mexico. Lincoln saw that Britain did not want war with the Union military, which was at its peak.[63]

There were other important factors that made Napoleon's plans a sham. By the end of 1863 all signs pointed to a stronger British-American relationship despite the continuing ravages of the *Alabama*. British national interest prevailed again to ensure cooperation over the second most heated issue in relations concerning the high seas. This time it was the construction of the Laird rams, which Russell lost no time in trying to curtail. In March 1863, he continued his outcry against Confederate raiders being built in Britain by remarking that the trade in such ships was "an evasion by every subtle intricacies of our law of foreign enlistment." His persistent singular actions in cooperation with the United States brought closure to the potential for war by the fall of the year. Yet except for Russell and Argyll (as far as is known) the rest of the cabinet remained quiet about the matter.[64] On 14 March, Russell voluntarily informed Adams that two more ships were being built in Scotland for the Confederates. This admission made Adams understand that the ministry was "without power to take the necessary steps" to prevent the construction of the raiders but was under pressure to do so.[65]

Russell yielded to Adams's evidence and public opinion about the raiders. Such machinations were popular in neither country. On 21 March, Lord Russell informed Adams that two Confederate ships were being built in Scotland, which caused Adams to expect support from the ministry. He was correct. Russell prepared for a debate on the United States and the Foreign Enlistment Act on 27 March. He informed Palmerston that "the fitting out and escape of the *Alabama* . . . was clearly an evasion of our law." Palmerston should speak of the government's disapproval of attempts to elude the law. In the debate, William E. Forster upheld Adams's argument that if the ministry lacked the legal power to detain the raiders, it should ask the Commons for more powers. Sol. Gen. Roundell Palmer spoke for the government against amending the Foreign Enlistment Act despite his belief that the law had to be widened to arrest for ship structure and intended use. John Bright asked Palmerston to mend fences with the United States, which fired Palmerston's nationalism. He castigated those "mouthpieces of the North," Forster and Bright, and he refused to amend the Foreign Enlistment Act. He was afraid to risk his slim majority on such a sensitive issue, which was his real reason for speaking against the pro-Northerners while he continued his wait-and-see approach to the Civil War. He also remembered that his government had been hurt in 1859 when he too hurriedly conceded to France's insistence that Britain pass a law to limit freedoms of radical political refugees in England.[66]

Two things blunted Palmerston's speech. Adams wrote Seward that if pressed by Northern privateers, some British groups would fight the North, and Seward should avoid giving Palmerston a "just cause of complaint" and resist "extreme measures" to help Confederates.[67] As a result of Palmerston's speech reaching the United States, Adams feared that danger loomed from the Union side because Congress had passed a privateering bill in February 1863, which authorized the president to issue letters of marque and reprisal to privateers to retaliate against the raiders. Welles and Sumner knew that this was a result of Seward's work to threaten Britain to get the latter to seize any suspicious vessels on the stocks, and the two argued that Seward's "rude schemes of private warfare" might lead to war if Northern privateers accosted British merchantmen. Welles rightly contended that fighting privateering was the navy's job because "private armed vessels . . . will be likely to be officered and manned by persons of rude notions and free habits." Sumner urged Welles to write Lincoln to stop any idea of Northern privateering. Welles obliged and Lincoln read the letter and visited Welles on 2 April. Welles spoke against Seward's letters of marque but at the same time argued that England was in league with the Confederacy. Lincoln "assented consequently to most that I uttered and controverted nothing" but remained conciliatory to Britain. He feared that since the South had few merchant ships the Northern privateers would raid British ships and cause a crisis. This conversation ended Seward's privateering threat.[68]

In the event, Seward had not needed to go so far with his threats against Britain because Russell continued to work against the Confederates. The foreign secretary helped allay the bad feeling created by Palmerston's speech, which Adams downplayed as resulting from senility. Lord Russell maintained goodwill by continuing to enforce the neutrality laws on the basis of the intent and structure of suspicious vessels in the shipyards. He decided to make a test case of the *Alexandra,* which had just been built for the Confederacy and, supported by the law officers, informed Palmerston of his intent. On 5 April 1863, with Palmerston's approval but without full evidence, Russell seized the *Alexandra* and requested American consul Thomas Dudley in Liverpool and British officials to collect evidence against the vessel. Russell's arbitrary action overturned Palmerston's speech of 27 March not to amend the Foreign Enlistment Act with the prime minister's prior assent and caused Adams to believe that the British wanted American cooperation against Confederate activities in the British Isles. The *Alexandria* case meant that Britain continued the policy of cooperation with the Union, for the ship's detention was a blow to the Confederacy. British policy did not go unnoticed: Henry Hotze wrote secretary of state Judah P. Benjamin that Russell's action "proves undoubtedly a strong desire to propitiate our enemies."[69]

As a further boon to the Union, Russell got the *Alexandra* trial moved to London because of Liverpool's Confederate bias. But most importantly, he had set out on a brave new course that put the ministry above the law on the raiders' issue, because national self-interest deemed it proper. In other words, if the lawyers balked, Russell decided to detain suspicious vessels and either negotiate with the owners or buy them. The government lost the case, but the prosecution of a ship built for the Confederacy sent Richmond the message to cease using England as its naval arsenal. Most important, Russell did not wait until the law was amended to modernize the neutrality policy to help him detain suspected raiders. After the *Alexandra* decision, the Confederates did not build a single ship in the British Isles, and the ministry made decisions without consulting the law officers to uphold peace and protect its interests. Finally, Russell saw that the *Alexandra* was captured at Nassau and held for the duration of the war.[70]

Seward and Russell also cooperated with the Northern blockade to safeguard British shipping gains. Northern shipping was in the doldrums when the war broke out because of the Southern-led withdrawal of Federal shipping subsidies in 1858 and the low-priced, iron-hulled British ships that carried goods cheaper than the old wooden American ships. Rising building and operating costs made American carriers less competitive than Canadian and British ships and caused Americans to sell their ships at low prices to Canadian and British shippers. Even without the antics of the Confederate raiders, the Civil War sped this process because of the cotton trade's disruption.[71] Seward diluted tensions by ordering the navy to be cautious about arresting foreign blockade-runners from Charleston to Matamoros.[72] He refused to bluster about the captures, and Russell allowed the cases to go through the American court system. Challenging the blockade meant abrogating neutrality and, perhaps, war.

British-Union tensions receded during the spring of 1863 with the mission to England of Federal agents. Millionaire shipping magnates John M. Forbes and William H. Aspinwall were funded with $10 million in new government bonds to purchase vessels being built for the Confederacy in Britain and Europe. Both Brahmins were ardent abolitionists and represented the chagrin of shippers and financiers about the depredations of the *Alabama* and the *Florida*. The friendly Barings loaned Forbes and Aspinwall £600,000 to go with collateral of $4 million in bonds. These funds enabled the two millionaires to fund a spy ring to gain evidence about the ships under construction, justify purchase, and stop them from sailing. The Barings' loan depended on the North not issuing letters of marque against British blockade-runners, a compromise between the British and the Union that erased potential incidents. The Forbes-Aspinwall Mission started Europeans buying Federal bonds. This fund reached $250 million by 1865 and swamped Confederate efforts to sell Erlanger Loan bonds in Europe, which raised only about $2.5 million.[73]

By mid-1863, Anglo-American cooperation subdued emotions about neutrality. They cooperated over British grievances about blockade-runners captured in the West Indies, where the runners picked up contraband to transship to the South. Welles refused to act, but Russell instructed Lyons to tell Seward that either Lincoln was trying to fool the British or else he had no control over Welles. Despite Lyons's reluctance to get into the middle of a spat within Lincoln's cabinet between Seward and Welles as principals, Seward talked Lyons into seeing Lincoln on 19 July. Lyons explained the complaint that the United States was abrogating the neutrality laws by intercepting British vessels on the high seas. Seward said that if right was not on his side it was best "to give up all the spits" to help Palmerston and Russell support the blockade. Lincoln put "in the strength of his hand" with Welles as he told Lyons on 20 July.[74] The president informed Welles on 25 July that the navy was to avoid neutral ports to watch neutral vessels, and then dart out and seize them, which was a practice that Charles Wilkes, the commander in the West Indies, had perfected. Lincoln responded to British complaints about seizures off St. Thomas by decreeing that the practice "is disproved and must cease." The navy was ordered not to detain the crews of captured neutral vessels except when needed as prize court witnesses. Lincoln's purpose with these abrupt orders was "while if it do no other good, it will contribute to sustain a considerable portion of the present British Ministry in their places, who, if displaced, are sure to be replaced by others more unfavorable to us."[75]

The gap between the cooperative president, secretary of state, and Welles was significant. Welles was unhappy because British law did not support Lincoln's instructions and because the president upheld Lyons's complaints about the spate of seizures during the previous spring. Welles believed that the prize courts, and not the president or the diplomats, had the jurisdiction to do this. In other words, Welles did not believe that executives, British or American, had any right to intervene in the interests of maintaining peace through cautious behavior. Having written so strongly, Welles then backed down out of loyalty to Lincoln: "I am not unaware of your strong desire to conciliate Great Britain and to make all reasonable concessions to preserve friendly relations with her. In this feeling I cordially participate." In an appendix to this letter to the president, Welles expressed his concern that Lincoln's orders were issued without any requirement by any neutral power to follow the same pacific procedures.[76]

The cooperative work of Seward and Russell, backed by their superiors, was challenged when on 11 July 1863 Adams informed Russell about the two Laird rams being built at Birkenhead. These ironclads had seven-foot underwater pincers to ram and sink opposing warships. Adams asked who had commissioned the construction of the rams. Owing to the controversy over his successes seen in the *Alexandra* case of a few months before, the Confederate agent Bulloch had shrewdly covered his contract with the Lairds. Russell's information indicated that they were to be sold to a French company to sell to Egypt as a ruse before turning them over to the Confederate Navy at sea. Russell was doubtful and consulted the law officers, who advised that nothing be done. In late August, he wrote a memorandum that defined his position. He wanted to continue procuring evidence against the rams being built "for the purpose of carrying on war agst a friendly power, viz. The United States of America." He wanted the *Florida* and the *Alabama* to be prevented from entering British ports anywhere in the world because they were built, equipped, and manned by Englishmen, had never put into a Confederate port, and "they are in substance tho' not in name, English men of war carrying on belligerent operations against a friendly power." Russell agreed with Argyll that the raiders were violating British neutrality.[77]

There was a larger split in Palmerston's cabinet than in Lincoln's on this central issue of relations. Russell's memorandum met with opposition from Palmerston, Newcastle, and Westbury. Colonial Secretary Newcastle said that preventing Confederate ships from visiting British ports but allowing Union ships to use the ports was a neutrality violation. Palmerston agreed: to bar the raiders was like allying with the North and breaching neutrality. Lord Chancellor Westbury (who had sided with Russell and Gladstone on intervention) was the most extreme anti-North minister and said that because there had been no trial or verdict against the raiders they could not be considered in violation of the Foreign Enlistment Act.[78]

Russell persisted as he had done in the intervention debate. He found out through Cowley that the rams were not for the French government and that there was no House of Bravay that had ostensibly purchased the rams for Egypt. The foreign secretary discovered Confederate naval officers in Liverpool. Finally, he doubted the communication from Robert Coloquhoun, the British minister to Egypt, that Bravay had been dealing with the pasha. Russell's decision to seize the rams was supported by Sir Austen Henry Layard, his permanent parliamentary undersecretary. For the second time in fewer than six months the Foreign Office acted on its own and assumed responsibility with the law officers.[79]

By 31 August Russell believed that the rams' situation was critical, and Adams and the Emancipation Society pressed him to act. He wrote both the Society and Adams that the law tied his hands. But as David Krein points out: "Russell's private thoughts . . . were far in advance of his official pronouncements." He informed Layard,

> I do not think we need wait for the opinion of the Law Officers for detaining the vessels if we have any evidence whatever to show there is reason to think they are intended for the service of the Confederates. In that case we might detain the vessels for further enquiry [as he had done with the *Alexandra*], & if that produces no certain grounds for a prosecution, then let them go to satisfy Seward & all rational men that we had done our best. . . . We are not to be frighten'd by a threat of war, & Seward is evidently not in earnest about it, as England, France, Mexico, & the so-called Confederacy would be more than he can manage.[80]

Fortunately, on 2 September Russell had the evidence to detain the rams. Another telegram from Coloquhoun indicated that the pasha denied making a deal with Bravay. Again acting on his own authority, Russell wrote Layard that the vessels were intended for the South and that he would present his case to the law officers if they refused to detain the rams. He issued the detention order to Layard on 3 September and wrote to Palmerston, "We shall . . . have satisfied the opinion which prevails here, as well as in America, that this kind of neutral hostility should not be allowed to go on without some attempt stop it." Powerful newspapers demonstrated part of this opinion. The *Saturday Review,* the *Morning Post,* and the *Times,* none of which had sympathized with the North, wanted the rams detained, showing that British opinion was changing. The *Times* publicized that "we cannot help feeling a certain degree of sympathy with [the Union's] remonstrances." This wording was a concession to public opinion and a warning that a precedent should not be allowed, because the United States or some other state might take advantage of it. Once again William Vernon Harcourt cautioned the ministry that England should accept the North's definition of neutral rights, which barred neutrals from furnishing England's enemies with commerce raiders. The *Spectator* further cautioned, "With the measure we mete it shall be measured to us again." Liverpool ship owners memorialized to the Foreign Office that not to detain the rams "would entail a serious danger to British commerce in the future."[81]

Therefore the issue was moot when Russell received Adams's "superfluous note" on 5 September that threatened war unless the ministry acted. Adams intended the note to be superfluous. Its lateness emanated from his trust in Russell who persuaded the law officers to redefine the Foreign Enlistment Act of 1819 on which the neutrality policy was based. He told them that the ministry was prepared to pay a fine if the law were broken. Palmerston agreed and suggested that unless a foreign buyer were found that the Admiralty purchase the rams for the Royal Navy. Somerset approved. Fearing that the rams might escape before a purchase could be made, he put sailors and marines on the first one that went out for tests. He wrote to Palmerston of his precaution that "such a trick as the *Alabama* must not be successful a second time."[82]

As Max Beloff wrote, "The real danger of an Anglo-American war disappeared." Palmerston's word was decisive because he "was a better defender of British interests, and of peace, the most vital of them, than the demagogues on either side."[83] Russell instructed Lyons to tell Seward that Britain opposed being a Confederate naval arsenal. To further vindicate Russell, Seward sent Russell a copy of Mallory's annual report on the Confederate navy in December 1863. The report indicated that Confederate vessels were being built in England and that there were plans for Confederate operations in Canada. Seward informed Russell, "The recognition of the insurgents without navy, ports, courts, or coasts, as a belligerent, was deemed by them . . . as an invitation to use the British ports."

It can now be said that the possibility of a British-American war over the Laird rams was not as imminent as Beloff believed when he wrote in the 1950s. So many cooperative acts long before the event said that no war would ever again be fought between John Bull and Brother Jonathan. In the event, Russell acted astutely for peace without ignoring the efficacy of British statutes.[84] As in earlier instances of cooperation, he persisted in assuring the Confederates and the Yankees that he meant business. To quell American complaints, on 10 September 1863 Russell first detained, and then saw that the government purchased, the Laird rams. With Palmerston's knowledge, the foreign secretary formally seized the rams on 9 October 1863 as a matter of policy rather than law. On 27 October marines boarded the vessels and work was stopped. Two British gunboats blockaded the rams. Adams's charges that the British were perpetrating the "gravest act of international hostility yet committed," and Russell's arbitrary seizures, brought an amicable conclusion.[85] Stronger neutrality resulted from Russell's acts to placate the North. Next to the *Alexandra*, Russell's seizure of the rams exhibited that the neutrality policy prevailed over domestic law.

The British seizures were even more complementary to Union diplomacy because, had the rams eluded Russell and ultimately escaped, they might not have caused any damage to the Union. This point underlines just how cautious the British had become. First, the Confederacy lacked skilled seamen and gunners to operate the new ironclad technology and perform the gunnery techniques that the two rams required for effective operations. Certainly, such experienced seamen could not be procured around European dockyards. Thus, as Warren Spencer points out, "This lack of trained and patriotic seamen raises a strong doubt as to the efficacy of the service the rams or any other ship of advanced technology could have rendered to the South." Second, there were problems with how the rams could be used by the Confederacy because of their construction and maneuverability. Third was the question of whether they could cross the three thousand miles of ocean between England and Confederate shores. Nevertheless, to prove strict adherence to neutrality and that policy dominated the law, the British bought the rams in a show of good faith to the North. Two things dominated the efforts to buy the ironclads. The first was to uphold the strict neutrality policy, and the second was to eliminate a sensitive issue with the United States. Palmerston and Russell acted so swiftly to buy the ironclads (Palmerston saw them adding strength against the French) that Somerset did not know of the purchases. When he found out what he was supposed to do, he quickly obliged and used them for coastal defense in Britain, Bermuda, and Hong Kong (which demonstrated that they could have gotten to North America). With the purchase, Somerset wrote to Gladstone that the rams added to the efficiency of the Royal Navy and that the principles of economy were met by the purchase price of £220,000 each. He said that the purchases finally put "an end to the complication of affairs which abroad was a source of difficulty, and at home a matter of party attacks." In light of these placatory actions, Anglo-American relations continued to improve. Seward was determined to maintain peace with Britain, and Russell refused to hurt Seward's cooperative position.[86]

Russell's seizures were the acts of a seasoned statesman because he knew opposition lay in wait. He took criticism from the Confederate lobby but explained that he believed that seizures were more desirable than war with the United States. On 5 September, he returned the barbs of Lord Robert Cecil and others in the lobby with the statement "I believe that I took a course which was necessary for the peace of the country." On 19 September Russell wrote Sir George Grey about a threat if the rams were not seized. He was thinking of the tables being turned if England and not the United States was a belligerent.[87]

In the midst of the rams issue, Russell ignored American cries to annex Canada, which surfaced for the first time since the early 1850s. On 7 September 1863, Palmerston wrote to Russell, "It is not likely that the Federals will attack us this year." References to war were scarce in Britain. Palmerston wrote to de Grey on 9 September that he agreed with Russell that there were not enough imperial troops to defend Canada and vetoed a plan to send reinforcements.[88]

There was no immediate vital interest worth fighting for in North America. Practicality again overcame the prime minister's emotions. Lincoln was pledged to peace with Britain whether the rams escaped or not. William Whiting, an American lawyer sent to Britain to observe the taking of evidence about the rams' construction, told Cobden that Lincoln "is determined whatever happens short of direct intervention not to have a rupture with England or France during the Civil War." Whiting continued that Adams was to stay in Britain even if the rams were allowed to leave. Yet the Confederates and Henry Adams held that the rams would have broken the blockade and harassed New York and Boston. British naval officer Capt. Cowper Coles, an expert about ironclad construction, challenged them. He downplayed the rams' potential impact. Cobden remarked, "The fact is that with 500 ships of war and 76,000 seamen voted this year [1863], we have not a vessel that would have a chance against one of those monitors on the American coast carrying their 15 inch guns projecting shot of the weight of three ordinary men." Cobden concluded that the Royal Navy could not break the blockade, let alone two untried rams.[89]

Somerset provided further evidence against the rams causing a British-American debacle. The First Lord echoed Coles and Cobden in not believing that the rams "were good for much." After he bought them, he wanted to test "a smaller class of vessels." When Palmerston handed the purchase order to Somerset, his mind was not on the United States but on using the rams against the French. In 1867, Charles Francis Adams looked back and agreed more with the unemotional response of the British leaders about the rams. He told his son that "I could not help a doubt whether she [one of the Laird rams he saw at a naval review] was really worthy of all the anxiety she had cost us."[90]

As exemplified by the rams episode, Britain and the United States were isolated and had to rely on their own scruples and proven diplomacy to overcome new difficulties. In other words, they were forced to interact peacefully. On 28 August, the *Times* worried about what episodes such as that of the *Alabama* could do to British commerce "if vessels were built in the yards of a foreign country of such a character and design as to be directly available against us. . . . we should probably remonstrate with considerable energy." The *Times* supported the ministry's precedent to outlaw building warships for belligerents.[91]

As the actions of the British government on the Laird rams proved, the Confederate cause was lost in Britain, and Benjamin ordered Mason to Paris to work for recognition. Benjamin Moran interpreted Mason's London mission as "fruitless of everything but evil to the rebels. Mason was the unfittest man they could have sent here," he continued, "and has proved an ignominious failure. His ante-cedents were bad, his associates were questionable, and his manners vulgar."[92]

The final piece of evidence that can be used to show the strength of British-American cooperation in 1863 came early in the ram's episode. Russell had con-fidentially informed the Washington legation a month before he actually seized the rams. With Lyons taking the cooler air in Canada to alleviate perpetual health problems, chargé d'affaires William Stuart told assistant secretary of state Freder-ick Seward of Russell's decision to seize the rams and that this information was "confidential and not official. Nothing was to be said of this matter until the con-firmation of it arrived!" Seward privately imparted his satisfaction to Stuart.[93] On 18 September he intimated the fate of the rams to alleviate Welles's anxiety. Seward explained that "[the rams] will be retained in port, but you must not know this fact, nor must any one else know it. Mr. Adams is not aware of it. No one but you and the President and I must know from here, and it is best that he should not know that you know it." Welles lamented that the president and the cabinet were being held up by Seward to protect Russell and enable the seizures to occur. Welles was a hostage to British-American cooperation. He knew he was still on the spot: if Russell decided not to seize the rams his career and not Seward's was in jeopardy because there was nothing written about their conversation. Welles was not a hostage for long because Russell's action vindicated the Union's cooperative foreign policy and ended the Confederate threat to the Union blockade.[94]

The foreign secretary did not stop with the rams. He applied the neutrality policy to Confederate ships being built on the Clyde while the rams were seized, which denied Number 61 and the *Canton* to the Rebels. In this event, Adams and Russell used the same plan that resulted in the rams' seizures: federal agents and informants gathered information in Glasgow. To obtain evidence, British of-ficials threatened subjects with long trials. On 26 October 1863, the same day the rams were seized in Liverpool, the *Canton* was detained and blockaded by a Brit-ish warship. On 10 December it was seized.[95] The bungling of Confederate com-mander James North, who signed the contract to build Number 61, allowed time to seize it also. The Confederates lost a great deal of money on both contracts.[96]

There was further proof of the growing cooperation throughout 1863. As a further gesture of goodwill and mutual purpose, Sir Alexander Milne, the com-mander of the North American and West Indies Squadron, visited New York and Washington. Milne had kept British subjects from becoming victims of the ex-panding land and sea war. He believed that better British-American relations in 1863 merited a visit, and Somerset agreed. Milne left Halifax on 24 September aboard his flagship, the *Nile,* with the *Immortalité* and the *Nimble* alongside. He met Lyons, returning from Canada, in New York City on 29 September where they were surprised to see six Russian warships, which had been ordered out of

the Baltic to avoid being lost to the Royal Navy or the French navy in case war
occurred over Russia's crushing the Polish revolt. Yet, as Milne and Lyons learned
from their American hosts, the Federals were just as surprised by the Russian
visit in addition to the antiquated conditions of the six warships. Lyons refused
to believe in an alliance between Russia and the North, but he worried about U.S.
aid to Russia in case England got into another war with Russia. Federal officials
in New York treated Milne with the utmost courtesy. He met Rear Adm. David
Farragut and Maj. Gen. Irwin McDowell, exchanged visits with Russian admiral
Stepan Lisovskii, and noted the coterie of Russian officers that could steer ships
purchased in New York out of port in the event of war with Britain.[97]

From New York, Milne entrained to Washington where he met Lincoln,
Seward, and Welles, who was impressed with the six foot two, strongly built admiral. Milne and Welles sat together at Lyons's dinner. The "exceedingly attentive
and pleasant" admiral said that he was the first top-ranking British seaman to visit
Washington in forty years because of the fear that the British crews might desert.
He remarked that he had tried to preserve harmony and prevent "irritation and
vexatious questions" surrounding the blockade-runners. He told Welles that he
admired the administration of Union naval affairs "and in his way sustained without making himself a party to our conflict."

Welles felt that the visit was "the harbinger of a better state of things, or rather
of a change of policy by the British government." Observing the guests at the
dinner table, Lyons noted that "even Mr. Welles thanked him [Milne] for the way
in which he had treated the questions concerning the two nations." Lyons wrote
Russell that Lincoln's secretaries expressed their high regard for Milne's "excellent
judgment, and to the firm but temperate and conciliatory conduct of the Admiral
in . . . the maintenance of harmonious relations between the two countries." Milne
was pleased as he left Washington on 12 October to return to Halifax via New
York. He wrote that the Federal officials were polite "beyond expectation" and
that Seward spent two days showing Lyons and himself around Washington.[98]

Milne's visit kept neutrality cordial. He made the visit because Britain had formal
diplomatic relations with the United States, whereas such relations did not exist
with the Confederacy. Federal officials were duly impressed by their first look at the
man responsible for the power behind Lyons's diplomacy. He made an unforget-
table impression on Seward, who wrote to Lyons on 3 December that "the just, liberal and courageous conduct of the Admiral in the performance of his duties while
commanding HM's Naval Forces in the vicinity of the United States, was known to
this Government before his arrival, and it therefore afforded the President a special
satisfaction to have an opportunity to extend to him an hospitable welcome."[99]

Lyons wrote that the Federal government was aware that "to nothing more than
to the excellent judgement and to the firm but temperate conciliatory conduct of

the Admiral is owing to the maintenance of harmonious relations between the two Countries." The admiral's actions merited these words: he kept his subordinate commanders in tow, and he refused to use his warships to convoy blockade-runners to diminish the chances of a collision.[100]

In something of a turnabout from his Radical ways as a cabinet member, after the Civil War, newly appointed Supreme Court Chief Justice Salmon P. Chase, ruled that the *Peterhoff* was destined for a neutral port with goods that could not be proven were intended for the Confederacy or for a blockaded port. Chase decided "that ship and cargo were free from liability for violation of blockade." Only the contraband cargo could be seized. But it was too late. The *Peterhoff* had been sold to the navy, which used it until it collided with another vessel off the coast of North Carolina and sunk. The court awarded the *Peterhoff*'s British owners $67,672.33.[101]

By this time, the majority of the population of the Western world supported a Union victory. Partly from the mutual support of both governments in 1863 on a broad range of serious issues, Lincoln was not far off in proclaiming the last day of November a day of Thanksgiving.[102] Just as Gettysburg had proved to be good ground for the bluecoat forces, so had 1863 established good ground for dependable British-American relations to confront disputes for the remainder of the Civil War.

8

Mutual Dependence in 1864

In 1864 Britain's strict neutrality was further challenged. Confederates operating out of Canada captured Federal ships on Lake Erie and raided the hamlet of St. Albans in Vermont. A further threat to neutrality also occurred when Congress, without the administration's support, gave notice that it was going to terminate the Reciprocity Treaty of 1854, which had expanded commerce on both sides of the border and allowed New Englanders to fish in Canadian inshore waters. The notice was given more to spite Britain's alleged breaches of neutrality rather than for sound economic reasons.

In all of these matters, Britain and the United States continued to cooperate. Russell and Seward remained patient and pacific. Russell worked for the unification of the Canadian colonies partly as a shield against U.S. revenge but primarily to bring to fruition his goal of responsible self-government under a confederation plan he set in motion in the late 1830s. Confederate acts of violence and robbery launched from Canada only made him impatient for a dominion of Canada. Like Russell, other British leaders were as afraid of Union reactions as they were dubious that the Canadians would ever quit their provincial differences and establish statehood without a substantial British investment. But the cooperation from the Americans helped the Canadians see, especially with the notice to terminate reciprocity that meant the return to fisheries problems, that they had better centralize the political and economic structures for historic purposes rather than for defense alone. Thus, from 1864 to 1867, Canadian leaders moved toward union just as the American Union was being resurrected.

The traditional interpretation is that Canada was a hostage to British-American relations during the Civil War and moved toward confederation in the war's last years in order to better face Union wrath. Fearful of a revengeful Union land grab, the British, it is said, moved Canada to unite against the expected Federal onslaught by forming a central government over Canada and the Maritimes, forming a trained militia to defend the frontier, and promising little else. The evidence shows that the only commotion along the frontier was by desperate Confederates trying to sway the British against the North. Their antics backfired and produced triangular cooperation. Thus a more subtle interpretation is needed.

First of all, the real dispute was between the Canadians and the British. Russell's generation knew since the 1830s that Canadian politicians were unreliable because of their provincialism. Nor were Canada's leaders eager to take advantage of the Union's plight when the Civil War broke out. If anything, they knew that the war was an economic boon. Only some conservatives supported the South. Moreover, Lincoln ignored the possibilities of cultivating Canadian public opinion in order to concentrate on the British people and British newspapers.[1] There was thus little reason for Britain to modernize fortifications at Montreal and Quebec because Parliament opposed military expenditures for Canadian defense, and there was never a majority in the United States interested in annexation.

Moreover, antebellum contingencies continued to play a decisive role. British-Canadian relations were precarious since the 1830s when Russell pressed for responsible self-government, economic growth, and self-defense. Fear of losing military and financial support caused Canadian leaders to procrastinate from the fall of 1858 through June 1864. At that point, the Duke of Newcastle, the colonial secretary, favored a legislative union of the Maritime Provinces rather than a larger union of the Maritimes with Upper and Lower Canada. As the Civil War began, Newcastle waited for the Maritimes to assume leadership of a federation of all of the provinces. The Maritimes were not only jealous of each other but also extremely put out by the greater sway of the two Canadas on the mainland in a larger confederation. Thus Newcastle's plan was exactly wrong for the confederation that he wanted. He was saddled with finding a new governor-general who blended civil and military into an advocacy for confederation, and he asked three candidates without success.[2]

Newcastle and his colleagues wanted to bring to fruition three decades of frustration about Canadian obstinacy and petty internal rivalries. Their long-range mission to make manifest a Canadian confederation coincided with Britain's military withdrawal that had begun in the 1840s. Withdrawal began with Britain's recognition of its inability to safeguard Canada, the French rivalry, and the Oregon compromise at the 49th parallel, all of which enabled Britain to neutralize the American threat to "its empire and influence in North America."[3] Pressure for the withdrawal of British regulars began in August 1846, two months after the Oregon Treaty. Federal military readiness for the subsequent Mexican War did not incorporate a strategy to turn on Canada. The eyes of Southern politicians were on the southern borderlands to expand slavery and to take advantage of free trade with Britain. Indeed, there was not a substantial American desire, among Northerners or Southerners, to annex Canada despite the pleas of leading Canadian merchants and bankers in the late 1840s and early 1850s when the economy weakened north

of the border. Even then, Canadian leaders could not bury their political and economic differences. The British attitude that the Americans were uninterested in
Canada was fortified by the rapprochement of the 1850s that included the Reciprocity Treaty.

At the core of the disagreement was the stubborn refusal of Britain to provide
financial support for a Canadian national railroad to strengthen the economic
infrastructure and for the defenses of Montreal and Quebec. From the beginning
of the withdrawal movement, Britain's military expenditures were debated, with
the militarists losing ground under the Conservatives Sir Robert Peel and Lord
Aberdeen in the 1840s and 1850s. The decision was to concentrate land and naval
forces at home against the French, and even here budgets were difficult to build as
peace and prosperity went hand in hand in Britain. This trend dissuaded the British from considering a military buildup against either France or the United States.
Russell's Whig ministry (1846–52) wagered that if trouble arose, troops could be
rapidly steamed to Canada, as they had in the *Trent* affair.

Under this defensive strategy, bipartisan pressure for imperial military withdrawal faced the Whig and Conservative governments of Russell, Derby, Aberdeen, and Palmerston from 1845 to 1861. By 1852, five thousand of an original garrison of eight thousand remained in Canada, and before the Crimean War there
were plans for reductions to three thousand. Similar severe reductions occurred
in the Maritime Provinces and the West Indies. To economize, in 1849 the office
of North American forces was abolished and control shifted to London. As far as
the Royal Navy as a deterrent was concerned, the same practice was followed: the
British refused to interrupt the neutrality of the Great Lakes as guaranteed by the
Rush-Bagot Agreement of 1817.[4]

The completion of the British military withdrawal from North America gathered
force at the outset of the Civil War. The movement did not suffer from the *Trent* affair because there were no Union battle plans discussed for invading Canada, little
in the way of a force to do so, and a lack of a resolve to break with tradition, and
Lincoln was hard-pressed to prosecute the war at home. He did not want to stir up
the British, and, as discussed earlier, British-American relations had improved after the *Trent* affair. This improvement reflected Whitehall's stance toward Canada
and the Maritimes. Palmerston and Russell feared a Union attack on Canada, and
they knew that the Canadian leaders were unprepared. They believed that London
owed the colonies financial aid to maintain their profitability within the empire
and should thus pay for Canadian defense. In reality, however, there had not been
an invasion threat by the United States, Canada had not built a national defense
force because there was no nation, and Whitehall could not defend Canada.[5]

During the *Trent* affair, steps were taken to organize the Canadian militia and
volunteer forces, but Whitehall was dissatisfied. Since little could be done militarily,
the British used conciliatory diplomacy to keep Canada from being held hostage.

Britain wanted informal empire, which required smaller expenditures, made profits, and kept controversial issues out of Parliament. Palmerston was furious when the Canadians refused to raise much of a military force during the *Trent* affair. Had the United States wanted Canada, the province would have been ripe. A year later there were only eighteen thousand volunteers, and Newcastle rebuked the provincial legislature but accomplished little.[6]

However, alleged threats to the frontier by the United States made a mark on Canadian leaders. Led by Conservative John A. Macdonald, confederation progressed from its infancy in 1864 to fruition in July 1867. The tensions surrounding confederation merged with the bad feelings caused by a Rebel raid on St. Albans, Vermont, on 19 October 1864, where three citizens were killed and the raiders escaped back into Canada. Montreal police magistrate C. J. Coursol found a loophole in the extradition law and paroled them. Matters worsened when $90,000 of the stolen money was returned to the raiders before the Canadian government could disapprove. Canada responded to American demands for stricter scrutiny by posting rewards for the Rebels. Two thousand volunteers and detectives guarded the border and provided intelligence about planned Confederate violations of Canadian neutrality. In November, Canadian officials and Lyons prevented a Confederate plan to capture steamers on Lake Erie, free Rebel prisoners on Johnson's Island, and attack Buffalo. Lyons notified Seward on 11 November, and a close watch was kept. The Confederates lacked authorization and abandoned the plan.[7]

Confederates kept causing trouble along the border. In December, Rebels tried to capture the Northern vessel *Chesapeake* for a commerce raider but failed. In January 1865 the Canadian Parliament passed the Alien Act to deport, fine, and confiscate arms of aliens involved in hostilities against friendly states. In light of these actions, the Federals refused to seek retribution, and the British and the Americans refused to increase their Great Lakes forces. The Liberals opposed Derby's statement in the House of Lords that British-American relations were "critical" and that the Great Lakes needed to be defended. Somerset supported Palmerston's argument for inactivity by saying that Seward's intent to increase his navy on the Great Lakes to protect against Rebel incursions came too late in the year to send reinforcements. Seward was in control and allowed tensions to move the Canadians to pass the Alien Act and to better protect the border while keeping Adams and Russell informed. Governor-General Monck was pleased with Seward, who knew of Monck's work on the Alien Act and the border in the midst of winter.[8]

The Union's objective for increasing its Great Lakes' force was to protect the frontier from Rebel incursions rather than to threaten Canada. Seward had implemented a passport system in 1861 that was difficult to enforce along the long frontier. After St. Albans he tried to breathe new life into the system but ran into the same problems. Like the British, Seward wanted the Canadians to protect their border and strengthen their neutrality laws. Canada responded with a program designed to do this, and Seward withdrew his order to enforce the passport system in order to remove a source of bad feelings. In the face of congressional pressure, he did not want the Rush-Bagot Agreement ended either. Despite the Confederate attempt on the *Michigan,* he persisted in his cooperative border policy when he did not overturn the Rush-Bagot Agreement. As Canada became more capable of safeguarding the frontier, Seward withdrew his notice in March 1865, thus winning a diplomatic victory with British assistance.[9]

In that same month Somerset introduced the Colonial Naval Defense Bill to produce a Canadian navy so that the Royal Navy could focus on the French. The bill demonstrated the cautious Admiralty policy of the antebellum and Civil War periods. The bill passed quietly through the House of Commons and was strongly supported in the Lords, and Somerset was applauded. For Britain the bill was an inexpensive step to safeguard British-American-Canadian relations (although the Canadians refused to contribute anything toward naval defense over the next forty years).[10] Somerset's concern was to strengthen the Royal Navy by building ironclads to protect the home islands and to continue the Royal Navy's protection of the empire.[11]

At last, the Canadians realized that they had to dissolve their internal differences and confederate to present a united front and extend their ability to cooperate with the United States. A naval armada was not coming to their rescue. Britain made that clear during the Civil War.

The Canadians were not so fortunate with the Reciprocity Treaty of 1854, which was due for notice of termination in 1864 and could then run until actual termination in 1866. Canadian agriculture and industry profited from the heightened Union need for war supplies. Yet the coincidence of the Northern feeling of Canadian duplicity in the St. Albans raid, disputes with Britain, and the American high tariffs made the treaty a mark for retaliation. Congress voted to abrogate the treaty in December 1864 and January 1865 just after the release of the St. Albans' raiders.[12] It was possible that the treaty could run another year, but there was no renewing it despite Seward's attempts. With the war winding down, high-tariff Republicans, led by Sen. Justin H. Morrill of Vermont, won the debate. Since secession had removed the block of free traders from the South, there was no stopping the revengeful Republicans. They needed tariff revenue to meet wartime debts, and they believed that they could get better terms with abrogation threats. Thus economic abrogation arguments were more critical than anti-Canadian or anti-British arguments. It was unfortunate that anti-British feeling about St. Albans occurred at the same time.[13]

This time it was Gladstone and his cabinet allies that contributed to British-American peace. Gladstone was confident about the maintenance of Canadian-American peace through the creation of a self-governing Canada that included confederation with the Maritime Provinces. His confidence was difficult for Clarendon and the Whigs to understand because they distrusted the United States. To cement the new policy, Gladstone relied on Edmund Burke, the late eighteenth-century British political philosopher whose liberalism implied strong self-government and self-defense. From Burke, Gladstone posited that Canadians needed to realize freedom and self-confidence. They needed to train a militia and modernize fortifications, although these developments were less important than developing strong central government.

Gladstone was more realistic about the situation in North America than were Clarendon and Russell. After decades of peace, the British still feared an American attack upon Canada. In that event little could be done except hold Montreal, Quebec, and the St. Lawrence lifeline until reinforcements arrived. Gladstone feared neither invasion nor peaceful annexation, and he tolerated ambiguity if it promised to sustain progress toward self-government.[14]

Sir Edward Cardwell was the unsung ally and administrator who implemented Gladstone's policy. Newcastle's retirement and death shortly thereafter brought Cardwell to the Colonial Office, which was his first major cabinet post. Since 1861, he had assisted Gladstone ably at the Treasury, where they had discovered similar ideas about domestic and imperial finances. Gladstone bowed to Cardwell's informed estimates of North America.[15]

Cardwell wanted confederation to reduce financial burdens. He stood between the Palmerstonians and radical imperial separatists such as John Bright, Richard Cobden, and Robert Lowe. On most Liberal issues Bright and Cobden were far from agreeing with the cantankerous Lowe, who felt that his views were informed because he had visited Canada. Yet all wanted a strong Canada, and they opposed anticonfederationists.[16] Just before Cardwell took the Colonial Office, his Oxford constituents unanimously returned him to the House of Commons, and he told them that colonists were stronger and needed freedom.[17]

Russell opposed a rapid solution. He helped originate Canadian self-government in the 1840s, but he had not written a timeline or method for self-rule. Compared to the "spacious sense of imperial destiny" shared by Cardwell and Gladstone, that of most ministers was narrow. Russell's draft for confederation in 1862 was abandoned. The plan provided that the imperial government should contribute half for defense, supplement the militia, and guarantee a loan for a strategic railway to transport troops from Halifax to Riviere du Loup. Russell allowed each confederated province its own tariff and defense. The sketch implied a loose federation, which Gladstone and Cardwell rejected for a strong central government that they thought was essential to nationhood.[18]

Neither Russell nor Gladstone acted further until Cardwell became colonial secretary in April 1864. Why should they not act impetuously? Since the Civil War began, the United States had not threatened Canada. In fact the conflict south of the border seemed to them to present a shield behind which confederation could be prosecuted. Cardwell's resolution for a strong central government to lead the

Edward Cardwell, colonial secretary, 1865–66, and secretary of war, 1868–74. British National Portrait Gallery

confederation attracted Lord de Grey, the minister of war, and Sir Charles Bowyer Adderley, a Conservative MP, who was to serve as undersecretary for colonies from 1866 to 1868. De Grey had moved closer to the Gladstonians' position on Canada for a year. Along with the strong central government, he supported a strong Canadian militia and was concerned when the Canadian legislature defeated the

Canadian Militia Bill in May 1862, forcing the resignation of John A. Macdonald, the Canadian Conservative prime minister. Macdonald's ministry had a small majority, the exodus of fifteen French Canadian members sealed his fate, and he used the militia issue to go out of office.[19]

The Canadians' political blunders distressed Newcastle and Monck. De Grey agreed that Canada had to defend itself and refused Monck's request for more arms. In August 1863 he instructed Monck to establish an efficient militia and to remain friendly with the North. Cardwell quickly agreed that the militia should be self-supporting; until this change occurred there would be no defense funds for Montreal. De Grey asked Cardwell to make Montreal the crucial defense point, because if the Canadians failed to defend the city, general defense was useless. Cardwell wanted a War Office recommendation about Montreal before he approached the cabinet, where paying for colonial defense was uncertain. De Grey was confident that Gladstone could carry the cabinet, got Cardwell's support, and informed Monck that imperial interests regulated imperial troops. Monck pressed Macdonald to fortify Montreal.[20]

On 22 June 1864, Adderley asked why nine thousand imperial troops stationed along the thousand-mile frontier were not concentrated at Quebec and Montreal. His argument was Gladstonian: the Canadians should pay half of the defense costs and defend the frontier with militia. He wondered why, if no danger existed with the Union, imperial troops should remain in Canada. Here Adderley raised another issue that had escaped Gladstone, but the speech stirred no opposition. Cardwell responded with the Gladstonian tenet that Britain must supply the defensive nucleus but that the Canadians must realize that their defense depended on their "spirit and energy." The House was satisfied, and the ministry was not compromised.[21]

Gladstone concluded that the United States desired peaceful, although unscheduled, annexation of Canada. Therefore the cabinet should create a nation better equipped to resist peaceful annexation. A stronger British military presence could increase Canadian security but might wound American pride and raise suspicions, but an independent Canada might arouse American admiration.[22] Palmerston differed with Gladstone: the prime minister did not think that Britons saw the colonies "as an encumbrance and an expense, and that we should be better without them." He wanted troops sent, and the cabinet concurred. Yet Gladstone wanted Canadian defenses inspected to determine the costs and to amass facts to support self-determination.[23]

The cabinet's decision to be cautious about funding Canadian defenses was an opportunity for the Gladstonians for good reason. The latest survey of Canadian defenses, made by the capable military engineer Lt. Col. W. F. D. Jervois, suggested that it was futile to defend the vast expanse of western Canada without command of the Great Lakes, and he concurred with the politicians that forces should be concentrated at Quebec and Montreal. He estimated £200,000 to modernize the works at Quebec and £450,000 for doing the same at Montreal. The decision that Jervois was to return to Canada to see if he had missed anything was Palmerston's compromise with Gladstone, and it went practically unnoticed by the cabinet. Palmerston had not prevented the work of Cardwell and Gladstone, who picked up additional support from Somerset, Argyll, and the Radical Milner Gibson.[24]

Ironically, before the cabinet meeting, de Grey withdrew three battalions from Canada for economy and "concentration," beginning the implementation of Gladstonian policy. No doubt the British-American cooperation of the times over Civil War problems assisted with the withdrawal design, as did European affairs, which were becoming worse year by year. Gladstone's planning coincided with the explosive Schleswig-Holstein question, which warranted stronger defense of the British Isles. In any event, the force in Canada was 8,200. On 12 July 1864, Cardwell ordered rigid adherence to concentration except for one unit at Toronto to train militia officers. On 16 July, he ordered future military movements in British North America for the "imperial interest." At that point Macdonald reentered office and had to decide how to pay for defense. Gladstone stated that the "center of responsibility" had to be shifted to the Canadians under the Colonial Office because "the Cabinet is not prepared . . . , and perhaps never may be prepared, to proceed upon such a basis."[25]

Macdonald had to show evidence of a strong Canadian militia and improve key fortifications before the Liberals matched forces. In a dispatch to Monck on 30 July 1864, Cardwell insisted that Quebec become the strongest defensive bastion, and he held Macdonald accountable. Britain was dedicated to giving all of the "professional assistance in our power" but not to force the Canadians to assume defense responsibility. The most important thing that the Canadians had to do, Cardwell implied, was to muster the spirit of dominionhood.[26]

The Canadians were leery about assuming frontline duties although they were proceeding with training the militia, which numbered 22,000. Gladstone amended Cardwell's dispatch of 6 August that he wanted strict economic accountability for supplying Canada and that the cabinet refused to act until the Canadians responded about self-defense. With the border quiet, Cardwell spurned Monk's renewed request for gunboats on the Great Lakes. In Washington, Lyons supported the Gladstonians' stance that Canada was indefensible unless the Canadians took a stand. But he did not think that Lincoln would attack Canada with the war, the impending fall elections, and the peaceful outlook toward Britain. With the situation apparently in his favor, Gladstone erased Russell's joint conference proposal. Knowing that they had begun a self-defense program, the former obliged the Canadians to decide on military and naval expenditures.[27]

Palmerston bowed to Gladstone when he insisted that the Canadians fortify Quebec. Even so, differences were still evident. Palmerston was interested in the tactical present while Gladstone looked to future responsibility for imperial defense. In a timely fashion, Jervois's latest recommendations were circulated within the cabinet. They were modest compared to his earlier mission. He believed that £1,754,000 should be spent improving defenses. Of this amount, £300,000 was to pay for gunboats for the St. Lawrence and the Great Lakes. Now with Palmerston wavering, and Jervois's evidence to support Gladstone, deeper inroads were made into Palmerston's policy.

Cardwell's resolution proceeded apace before Jervois's return. By 28 September 1864, Cardwell gave Canadian confederation top priority. His decision was reinforced by the *Times* on 24 October, which declared, "Our colonies are rather too fond of us, and embrace us, if anything, too closely." The colonial secretary urged the provincial governors to gain legislative support for confederation and denounced a mere union of the Maritime Provinces. The conventions at two of the maritime capitals, Charlottetown and Halifax, pondered such a union with delegates from Prince Edward Island, Newfoundland, Nova Scotia, and New Brunswick. Macdonald attended both conventions and was relieved that no results were reached. At the Quebec conference his plan for the larger confederation succeeded, with all in agreement except Prince Edward Island.[28]

Then the St. Albans raid occurred. Ironically, the raiders served peaceful British-American relations and Canadian confederation. St. Albans ignited a new period of cooperation to protect the border at a serious juncture. Leaders on both sides of the common frontier realized that Confederate desperation was in direct proportion to declining military fortunes. The raid renewed the Canadians' efforts to organize a militia and pay for defenses. The militia rounded up the raiders, and Seward countermanded General Dix's orders to chase the raiders into Canada to avoid further incident. He waited quietly for the Canadians to uphold their neutrality.[29] Macdonald reacted by writing, "The true way to succeed is for the Canadian Government to assume an indifferent tone in the matter." No further raids occurred. Several months later Seward recalled border guards and refused to terminate the Rush-Bagot Agreement by militarizing the Great Lakes.[30]

Britain's response supported Seward. Cardwell received news of the raid on St. Albans on 10 November 1864. With what must have been some trepidation, he thought Anglo-American relations were good. Like Gladstone, he felt that Seward had every right to increase surveillance on the Great Lakes and along the common border. It was too late to alter the cabinet's decision on Confederation. Priorities were established. Seward's behavior was unprovocative.[31]

In fact, St. Albans won more adherents for Confederation in London. In mid-November, the press said a union was essential for peace. Palmerston's newspaper, the *Morning Post,* was a leading supporter; the *Times* and *Daily Telegraph* agreed. Argyll again backed Gladstone, and soon the cabinet agreed that confederation remained a top priority. There was little to do but monitor Macdonald's work.[32]

The dispatch authorizing Confederation went to Monck on 3 December. It expressed full approval of the Quebec conference and recommended that larger

powers be vested in local bodies to sway the Maritimes and with final authority
in the central government. Monck was instructed to send a deputation to London
to discuss details. Progress toward the implementation of a Liberal North American policy was now being made. Neither Palmerston nor Russell argued for more
troops after the St. Albans raid or for the mobilization of Canada's militia.[33]

In December 1864, Russell asked what would happen if the South allied with
the North and cut the Civil War short? There was a rumor that Jefferson Davis
had been plotting with Lincoln. Russell informed Palmerston that he questioned
the verity of this rumor, but he counseled that if it came to anything, the defense
of Canada would be urgent. Specifically, Russell felt that "the responsibility [for
Canada] in case of war is enormous." He wanted Halifax "made so strong as to be
impregnable—and the railroad to Quebec at once undertaken on joint British and
colonial credit. This is the great question for the next session."[34] As with the San
Juan Island water boundary dispute that had flared up in August 1859, Palmerston
became alarmed without checking the facts. He refused to listen to the soothing
reports from chargé d'affaires Burnley in Washington, who wrote that Seward was
docile about St. Albans and the incidents on the Great Lakes. "I think we have got
safely out of Canadian troubles thanks to Lord Monck's extremely energetic and
conciliatory policy towards this country, which has been duly appreciated by Mr.
Seward & the cabinet."[35]

Late in December, Gladstone informed Cardwell that he was uncertain that the
Americans had an invasion plan. If such a plan existed, British authorities had not
tried to ferret it out or counter it. With that logic on his side, Gladstone defended
confederation and won important concessions. He objected to fortifying Quebec,
and he insisted on large naval reductions. Only Milner Gibson and Argyll supported him. Cardwell hesitated, and de Grey was cautious. But again bowing to
Gladstone, Palmerston formed a cabinet committee to determine reduction of the
naval estimates composed of Cardwell, de Grey, Somerset, and Gladstone himself,
which was a further concession. The only specific decision that the committee
made about Canada was to include £50,000 for Quebec in the army estimates for
1865. This amount was hardly enough to stop an American invasion. Gladstone
wanted more specific information about American plans, and he desired to establish "a frank understanding" about Canadian defense responsibilities. The cabinet
committee recommended that Canada fortify Montreal and that Britain pay for
modernizing the defenses of Quebec and for arming both sites. Gladstone, however, refused to act unless Macdonald pressed confederation, trained the militia,
and kept the imperial government informed about his progress.[36]

Then Britain's concerns about an American invasion seemed to abate as quickly
as they had arisen. One reason was Grant's grip on both Richmond and Lee's army.
"There seems a gleam of peace from America," Russell informed Palmerston in early
January 1865.[37] Nevertheless, the prime minister and foreign secretary remained

suspicious of American schemes about Canada as the Civil War ended. Cardwell ordered Monck to supervise defensive operations to get something done because "there was remarkably little evidence of the sense of acute peril, or desperate urgency, in Great Britain." Palmerston, Russell, and the cabinet majority disapproved of Gladstone's cautious policy, but it remained the government policy anyway. In that regard, Monck was instructed to use provincial officials to administer garrisons to loosen administrative ties with Britain "progressively."[38] But there was another wrinkle. On 19 January 1865, Palmerston believed that the *Alabama* dispute made war possible once the rebellion was quashed. He wrote the queen that Gladstone objected strongly to fortifying Quebec and insisted upon a reduction of five thousand naval personnel. The entire cabinet opposed Gladstone except for Milner Gibson and Argyll and concluded that £50,000 should be added to the army estimates to begin the fortifications. This was a cut of £350,000 from the original estimate. In return, the Canadians were to spend £450,000 to fortify Montreal.[39]

Despite the friendly tone of Adams's communications to Russell in their interviews at the Foreign Office, fear of a Federal invasion continued into March. In their meeting on 27 February, Adams had apprised Russell of the alleged Confederate plan to stop the Civil War so that the North and the South could concert in a war against France in Mexico or against Britain. In the same breath Adams downplayed this Confederate attempt to hurt Anglo-American relations. He told Lord Russell that Richmond was also "coquetting" with France and promising to support Mexico against the United States.[40]

On 13 March there was a long discussion in the House of Commons about Canada. Conservative Seymour Fitzgerald tried to use the perceived threat of war against the government. Forster rose in defense and said that war was unlikely and to continue with the policy of peace. Cardwell said that Canadian-American relations were friendly. Disraeli echoed Forster that war was unlikely. Bright praised the Federal cause and urged peace. Palmerston summarized this bipartisan consensus by now saying that he discounted a Union attack on Canada after the Civil War.[41]

In this Parliament the Liberals outlined their plan for Canadian self-government and self-defense. In February 1865, de Grey remarked on the central matter in the plan: "We take a share of the expense [for Canadian defense] upon ourselves. We ask them to take the larger." Russell and Granville answered Conservative criticism that in the event that Canada was attacked, England would come to Canada's defense. The outcome of the Canada debate was positive for Anglo-American relations. The House of Commons agreed that there was no immediate threat to Canada and that they should not act hastily about Canadian defense. Disraeli approved of concentrating imperial forces at Quebec and Montreal. Echoing Adderley, the Conservative leader said that the fifteen-hundred-mile frontier was impossible to defend. Speaking for the Radical Liberals, John Bright shared the protestations of peaceful intentions that he had received from Sumner. Bright revealed, "There is not a man in the United States . . . whose voice or whose opinion would have the smallest influence in that country, who would recommend or desire that an attack should be made . . . upon Canada with a view to its forcible annexation to the Union." Bright believed that "there was the greatest possible calm on the frontier. The United States has not a word to say against Canada." He concluded that Lincoln's government favored peace more than any American administration since the Revolutionary War. Culling up a theme he had used in the 1840s to advocate peace with the United States, Palmerston said that common ancestry prevented war, and he repeated that he expected friendly relations when the Civil War ended.[42]

Support for his Canadian plans was so strong that Gladstone did not have to speak in the Commons as the Canada debate continued. Forster summarized Gladstone's policy as an alliance between two self-governing states with a common sovereign, and denounced Conservative leaders who feared war. He argued against the possibility of an American attack on Canada because the demands of the American Civil War debt were too great to support an adventurous policy. Cardwell rose and pointed out the government line that relations with the United States were "perfectly friendly." The Americans had not served notice of invading Canada when they abrogated the Fisheries-Reciprocity Treaty of 1854 or threatened the same for the Rush-Bagot Agreement of 1817. Nothing had come of Confederate actions along the border, he reminded. The passport system was withdrawn as a defensive measure at the behest of the American government. Yet in the long term, Cardwell concluded that "war with Canada is war with England," but the less said about war the better.[43]

With the Liberals' plan for Canadian self-determination clear to Parliament, the Gladstonians confronted Canadian leaders in London from April through June 1865. Cardwell thought such a confrontation "a delicate matter" because, by 1 April, the Canadians had not responded to Cardwell's dispatches since 21 January, and the cabinet and Parliament were uneasy without Canadian plans, which was, in fact, the core of the imperial plan.[44] For this reason, Whitehall withheld defense funds until a Canadian plan was approved. Cardwell and de Grey disseminated this message while trying to convince the Canadians of British regard for the imperial connection. On 23 May, Gladstone wrote that if Canada wished to remain British and to fight for the connection, "as men fight for their country, I do not think we can shrink from the duty of helping her" and thought that Lowe's desire to release Canada immediately was uncourageous. Gladstone's third policy guideline was caution, which stemmed from his conviction that the United States was preoccupied with rebuilding and had no time for international disruptions. He noted that the United States quickly disbanded its standing army because of the requirements of reconstruction and economy. He concluded that if an American attack transpired, Britain and Canada had no time to build extensive fortifications anyway. All that could be done was to prosecute the defense works at Quebec with "all dispatch." Meanwhile, Gladstone gathered more intelligence about American intentions and told the Canadians that there was little reason for their "feverish impatience" for British funds. During confederation Canada was treated "as morally in the attitude of an independent Power."[45]

At the London conference in June the Canadians wanted to begin new fortifications immediately. This plea was rejected in favor of assistance if attacked. Otherwise, the Liberals refused to be dislodged from their position of self-determination for Canada and a spiritual tie to the mother country. The Conference closed, and Gladstone expressed the magnitude of the decision to Argyll as "one of the weightiest questions I have ever discussed." Defense had to "stand over for a future period, while we push to the best of our power the formation of the Confederation." This decision satisfied Parliament and the separatist Radicals.[46]

After the conference, Cardwell managed the principles given to the Canadian delegates. They were working more for what they thought was Canada's benefit and less because of a fear of an American invasion. He wrote Monck, "I am anxious to turn the screw as hard as it will be useful but not harder." A week later he instructed Lieutenant Governor Macdonnell of Nova Scotia, long regarded as a nuisance by the Colonial Office, and who faced removal if he persisted in blocking confederation, to inform his parochial legislature about the priority of Confederation and national defense. Until they had achieved union, the provinces were considered a "quasi-independent country financially responsible for its defense measures." Gladstone wrote Cardwell that Canada must be ready to devote "all her resources both in men and money to the maintenance of the connection with the Mother Country" to keep the relationship. Cardwell then informed Monck that the vacillating colonists must realize their "duties as well as their rights, and that they must act with courage and build a nation or any consequences would be of their own making."[47]

Sensing trouble about this straightforward policy, Gladstone informed Russell not to mention confederation in Parliament to allow time for the Maritime Provinces to accept the understanding. Russell wanted to coerce (whatever that meant) the colonists into understanding what was for their own good. Gladstonians said that force countered the spirit of confederation that was critical to success. Gladstone refused to castigate Russell, as he was working for the union of all of the provinces and had ordered Sir Frederick W. A. Bruce, Lyons's successor as British minister to the United States, to induce Nova Scotia to support confederation. The picture brightened considerably in August when Russell learned that Seward canceled his notice to terminate the Rush-Bagot Agreement and promised that only American revenue cutters were being built for the Great Lakes. Just before his death on 18 October 1865, Palmerston told Sir William Fenwick Williams, the new lieutenant governor of Nova Scotia, to influence that legislature for confederation.[48]

Palmerston's demise did not disrupt the cabinet's movement toward confederation. Russell became prime minister and Clarendon returned as foreign secretary. Both supported Gladstone's plan for confederation and self-defense, thus maintaining continuity with his predecessors. Nor did Russell anticipate a war with the United States. The British knew that the U.S. Army and Navy were rapidly disbanded to save expenditures to decrease the huge war debt.

Despite these American professions of good faith, Clarendon, foreign secretary for the third time, was apprehensive. In early September, he wrote Undersecretary Hammond that Anglo-American relations were his top priority, that he was suspicious of the United States, that he expected a rapid American recovery from the Civil War, and that anything might happen.[49]

The immediate threat to peaceful relations was a dispatch from Capt. John Bythesea, the British naval attaché in Washington. Bythesea wrote that three gunboats each were being built for the Great Lakes at Buffalo and Cleveland and that two more were being constructed at Baltimore and New York. When all were finished, Bythesea warned, there would be six armed American naval vessels on the Upper Great Lakes and two on Lake Ontario. These vessels would carry twenty-nine light guns and armament that allowed an increase to fifty-four or a corresponding weight of heavier caliber. There were no competitive British naval vessels on the Great Lakes. Learning of Bythesea's report on 29 September, Russell asked Bruce to query Seward about the authenticity of this program, and he sent a note to Somerset asking if Britain could launch similar vessels. Somerset replied that vessels of the *Plover* class, which were nearly the same size as the American vessels, could be sent. They were strongly built and heavily armed. Russell ordered that they be readied. The old balance of power politics in which the Whigs were so practiced again threatened Gladstone's North American policy.[50]

In support of Gladstone, Foreign Secretary Clarendon disagreed with Russell's fears and followed his usual cautious policy of patient indifference. Clarendon trusted Seward's assurances that the new American vessels were exclusively for revenue and within the armament stipulations of the Rush-Bagot Agreement of 1817. The foreign secretary did not believe that Bythesea's reports to Russell evidenced hostile intent. In Washington, Sir Frederick Bruce, who was selected for his office because of his desire for friendly relations, supported Clarendon's position. He explained that Seward, who was now faced with the stern political struggle against the Radical Republicans over Reconstruction, did not want complications and expressed that "time" was the "great agent" for resolving the *Alabama* dispute and other problems. Seward told Bruce that "the interest of the two great branches of the Anglo-Saxon race on both sides of the Atlantic was to go together." These statements caused Bruce to think that Seward was for "peace with all the world and especially with England."[51]

This private consensus caused Clarendon to wait for Seward to initiate closer relations. The minister in Washington's opinions had become Clarendon's watchword since the 1850s. On 9 December, he informed Bruce privately, "More good is to be effected with him [Seward] by friendly and private communications than by official representations requiring written answers that must either be offensive to us or make him unpopular at home." Bruce was to maintain cordial ties to Seward and flatter him with the news that British-American cordiality was top priority. Clarendon's messages eased some of Seward's burden, because the foreign secretary was also concerned about France in Mexico. Clarendon further thought about giving Bruce precise information about the number, tonnage, and armament of the total American naval force, and whether it was calculated for war or for revenue. And if Seward thought additional vessels were necessary, Bruce was to propose a modified arrangement similar to Russell's that limited the number of warships of either side on the Great Lakes. Clarendon's idea was to expand on the agreement of 1817. If Seward was unreceptive, Bruce was not to bring the matter up.[52] To keep the matter in the Foreign Office so as not to cause a squabble, Clarendon stopped the Admiralty until he received more news from Bruce. If that information was troublesome, Clarendon instructed Bruce to dissuade Seward from increasing the American Great Lakes fleet. Failing that, Bruce was to find out about the size and capabilities of the U.S. vessels proposed for the Great Lakes.

Bad news threatened Clarendon's accommodation. On 20 January 1866, Bruce received intelligence about the American navy from Bythesea recommending that Britain should build gunboats. The American vessels on the Great Lakes, Bythesea wrote, were bona fide revenue cutters, and they could damage shipping and Canadian towns. If unopposed, they could transport soldiers to Canadian battlefields and impede troop movements.[53]

With Seward agreeing not to raise an issue over the situation in the Great Lakes, the matter rested to Clarendon's satisfaction. Certainly, both governments seemed now to be supportive of a lull in the best interests of the rapprochement. Their cooperation went a long way in allowing Canadian confederation to occur on 1 July 1867, over two years after the Civil War ended, and testing whether the United States would use force to stop it. As force was not attempted, or even discussed, in Washington, Canadian confederation symbolized the strength of the Anglo-American rapprochement at the end of the Civil War. Neither jealousy nor territorial ambitions drove the United States to try to interrupt Confederation. American national self-interest was internal and not directed north of the border, just as it had been in the antebellum era. By the same token, parallelism existed between British and American policies: Britain's national self-interest kept it from acting militarily in Canada despite some suspicions of an attack at war's end, and national self-interest kept the United States from considering military annexation of Canada. As Confederation moved ahead peacefully, Seward cooperated along the border and refused to use the *Alabama* claims or other disputes to halt confederation by threats or by support for an attack. Frankly, the Americans had their hands full with their own political, social, and economic problems of readjustment.

Thus American national self-interest had no serious interest in Canada except to cooperate to defeat the Confederacy—and that was achieved. Canada was strategically located, along with the West Indies, to deter the Federals from victory over the South. However, except for blockade-running and a few Confederate border raids that backfired on the Southerners, the strategic worth of these British colonies was ignored. Lincoln had no interest in using the Civil War to strengthen the North American balance of power in his favor except to defeat the South. Nor did the British use American distractions to resurrect its earlier prowess with the balance of power. Conversely, the war convinced the colonials to make a nation in order to receive help from Whitehall. Thus national self-interest explains much of what happened during the Civil War in British-American diplomacy. And this interest time and again worked to benefit the rapprochement.

9

The Failure of Confederate Diplomacy
and British Pro-South Impotence

"Observing the interaction between the sea and land along the rocky Maine coast [Jefferson] Davis watched the waves rush onto the cliffs, only to be thrown back. But when the tide receded, 'I saw that the rock was seamed and worn by the ceaseless beating of the sea, and fragments riven from the rock were lying on the beach.'"[1] Far from any sea, the Jefferson Davis Monument looms up from the flat landscape west of Russellville, Kentucky, at Fairview, his birthplace, as a granite monument to a marble man. Seen for the first time, the edifice does not seem to belong to the environment. It seems misplaced, a concocted relic to the past. He was no doubt out of place on the Maine coast, and, similarly, the monument appears to be as awkward, troublesome, and unsuccessful as Davis's diplomacy and as out of place as his diplomats were abroad. Except for France, Britain and other governments ignored these unaccredited agents just as they ignored the opinionated Davis. Despite what one might think of the merits and demerits of the monument at Fairview, Confederate diplomacy was anything but monumental.

The failure of Confederate diplomacy advanced British-American caution and cooperation. Jefferson Davis's prewar vision that the South showed the way to true union, based on the ascendancy of states rights, stultified his diplomacy. He lacked the ability to see that the Northeast and the Midwest were developing diverse industry and agricultural practices superior to those of the slave-labor-intensive South and that free societies were economically superior to slave societies. In failing to comprehend these realities, Davis's foreign policy was unlike the realistic policies of Lincoln and Palmerston. Confederate diplomacy was unrealistic, with its reliance on cotton to leverage the European powers. Davis also could not see that, almost from the beginning of the Civil War, Confederate diplomacy lacked legitimacy, as the European powers refused to recognize it. Conversely, Union diplomacy was recognized. The goals underpinning Union diplomacy were abundantly clear from the outset of the Civil War: complete Confederate defeat and the restoration of the states to the Union. When general emancipation was added in 1863, the powers could clearly see the Union's resolve. They were further deterred by the tough stand that Lincoln and Seward took on defeating the Rebels and drawing the line against recognition of the Confederacy.

Davis failed to see the respect of the European powers for the Union's position. He was a stubborn man. A recent analyst records the remarks of the eighteen-year-old Varina Howell, who married Davis soon after their first encounter at Hurricane, the Mississippi River plantation of Davis's older brother, Joseph. Brian Dirck writes that in "perhaps the most accurate assessment of his character ever written," Varina wrote, "He . . . has a way of taking for granted that everybody agrees with him when he expresses an opinion, which offends me. He is the kind of person I should expect to rescue one from a mad dog at any risk, but to insist upon a stoical indifference to the fright afterward."[2] In other words, Davis victim-ized himself with his pride. Lincoln and Palmerston were much more realistic in overcoming this weakness in themselves.

Nor was the picture that the British had of the South conducive to supporting Confederate diplomacy. London *Times* correspondent William H. Russell, writ-ing on his travels through the South early in the war, disclosed his view of the region as a social backwater, and his pro-North articles reached a goodly number of the British middle class and aristocracy. He was most disappointed at his failure to find a refined civilization there. He argued that the South was unreliable as a financial partner because several states had repudiated debts owed to Europeans and that Davis was the worst offender of all. (Lincoln used this material in his propaganda campaign in Europe.) In addition, Russell described the horrors of slavery so vividly that no self-respecting Briton could support political recogni-tion of a slavocracy. In general, the picture that Russell sent back to England was one of a prideful, rude people living in a decadent, reactionary society that was closed to modern ideas. This society, he believed, was raised on the twin evils of property and violence that were prized above human life.[3]

Despite these fatal flaws, this selfsame pride that the South was unique and deserved its independence kept Davis from adjusting his diplomacy to the reali-ties of the times. Henry Steele Commager suggests that the South believed that it did not need to "win in order to win." Davis's goal was to keep the war going, preferably with European support, long enough for the North to grow war weary and sue for peace. Conversely, the North had to defeat the South by marching through the Confederate army on its home territory. Union armies had to pos-sess the South, in other words, and in 1861 this seemed to both the Confederate government and foreign powers to be a distinct impossibility.[4]

If Davis intended to place any emphasis for victory in his diplomatic goals, he was bound to fail because they were inflexible. He refused to adjust to the requirements for independence that the powers required. He believed that he held the upper hand from the beginning of the Civil War. He could not let go

of this self-protective device. His leverage was cotton, but he failed to use cotton
to sway the powers to his design. Thus bad cotton management fed bad diplomacy and political generals who refused to coordinate with each other. Davis's
prideful personality and management style caused him to rule all aspects of the
government and the military. He was unable to get along with many of his commanders (with the exception of Robert E. Lee), state governors, and congressmen.
Historian Charles H. Wesley believes that the loss of virtue was more important
than weak economics in explaining the collapse of Davis's government.[5] In other
words, Davis could not recognize that abolitionist Europe could view the Rebels
with disdain. A strong reason why the Europeans refused to intervene was because Davis could not offer a national plan that showed abolition and the development of a democratic state.

Following the dictates of their leaders, the Confederate envoys' "King Cotton
Diplomacy" failed to turn the heads of the British. In Washington, British minister Lord Lyons observed early in the war that "the very exaggerated and very
false ideas they have in the South about cotton will lead to very foolish conduct.
It is true that cotton is almost a necessity to us, but it is still more necessary for
them to sell it than it is for us to buy it." Lyons was saying that if the South tried to
coerce Britain by withholding its cotton from export, "other cotton would be got
elsewhere or a substitute found."[6]

In fact, the failure of Confederate diplomacy increased the cooperation of British and American diplomats as the Civil War progressed. Their answer to trouble
was the antebellum solution of give-and-take. Only Davis refused to give. Thus
Confederate diplomacy was stymied from the beginning because of slavery. Foreign Secretary Russell asserted that "in my opinion the men of England would
have been forever infamous if, for the sake of their own interest, they had violated
the law of nations, and made war, *in conjunction with these slaveholding States
of America*, against the Federal States." Along with Russell's concerted effort to
ignore the Confederate emissaries and Parliament's refusal to take up the cause
of the Confederate lobby, by late 1862 Davis's pride was hurt, and he despised
the British. He was certain that the Confederacy had to go on alone. From then
on, his tone often threatened Britain. This tactic was in strong contrast to Lincoln's refusal to use anger and his desire to cooperate with the British. As Brian
Dirck points out, "Davis was a president who knew; Lincoln was a president who
hoped." Davis seemingly made no effort to face the obstacles his pride presented
to him as a statesman or to negotiate about slavery with the United States, Britain,
or France until early 1865. His attempt to settle with the Union in February at
the Hampton Roads Conference on the basis of Confederate independence while
concomitantly trying to obtain British and French support in return for gradual
emancipation were desperate acts. Davis was too immersed in the righteousness

of his cause to act otherwise. Allan Nevins describes him as obstinately "clinging to fixed ideas and prejudices that were quite erroneous."[7]

He started off on the wrong foot. When the Civil War began, Davis believed that the Europeans would ultimately recognize the independence of the Confederacy because they needed cotton. He refused to ship large quantities of the bumper cotton crop of 1861 to store in British and European warehouses to amass credit to pay for the war. Instead, he squandered his credit by keeping the cotton and destroying much of the crop to keep it from the Union armies and as leverage in bringing about Europeans' recognition of Confederate independence. This embargo showed that Davis was oblivious to the British industrial diversification in the textile industry that weakened his blackmail scheme. Nevertheless, he continued to believe that the British would respect his free trade philosophy against the high tariffs of the North and see the moral imperative in the Rebel fight against what he decried as the oppressive, money-grubbing, imperialistic, industrialized North.

Furthermore, Davis failed to learn from the British press. By the fall of 1861 Confederate "King Cotton Diplomacy" was repudiated by the London *Times,* the most widely distributed British newspaper. At the same time, he seemed to be unaware of the *Times'* antipathy against the North. Instead, the *Times* argued that the failure of cotton to reach England was as much the fault of the Southerners as it was of the Federal government. In October, the newspaper commented on the Southern embargo on cotton exports. Britons read the *Times'* leader urging them not to be coerced by "King Cotton." It continuously pressed for the need to develop Indian cotton to reduce dependence on the South. Despite its growing antagonism toward the Northern animosities against neutrality, a leader writer supported Palmerston's cautious policy with "We shall get all we want to supplement the enormous stock in cotton and from other sources without breaking the blockade or interfering in any way whatever." Foreign Secretary Russell expressed the same sentiments when he wrote of his frustration at the North's emotional interpretation of neutrality as a pro-South action, "but I wonder that the South do not see that our recognition *because* they keep cotton from us would be ignominious beyond measure."[8]

Thus Davis's diplomacy was understood early in the Civil War. It was easy for readers of the *Times* to see what he was up to. In addition to his fixation on cotton, there is no evidence that he thought about the antislavery proclivities of Britain and France. Moreover, in thinking about how to establish supply lines through the back door of Matamoros, he had to struggle with the Mexican leaders' recent memory that Southern politicians and soldiers were in the forefront of the expansionists who fought the Mexican War. Nor, when Davis sent the unscrupulous John T. Pickett as his agent to Mexico in 1861, did he realize the antislavery, republican proclivities of the Liberal government there. Pickett was a poor choice, just as the Rebel agents Davis sent to Britain and France were. Pickett was an ex-Cuban

Jefferson Davis, president of the Confederacy, 1861–65. Library of Congress

filibuster and schemer, despite having been the U.S. consul in Vera Cruz. Davis's instructions to Pickett were just as bad as his choice of minister. To his narrow way of thinking, Davis reasoned that there was a connection between the Confederacy and Mexico because both governments allowed human bondage. Little did Davis realize that Juárez was fighting to overthrow forced labor. Davis thought the Juárez government supported the Union and decided to support the conservative Church Party against Juárez. Nor did Pickett's statements that foreign intervention was needed to save Mexico sit well with Juárez. Pickett advocated an alliance between the Confederacy and Spain in order to divide Mexico. With these naive statements, Pickett's mission failed by November 1861, at the same time that the *Times*' vendetta against the South was gathering momentum. To make matters worse, Pickett was arrested in a bar for disorderly conduct with a Yankee vendor who supported the Mexican liberals and spent thirty days in jail. He then bribed a local judge to gain release. He wrote numerous criticisms about Mexico, which Union agents intercepted in New Orleans and gave to American minister Thomas Corwin and to Juárez. In these ways, Pickett's mission did nothing to advance Davis's contention that Mexican support for Confederate trade at Matamoros was successful and formed a solid base for Confederate diplomatic and commercial activity.[9]

Confederate diplomacy failed to gain the support of the powers to surmount the logistical challenges presented by the Civil War. The British and French recognition of the Union blockade at the beginning of the war doomed the free transport of war supplies into the South. The ever-tightening Northern blockade prevented war materiel from reaching the South and raised the costs of the goods that got through. It forced expensive overland transportation of materials through Matamoros and then the long haul through Texas to the battle lines with all of the attendant hardships and dangers. The blockade also made it more difficult for Southern civilians to obtain goods from the North and Europe. The incipient shortages and higher prices contributed to civilian discontent.[10]

Confederate diplomacy suffered as the blockade broke the transmission and receipt of intelligence, dispatches, and instructions between Richmond and its overseas emissaries from late 1861 to mid-1863, a critical time for the Confederacy to gain credibility abroad. Even had communications succeeded, the six staff members of the Confederate State Department could not have kept pace. They were forced to gain intelligence from Northern newspapers, old European papers, journals, and parliamentary papers. They lacked basic reference books. Their dispatches were lost or captured and often printed in Northern newspapers. Pickett's blundering was only one example. Until Judah P. Benjamin, the secretary of state, began to use fast steam blockade-runners from Nassau or Bermuda after mid-1863, it was common to wait six months to mail and receive documents back.[11]

Confederate diplomacy made no trouble for the British-American rapprochement during the rest of the Civil War except to try to use Maximilian's regime to obtain French recognition of Southern independence. Yet a formal relationship between the Davis administration and Maximilian never reached the table. In fact, Confederate agent to Belgium A. Dudley Mann wrote Benjamin in September 1862, "I shall be agreeably disappointed if we do not, in after years, find France a more disagreeable neighbor on our Southern frontier than the United States, at any time prior to their division, ever found Great Britain on their northern border." Mann believed that the people of the South would be uneasy over the French-backed regime in Mexico. Confederates were suspicious that Maximilian might try to annex Texas to revive the historic Mexican boundaries. Benjamin's inquiries to Slidell in France were captured and read by Seward, who forwarded the documents to American minister Henry Sanford in Belgium. Sanford believed that "the idea of making the new Empire embrace the ancient boundaries is not an idle one" and that the probes that French consuls were making in Texas and Virginia were real ones.[12] The South's skepticism about Napoleon's "grand design" never flagged after that. In these ways, Davis was encircled in the diplomatic arena several years before Grant encircled him militarily.

Davis's British policy was similar to his superficial Mexican policy. He never seemed to think about the backlash on the South regarding the use of British resources to build a Confederate navy. His strategy of making Britain his naval shipyard quickly backfired in 1862 and 1863 and coincided with the demise of Confederate diplomacy. In believing that he could build a navy abroad, he was deflecting irresolvable domestic problems. He was naive to believe that the British government and public opinion would stand for this activity against Union diplomatic leverage. But he had little other choice if he wanted a navy. The chief deficits at home were lack of iron for shipbuilding and railroad expansion and a poor transportation system to get these materials to the few heavy industries that lacked the heavy presses to turn the iron into plating for warship construction.

Confederate diplomacy suffered from the agrarian culture. Modernization was impossible because of slavery. In addition, it suffered from a worn-out economy and a destabilizing government. Davis seemed to care little about stabilizing and strengthening his government. His poor leadership reinforced popular resistance inflamed by the worsening economy. In experiencing all of these signs of defeat, he continued to believe that he was above the laws of nations. His penchant to run everything (or attempt to) made him unpopular with the inner governmental circles and state governors. The government was always in flux. As an example of how difficult he was to work for, fourteen cabinet ministers served the six cabinet offices during the four years of the war. In 1862, the number of Davis's critics increased as pressures mounted on the government. His management style was a far cry from that of Lincoln and Palmerston, who allowed their secretaries and ministers to run their own offices without constant interference. Still, Davis's pride prevailed, and he did nothing publicly (as Lincoln would do) to show that he had listened to his detractors. He "preferred the role of silent martyr."[13]

Davis, on the one hand, trapped himself in the details of establishing a new government and bureaucracy accountable only to him. These challenges gave him little time to face realities. He worked harder and harder and achieved less and less. Lincoln, on the other hand, was a realist in foreign policy and succeeded in making the European powers clearly understand the limits of his policy without incurring a fight. Conversely, Davis proved as incapable of securing intervention as Lincoln was successful in understanding how to keep it from ruining his vision for victory.

Despite all of these pitfalls, Davis tried to mount a convincing diplomatic front. He invested substantial time and money to win British recognition of Confederate independence, especially in the first few months of the war. But his chances of success were based on ducking the slavery issue. He tried to convince the British people that the war was caused by factors other than slavery. Yet he set another trap for himself in taking this direction. As R. J. M. Blackett points out in his study of British opinion about the warring sides, "Try as they might, however, none of the Southern spokesmen could escape the fact that one of the major pillars of the new polity was an institution that most in Britain found abhorrent. Nor could they skirt the issue of slavery and at the same time palliate, if not openly endorse, the right of the new nation to continue the offensive and outdated institution."[14]

Under these circumstances, Confederate diplomacy was only a perceived threat to the Union rather than a reality. Palmerston recognized its failure when he argued that decisive battlefield victory alone could sway his government to recognize Confederate independence. Even here he was omitting a long-held tenet that prohibited him from recognizing the Confederacy. Left unsaid was the prime minister's long-time position as the most fervent antislavery leader in Europe. Even if the South had won on the battlefield decisively enough to satisfy him, what would Davis have done about slavery to move Palmerston to recognition? The prime minister's silence is itself a comment on his opposition to the Confederacy and his refusal to give up the lucrative commercial and cultural relationship with the Northern states.

Thus Confederate foreign policy hinged on "wishful thinking," as Dean B. Mahin surmises. In addition to the "King Cotton" conundrum, Davis and his colleagues believed that they could attract the European powers' support by portraying themselves as freedom fighters against a monstrous tyranny that they propagandized was destroying an independent and prosperous way of life. In an arrogant manner, Confederate diplomacy consistently conveyed to the Europeans that it was their "duty" to support the South to end an unjust war of the tyrannical, imperial, industrial North against the upstanding, peace-loving, agrarian South. This argument never captured a significant base of opinion abroad and faded in early 1863 when the Emancipation Proclamation was pronounced and pitched human freedom squarely onto center stage, and at a time that British-American cooperation on wartime matters was moving ahead. This marked the point at which Britain and Europe could understand the North's goals for the first time. From here on, the powers could not support a slavocracy against an established, abolitionist republic.[15]

Even had the Confederates had a viable foreign policy explanation, their propaganda arm was weak in Europe. Confederate diplomats were unsuccessful in 1861 and 1862 in England and in Europe. Confederate foreign policy lacked propaganda value after the Emancipation Proclamation and the eruption of support for the North by the British workers. Confederate propaganda continued to appeal to supporters it had won over early in the war, but it failed to expand its public base.[16]

The foregoing explanation of why Confederate diplomacy defeated itself from the beginning was tied to its poor strategy, arrogance, and unfortunate timing throughout the war. The first diplomats that President Davis sent to Britain and France were hamstrung by not being from a recognized government.[17] Moreover, from May 1861 onward, the Confederate commissioners made no inroads with British leaders. The

first group, Pierre A. Rost, Dudley Mann, and William Lowndes Yancey, lacked
diplomatic talent. Yancey, the best known, had a reputation for oratory but was such
a "fire-eater" secessionist that he alienated Europeans immediately. He had actually urged the reopening of the slave trade on the grounds that the Federal government had acted unconstitutionally in abolishing the trade. Thus, as Frank Owsley
remarked, they were "about the poorest choices possible." Nor were Confederate
diplomats who followed the first three any better. The *Trent* episode represented the
most notoriety that James A. Mason and John Slidell received on their missions to
Britain and France. Like the first three Confederate agents, neither had significant
diplomatic experience. Furthermore, Mason's reputation was damaged because he
was well known as the author of the Fugitive Slave Law of 1850. Slidell had more tact
and finesse but could do little because of his defense of slavery.[18]

Among the activities of the first group, Yancey's antics constitute an example of
the failure. He met with British Liberal officials and tried to raise support among
Conservatives. He did not succeed in drawing either Liberals or Conservatives into
support for the Rebel government. He was able to speak at Fishmongers' Hall in
London with the mayor present. Yet his speech produced such heavy opposition
that he was intimidated and avoided the limelight during the rest of his stay. Moreover, Yancey was an easy mark for Union representatives in England. Union propagandist J. Sella Martin condemned Yancey as a slavery advocate, and Martin's colleague, George Thompson, reprinted one of Yancey's letters that condemned the law
abolishing the African slave trade as unconstitutional and a radical revolutionary
document. Frustrated, Yancey returned home in early 1862. R. J. M. Blackett therefore concludes: "There is no evidence that other Confederate representatives were
having any more success than Yancey" in the critical early months of the war.[19]

Further evidence became plain during the Polish Crisis in 1863, when Britain
and France watched helplessly as Russia battered Polish nationalists. Coinciden-
tally, Lucius Quentin Cincinnatus Lamar, acting as Davis's special commissioner
to Russia, never made it to St. Petersburg because of the Polish revolt. He probably
would have had worse luck in Russia than Yancey had in England, owing to the
czar's support for the North. As it was, Lamar found no favor in London, writing
Benjamin that Palmerston was more absorbed with European problems than with
the American Civil War. In June 1863 Confederate diplomacy received a further
shock when the House of Commons shelved the idea for an international congress to ameliorate the Polish and American questions.[20]

The Confederate raiders constructed in Britain backfired on Confederate diplomacy also. The Rebel diplomats never tried to justify the depredations of the *Alabama* and its sister raiders as part of a general diplomacy. The fact that they tried
to hide their culpability while the raiders were being constructed caused Britain
and the Union to cooperate against the Confederacy to protect Britain's neutrality.

Here again diplomatic questions were raised that Confederate emissaries could not explain away. The more the *Alabama* and its consorts destroyed Union shipping, the more the ministry was consumed by fears of Federal retribution. To avoid a military struggle, Palmerston and Russell pursued strict neutrality and adjusted their high seas policies to cooperate with the Federal government. Said another way, for self-protection, whatever British partiality existed toward the Confederacy stopped short when it came to international maritime law.[21] In these respects, there was nothing about Britain's policy or the statements that ministers made that could not be undone at war's end. Thus the Confederate shipbuilding program in Britain and the considerable damages by the raiders to Northern merchant vessels drew the ire of many nations and weakened Confederate diplomacy.

Britain and France saw through this obvious scheme and reinforced their neutrality and estrangement from the Confederacy. Moreover, Davis's inexperienced diplomats failed to convince British leaders that the Confederacy could help Britain surmount its frustrations emanating from the Civil War, but instead remained "insensitive and inflexible." For example, British tempers flared when Richmond refused to offer protection for British subjects who had been conscripted in the South. As a result, all of the British consuls protested the desperate conscription law and were expelled in 1864.[22]

Conversely, the Union's diplomats and consular agents in Britain and France worked hard, and often successfully, to prevent Confederate agents from violating the neutrality proclamations. American minister Charles Francis Adams and Consul Thomas H. Dudley in Liverpool and Minister William L. Dayton and Consul General (later Minister) John Bigelow in Paris prodded their host governments to enforce their neutrality. Through a sophisticated group of spies and agents they detected Confederate attempts to circumvent neutrality and pressed Russell to act with increasing success throughout the war.[23] They kept the lines of communication open and defused anger that might have been spawned by surprises had intelligence gathering not been constantly employed.

Moreover, the Confederate agents refused to combat the growing European dependence on Northern grain. From 1861 to 1863, the Northern states supplied almost half of British grain imports, compared to less than a quarter before the war. "King Corn" became more important than "King Cotton," coinciding with the onslaught of superior Union mass and the hard war that dampened the Confederate war effort.[24]

The final irony for Confederate diplomacy came from January through March 1865. Davis sent a special emissary, Duncan Kenner of Louisiana, a close friend of Rebel secretary of state Benjamin, chairman of the Ways and Means Committee, and a wealthy owner of five hundred slaves, to England and France to request recognition of the Confederacy in return for gradual emancipation. Kenner had

advanced this notion since the fall of New Orleans in 1862 and was enthusiastic about the new direction that President Davis was taking. This Confederate
congressman was an adaptable man, unlike many of his peers, and he believed
that the plantation could continue to prosper with free labor. Davis made him a
minister plenipotentiary to stop Mason and Slidell from frustrating the British
and French governments with the new Confederate position. Davis reasoned that
Kenner might convince the British Conservatives that a Confederate government
based on free labor was preferable to democracy.[25] But Davis and Kenner were
much too late. Napoleon III continued his line that he would help the Confederacy only if Britain took the lead. The British bluntly refused Kenner's offer, consistent with their position since the beginning of the Civil War. More importantly,
both governments told Kenner that the slavery issue had never controlled their
thinking about the Confederacy. It would have made no difference if the offer had
been made several years earlier, and in 1865 it was embarrassing to make such an
offer when the Confederacy was close to defeat. Kenner was still in Europe when
the end came just a few weeks after he had made his offer. This last Confederate
act was symbolic of the impotence of Confederate diplomacy. It also manifested
Davis's persistence, misplaced idealism, and even something of his arrogant nature that broke out in times of stress throughout his life.[26]

Napoleon's arrogance was muted this time to the detriment of the Kenner mission. Kenner had experienced many rejections to his initiatives to intervene and
could not endure another snub by Palmerston. He therefore wisely turned down
Slidell (acting in Paris for Kenner), saying he had to follow England's lead. Slidell
misjudged French self-interests throughout the war and never understood the
relationships between Napoleon and his ministers.[27]

Nor did Slidell ever grasp the niceties of Seward's diplomacy and how it affected
French policy. Seward said near war's end that the United States would remain neutral toward Napoleon's Mexican adventure. (There were crazy rumors stemming
from a plan of Francis P. Blair Sr. of an alliance between North and South against
Napoleon's puppet government in Mexico, and even of an "allied" invasion of Canada.) Lincoln heard of the same plan in his conference with Alexander Stephens at
Hampton Roads in February 1865, where the Confederates tried to secure peace
to save their government. Lincoln refused Stephens's suggestion to call a truce and
together go after France in Mexico. Thus the emperor used rare common sense in
what he knew was a lost cause, for on 14 March 1865, Palmerston told Mason that
the South's lack of military success had prevented British recognition of Confederate independence and that nothing could be done to save the Confederacy. There
had been no threat to the vital interests of the Europeans to merit recognition.[28]

Confederate diplomacy lacked substance and tact from the beginning and
never maneuvered the British or the French to a diplomatic Antietam, let alone
a Gettysburg. It clearly symbolized the upstart nature of the Confederate nation

and consistently detracted from achieving European recognition. It was like a new company that wanted immediate profits and quickly failed from inexperience, immaturity, and the arrogance that both foster. There was a childishness about it. These liabilities were hardened by Confederate inability to create converts in Britain, France, and elsewhere in Europe.

In addition to Davis's narrow-minded diplomacy and the woeful showing made by Confederate diplomats, there were many reasons why the British failed to support the South and drew closer to understanding Union foreign policy as the Civil War reached its third and fourth years. The British Liberal government and the aristocracy provided little solace for the pro-Confederates in Britain. Palmerston never encouraged the South. He was restricted from supporting the South even had he wanted to, and there is no strong evidence that he did, as he was immersed in European and domestic problems. Under such pressures, he was too wise politically to cause a stir over the South. There was not a tradition of aggression against the United States. He had always resorted to deterrence at best and indifference when there were not crises. He was a leader for British-American peace and an influence on the maintenance of the antebellum rapprochement. Moreover, the pro-Union lobby was well organized with John Bright at its head. Bright was untouchable. He had long advocated drastic parliamentary reform, and the war stimulated his crusade. His restraint upon Palmerston redounded also to the pro-South flock in England, because pro-Southerners were compromised without the prime minister's support.[29]

Palmerston was on firm ground with his cabinet in his refusal to support the South. At no time during the Civil War did the cabinet or the aristocracy, including the Conservative opposition, give the South much hope of support. Herbert C. F. Bell, Palmerston's biographer, puts it succinctly:

> The day of success for Palmerstonian policy had virtually passed. No longer would haughty words, orders to the fleet, and patronage of the smaller continental states give England a pivotal position in international affairs. Developments on the continent and among her own people were co-operating to diminish her influence. . . . But England, every year more businesslike, was yielding to the persuasion of her Cobdens and her Brights that it was better to economize on armaments, and to avoid so much as risking her blood and treasure for issues in which her own interests were not obviously concerned. A change was noticeable, too, in the conduct of British diplomacy. Palmerston's astuteness, his adventuring spirit, even his desire to take an active part, seemed gradually to be deserting him; and Russell could do little to supply the loss.[30]

Britain was more detached from American affairs in 1863 because of European crises. Palmerston maintained the tradition of staying out of Europe militarily and remained on the sidelines watching as reactionary movements spread over the Continent led by Russia, Prussia, and France. It refused to mount significant military spending to keep up with the armed might of the European powers and the United States. With this perspective, British leaders certainly thought that supporting the Confederacy was a poor bet. They saw many of the same things in North America as they saw in Europe. They recognized that the Federal government possessed the greatest army that the world had ever known. Its navy increased from a handful of old wooden ships to a modern navy of nearly seven hundred vessels. As a result of his realism, Palmerston wrote to Russell in 1863 about British-American relations saying that he surrendered an active role in influencing the Civil War after intervention was defeated in October 1862.

The Confederate cause also failed to draw British support because Britain maintained strict neutrality. This tenet fostered cooperation with the Union to the detriment of Confederate diplomacy. In 1863, neutrality was preserved by conciliatory actions of the British and Federal governments. Palmerston was conciliatory about the Laird rams and blockade-runners, just as Seward refused to cause incidents over the Union seizures of the *Peterhoff* and other British blockade-runners. He said that to allow Confederate shipbuilding to continue would be suicidal if Britain became involved in a war and the United States built raiders for England's enemies. He wanted no "diplomatic wrangle with the Federals."[31]

He was assisted by the weakness of the pro-Confederates. They made no attempt to link forces with the pro-Polish insurrectionists to press the Palmerstonians for support. Neither movement was prominent enough to capture the imaginations of the British people. Palmerston and Russell were indeed fortunate that the pro-Confederate opposition was weaker than they were.

There are a number of reasons why the pro-Confederates were unsuccessful with Palmerston. In 1861, Conservative reviews disseminated the theory that the Southern planters resembled English country gentlemen so that there was a feeling of kinship based on the traditions of the landed gentry. This theory never gained enough strength to impact the arguments of Confederate sympathizers in England. There was some affinity of one group of gentlemen farmers to another, but the cotton planters of the South were bound to the manufacturing class of Britain who were the enemies of the English gentry. Moreover, there is little good evidence of strong feelings for the South among the English aristocracy.[32] It was thus a safe bet for Palmerston to remain indifferent.

To begin with, any aristocrat who was pro-South had little political clout. That said, they had a difficult time getting the government of the day to support their pro-South credibility. The charges of pro-South Conservative aristocrats such as the eccentric Lord Robert Cecil that the ministry retained power by paying off the Conservatives and the Liberals fell on deaf ears. The opposition charge that Palmerston had an affair with a young woman and paid perhaps £20,000 to avoid a lawsuit did not decrease the prime minister's popularity. England abounded in prosperity, and any antigovernment causes as spurious as these were difficult to support. Moreover, although Palmerston and Gladstone were never on agreeable terms, Gladstone's tax program had yielded excellent returns. Despite the economic dislocations caused by the Civil War, Gladstone ended the 1862–63 fiscal year with a surplus of £3.5 million, which was massive for the times. The army and navy expenditures had been reduced considerably, the income tax was decreased, and the tea tax was lowered. All of these measures were approved without cabinet debate.[33]

In the face of Palmerston's popularity and the prevailing prosperity, Derby had announced before Parliament opened in February 1863 that there would be "no serious fighting," and the Conservatives did nothing of importance to overthrow the ministry during the Civil War. They were thus not about to support the Confederacy against the government. "It seemed," the *Annual Register* proclaimed as the session got underway, "as if the long and warm contentions, which had resulted in the great reforms of the preceding thirty years, had been succeeded by a season of reaction and repose . . . an indefinite portion of professed conservatives in Parliament . . . felt that the veteran statesman, with his great tact and knowledge of the world, his large experience and skilful management of affairs and men, was, of all whom the times afforded, the person best adapted for the situation which he filled . . . no Minister of late years has possessed so great an ascendancy in the House of Commons."[34] At the lord mayor of London's dinner for Palmerston, he was introduced as the most popular prime minister since Earl Grey in the 1830s. In his remarks, Palmerston invited the audience to approve of his government's restraint in resisting the "blandishments on the one side and threats on the other" for a British-American war.[35] In the afterglow of these tributes, the ministry continued. The pro-South faction of the Conservative Party supported Palmerston and was not a legislative force for the Confederacy.

The aristocrats who could not cast off the South's cause rivaled Confederate diplomacy in ineptness to press the Rebel cause in Britain. The Confederacy's aristocratic friends and their commoner allies never moved Parliament for many of the same reasons that Jefferson Davis manifested. They could not separate personal interests from a sincere desire to help the Confederates. Many were moved more by fears of Bright's radicalism and of democratic institutions than dislike of the North. In any case, Palmerston's power was overwhelming, and we have seen that Lincoln's government worked consistently throughout the Civil War to keep Palmerston in power by caution and cooperation over a number of volatile issues. Lincoln was aware that most of the aristocratic support for the South was within the Conservative Party, although its leaders, Derby and Disraeli, supported neutrality and Palmerston's nonintervention policy, and they certainly did not want to be in power during the Civil War, because they would face the same threats that the

Liberals had had to wend their way through. Just as the Americans knew, to create a situation over any number of issues discussed earlier could have toppled Palmerston and his circumspect ministry and supporters who professed either neutrality or kept their pro-Confederate sentiments to themselves. The president knew of Adams's statement to Seward that the core of the Conservative Party "continues to be animated by the same feelings to America which brought on the [American] revolution and which drove us into the War of 1812."[36] Yet the chief Confederate propaganda journal in England, the *Index,* pointed out on 28 May 1863 that while Palmerston remained in office "the cabinet in Washington has nothing to fear, and the Confederate States nothing to expect."[37] Those Conservatives who still vented about the War of 1812 were compromising themselves because it was a war that the British people, whose support was badly needed, cared little about.

The pro-Southerners failed to make anything of latent aristocratic feelings about 1812 or any threat the British government made toward the North (as in the *Trent* affair) that might have been taken as a pro-Confederate move. Rebel sympathizers were allowed by Conservative Party discipline to gain prominence in Parliament but were checked during the recognition debate in July 1862. Aristocratic outcry against the North crested during the cabinet's intervention debate that autumn and subsided thereafter. There was no attempt by the interventionists to recruit the pro-South aristocrats. Thus the pro-Southerners were forced to work alone. An attempt by John Roebuck and William S. Lindsay, two pro-South MPs, was made from 30 June to 13 July 1863. Roebuck was raised in Canada, where he had acquired a strong dislike for the Yankees. He was an anxious, vain, and dogmatic person and a firebrand reminiscent of the Confederate emissaries sent to Britain. Charles Francis Adams thought he was a madman, but Mason thought he was "a statesman of great intelligence and experience." Lindsay was self-interested in another way. He was Britain's largest ship owner and a confidant of Napoleon III. His pro-South stand was as financial as it was ideological.[38]

Roebuck and Lindsay's mission to get Parliament to recognize the South's independence was doomed from the beginning. The Conservative Party leadership of Derby and Disraeli remained pro-North and refused to support the pro-Confederates. In May 1863, Roebuck gave notice of bringing in a motion to recognize Confederate independence. But he was too late because "by this time the South did not command the support of any British party. Before Roebuck could bring his motion to the floor for debate, Russell "confidently" wrote Lyons, "I think it certain that neither Lord Derby, nor Cobden will support it, & I should think no great number of the Liberal party."[39] At any rate, Roebuck and Lindsay unilaterally visited Napoleon on 20 June to obtain his support. Carried away by the occasion, Napoleon told them that he could not make a formal pro-South statement because, when he had before, Russell had told the United States. The emotional emperor asked the two MPs to tell the House of Commons about that.

Neither Roebuck nor Lindsay was fit for what they were trying to do, and their tactic backfired, to the benefit of Anglo-American peace. Despite what the South thought, Roebuck was not respected among his peers. He "was a favorite subject for *Punch* to laugh at," and he was frequently ridiculed as "Don Roebucco the smallest man in the House [of Commons]." In 1862, he became anathema when he accused workers of being "spendthrifts and wifebeaters." Henry Adams believed that most reasonable politicians regarded him as generally mad. What was worse, he was clearly swept away by his audience with Napoleon III and forgot that he had gotten nothing from the opportunist. On 30 June, within hours of the first shots at Gettysburg, Roebuck told the House of Commons that Napoleon III had commissioned him to make a motion that Britain join with other powers to recognize Confederate independence. Caught up in his pretentious nature, Roebuck forgot that he might be perceived as a French errand boy dictating to the House of Commons. Both Liberals and Conservatives roundly criticized his speech. Disraeli withheld his support. In addition, Roebuck made two more tactical errors. He could not prove the French cooperation to recognize the Confederacy, and the motion was an attempt to oust the Liberal ministry without getting any Conservative support (as Disraeli's position indicated). The debate brought out that the Conservative leaders and members were not ready to force the recognition issue. Henry Adams was present in the gallery and noted that after Roebuck had spoken, Bright spoke up and "with astonishing force, caught and shook and tossed Roebuck, as a big mastiff shakes a wiry, ill-conditioned, toothless, bad-tempered Yorkshire terrier." Moreover, Palmerston was ill during the debate, but he returned to the floor as the speeches dragged on. The matter was deferred amidst sharp criticism from the French press of Napoleon's desire to recognize the Confederacy with Britain. The majority of British opinion wanted to stay out of the American debacle. Southern propagandist Henry Hotze said that at this point the Southern cause was defeated in England. Parliament never again seriously considered the recognition question.[40]

Moreover, Roebuck's plans for a joint British and French intervention provided grist for the mill of pro-North societies. There was a significant increase in pro-North petitions. These emanated from large public meetings in London, Liverpool, Manchester, York, and sixty other towns under the leadership of the London Emancipation Society. The society began its anti-Roebuck campaign in May 1863, a month before his speech in the House of Commons. The petitions condemned the South and expressed concern about the Confederate warships being built in Britain. They called the ministry's attention to the need to strengthen neutrality. In late June, the London Emancipation Society brought up another petition supporting emancipation and reinforcing the plea of the Union and the Emancipation Society that had expressed concerns about possible recognition of Confederate independence. The petitions of the two pro-North organizations outdistanced the efforts of eccentric Roebuck and his Confederate propagandists because they raised serious questions about the consequences of a retreat from neutrality.[41]

The cause of the Confederacy in Parliament had never amounted to much, and now it was dead. The House of Commons was neutral ground throughout the war. At the war's outset, William H. Gregory met with little success when he gave notice that he intended to submit a formal motion to recognize the Confederacy. The House compromised itself over that issue, as Palmerston pointed out. On the one hand, if the motion was made, "all the Americans will say that the British Parliament has no business to meddle with American Affairs." On the other hand, he said that in the ensuing debate on the motion, Gregory's friends would praise the South and malign the North. Friends of the North would do the reverse, and, overall, in America "each party will be offended by what is said against them, and will care but little for what is said for them." Therefore, the prime minister concluded, England had to stay "aloof" from the war to maintain its freedom of action in the future.[42]

Outside of Parliament, one reason for growing aristocratic silence during the last several years of the war was the concomitant upsurge in popular support for the North. The aristocracy was further dashed by Bright's oratory against slavery. As Bright and the workers became resolute for the North in the first half of 1863, so did Parliament.[43]

The British aristocracy's threat to the Union was less powerful throughout the Civil War than American leaders believed. After the victories at Gettysburg and Vicksburg, Union leaders such as Navy secretary Welles still believed that the aristocracy was far from surrendering its hope for "our national dismemberment." Welles believed that the aristocracy hated the United States government and the American people. He did not say why, however, and he did not seem to notice the British aristocrats who supported the Union throughout the war. He believed that aristocrats listened to the pro-Confederate journals that were unwilling to print that the twin Union victories had broken the Confederate will to win. In sum, Welles thought, "Palmerston and Louis Napoleon are as much our enemies as Jeff Davis."[44]

Proof of Welles's mistaken belief that the British upper classes were opposed to the Union en masse came a few months later. After the 24 September 1863 issue, the *Times* and other leading British newspapers quit talking about democracy's failure in America. In this atmosphere, Bright's crusade for the North silenced many aristocrats from making public antidemocratic utterances. Adams believed that Bright would become a major British politician at war's end because he had placed the question of democracy in the forefront of British politics. That is why Adams began to accept memorialists for the Union cause at the American legation, after at first believing that such an activity was beneath his charge. By early 1863, Adams was visiting with delegations from antislavery societies. As R. J. M. Blackett points out, "Every delegation that visited the legation was a public relations victory for the Union."

Members of the delegations usually included some of Britain's primary politicians. Bright and Charles Sturge (the mayor of Birmingham), for instance, brought the address from Birmingham. Delegations that could not travel to see Adams visited American consuls in provincial cities and Glasgow, where a deputation from the Parliamentary Reform Society of Paisley addressed the consul in the summer of 1862. All of these meetings were widely publicized and carried much more weight in English society than the friends of the Confederacy. They could not go before the public like the Union's supporters and formally use the American legation. Neither Palmerston nor Lincoln had anything to do with peace addresses written by Confederate sympathizers during the last two years of the war. In fact, Sir Henry Holland, Palmerston's personal physician, who was in Newport, Rhode Island, and visited with French minister Mercier soon after Gettysburg and Vicksburg, said that neither Britain nor France would do anything but watch the Civil War.[45]

Adams kept the aristocracy from becoming more emotionally attached to the South. He urged Seward not to emphasize the split in English society between the aristocracy and the workers over the reform question and over the Civil War. Why should he? In the wake of Roebuck's failure to raise the House of Commons, the pressure on the American legation in London receded. Pro-Unionist Monckton Milnes, Lord Houghton, rushed through a throng at a party saying that Palmerston's government would remain in office with the problem of Confederate recognition out of the way. He triumphantly threw his arms around Henry Adams and kissed him on both cheeks. Buoyed up by the victory in Parliament, Charles Francis Adams believed that he was equal to anything, especially now working with Russell to stop the Laird rams and any other Confederate projects that might be underway in Britain.[46]

Not only did Confederate propaganda fail to sway aristocrats or British society in general, but also it was blocked by the formation of a popular reform movement that the Confederates could not emulate. The war ignited massive popular support for reform, which immediately distracted both parties about how to deal with the outburst. The failure of the pro-South aristocracy and Confederate diplomacy on the one hand, and the rise of the working classes on the other, caused the Civil War to end with a surge for reform in Britain. Palmerston wanted no more reform and saw the obvious change in politics coming closer to his councils when the elections of July 1865 returned all of the pro-North MPs and elected several new reformers. Some outspoken leaders of the South were not returned. Adams believed that the elections weakened the aristocracy and disclosed the influence of American institutions on English politics. The elections caused Russell to desert his "Finality" position on electoral reform unwillingly. Both parties realized that they had to confront the issue.[47]

The decisive Union victory shattered the paternalistic culture of the South and with it the myth of aristocratic predominance. The American Civil War was a decisive turning point for the aristocracy not only because some of them had chosen the losing side out of pride. The conflict further weakened their grasp on nineteenth-century England. The brightest of the Whigs, such as Granville, donned Liberal robes to do what had to be done to maintain political office. Whig statesmen such as Clarendon, who were too old to adapt to more reform, knew that they were on their last legs and governed only to hold onto Old England as long as they could. Granville and the newer Liberals were too smart to let the Civil War influence their proclivities to rise in politics, business, and finance. They knew that support for the South would not help them achieve their goals. In these ways, the Civil War underlined an antebellum movement toward reformist Liberalism. The lack of aristocratic ability to press the Confederate cause decisively illustrated that the British-American antebellum rapprochement did not die during the American war but rather was cast into new and deep philosophical shapes because of it.

10

Cooperation to End the Slave Trade and

Promote Commercial Expansion

Cooperation overseas was one of the new shapes of the British-American relationship that continued in spite of the Civil War. There were two primary regions of cooperation away from the battlefields that conditioned how Britain and the Union thought about the fighting. First, behind the refusal of Britain and the United States to fight over some reason connected to the battlefield tensions and potential rivalries on the high seas was the agreement that a free society allowed for the realization of a nation's true productive powers. In addition to its intrinsic wrongs, slavery barred modernization and had to be removed. Slavery's inhumanity enabled European leaders to help Lincoln realize that he had to abolish slavery for his war goals to be understood abroad, and emancipation of African Americans in areas of the South not held by Union armies convinced the Europeans that his goals were honorable. He agreed with Seward that to avoid violence and to maintain his political majority he had to wait for emancipation until 1863. Second, emancipation occurred at the same time Britain and the United States were continuing their antebellum cooperation to expand overseas commerce. The continuation of their informal partnership in the Far East echoed their cooperation to stop the slave trade. Historians of Civil War diplomacy have generally overlooked this dimension of the British-American Civil War relationship.

One reason that the partnership to end slavery did not occur in the first two years of the Civil War was Lincoln's refusal to act decisively on the question. European leaders could not understand his position on slavery. Watching a Europe that was breaking up into new nations, the British and French believed that the Confederacy was another example of liberal nationalism. Russell and Gladstone thus had a hard time understanding that the Union was fighting for its freedom. Britain was moving its colonies to independence, and the Liberals believed that the Union cause was imperialistic. They did not appreciate Lincoln's tenet that freedom and slavery could not coexist under the U.S. Constitution. After the autumn of 1861 Lincoln tried to allay European suspicions that the Union was fighting a selfish, imperialistic war.[1] He made emancipation a predominant war aim because he agreed with the extreme abolitionists, whose power was growing in Washington throughout the second half of 1862, that to cement good feelings with Britain he had to make a strong statement about obliterating slavery.

Unionist antislavery actions occurred first in the late summer and fall of 1861. In early August Congress passed the Confiscation Act to seize property—including slaves—that aided Rebel war efforts. In September, minister to Spain Carl Schurz, a German refugee from the revolutions of 1848, persuaded Lincoln to include slavery in his justifications for the war effort to Europe against the South. Early in 1862 Schurz returned from Spain and recommended that Lincoln block European intervention with an emancipation proclamation. Lincoln responded, "You may be right. Probably you are. I have been thinking so myself. I cannot imagine that any European power would dare to recognize and aid the Southern Confederacy if it became clear that the Confederacy stands for slavery and the Union for freedom." At the same time, the son of former king Louis Philippe of France, the Prince de Joinville, prodded Lincoln on emancipation. Joinville's plan aided Lincoln's gradual emancipation plan to arrest the chances of a bloody slave insurrection that frightened the Europeans. Joinville remarked that the feelings of repugnance for a slave state kept the Europeans from intervention, but they could not understand why Lincoln delayed. Lincoln was also prompted by news from Charles Francis Adams that Mason and Slidell were hinting about the South's willingness to approve gradual emancipation in return for recognition. Adams thought they were creating a deception and believed it was serious enough to merit countermeasures to extinguish Russell's perception that the North was fighting an imperialistic war. In response, the president did what he felt he could safely do without arousing the Democrats and others who did not want a war on slavery. Lincoln's antislavery actions made a difference over the next several months. On 16 April 1862, representatives of the British Anti-Slavery Society met with Adams to praise the Federals for opposing slavery.[2] Since the war was not going well, Lincoln was aware that general emancipation reflected desperation, and he had not disguised his feeling and his opinion that slavery was a primary cause of the war.

Each new antislavery measure drew Union foreign policy closer to the European powers. Lincoln signed a law prohibiting slavery in all the national territories that overturned the Dred Scott decision, which had declared excluding slavery unconstitutional a few years before the Civil War. The issue of resettling runaway slaves was growing into the need to abolish slavery in the Border States of Maryland, Kentucky, Delaware, and Missouri where state laws prohibited runaways, but Union military commanders were reluctant to return them. Lincoln knew that, as long as slavery remained in the Border States, they might join the Confederacy. This threat impinged on his foreign policy because while slavery remained in these states the Europeans could not view the Union's efforts as united in waging a battle between freedom and slavery. Lincoln worked with "exceptional finesse" to disarm Radical Republicans by listening to Charles Sumner's abolitionist talk to ease tensions. By the end of the summer of 1862, Lincoln was compelled to begin emancipation to strengthen the Union in Europe and to relieve friction with the Border States.[3]

Lincoln also used the prewar tradition of private treaty making to assault the slavery issue in the pre–Emancipation Proclamation months. This initiative was seen in the Anti-Slave Trade Treaty of 1862, which Lincoln believed was another gesture to gain the powers' understanding. The treaty manifested national interests of both the United States and Britain. It culminated a long period of calumny about the British right to search American vessels suspected of carrying slaves and a briefer period of cooperation up to 1861. Southern congressmen had been powerful enough to prevent the U.S. Navy from enforcing its anti–slave trade laws, which put more pressure on the British to stop the slave trade. In 1818 Britain proposed a convention to the United States for searching suspected slavers and for establishing an international police force. A law of 1820 slated the death penalty for slavers but was not enforced until Lincoln's presidency. Another law, which cut arrests in half, allowed seizure of ships with slaves aboard but not if the ships were fitted out for slaves and were caught heading to West Africa for cargoes. The British were prohibited from searching suspected American slavers, which Southern lawmakers interpreted as flagrant violations of peacetime neutral rights. In response, the British suggested how they could police the seas without infringing on the American flag. An agreement to search American vessels without irritating republican pride became the goal of British slave trade diplomacy. In 1824, a second British proposal to extend the right of search requested the Americans to regard slaving as piracy. The Senate restricted search areas severely on the first proposal, and the British dropped the second. In 1842, Article 8 of the Webster-Ashburton Treaty provided for squadrons to operate independently off the West Coast of Africa to stop ships bearing their own flag. Yet Southern political pressure kept the United States from acting without urgency.[4] Slaves landed at Cuba in the 1850s brought the need for closer cooperation. In 1859, Britain and the United States agreed that the Royal Navy could board suspicious vessels. If a mistake was discovered, Britain agreed to admit trespass and pay reparations.[5]

At the same time, Russell tried again to increase cruisers around Cuba, a hotbed of the slave trade. Somerset, however, feared arousing the United States' ire but wanted his view kept private. Unless the British contacted ships flying the American flag, their vigil was difficult to execute. Palmerston was cautious and told the House of Commons that he had withdrawn cruisers from Cuban waters because Southern slave interests pressed Washington. Yet he refused to verbally attack the United States and said that a British warship seizing a slave ship without papers had to be judged by an Admiralty court and condemned by British law while American warships had no recourse under U.S. law. The prime minister commented that Southern officers commanding naval vessels refused to make searches while Northern captains "gave them 'very effective and vigilant co-operation.'" On the eve of the Civil War Palmerston did not believe that many Cuban slaves got to the United States. Yet he needed American cooperation to stop the Cuban slave trade.[6]

American cooperation occurred as sectional tensions mounted. The Admiralty received reports from the West African station (where steps were taken to block the coast from the interior slave chiefs) that the American navy was trying to suppress the slave trade. British officers' comments were promising because they had been critical of the lackadaisical American attitude. This situation changed when the Civil War broke out and the American patrol was recalled for blockade duty. In July 1861, British consul Robert Bunch in Charleston warned Russell that Southerners might take advantage of the United States African Squadron being withdrawn for blockade duty. Once the patrol ships were withdrawn, the Southerners might begin to run slavers between Africa and Cuba under the Stars and Stripes to escape capture by British patrols. On hearing this, Russell ordered Lyons to ask Seward to prevent slaving under the American flag.[7] Seward complied, and a significant movement in the antislavery partnership occurred on 5 October when the Foreign Office informed the Admiralty that Lincoln's cabinet was willing to allow British cruisers to stop American ships suspected of being slavers. Moreover, Seward informed Russell that slavers would no longer be permitted to fit out at New York. Seward believed that these steps made possible the final liquidation of the African slave trade. He replied to Lyons that he wanted some Union warships to return to African waters and reiterated Lincoln's support for properly conducted British searches.[8]

As the anti–slave trade partnership developed, private steps were being taken to negotiate an anti–slave trade convention until the *Trent* affair. Palmerston wrote Russell on 24 September to press for Union help against the slave trade "by giving us facilities for putting it down when carried under the United States flag." Accordingly, on 19 October Russell instructed Lyons to discuss the matter with Seward. Their conversations were agreeable. Indeed, on 12 November 1861, Lyons acted on Russell's instructions and signed an "informal memorandum" with Seward. With this agreement, Seward accepted Russell's desire for British warships to search and detain American ships within thirty leagues of the African coast for reasonable cause that slaves were on board under the precedent that this activity could not be prosecuted elsewhere. Despite Seward's help, Lyons still thought the former's motives were suspect and wanted a formal treaty to hold the American at his word. Russell agreed and held out for a convention.[9]

Negotiations were revived on 10 February 1862 in the wake of the relief and cooperation produced by the *Trent* affair. The questions of search and seizure on the high seas were difficult. A slaver could still escape the British search by hoist-ing an American flag. To erase this unsavory act, Lincoln proved that he meant business against captured slavers when he refused to commute the death sentence against the pirate Nathaniel Gordon, convicted as a slave trader four times. Gor-don was hung on 7 February—the first captain of a slave vessel to be executed in the United States. Lincoln's action was popular in England. Russell gave Seward "full credit for his sincerity" and repeated that bad feelings from British arrests of American vessels required a formal agreement. He continued to prod Seward by recalling that the Webster-Ashburton Treaty had promised eighty American cannons off Africa and noted that there was currently but one American patrol vessel with twenty-two cannons on station. The Royal Navy on the West Indies station had not stopped a vessel flying the America flag since 1858 when a naval war almost erupted over a British seizure of an American ship. The Civil War made seizures more difficult. Russell noted that the American vessels withdrawn for blockade duty inflicted damage on British commerce. The least the Americans could do, Russell argued, was to cooperate in an efficient anti–slave trade treaty enabling a sufficient number of British warships to compensate for the loss of American vessels on the African station. He was encouraged by Seward's coop-eration. Palmerston supported a formal pact by using as leverage the argument of British Unionists that the Civil War was fought to extinguish slavery.[10]

Lincoln's leadership in making the Anglo-American Treaty of 1862 was as criti-cal as Seward's and Russell's. American foreign policy made a "radical change" because Lincoln wanted a treaty even if Britain did not change its nationality laws, which had long been an obstacle to settlement. The president saw the treaty as an indirect method of spreading his desire for eventual emancipation. The senior leaders of both governments had cleared the way for private negotiations. Lyons presented Russell's treaty draft to Seward at the State Department on 15 March 1862. Because Seward thought the United States should be the cornerstone of the treaty, he rejected the draft on 21 March, as it gave the Royal Navy the right of search and seizure of American ships, and the negotiations had to be perceived in the Americans' favor to pass through Congress. Yet Seward realized that, other than the nationalistic issue, Lincoln's cabinet and the Senate approved of the treaty. Antislavery feelings were strong in Congress, as even then it debated freeing the slaves and not returning fugitives. Lincoln read a speech to Sumner enjoining Congress to help fund states gradually abolishing slavery. It was an overwhelm-ing success in both Congress and the newspapers. The usually critical *New York Tribune* maintained, "We thank God that Abraham Lincoln is President of the United States, and the whole country, we cannot doubt, will be thankful that we have at such a time so wise a ruler."[11]

As with the antebellum treaties, the Anglo-American Treaty of 1862 was made quickly in Washington. Lyons speedily redrafted the treaty and was confident of

Russell's approval. To avoid the impression that Seward submitted to the British, Lyons gave Seward the credit for drafting the treaty and consented to Seward's provision that search and seizure run for a decade. This was a "manufactured conflict" to make it seem that the Americans had gotten better terms.[12] On 7 April 1862, Seward and Lyons concluded a treaty that provided for mutual search and trial by mixed courts. It armed British and American warships with special anti-slave warrants to search suspicious ships in specified areas. Slavers were to be sent to mixed Anglo-American courts. Seward wrote Lincoln a congratulatory note on 24 April for the "unanimous ratification" of the treaty, calling it "the most important act of your life and of mine."[13] Ratifications were exchanged in London on 25 May 1862, and Lincoln signed it in July. To enforce the treaty, the United States reinforced its squadron off the West African coast.[14] The treaty met Palmerston's goal for the mutual right to search ships off Africa and Cuba. (Seward remarked that if such a treaty had been concluded in 1808 there would have been no Civil War.) The treaty gave Lincoln political favor with antislavery Radical Republicans and encouraged British abolitionists. James A. Rawley believes that the treaty was part of the "second American revolution." It did not change the British attitude about intervention. The ministry viewed it as a feeble attempt to weaken the Confederacy, but it cleared up British confusion about Union war aims and it moved cooperation to a new level.[15]

The treaty kept the private diplomacy behind the rapprochement. It was popular on Capitol Hill because it ended the slave trade and pledged goodwill between Britain and the United States. Sumner worked closely with Seward to obtain unanimous Senate approval on 24 April and wept when he told Lyons that it passed unanimously. Lyons visited Sumner that evening "in great joy, happy that his name was signed to a treaty of such importance—perhaps the last slave-trade treaty which the world will see. He overflowed with gratitude & delight." Earlier that day Sumner had rushed from the Senate to give Seward the good news and found the secretary lying on his sofa at the State Department. Upon being told that it put an end to the slave trade and was a "pledge of goodwill & friendship between the U. S. & England," Seward cried "Good God! The Democrats have disappeared! This is the greatest act of the Administration." Seward exclaimed in similar fashion to Lincoln. Moreover, the treaty drew good feelings from the House of Commons, which was busy dashing the Confederate lobby, and helped change British opinion toward the United States when the Union's military fortunes were not faring well. Henry Adams said that Seward's diplomacy altered British opinion in the Union's favor. Seward took advantage of the treaty's transatlantic popularity to write a dispatch to the elder Adams on 14 April 1862 that included a map showing how the Union army was strangling the South. He argued that the North was victorious everywhere, that the chief Southern ports were about to be opened, and that Britain and France should announce that they did not intend to recognize Confederate independence. Russell echoed the ministry's position that it was too early to determine a victor. He remarked that the British economy suffered from the blockade. Lincoln was on his way to making emancipation one of the main reasons for fighting the war, but he had more to do as the Anglo-American Treaty of 1862 was not a substitute for emancipation.[16]

Only one member of Lincoln's cabinet disapproved of the treaty. Otherwise the cabinet was unanimous in support, as was Congress. Despite the cabinet's support, Secretary of the Navy Welles criticized Seward for not consulting the cabinet about the treaty. The capable secretary believed that Lyons had maneuvered Seward into agreeing to a limited Union right to search suspected slavers instead of enemy warships, and then only in certain areas. Welles believed that the British took advantage of the Union's poor military performance to get the treaty concluded privately when Lincoln's government needed popularity. (It seemed to escape Welles that Palmerston's ministry, with its narrow majority, needed the treaty for the same reason.) Welles believed that Seward thought primarily of his self-interest in making the treaty, and "he has been inconsiderate or duped, perhaps both." For these reasons, Welles refused to furnish cruisers under the treaty despite Lyons's clarification that treaty powers were in addition to existing belligerent rights. Although Welles retreated after Lyons's explanation, he still suspected Seward of going too far to conciliate Britain. (Certainly Sumner had not, which meant that the Radicals supported the treaty.) Seward retorted that Welles was unable to think beyond the Navy Department. In reality, Welles had lost his usual objectivity when it came to Lyons, whose relations with the Navy Department were never good. Welles and his staff believed that Britain was helping the Confederates build a navy and blockade-runners. But Welles was isolated, and a stride had been made toward helping Britain control the slave trade because slavers could no longer hide beneath the Union Jack.

The Anglo-American Treaty of 1862 seemed to produce immediate results, arbitrating against the odds of British and French intervention early in this pivotal year for relations. On 8 August 1862, Somerset announced to Palmerston that the slave trade had ceased for the time being. By early 1864, First Naval Lord Frederick William Grey wrote that the United States was "able and willing" to use cruisers to execute the treaty. Somerset wrote to Palmerston that since the American flag no longer shielded the slavers from search, chances of ending the trade were better than ever.[17] Although Sir Alexander Milne's fleet never captured a slaver in his four years on station, the treaty helped with the dramatic decline of the slave trade during the Civil War years. By mid-1862 prices for slaves had declined. It was no longer good business to try to bring slaves to the South. The system of capturing Africans and getting them to the slavers began to rot away in West Africa. As Philip Van Doren Stern writes, "Victory against slavery had been achieved on the African front before it had been won at home." In 1862 more than two thousand slaves were reported by British authorities to have been landed in Cuba and sold for $306 a person. But in 1864–65 only 143 slaves were landed in Cuba, and all were rescued. Landing slaves was made extremely difficult by stepped-up naval vigilance and the prosecutions of the captain-general of Cuba. In 1864, Eardley Wilmot, commander of the British West African Squadron, reported to the Admiralty that plenty of slaves were brought to the coast, but dealers were afraid to buy them because of the increased patrols under the treaty. Thus Wilmot believed that "the year 1864 will be recorded in the annals of slave-trading history as one of complete success over the well-contrived plans of the slave-dealers." Royal Navy historian Colin Baxter believes that the British annexation of Lagos (a hotbed of slaving), the treaty, and increased vigilance along the coast "virtually abolished" the African slave trade in 1865. Somerset contributed by refusing to use the Royal Navy to arouse the United States to cooperate in making and enforcing the treaty. By 1870 the transatlantic slave trade had disappeared.[18]

With the treaty in hand, later in April Seward advised Lincoln against a hasty emancipation without decisive battlefield victory. Neither leader feared that Britain needed such a clear edict to support the Union. They could buy time until the political climate improved for the Republicans, and they could withstand the Radicals in their own party and the peace Democrats. Seward displayed courage when he argued that a premature emancipation proclamation looked like desperation. This time it was Lincoln who heeded Seward's advice to wait for a decisive battlefield victory. Seward's act converged with British fears of a massive slave insurrection once emancipation was proclaimed. Their trust in him grew to the point that John Slidell wrote on 23 June 1862, "I think that it is now more evident than ever that England will do nothing that may offend the Lincoln government."[19]

Seward again drew Lincoln's approval on 22 July 1862 when the president presented the first draft of his Emancipation Proclamation to the cabinet. The draft held for general emancipation on 1 January 1863 in all areas not held by Union forces. The secretary of state approved the draft but again recommended that Lincoln postpone it. Things were not going well on the battlefield, with McClellan's inability to see the battlefield and the composition of enemy forces that he greatly outnumbered. After getting within five miles of Richmond, Robert E. Lee rallied the Rebels, and "Little Mac" lost whatever courage he had been able to muster to advance to victory. McClellan's failure to take Richmond and his subsequent retreat across the Virginia Peninsula with great losses from disease and heat, with Lee's army in pursuit, moved Seward to warn the president that a proclamation of emancipation coming under any circumstances except clear military victory "would be considered the last shriek of the retreat." "I suggest sir," he continued, "that you postpone its issue until you can give it to the country supported by military success." Lincoln immediately accepted Seward's advice.[20]

Seward was on the mark. The country was not ready for a general emancipation, as evidenced by the elections of 1862. The Republicans lost four states to the Democrats in the elections to the House of Representatives (New York, Ohio, Indiana, and Illinois), and Pennsylvania, which Lincoln carried in 1860, split the vote. There were 102 Republicans and Unionists and seventy-five Democrats in the House in the Thirty-eighth Congress. Lincoln therefore lacked a firm majority to declare emancipation, and the returns disclosed the public's dissatisfaction with the conduct of the war. The president's hesitations on emancipation weakened the Republican Party and pleased nobody.[21]

And despite their support for the Anglo-American Treaty of 1862, Lincoln's cabinet members were disdainful of Seward because of the private diplomacy that he used to hatch the pact. As Welles had demonstrated, they felt deprived of inside information (often with good reason). Yet Lincoln was fully in support of Seward's conciliatory policy. As Lyons was about to embark for England on leave, Lincoln told him, "I suppose my position makes people in England think a great deal more of me than I deserve, pray tell 'em I mean 'em no harm." While he was home, Lyons told his superiors that Lincoln and Seward complemented each other so that when one blew hot against Britain, the other blew cold. Lyons understood that the previous year the president had restrained Seward's chauvinism to negate a foreign war, but he had observed firsthand how Seward had resolved the *Trent* affair.[22]

With Lincoln behind him, Seward did not hesitate to maintain friendly relations with Britain after the anti–slave trade treaty. On 10 October 1862, the secretary of state asked Welles to modify the latter's instructions concerning the treaty. Seward wanted to be relieved of the responsibility of sending cruisers to help the British off the coast of Africa. Welles did not object to Seward's request even though it was not to the navy's advantage against the Confederacy, as combined tactics to defeat the Rebels were becoming more important. Welles believed that Seward had hatched the treaty to curry popularity for himself with the abolitionist and antislavery groups and to flatter his "vanity and egotism." He also "has undertaken an ostentatious exhibition of his power to the legations." Welles reasoned that the British detected Seward's drive for power and took advantage of it because it weakened the navy's abilities. He worried that the treaty caused the United States to surrender its right of search, which gave up American belligerent rights at a time when the Confederates could take advantage of it.[23]

Back from leave in November, Lyons displayed further cordiality when he told one of Welles's assistants on 12 December that "he well understood and rightly appreciated" Welles's position not to surrender the right of search to the British. Asst. Sec. of the Navy Gustavus Fox, who was as critical of the British as his superior, told Welles that Lyons wanted "a declaratory or supplementary clause to make the belligerent right of search and the treaty right of search compatible." Welles sensed that "this whole roundabout proceeding is one of Seward's schemes ... to get his mistake rectified without acknowledging his error. Lord Lyons is no more blind to this trick than I am."[24]

Despite what Welles thought, private diplomacy continued to make the difference. The Lincoln-Seward collaboration grew into the Lincoln-Seward-Lyons collaboration, which gained strength in 1863. Lyons tipped off Seward about a Confederate plot to release prisoners of war from an island on Lake Erie. The two diplomats met at Seward's small dinners to informally discuss problems. Lyons often encountered Seward on his walks, and Seward often asked the British minister to join him in his carriage. Charles Sumner was a frequent dinner guest at the British legation. Knowing all of this, Welles claimed sarcastically that Lyons shaped American foreign policy.[25]

Despite what Welles and other members of the cabinet thought about the motives of Lyons and Seward, Lyons and his consuls supported neutrality and nonintervention throughout the war that assisted the Union's foreign policy and diplomacy. Lyons had good reasons for consistently recommending against intervention (such as he had done to Russell during his leave in Britain) no matter how awful the bloodshed became. Throughout 1861 and 1862 Consul Bunch wrote from Charleston that the South was overextended and weakly led. He warned Russell not to be fooled by Confederate advocates in Britain. Moreover, several consuls wrote that the Union blockade had little effect on cotton exports. What caused a shortage was the self-imposed Confederate embargo and destruction of cotton to force Britain and France into the war. Southern planters and cotton traders prevented cotton from being loaded on British blockade-runners. Southern newspapers and the Confederate Congress voiced unanimous support for the embargo. These tactics aroused the British before the war was six months old when the cotton embargo began the South's implosion. The consuls' warnings were coupled with the ministry's belief that the North was peaceful toward Britain. At no time during the Civil War did Britain need much Southern cotton for a number of reasons.[26]

For all of his misgivings about the North's war prospects, Lyons upheld Seward's confidence in him by refusing to support intervention schemes in Washington. Clearly aware of the South's weaknesses, Lyons refused to listen to Mercier's idea for a cease-fire to give the fighting emotions a chance to subside, to end the blockade, and to enable Britain and France to recognize Confederate independence. Lyons told Mercier, who had Rebel leanings, that Britain could not recognize the Confederacy. The British cabinet took Lyons's recommendation not to rankle Seward. Russell assured Lyons of Britain's continued neutrality on 2 November 1861.[27]

Russell knew that if he did not comply, Britain might someday be in the North's position. In early February 1862, Russell told Adams that British merchants were on their own recognizance. The foreign secretary told Mason that Britain continued to recognize the Northern blockade's effectiveness. This disclosure moved Mason to believe that Russell did not support the Confederacy and wanted to continue inaction. Lyons was equally careful with Seward, and the blockade issue vanished.[28]

With the large issue of the blockade agreeable, Britain and the United States were freer to concentrate on overseas commerce together. A further reason for the rapprochement came with the continuation of geopolitical convergence in China and Japan that had begun during the antebellum period. In China there were common commercial aims and agreements stemming from the 1840s on the use of force to keep that ancient country open to the West.

From 1850 to 1865, British and American mercenaries and sailors helped the Chinese government quell the Taiping Rebellion in southern China and the Yangtze Valley. An American commissioner was recalled in 1853 for following an antiBritish policy in China, and a new man was sent out to cooperate. Robert M. McLane, son of an American secretary of state, was instructed to help the British obtain commercial concessions through a renewal of its treaty with the Chinese.[29] Although proclaiming official neutrality, the United States had offered assistance to the British and the French against the Chinese from 1856 to 1860. Nearly one hundred British sailors and marines were killed on the Pieho River in June 1859 while taking a treaty to Peking. The Chinese denied further entry to the British and French diplomats who wanted to reside at Peking. The senior American officer in China helped the British recover their wounded, saying, "Blood is thicker than water." News of this incident reached Britain two months later and caused widespread dismay at the atrocities.[30]

In the Pieho River incident the cabinet lines formed around inactivity and neutrality. Lewis, Gladstone, Sir Charles Wood, and Somerset wanted caution. Lewis thought that Britain should have remonstrated before fighting. Gladstone doubted Britain's right to continue without further talks with the Chinese. Somerset thought that the navy and the diplomats made judgment errors. The unauthorized fighting placed the cabinet in a precarious position. The first lord felt that Sir James Hope, the British naval commander, acted brashly in commanding from the lead warship where he could not see the action and was wounded as a result and recommended that he not receive an award for gallantry. The ever cautious Somerset continued to work for Anglo-Chinese collaboration because the French were untrustworthy allies, the British public did not want a war, and British forces were needed at home to watch France as Napoleon III annexed Savoy in March 1860, when British regulars from India reached China. The Chinese campaign was costly to the retrenchment-minded Gladstonians. The House of Commons was moved by John Bright and Thomas Baring to question expenditures and settled on a sum of less than £500,000.[31] As we have seen before in such incidents, Palmerston and Russell wanted a stronger policy. They believed that their diplomats had acted correctly in refusing to use any other than the usual

Pieho River route. On 24 September 1859, the cabinet majority upheld them to pursue additional war with the Chinese. The two old leaders seemed to be upheld in late October when news reached the ministry that the Chinese had mistreated an American representative who had used an alternate route to Peking. A successful war effort was prosecuted and a British legation was established in Peking by the treaty of 24 October 1860.[32]

As the Civil War began, the United States benefited when the British and French defeated the Chinese and established new treaties. Behind the Anglo-French military shield, the Americans widened their commercial corridor in the Yangtze Valley, which in turn enhanced American coastal shipping. The Americans promised to act as brokers of relations between the Chinese and any third power that might threaten the government. The Civil War disrupted American trade in China while the British moved to exploit their new treaty advantages and monopolized trade by the 1860s, a further reason that made peace with the United States necessary throughout the Civil War.

Similarly, the United States needed peace with Britain because it became more involved in the Far East before the Civil War and wanted to continue its advances during the conflict. In this regard, Seward's imperial vision held that slavery was a hindrance to an outward thrust. He promoted peaceful commercial expansion to fulfill America's "higher destiny" to project republican principles abroad. His argument unfolded as follows: Slavery had to be removed because expansion needed a supportive federal policy, domestic peace, rapid and efficient use of resources, and a thorough revision of American political economy. Slavery prevented an efficient labor system and was an obstacle to modernization. Increasing freedoms, western railroads, overseas commerce, and peaceful acquisition of contingent areas, such as Canada and Mexico, could attain these dynamic goals and avoid a depression. Slavery might not be contained unless the North won the Civil War. Otherwise, the continuation of a government of parochial slaveholders might oppose expansion to save the South's economy.[33]

This rationale moved Seward's cooperative British policy. In addition, he was planning postwar expansion in China. He based his plans on China's commercial potential and "peaceful cooperation with European powers to support Chinese independence, stability, and receptiveness to Western civilization, including trade." Britain was a part of his plans. He implemented his plans through Anson Burlingame, a young Republican, whom he dispatched as minister to China in 1861. Burlingame established such a positive reputation that at the end of his mission in 1867 the Chinese asked him to lead a team of British and French diplomats to establish better relations between the imperial government and the nine treaty powers. British supporters abetted his selection. Burlingame contracted amicable relations with Sir Frederick Bruce, the British minister to China, who ameliorated Britain's aggressive policies. Burlingame and Bruce met daily. They agreed to a "cooperative policy" to assist both traders and humanitarians. Bruce represented the strongest influence in China, but Burlingame's amiability and talent gave him power beyond American means. They succeeded in getting the French and Russians to approve a policy that did not threaten Chinese territory or jurisdiction and caused the Western powers to stay out of Chinese internal affairs unless the government breached the treaties. Their personal diplomacy extracted further commercial concessions from the Chinese. Burlingame convinced the imperial government to warn the *Alabama* and its sister ships away from the coast. He helped to initiate surveys of coal deposits and a translation of Henry Wheaton's *Elements of International Law* to facilitate future negotiations.[34] As we will see in a later chapter, the British government rewarded Bruce for his close personal diplomacy with Burlingame and his desire for friendly relations by appointing him to succeed Lyons in 1865.

Burlingame served as United States minister until November 1867, when he resigned to become the first diplomatic representative of the Chinese government to the West, where he gained Western respect and understanding for China. In 1868, Burlingame's mission to the United States with Chinese delegates emphasized Chinese modernization. In 1869, the mission visited London, where Foreign Secretary Clarendon upheld Bruce's policy by writing that Britain did not intend to infringe on the Chinese for commercial advantage, which he later retracted in the face of popular opposition. The departure of Burlingame and Bruce from China and Clarendon's death in 1870 caused the cooperative policy to lose some of its force. However, Clarendon's support for Burlingame and Bruce breached Britain's war policy for concessions and enabled the cooperation in China to the benefit of both Western governments. The alternative was the sharper policy offered by British merchants. They wanted a return to the aggressive policy of the 1850s, which had brought commercial gain. As David Pletcher points out, "British policy never rejected Burlingame's goals of cooperation and conciliation outright but tried to reconcile these goals to British interests."[35]

As in his support for British-American cooperation in China, Seward's drive for commercial expansion caused him to refuse to use the slavery issue to embarrass Palmerston in Europe where Britain was severely compromised.[36] In February 1864, Seward thought that Palmerston might revoke recognition of Confederate belligerency to shed American complications. The secretary of state had good reasons for his thinking, because Russell severely mismanaged the Schleswig-Holstein affair and ended up isolated in the cabinet with Palmerston and Lord Chancellor Westbury as the only ones who wanted war against Prussia and Austria. Observing this split, Derby made his contemptuous "meddle and muddle" statement that broke the truce between the two parties. British prestige was the lowest of the century, and the Conservatives tried to oust the Liberals over foreign policy. Derby and Disraeli won in the Lords by nine votes but ended up eighteen short in the Commons, and Palmerston survived.[37]

While Palmerston faced his sternest foreign policy test since the Civil War began, another American ally came to his aid to douse an attack against Lincoln's conciliatory foreign policy. On 11 January 1864, as chair of the Senate Foreign Relations Committee, Sumner buried James A. MacDougall's resolution to declare war on France if its troops were not withdrawn from Mexico by 15 March. Since the previous January, Sumner had told the California senator "not to present anything offensive to France." The *Chicago Herald* and the *New York Tribune* regretted Sumner's action, but Lincoln was thankful for it. In April, Sumner prevented passage of another punitive resolution aimed at France by Rep. Henry Winter Davis of Maryland after it passed the House of Representatives by 104–0.[38]

For once, Sumner and Seward were political allies. In early September 1865 Seward wrote John Bigelow, American minister to France, that Americans were "strongly disincline[d] from seeking aggrandizement by means of military conquest." Territorial expansion could only occur by the "annexation of adjacent peoples . . . through their own consent."[39]

On 30 November 1865, Napoleon proposed a mutual defense alliance with Britain against potential American invasions of Mexico or Canada, which the British quickly rejected because they distrusted Napoleon. As Henry Blumenthal points out, "Such an alliance would, therefore, not only be inoperative, but might provoke the injury it would be designed to cure." Seward; Montholon, the new French minister in Washington; and Foreign Minister Drouyn de Lhuys opposed Napoleon. Mexico was unpopular to the French opposition, and the United States continued to recognize Juárez. The Mexican civil war continued, and war clouds hung over the Rhine. In the face of France's European enemies and Britain's inability to help, even Napoleon's wife agreed that Mexico was a costly mistake. On 15 January 1866 the emperor issued the withdrawal order.[40]

By this time Seward knew that Napoleon was going to withdraw from Mexico. James Watson Webb's secret mission to Napoleon's court in November 1865 convinced Seward that Napoleon was going to evacuate his troops over the next two years and leave Mexico to the people. Webb divulged this confidence to Seward in early December, and Seward asked Webb to inform Napoleon of President Andrew Johnson's "cordial approbation" for Napoleon's solution to the Mexican question. Seward safely and openly pressed France to withdraw in order to silence his political critics who wanted him to get tough with France.[41]

The *Moniteur* announced the completion of French withdrawal by November 1867. Seward refused to interrupt because he wanted France to extricate itself "voluntarily." He even tried to obtain clemency for Maximilian through Juárez but could not stay the former's execution on 19 June 1867. Maximilian's wife, Carlotta, escaped to "wander insane over the face of Europe for the next sixty years." Despite Seward's soft touch, Franco-American enmity remained, and the National Assembly feared that in a "moment of peril you will find the Americans against us."[42]

Napoleon's utterances confirmed Seward's belief that he need not fear European recolonization threats in the Western Hemisphere. He first took this position in 1852 when he reaffirmed the Monroe Doctrine in refusing to support Lewis Cass and others who believed that Britain and the Europeans were intent upon reconquest. Seward remarked that the Eastern Hemisphere was the site of future international commercial and territorial rivalries. He was interested in continuing Franklin Pierce's move to annex Hawaii, for instance, while predicting that the Pacific was "the chief theatre of events in the world's great hereafter." In 1856, Seward believed that rivalry depended not on armies but on "invention and industry"; moreover, Russia was the ultimate rival in the Far East because he believed that Britain and France were "temporary" and "ephemeral" European powers. For the time being, Britain was the chief obstacle to Asian trade and the model to be emulated. Seward showed the same appreciation for Britain's method of empire building for two decades. "Wise old England!" he then wrote. "How she fortifies her island Realm, and yet all the while develops and improves the energies of her people, while she does not hesitate to undertake the police regulation of the world!" The envious Seward wanted New York to ultimately replace London as the world's financial center, but he needed British products to carry across the United States to the Pacific and Asia. Because of this need he saw Britain and the United States as commercial partners rather than as enemies.[43]

Seward was the leading American expansionist from the 1840s onward, with an original vision. He saw the unity of land and sea transportation and he supported maritime interests such as whaling.[44] He saw the continuity in American history and its destiny through commerce more clearly than even John Quincy Adams had. In the 1840s Seward believed that the Pacific Northwest was "part of the larger 'battle . . . for Asia.'"[45]

Seward continued to shape his vision in the 1850s, to the point that it paid dividends during the Civil War, as already seen with British-American cooperation in China. As a Republican senator he supported a transcontinental railroad and annexation of Hawaii. In 1852, he and William McKendree Gwin were granted federal funds to survey the Bering Strait and the northern Pacific "for naval and commercial purposes," that is, to expand the whaling industry and Far Eastern commerce. He talked about buying or conquering Russian America. When he ran for president in 1860 he spoke of eventual annexation of Alaska. Part of his plan was the link to be provided by Perry McDonough Collins's intercontinental telegraph line. Collins became imbued with expansionism as a shipping clerk in New Orleans, where he met Gwin and Robert J. Walker. With connections that reached from J. W. Dent, Ulysses S. Grant's father-in-law, to President Franklin Pierce, in 1856 Collins became American commercial agent for the Amur River District in Siberia with the approval of Pierce and Stoeckel.[46] Seward and Collins held that North America was the vital link between Europe and Asia. Seward advocated federal aid for Collins's plan to tap

Siberia and create overland and communication links between the Amur District and St. Louis to make the United States the world's communication and commercial center. He supported Collins during the decline of public interest in expansion just before the Civil War and during the conflict.

As secretary of state, Seward urged Congress to subsidize Collins, and he instructed his ministers in London and St. Petersburg to obtain grants from both Russia and Britain. The Russian grant was tendered in July 1863. It was to enable the construction of a telegraph cable from the Amur's mouth to Russian America. Collins then traveled to London after Seward instructed Adams to negotiate the right-of-way through British Columbia. Collins discussed the plan with Palmerston, Newcastle, and the governor of the Hudson's Bay Company. They approved the British investment in February 1864, with Newcastle being "constantly courteous and favorably disposed." The agreement authorized Collins to construct a telegraph line through British Columbia to connect Russian America with the United States. Collins's bill passed Congress, and Lincoln signed it on 1 July 1864. Unfortunately for the diplomacy that had occurred, Collins's dream ended with the opening of Cyrus Field's Atlantic Cable on 26 August 1866, which allowed messages through Europe, less than a third of the Amur distance, and Russia's refusal to grant an adequate rebate. Meanwhile, due to the exigencies of the Civil War, work lagged on the intercontinental railroad, Seward's link between Europe and Asia.[47]

Commerce was aided by liberal geopolitics in Republican and British Liberal politics. Neither party was interested in conquest. Seward and Gladstone supported extending the Reciprocity Treaty after it ended in 1866 but failed in the chaotic post–Civil War politics and grievances over the *Alabama* claims. But by this gesture Seward showed that he was uninterested in Sumner's idea of annexing Canada for the *Alabama* reparations. Gladstone and Seward understood the economic codependency. Throughout the Civil War, Seward had no desire to use force to annex Canada because he believed that it would naturally join the United States. Adams explained this vision to Russell in December 1861. Adams's point was that nowhere in Seward's speeches was force mentioned.[48]

The mutual peaceful commercial competition was illustrated in Japan as well. In the early 1850s Britain supported American leadership in Japan because British governments had long opposed trade monopolies. Once the Americans broke through, British trade could follow. Britain had facilitated American trade in China, and now America could do the same for the British in Japan. In the late 1850s Seward espied that the breakthrough by Adm. Matthew C. Perry was working. This most "Asia-oriented" secretary of state of the century said that the Japanese were accommodating their institutions and customs to the commerce of the times and to the law of nations.[49]

Since the 1840s Britain wanted to cooperate with the United States to gain more inroads into Japanese commerce. When serious American inroads were made in the 1850s, the British did not intervene for several reasons. First, merchants were content to take advantage of existing trading opportunities in China and were uninterested in Japan. Second, the Admiralty doubted that it had the naval strength to protect commercial expansion into Japan. Third, Britain became engaged in the Crimean War in March 1854 when American Admiral Perry was about to make a historic commercial treaty with the Japanese. Fourth, Chinese affairs challenged the Foreign Office, and it was not anxious to create more diplomatic incidents.

Despite the Foreign Office's attitude, the London *Times* supported the United States in Japan. The *Times'* American correspondent argued that Perry's maneuvers were apt because the Anglo-Saxons constituted a master race resigned to civilize the "besotted Oriental nations." The *Edinburgh Review* was supportive also. In October 1852 it argued that the Japanese should allow Perry to establish treaty ports because the Japanese could not succeed against modern Western armaments and must be saved for civilization. Nevertheless, the British remained inactive under foreign secretaries Palmerston and the Conservative Malmesbury. The latter refused Russia's requests to unite against American incursions in Japan in 1852, and he refused to allow Sir John Bowring, British consul at Canton, to negotiate directly with Japan. In July 1852 the foreign secretary wrote that he "would be glad to see the trade with Japan open; but they [Her Majesty's government] think it better to leave it to the Government of the United States to make the experiment; and if that experiment is successful, her Majesty's Government can take advantage of that success."[50] In December, Malmesbury informed the British consul at Canton, Sir S. G. Bonham, who replaced Bowring, that Britain appreciated the United States' remaining aloof when Britain opened the China trade. Now they awaited the results of American diplomacy with Japan.[51]

Clarendon became foreign secretary in 1853 and continued inactivity in China and Japan. He wanted to revise Chinese treaties, and he sent the instructions to the new permanent British consul to China, the aggressive Bowring, to the Department of State to show his support for Perry's mission. Clarendon did not want Anglo-American rivalry in the Far East. His instructions to Bowring emphasized that any British action was to be contingent on American commercial successes. Clarendon corrected permanent undersecretary Edmund Hammond's dispatch to Bowring of 8 June 1854 to state that under no circumstances should force be used except in self-defense. He also instructed Bowring to cooperate with the French. Otherwise, Clarendon ordered on 3 July to consider Japan only "when there shall no longer be any danger . . . to Her Majesty's possessions or to British Trade."[52]

With the Crimean War over, Clarendon remained conciliatory toward the United States. During that conflict he had helped bring about the Canadian-American Reciprocity Treaty, while the British concentrated on defeating the Russians in the Near East. In 1855, as Anglo-American tempers flared over the Crampton affair, he remained conciliatory with the United States in China and

Japan. On 8 December, for example, he wrote Bowring that "joint action with the U.S. Commissioner and Naval force would be the best means of bringing the Japanese to view us with favor."[53] For the time being, war with the United States was possible over the Crampton affair, and Clarendon saw that more warships were sent to the China coast to oppose the American navy. He reasoned that if an Anglo-American war did not occur, the British warships might be useful in negotiations with China and Japan. In reality, Clarendon did not want naval diplomacy, and the end of his secretaryship in 1858 showed no change in his conciliatory policy, despite the fact that the United States remained noncommittal to British feelers for cooperation. Since Clarendon had not acted aggressively in Japan, the United States had no reason to become vindictive. Malmesbury took Clarendon's place under the Conservatives and proclaimed to all of his diplomats and the governments to which they were accredited that peace was his leading principle, that he opposed territorial expansion, and that he had no wish for exclusive privileges anyplace in the world. Britain continued with the "extension of commercial and social intercourse between nations."[54]

The bipartisan British "cooperative policy" supported the most-favored nation clauses in treaties with China and Japan. Britain's cooperation was clarified with Perry's treaty with the Japanese in 1854, and not when Perry's expedition was announced, which is an important point. Britain's cooperative policy was announced at the time of Bowring's appointment and took effect only after London heard about Perry's successful diplomacy with the Japanese, which showed the Foreign Office that productive results could be achieved.[55]

In China, in the 1850s an international settlement of British, French, and Americans grew up in Shanghai, the center of trade in the region. Americans lived and worked in British settlements. Yet the usual American Anglophobia injured prospects of long-term cooperation. The Department of State wavered between joining with the British to press for additional commercial concessions and supporting independent initiatives with the Chinese government. There were more reasons to cooperate because Chinese officials treated westerners as "foreign devils."[56]

During the Civil War, Britain and the United States cooperated to maintain their commercial interests in Japan. That ancient kingdom was engaged in a civil war of its own between Japanese government leaders who wanted to open Japan to the West and the popular followers of the ruling classes outside of the government who wanted to keep Japan closed. Seward viewed Japan as an ultimate American trading domicile, and he wanted to work with Britain and France to force the Japanese into the Western commercial sector. The United States promised to build warships to support the Japanese government, although the challenges of the Civil War allowed only one warship to be built. The Japanese were so unskilled at navigating the world oceans that a U.S. naval officer had to take it to Japan.

Seward worked with Townsend Harris, the minister resident in Japan from

1855 to 1861 at the outset of his secretaryship. Harris cooperated with British negotiations with Japan in 1858. He spoke with Lord Elgin, the British negotiator, and
he solved the interpreter problem by loaning Elgin his private secretary. This secretary became almost first secretary to Elgin's mission. Elgin's successful commercial treaty "confirmed the fact of American leadership in the opening of Japan."[57]
Neither Clarendon nor Malmesbury wanted a forceful policy, and Palmerston
showed that he was changing his policy from those of his days as adventurer in
weak states to a realistic policy of nonintervention by not contesting Clarendon's
peaceful Far Eastern policy. (There was remarkable consistency in the devaluing
of Japan by all of the British foreign secretaries of the 1840s and 1850s.) Harris
used his coordination with Sir John Bowring to convince the Japanese to open
their commercial doors. At one point, when his negotiations were breaking down,
Harris quoted Bowring that Britain had hung back from Japan to maintain peace
and because a fleet of British warships appearing in Japanese harbors was not
the way to negotiate. This quotation supported Harris's purpose to convince the
Japanese that they needed the West just as the West needed Japan, with the threat
of the British fleet hovering in the background if he did not get his way.[58]

Harris's inroads were threatened in January 1861 when Henry Hensken, the secretary of the American legation in Japan, was murdered. Seward proposed a naval
demonstration, but Harris talked him out of it and resigned in ill health. Seward
appointed a friend from Albany, Robert H. Pruyn, to replace Harris. Seward told
Pruyn that Japan was semibarbarous—that the government was enlightened but
that the people and the ruling classes were fearful of the West. Pruyn would be
dignified but firm in establishing good relations with British, French, and Russian diplomats in Japan. This position maintained a foothold to accomplish his
commercial goals. Seward instructed Pruyn to take no advantage of American
relations with Japan to gain advantage over the Europeans but to join the powers
if the Japanese became difficult about trade and Christianity, the two prongs of his
Japanese policy.[59]

Pruyn's mission began well because his course was less animated than the other
powers that had commercial treaties with the Japanese. When the Japanese resisted
further commercial incursions by the British and French, there were more mur-
ders and persecutions, and Britain and France used naval force to extract indem-
nification for the losses. Seward had no intention in the midst of the Civil War to
become involved in the Europeans' actions because the United States had no grievances. He wished to stand behind the offensive shield of the British and the French
because their achievements against the Japanese assisted with American security.
Other than that guidance, Pruyn had wide discretionary authority.[60]

Caution was the best policy, because it took three to four months for messages to travel back and forth from Japan to Washington, or two months when
transmitted by telegraph from San Francisco to Washington. This caused Pruyn

to be resourceful and exercise good judgment during a crisis when he had no time to explain the crisis or to await instructions. The first American crisis hit in 1863 when uprisings against foreigners included American nationals. Britain stemmed the crisis by threatening another naval demonstration to elicit indemnities for the injured. Pruyn agreed with the forceful British policy and informed Seward. Pruyn believed that he was easily justified in supporting force when the Japanese burned the American legation buildings at Yedo and attacked American merchant ships. Pruyn cooperated for the first time with Britain and France in a show of force. He ordered the American warship *Wyoming* to demolish attacking Japanese vessels. He wrote Seward on 14 July 1863, and Seward received the account in early October.[61]

In 1864, Pruyn upheld Seward's policy despite the lag in communications. The secretary of state had been wise to give Pruyn extensive discretionary powers. Seward approved of Pruyn's description of the way he had helped stamp out the uprising. Pruyn had by then worked out a program of joint action with the British and other powers by which the Japanese government agreed to pay $3 million and to open another commercial port. Seeing that another warship being built for Japan in the New York yards might be used to strengthen the resistance to Westernization, Seward refused to release the *Fusiyama,* a twenty-four-gun vessel.

Pruyn allied with Britain, France, and Holland by signing an agreement of 30 May 1864 to help the central government of Japan against the warlords. Their objective was to assemble a fleet of warships from each of the navies, reopen the Inland Sea, and attack Choshiu, the gateway to dominating the Straits of Shimonoskei. The leader of the Westerners, Sir Rutherford Alcock, returned to Japan after a two-year absence in England. Alcock acted on his own after informing Russell of his intentions. The seventeen-vessel fleet defeated the warlords and accomplished the alliance objectives before Alcock arrived, and Alcock received Russell's harsh rejection of his punitive plan and was recalled for insubordination.[62]

Seward wanted Pruyn to employ a nonpunitive policy, but he gave the latter wider discretion than Russell had given to Alcock. Pruyn dedicated a rented steamer, the *Ta-Kiang,* to the fleet. An officer and seventeen seamen from the *Jamestown,* an old U.S. warship in the area, manned it. During the fracas against the warlords from 5 to 8 September 1864, the thirty-pound guns aboard the *Ta-Kiang* assisted with the reduction of the fort at the entrance to the Straits of Shimonoseki. The United States thus was very much a part of the offensive naval action, and Pruyn reported that the fleet secured American security in Japan.[63]

Seward's Japanese policy had its critics. On 30 November 1864 Welles was annoyed because Thurlow Weed, Seward's agent and Pruyn's brother-in-law, had secured contracts to build several gunboats for Japan. The exigencies of the Civil War enabled time to build only the *Fusiyama.* Welles smelled corruption and was critical of getting involved with Britain and France in a "war" with Japan with whom he believed the United States had no quarrel. He thought it "wicked" that he had to buy the ship for "such a private purpose, and to impose on the Japanese who have trusted us." He informed Lincoln and Seward that they should not partake of this "swindling" activity.[64]

Nevertheless, Japan was another instance of Seward's cooperation with the powers during the Civil War and puts British-American relations in a larger perspective. It helps to explain why diplomacy retained its antebellum dependability and its private nature. Commercial aims were similar and another reason why Seward evinced international cooperation and eluded international disputes. Lincoln's "One War at a Time" statement was a myth, because he and Seward never intended to fight another war with Britain or anyone. Any such war blocked empire and emancipation. This explanation points out an underlying reason why the United States was anxious to return to a peaceful existence after the Civil War.

11

War's End

Retrenchment and Commerce Ascendant

The Civil War's end brought the rapid disbandment of the Union military and a return to a peacetime economy. Obviously, this event would not have occurred if the United States had wanted to settle its disputes with Britain with force. After Lincoln was assassinated, his plans for peaceful foreign and domestic postwar policies remained in place. The British-American relationship did not falter when Palmerston passed away six months later, on 18 October 1865, and Clarendon, back at the Foreign Office, struggled in the short-lived Russell government that failed to pass a reform bill and went out on 18 June 1866.

With the deaths of two great leaders, the instability in both governments was fortunately not emulated in their diplomatic relations because of the proven co-operation on a host of disputes before and during the Civil War. The stability in relations proved strong enough to withstand outcries in the United States after the war. During the postwar period, American problems headed by the *Alabama* claims caused the continuation of cautious diplomacy. Queen Victoria was often militant toward France and Russia, but she "remained remarkably temperate vis-à-vis the United States, and she never criticized Gladstone for appeasement of the United States." She urged her ministers to be understanding about the *Alabama* claims, thinking that the United States "have just cause of complaint" and not to become upset at the bluster of American senators such as Sumner; she also encouraged Gladstone to continue the wartime rapprochement.[1]

The queen's instincts were correct. Americans showed no interest in invading Canada or annexation. Only Sumner and a few Radical Republicans pressed Seward for annexation. Sumner's idea that Canada be annexed as payment for the indirect damages of the Confederate raiders fell on deaf ears, especially when he mentioned the sum of more than $2 billion for the damages. But even Sumner did not want to take Canada by force, and he of all people did not want war with England no matter how loud he ranted about Britain's supposed support for the Confederacy. Seward toyed with annexation, partially to keep Sumner at bay, and by the last months of his secretaryship in 1868 and 1869, he had discarded the idea in favor of a convention to settle all of the main questions to cap his cooperative history with Britain. He failed for a number of reasons, and the Senate refused to approve the Johnson-Clarendon Convention of 13 January 1869, with the chief elements of a comprehensive treaty contained within it. Private diplomacy in 1869 and 1870 moved in that direction. Thus, instead of moving steadily toward conflict, relations focused on peaceful settlement.

On the *Alabama* claims, Russell and Clarendon refused to accept British responsibility and stalled for good terms from Seward. As in 1850s, Clarendon wanted an entente with the United States to smooth the way to negotiations, and his policy met with a modicum of success. From 1865 to 1871, the *Alabama* claims kept the rapprochement alive because both governments wanted to settle in peace. In other words, as had happened so often before, the longer the dispute went unsettled, the more that fact said about the stability of relations. Indeed, the foreign policy of both powers had by now become exceedingly similar. Both were forced to practice patience and indifference before a vexatious Congress, split apart by the battle over the form of Reconstruction, and generally in opposition to President Andrew Johnson's moderate Lincolnian plan. In support of this interpretation is the reality that along the Canadian-American frontier private cooperation erased Fenian threats midway through 1866 and 1870 and kept the fisheries peaceful after energetic Canadian efforts to impose a tax on Americans fishing in Canadian inshore waters in the wake of the abrogated Reciprocity Treaty. Britain understood that Seward and Johnson could do nothing public to show the Fenians or the New England fishing interests that it meant business because of the impact that Reconstruction politics was having on them. Seward especially did not want to lose political ground, as he still had aspirations of being president. Moreover, his longtime battle with the Radicals continued unabated, and the latter group was sensitive to all that the secretary of state enacted publicly for ammunition to oust him. Thus, as disclosed in the many private letters of Sir Frederick Bruce, Lyons's successor as the British minister to the United States, the British object was to let Seward lead in private and trust that in the last resort he would act with the British and Canadians against the Fenians and support joint policing of the fisheries.[2]

Therefore, despite contentions that British-American relations were at their nadir when the Civil War ended, one development must not be forgotten. Over the next six years the two countries engaged in an all-or-nothing diplomacy whereby all of the antebellum and wartime disputes were merged into one agenda for negotiations. There were numerous reasons to loosen tensions as the Civil War ended. In March 1865, Disraeli explained to the House of Commons that Northerners were tired of war physically and financially and wanted to pursue their own business, for which British loans were needed, and Reconstruction consumed the Federals. Walter Bagehot drew attention to the expense and personnel the Federals needed

Sir Frederick William Augustus Bruce, British minister to the United States, 1865–67. Library of Congress

to occupy the Southern states. There was no united spirit, time, or money to punish England for its alleged misdeeds. The convergence of interests against war saw Britain remaining docile as Jefferson Davis and his tattered government fled from Richmond just before Lee surrendered his starving army at Appomattox on 9 April. As Davis fled into North Carolina, where he was coolly received, John C. Breckinridge of Kentucky, the new Confederate secretary of war, worked for peace with generals Joseph E. Johnston and Pierre Beauregard, two of Davis's greatest antagonists.[3]

Similarly, the British were consumed with domestic issues. The Conservatives had been out of office since 1859 and wanted back in with an electoral reform bill. Throughout the war Palmerston had opposed reforms and opted in that direction only if pushed by his rivals. In fact, interesting tactics were at hand in the passive House of Commons. Conservative leader Disraeli surprised Palmerston by supporting abolition of the income tax by citing the large budget surplus that Gladstone's policies had amassed amid peaceful foreign affairs. To add further credence to Disraeli's position, British leaders sensed that peace continued because they understood the Union's postwar predicament. Speaking for the government, Russell agreed with Disraeli that the Americans were going to be satiated with Reconstruction and remained on the best terms with Charles Francis Adams. Adams was accepted in British society with great warmth as a kind of local hero of the war's success. Britain had only to remain "prudent" to maintain peace.

Lincoln's assassination strengthened Russell's outlook. The president's death had a strong impact on British feelings because his untimely demise magnified his unprecedented accomplishments to preserve the Union and to emancipate African Americans. Russell believed that British shock, the cabinet's successful request to the queen to express sorrow to Mrs. Lincoln, and the outpouring of condolences from the British people curbed further ill will. The London *Times* joined the chorus for peace. News of Lee's surrender and the impending collapse of the Confederacy was received on Sunday, 23 April. Three days later, news reached Britain of Lincoln's assassination and what was thought to be Seward's assassination. The *Times* now bewailed the loss of Lincoln as "a man who could not, under any circumstances, have been easily replaced" and "slowly won for himself the respect and confidence of all." Englishmen, the writer continued, "learned to respect a man who showed the best characteristics of their race in this respect for what was good in the past, acting in unison with a recognition of what was made necessary by the events of passing history." The *Times* also lamented the loss of experience if Seward passed away from his wounds.[4]

Disraeli and Russell were correct that Americans were uninterested in debating Reconstruction or starting another war. Only a few isolated senators, such as Sumner, and Northeastern merchants demanded that Canada be annexed to repay the *Alabama* claims. To quell this outcry, once he had recovered from his wounds by midsummer and was back at work, Seward worked to settle the *Alabama* dispute by swapping British Columbia for the claims, but he had little support either in the United States or in Canada, where nationalism was growing as Confederation moved forward. Nobody wanted to annex anything north of the border. He acquiesced to Adams's advice that Britain refused to cede any of its North American territory, and in 1867 he said that the *Alabama* dispute had to remain unsettled until Britain and the United States worked out a peaceful settlement. In 1868 he said, "It is a truism that commercial and industrial interests continually exert a powerful influence in favor of peace and friendship between the government and people of the United States and Great Britain."[5] Peace was further validated in the July 1865 parliamentary elections. All of the pro-North members were reelected.[6]

Sir Frederick Bruce saw difficulty in the diverse regions of the United States supporting an English war. Instead he viewed the "destruction of the Southern propri-
etary class" as favorable to a peace. Bruce's observation was astute. The war nearly
turned the South upside down. It extinguished one fourth of white men of military
age, half of its livestock and farm implements, tens of thousands of small farms and
large plantations, and thousands of miles of railroads and telegraph wires. "At its
best," Jay Winik tells us, "the Confederacy has the look of a deserted fairground."

> But for the most part, the sights and colors are ugly, even ungodly. . . . dismem-
> bered corpses lie scattered about, their stinking, bloated remains eviscerated
> by rats and scavenger birds, their decaying flesh staring up at the stars at night.
> Where proud antebellum homes and mansions once stood, there is rotting
> wood and cracked paint and weed-choked grass; where Southerners once took
> evening promenade walks down hundred-foot-wide boulevards and through
> acres of rich green parks, there is the stench of urine and feces and decaying
> animal carcasses; and where there was once the clamor of commerce . . . there
> are now ghost towns and equally ghostly urban pockets.[7]

In contrast, Northern economic self-interests concentrated on continuing the
wartime boom in production, and these agricultural and urban interests engaged
in sectional wrangling and thought less about foreign affairs. The Midwest and
West wanted low tariffs instead of the high tariffs in the Northeast. The national
debt was £555.6 million, and British money was needed to repay the debt and
encourage economic growth. Cotton production was ruined. Despite the positive
glow in relations, European bankers refused to loan the United States money, and
financiers failed to pay the debt or lower interest rates until the *Alabama* claims
were settled. The Midwest and the West needed money and trade from their British partners. British confidence returned with the Barings' assumption of "28.7
percent of North American railroad stocks issued through London merchant
banks, worth £34.68 million." This was the largest responsibility of any house for
American finances.[8]

In June 1865, Britain and France withdrew recognition of Confederate belligerency, which dimmed the possibility of a third Anglo-American war. The Franco-
British entente grew closer because of the fear of Federal retribution, but without
a threat by late 1865 the mutual suspicions between Britain and France returned,
although the naval rivalry remained dormant.[9]

The Europeans' concerns about continued violence in the United States were
also eased when it became evident that the Southern states were not held in military subjugation. A nonmilitaristic policy was followed to readmit them. They
were further comforted when the volunteer army was disbanded. Allan Nevins
explains that the anti-martial spirit quickly returned: "The military policy would

have been a death-knell for the political system which American people . . . had inaugurated in 1789, and which had since then been the admiration of the civilized world." The war's tragedies brought a profound sense of human loss. Americans wanted to forget the domestic and international ramifications of the Civil War.[10]

A further reason not to fight over the *Alabama* or other disputes was that British trade with the North grew immensely during the war. The twenty-six MPs for Lancashire sat silently during the parliamentary debates on recognition because the production spawned by the war prevented bankruptcy and a long period of suffering by the workers. Instead of total ruin, the war brought "undreamed of profits." Even the workers worried about being ruined if the war ended. Board of Trade records show that the North and South bought more than $100 million in war supplies from Britain. Confederate privateering enabled England to take over the merchant marine trade from the United States. Transfers of American vessels to the British flag resulted from the Confederate raiders' sinking more than two hundred ships and destroying around $30 million of property. American and European shippers grew afraid to consign cargoes to American ships. Most of the American merchant ships were sold off by 1 July 1864, with England buying $42 million out of a total sale of nearly $65 million. As Owsley points out, "England has fought wars for less than the destruction of the rival's merchant marine." With these gains, both direct and indirect, the peace had to be kept.[11]

This development was not one-sided, which deflected American wrath after the war. British and French businesses were bound to Northern industry. Britain invested heavily in building the Northern infrastructure of canals and railroads. British financial houses funded land development, banking, and public securities. In the 1850s there was a massive expansion in British imports of grain and foodstuffs from the Midwest, which increased during the war. Mechanization and expanded acreage increased grain exports 50 percent from 1861 to 1863 to compensate for poor British and French harvests. In 1863, Sumner wrote Bright that the North was prospering, that travel was increasing, and that incomes were large.[12] Bright knew that 3 to 4 million Britons depended on American foodstuffs.[13]

Part of the North's prosperity during the Civil War resulted from Britain's having to maintain the grain trade to remain the world financial capital. Between 1855 and 1865, Britain's American exports increased by £7 million, and it remained the primary receptacle for American products. The British textile industry lost prominence to heavy coal and iron industries by 1850, meaning that cotton was no longer king in the arena of British needs.[14]

The Federals had further reasons for keeping the rapprochement that trumped the hard feelings about the *Alabama*. Lord John Russell intimated this point when he said that war was impossible because of the massive internal problems of Reconstruction, economic recovery, and territorial expansion. Peace was needed to rebuild and expand the infrastructure. The continuation of manifest destiny to develop the trans-Mississippi West, and Seward's devout interest in humanitarianism and geopolitics, meant expansion of the railroads and establishing dependable communications with the Northeast. Governmental attention was directed at Reconstruction and solving the racial and political problems.[15] Finally, Northern resentment against Britain was precluded by American awareness that Palmerston kept Napoleon III from intervention.[16]

Another mutual reason that precluded fighting was that military retrenchment possessed both countries after the war. Britain was not on a war footing in the 1860s and 1870s, despite the French naval rivalry. First Lord of the Admiralty Somerset followed Gladstone's retrenchment policy to the hilt. The Royal Navy reduced its strength from 85,000 in 1860 to 61,000 in 1870. The Royal Navy in American waters was reduced during the Civil War from forty-two warships during the *Trent* affair to thirty-one by 1864. The number of sailors was reduced from 14,088 to 7,135. The first lord believed that Britain's ironclads were superior, so there was no need for extensive naval modernization.[17]

Retrenchment also dictated British policy toward its North American land force. The British military contingent in Canada was not a threat to the United States either before or after the Civil War. Nor was the U.S. Army a threat to Canada. By 1870, Prime Minister Gladstone and Colonial Secretary Cardwell had withdrawn most of the imperial garrisons from Canada and forced the new Dominion to raise a trained militia to protect the frontier. As cabinet ministers they had begun military withdrawal in 1864 when Cardwell took the Colonial Office. He succeeded in pressing the British North Americans to enter a confederation. Canadian dominionhood in July 1867 was a product of a long-term policy and imperial retrenchment during the Civil War years and not a threat to the Union. The upheaval south of the border helped the Canadians see the need to reconcile provincial disputes for a new central government to deal with the United States on reciprocity, fisheries, and boundary issues. As they preferred to do in the early 1850s under Clarendon, Britain tried to bring the North Americans together for talks. This action was taken after the trying fishing season of 1870, which was a culmination of years of tensions between New Englanders fishing offshore of Newfoundland, Nova Scotia, and in the Gulf of St. Lawrence. Because of the Civil War, the imperial government took another giant step back from direct interference in the North American affairs, just as it had in the late 1840s.

Other factors benefited Anglo-American relations after the Civil War. The Union army was rapidly disbanded. Four days after Lee surrendered, the War Department stopped all recruiting and drafting, and mobilization machinery was reversed. By 28 April orders were issued to quickly reduce military expenses. Purchase of war animals, wagons, and forages halted. Unneeded ocean and river transports were sold, and all requisitions for railroad construction and railroad work stopped. The government decreased its orders for weapons and supplies. Work on

General Ulysses S. Grant, 1863, Lincoln's primary military agent for pursuing the hard war that resulted in victory for the North. Library of Congress

field fortifications ceased. All bureaus curtailed operations except to maintain the regular army and to help disband the volunteer force. The number of generals and staff officers was reduced. Military restrictions on trade and commerce ceased.[18]

Secretary of War Stanton and General Grant planned the disbandment in fewer than two hours in mid-May 1865 because Southern resistance to the surrender was nonexistent. Over the summer the army was reduced from 1 million to 80,000, and eventually to 27,000.[19] On 1 May the volunteer army numbered

1,034,064. On 19 July, the last regiment of the Army of the Potomac was sent home, and by 1 August, the last of Sherman's regiments left Louisville. By the end of the first week of August, 640,806 troops had been mustered out. By 15 November, nearly four-fifths of the total, or 800,963, had been demobilized. By 1 November 1866, the regular army contained only 11,043 volunteer soldiers, of whom 8,736 were African Americans.[20]

Grant wanted rapid disbandment because he harbored no grudges against the British. He was not a political warrior like so many failed commanders such as McClellan and Frémont. He was content with the regular army, which remained three times larger than the prewar army. Yet it was a long way from the 1 million soldiers of May 1865. By the fall of 1866, the regulars numbered 54,302, which was 20,000 below the maximum of 75,382 authorized by Congress. In 1864–65, the army cost more than $1 billion, but in 1866 it cost less than $100 million.[21]

Naval disbandment followed a similar pattern. Steps to cut the navy to a coastal and riverine force began in February 1865 after all of the Southern ports were taken. This was a large undertaking, considering that by 1864 it had surpassed the British and the French navies with 671 ships, including 71 ironclads and 51,500 seamen. France had a fleet of 376 ships that included 18 ironclads, and 51,998 men. Britain had 417 ships with 30 ironclads and 68,811 men. In May 1865 Welles reduced the navy to 10 warships on the Atlantic and 12 in the Gulf of Mexico. The rest of the navy was rapidly reduced to save money.[22]

By 1 May, home squadrons were cut in half and greater cuts were made that month. The Potomac Flotilla and the Mississippi Squadron were disbanded. The monitors were docked. By mid-July cuts of 471 ships on blockade duty left only thirty steamers and receiving ships afloat. The navy had 530 vessels with 2,000 guns in early 1865. A year later it was reduced to 117 with 830 guns. Foreign squadrons were reestablished in European, Brazilian, and East Indian waters, and a new squadron was initiated in the West Indies. The Pacific Squadron remained. Yet navy manpower was reduced from a top number of 51,500 sailors and 16,880 artisans, to only 12,128 by December 1865. To cut down on dry dock work, 340 naval vessels were sold on the cheap.[23]

Arguments could be mounted that disbandment and retrenchment could have been quickly reversed if British-American bad feelings had threatened armed conflict. Yet neither government wanted this to happen, and the hatred that the Radical Republicans, a minority to be sure, and others felt for the British never took hold. And even their leaders such as Sumner did not want another military conflict. Instead, popular feeling prevailed that Britain's neutrality had been more beneficial to the Union than to the Confederacy. It was noted from 1863 to 1865 how completely the British had ignored the South by making the neutrality laws more restrictive in favor of the North. The blockade tightened, and successful blockade-runners carried little to help the Rebel army.

The American people were further focused on the economic boom that absorbed the returning veterans and the legal oceanic commerce that both governments badly needed. The Civil War fostered a tremendous growth of industry and agriculture. Railroads joined the East and West. Telegraphic communications improved across the Atlantic and in North America. Britain and the United States looked to informal empire and eased into the post–Civil War era dedicated to prosperity. Both societies wanted to forget. Returning to America after spending the war and its aftermath in London, Henry Adams opined: "The new Americans, of whom he was to be one, must, whether they were fit or unfit, create a world of their own, a science, a society, a philosophy, a universe, where they had not yet created a road or even learned to dig their own iron. They had no time for thought; they saw, and could see, nothing beyond their day's work; their attitude to the universe outside them was that of the deep-sea fish."[24]

The British venture capitalist, Sir S. Morton Peto, who toured the United States with potential British investors in the fall of 1865, wrote of the boom. He emphasized the wonderful "elasticity" of American resources: "Throughout the war, the nation gave evidence of rapidly increasing wealth. . . . America, which in so many respects has shown herself superior to ordinary rules, has, in regard to the effects of the war, shown that the heaviest and most costly conflict can be borne not only without exhaustion, but even with an increase of national prosperity."[25] Through Peto's book, *The Resources and Prospects of America*, British leaders knew that the United States developed and was thankful that Britain had not taken on Brother Jonathan. Gladstone read it from 17 to 20 April 1866, soon after its release.[26]

Peto's observations were astute. Neutrality enabled the *Alabama*s to sink a hundred or so American merchant vessels and forced hundreds to seek foreign flags for protection. Britain profited the most from this shakeup, which increased bad feelings. Yet the Confederate raiders may have been a blessing, as Allan Nevins points out: "Because of the lack of shipping, local needs and energies, the war had broken down whatever dependence had existed upon European manufacturing and had stimulated national industry. This was possible because the nation found it could simultaneously support a great war and a burgeoning civilian economy too." Iron and steel industries underwent tremendous expansion. New machinery increased the production of clothing and other daily war necessities. Northern industry "was generally immune from wartime damage" and surged ahead into the late 1860s. Markets multiplied, and internal and external capital investment—mostly from the British—caused the ebbing of British-American enmity. From reading Peto, Gladstone believed that American resources were, in Nevins's words, "inexhaustible, and would ensure prosperity."[27]

At war's end, the strength of British-American commerce and British finance was not matched favorably by British diplomatic power. But the United States refused to threaten military retribution for the latter's alleged Civil War infractions.

Instead, relations quickly reverted to common needs and took an economic course, which enabled Britain to await negotiations in the best antebellum tradition. The British leadership that emerged was fortunately strong enough to nourish the prospect of general negotiations. An analysis of the actions of these individuals for what they did to stave off a British-American war and how these men envisioned the rapprochement after the war provides valuable information in a study of postwar relations.

Conclusion

Accommodations and Rapprochement

British-American relations continued on their traditional path during the Civil War despite what historians have written about their tenuous nature. This unsettled atmosphere was established from the spring of 1861 through the early winter of 1862. In this period, Britain declared strict neutrality, began to court the new American minister, and refused to take advantage of the Union's military weaknesses demonstrated by its retreat from Bull Run on 21 July and its inability to mount a campaign against the Rebel forces. Moreover, Britain was distracted in Europe where France was its primary enemy. Fears remained of an ascendant French iron and steam navy spearheading a cross-channel invasion that was independent of the tides. In the fall of 1861, the British cast suspicious eyes at Napoleon III's intervention to gain military control of Mexico. Britain halfheartedly participated in the intervention to extract concessions for Mexican robbery and murder of its subjects and seemed perplexed when the United States refused an invitation to join the expedition as a counterweight to the French emperor's ambitions. Finally, the *Trent* affair was quietly settled in two months of cooperative diplomacy in November and December. Cooperation continued in the winter of 1862 and, more often than not, throughout the entire year. As in the antebellum period, relations remained cautious to promulgate cooperation when events threatened the traditional peace.

From early in the Civil War onward, Palmerston aided the Union by refusing to support the South in Parliament and never tried to stir up public opinion to fight a war. By the end of the Civil War he had gained a grudging respect for Lincoln and the Union. Russell particularly expressed this newly found faith. The outpouring of sympathy after Lincoln's assassination was especially strong from the queen, Russell, and other leaders.

Reflecting the parliamentary preference, the vast majority of the British cabinet remained noninterventionist throughout the entire conflict despite disputes that could have upended relations. Canada was left primarily to fend for itself, and it was the home government's indifference that moved the colonists to dominionhood more than misplaced fears of Yankee invasion threats, of which there were none beyond the bluster of a minority of Anglophobes. The Lincoln and Johnson administrations made no such threats. Britain refused to take drastic action against the Union over seizures of its merchantmen who tried to run the Union blockade for profit throughout the war. Russell was comfortable with letting American prize courts settle the claims. After all, Britain had put the runners strictly on their own responsibility with the Proclamation of Neutrality. Neither on that nor on other matters did Whitehall rally the Royal Navy in North American and West Indian waters except briefly during the *Trent* affair, and that was a traditional deterrent rather than a deliberate war preparation. The expense of maintaining a large armada in North American and West Indian waters while watching France in the English Channel and the Mediterranean was too much to bear. Thus, the antebellum deterrence policy was exactly right for the challenges the Civil War evoked.

Comparable to Britain's realistic policy, the Union never planned to fight Britain. In the first month of the Civil War Lincoln modified Seward's so-called and short-lived foreign war panacea; it was directed against Spain and France and not Britain anyway. On reading Seward's vindictive dispatch of 1 April 1861, Lincoln toned it down and took control of foreign policy. In reality, their direst enemies were the Radical Republicans and not the British Liberals. The president had to quell Radical Republican interventionist attempts to take over Union foreign policy, and these attempts might be considered more significant for British-American relations than the British intervention debate. Since Lincoln kept the Radicals, who would have pressed a more vindictive British policy at bay, he was able to maintain control of foreign policy to the benefit of British-American relations. Lincoln and a dutiful Seward became fixtures of Anglo-American caution and cooperation throughout the conflict, even at the risk of ostracizing the members of the cabinet, such as Welles and Chase, and the senate. When the blowup occurred between Lincoln and Seward on the one hand, and the Radicals on the other hand in December 1862, Lincoln's astute understanding of men and motives enabled him to emerge, with Seward retracting his resignation. This political victory put them on firmer ground to cooperate with the British. Like Britain, the Union had preferred isolation from world conflicts, and that policy continued during and after the Civil War until the end of the century.

As they were used to doing when tensions arose during the antebellum period, Britain and the United States continued making treaties and agreements despite the tensions of the Civil War. With the conflict not a year old, Seward and Lyons privately concluded an anti–slave trade treaty in Washington, thus updating the Webster-Ashburton Treaty of 1842. In less than a year, the antislavery parallel continued after the Emancipation Proclamation impressed on the Union military and the British that the war was being fought to end slavery. The proclamation increased British understanding and respect for Lincoln's prosecution of the Civil War and Britain's public sympathy for the Union as a partner in the antislavery struggle. Emancipation coincided with the British decision (once and for all) not to intervene, which was a diplomatic victory for the Union. In 1863, the long-standing claims of the Hudson's Bay Company and the Puget Sound Agricultural Company were resolved. Meanwhile, for the first time since the Webster-Ashburton Treaty evinced it, the U.S. Navy assisted the British against slavers along the West African coast. Indeed, the war strengthened these proven methods behind dependable relations. They were dependable enough to withstand the congressional decision not to renew the Canadian-American Reciprocity Treaty in 1864. That decision led to its termination in early 1866 per the agreement. Seward's cooperation was again seen in his unsuccessful attempt for its renewal. However, the end of this treaty did not sidetrack Anglo-American relations. Moreover, historians often overlook the fact that both powers remained expansionist and continued to cooperate for commercial gains in China and Japan. Both sought new markets through negotiations and gunboat diplomacy, but not full-blown military force, to establish informal empire.

Such diplomatic trends resulted from the national self-interest of both powers before, during, and after the Civil War. Britain's "accommodationist sentiment toward the Union" revealed its national self-interest, which assisted the rapprochement's growth. The Union's national self-interest paralleled Britain's need for peace and cooperation. Foreign policy realists, such as Lincoln and Palmerston, had no other safe alternative.

For the rest of the conflict, and during the following six years, the rapprochement was apparent. Conservative foreign secretary Lord Stanley contributed to cooperative relations with the United States by successfully negotiating a long-needed Naturalization Treaty wherein Britain abandoned its old laws and agreed to allow British subjects to become American citizens quickly instead of the established five-year waiting period. For immediate purposes this treaty helped to extinguish tensions between Irish-Americans and the British because Fenian revolutionaries captured in Britain, Ireland, or Canada could be returned to the United States. It was ratified by both powers in 1870 under the Liberals, another example of British bipartisan foreign policy of this era.[1]

During the brief Derby ministry from mid-1866 until the end of 1868, Gladstone replaced Russell as the leader of the Liberal Party and led his first ministry into office in December 1868 on a platform of domestic reform and peaceful international relations. He selected the Union's push to extinguish slavery as a profound example of liberal reforms for the good of the people. Gladstone's reforms were stimulated by the Union victory over the Rebels, and these reforms provided definition for the Liberal Party's electoral, educational, and military reforms during the early years of Gladstone's first ministry. So the converse of the early belief that Union tyranny was fighting an incipient states' rights nationalism won out.

Furthermore, Gladstone's Liberal Party interpreted the war as a victory for the continuation of British-American cooperation in industry, commerce, and finance.

The essentials of a comprehensive treaty were spawned from this mutual dependence. Britain and the United States continued to complement each other, with American exports of raw materials and agricultural products and British exports of finished goods. Transatlantic trade flourished and continued to grow after the war along with the return of profitable British finance and the growth of American finance until it was second only to Britain in its credit rating. For immediate purposes, the United States needed British loans to refinance its massive national debt at lower interest. Upon taking the Foreign Office for the third time in December 1868, Clarendon realized that the two powers needed each other for foreign policy and commerce. He privately suggested that his minister to the United States, Sir Edward Thornton, explain Britain's willingness to cooperate to Sumner and his clique, who had continued to criticize Britain about Civil War disputes. Thornton was to suggest that "there has not for years been a govt. in this Country so friendly to America as the present one, including many prominent members['] own personal friends [of Sumner] the D. of Argyll and Bright. I hope that he [Sumner] will . . . meet us halfway in establishing a cordial Entente between our respective countries which really would be the most important event of modern times and more fraught with advantage to the civilized world."[2] By April 1869 Clarendon was moved to write Thornton confidentially that "we trust to time to produce a desire in the U.S. for a more liberal commercial system; and our patience in that respect will not be wholly without its fruit in asmuch [*sic*] as a large portion of the American community will be clear-sighted enough to see that, in this respect, their interests are identical with our own; and between nations and communities a bond of common interest is more valuable than any other that can be devised."[3] He did not stop there. On the same day, he instructed Thornton through another private letter that "one matter . . . on which . . . it has been the dream of my life [,] . . . [is] a close alliance between the U.S., England, and Germany—the three countries in which thought is free and progress certain. . . . I wish you would recur with [Secretary of State Hamilton Fish] . . . to this Protestant alliance as an idea that had originated with himself and see if anything could be made of it."[4]

Clarendon followed up in sending Sir John Rose, a Canadian financier, to see Fish privately in Washington in early July 1869. Fish showed that he was moving rather quickly toward closer relations with Britain and Canada by promising that he would cooperate to extinguish the Fenians who threatened the common frontier. Rose wrote to Canadian prime minister Sir John A. Macdonald: "I really think that so long as he is there, we have nothing to fear;—if vigilance and good health can prevent it."[5]

Clarendon's work harkened back to Lyons's method of giving Seward credit for diplomatic transactions, and it fostered private talks to establish the grounds for negotiating a comprehensive treaty with the private, informal methods used to make the antebellum treaties as the model. The U.S. Treasury's need for low-interest

Sir Edward Thornton, British minister to the United States, 1868–81. Thornton symbolized the caution and cooperation in British policy by working privately to create the Treaty of Washington negotiations of 1871. Library of Congress

foreign bonds was intricately bound up with the movement to settle the *Alabama* dispute as a part of the talks. This mutual self-interest driven by international finance characterized Anglo-American relations after the Civil War, and particularly from 1869 to 1872. Once the *Alabama* dispute was resolved, the U.S. Treasury and a consortium of London bankers were able to place low-interest bonds in Europe to fund the American debt and solidify the post–Civil War rapprochement.[6] Thus, as antebellum politics and economics had already indicated, the Civil War and its

Hamilton Fish, American secretary of state, 1869–77. Library of Congress

aftermath continued to develop the materialistic relationship that undergirded the cautious and cooperative foreign policy of both governments.

Therefore, from the beginning of the conflict the antebellum traditions supporting the relationship remained stronger than the tensions and tendencies of the Civil War. In other words, wartime diplomacy never escaped from antebellum traditions but used tradition to advantage. The antebellum traditions overpowered Anglo-American disputes during the Civil War so that the event was incarcerated within antebellum diplomacy and was incapable of causing an international conflict.

This point is seen in the rapidity with which the cousins worked for normal relations after the South's surrender. On 6 July 1865, the *New York Times* carried Russell's letter to Bruce that the United States could confiscate any Confederate vessel; the letter also announced the liquidation of belligerent rights. Russell continued that Britain was "gratified" that the American government "no longer claim[ed] belligerent rights against Britain, and that "normal relations between the two countries are practically returned to the condition in which they stood before the civil war." Sumner informed John Bright that General Grant wanted normalcy. People listened to Grant, the national hero, and he wanted the *Alabama* claims dropped altogether to calm relations. Sumner, playing his usual political game, disagreed but was quick to say that the American aim should be to bring the two countries into a profound harmony by removing all questions in dispute to the *Alabama* claims, the fisheries, the San Juan Water Boundary, Canadian-American reciprocity, and the Fenian menace to the common border. In this idea, Sumner was heartened by Russell's "tone of Equality which I hail as a harbinger of better days."[7] Sumner foresaw the development of a movement for private talks for a general settlement despite his outcries against Britain over the *Alabama* claims after the war.

In actuality there was no substance to Sumner's postwar threats of an American war of revenge for Britain's alleged pro-South acts. Prewar trends along the Canadian-American boundary continued with the almost total mutual disregard for building or refurbishing fortifications. Joseph Schweninger, a scholar of Canadian-American frontier defenses, wrote that during the post–Civil War era American "attention was focused elsewhere, and the possibility of war with Britain decreased with each passing year." British Liberals said the same in the Commons. Forster remarked that the only threats to the border were from desperate Confederates. He debunked the fears of a war with the United States and uttered the same about a French invasion of Britain. As late as "two or three years ago . . . we were afflicted with a French panic. I believe there is nobody now who is not ashamed of having believed that the French Emperor would come over like a thief in the night and land an army on our shores." Forster's speech paralleled Britain's long-term desire to stop defending its colonies and withdrawing honorably. Instead of growing vindictive about Canadian confederation two years after the Civil War ended, a stronger system of Canadian border defense enabled the United States to reduce its small military units on the northern frontier and leave fortifications to decay. In 1870, the U.S. government ceded parts of several forts for use as public parks. From 1868 to 1873, during his reform ministry, Gladstone and Chancellor of the Exchequer Robert Lowe reduced defense expenditures by £4 million, which was "the lowest level of defense spending since before the Crimean War." This reduction in force was exemplified in February 1870 when Whitehall informed the Canadians that European unrest dictated withdrawal of all imperial troops except for small contingents at Québec and Halifax. Cooperation to protect both sides of

Baron Eduoard de Stoeckl, Russian minister to the United States. Despite his government's good relations with the United States, Stoeckl was a critic of the Union throughout the Civil War. Library of Congress

the border dictated the use of troops by then. President Grant moved troops to the border to confiscate Fenian arms shipments and, along with British-led Canadian militia, stopped them from an early spring raid, while from its side of the border the Canadian militia repelled a Fenian raid from Vermont in May. By 1871, the Fenians were humiliated, and there has never been another threat to the common boundary. In fact, because Britain paid Canada for the minor Fenian disruptions and for placating American leaders, nothing was said about them in the Treaty of

Washington talks of 1871. Meanwhile, France had withdrawn from Mexico, and friendly relations continued between the British ministers to the United States, Bruce and his successor Sir Edward Thornton, and Hamilton Fish, Seward's successor. Schweninger writes, "After 1871, British planners tended to consider a war with the United States to be only a remote possibility."

Others debunked the possibility of war. In late August 1865, Gladstone wrote to Sumner: "On the whole the history of your great war impresses me with no feeling so much as this; that it is, as I now learn, hazardous in the extreme for us to pronounce upon America of questions of the future." The Union's perseverance revealed an ethic that "surpassed our scale and measure." In Liverpool in 1866 Gladstone said that he and others had erred in describing the American constitution as a failure. The war changed that belief, showing instead the virtues of "extended franchises." In 1871, cabinet ministers remarked that Gladstone believed in Cobden's theory that the world was too civilized for war. Gladstone's parliamentary reform ideas surprised many of his supporters because he acknowledged Civil War lessons in showing the strength of democratic governments implementing the national will. He was also impressed by the earnest manner in which the Americans overcame wartime financial problems and no longer condemned Lincoln's paper currency. Gladstone now saw the debt redemption measures underway as ingenious examples of how to obliterate a national debt. Ironically, although he misunderstood the first principles of the Civil War until it was well advanced, it helped to make Gladstone a popular leader. Both British parties began to quote the American example as they competed to pass a voting reform bill.[8]

The politics emerging from the Civil War implied progress on both sides of the Atlantic. Gladstone's reformist post–Civil War perspective was infectious. During the next twenty years he talked about the "commanding moral influence of the North" and how it extinguished slavery almost as an act of providence. He talked about the natural Anglo-American community, and he is credited with being the first to use the phrase "the English-Speaking Peoples." In his article "Kin beyond the Sea" in the *North American Review* in 1878, he wrote that the United States and Britain were the two most powerful nations in the world. He conceded that Brother Jonathan was ascending over John Bull. He applauded the commonality of self-government, freedom of speech and thought, and the different institutions that emanated from the two countries. He praised the stubbornness and creativity of how the U.S. Constitution survived and was perfected for freedom. Most important, he disparaged the fears that had existed in 1865 of the military dominating postwar American society. With his deeds since the war demonstrated in "Kin beyond the Sea," Gladstone joined Lincoln as one of the two progenitors of the British-American Liberal tradition of the nineteenth century. They took their countries beyond the "hold the line" inactivity of Palmerston to a philosophic realism that dismissed war as a solution to international conflict. In the end, Gladstone carried on the burgeoning Anglo-American liberal-democratic tradition to which he and Lincoln contributed so much.[9]

There was no place in Gladstone's orderly view of the universe for disorderly British-American relations, and his diplomacy buttressed the rapprochement. His vision for his first ministry was peace, retrenchment, and reform. The prime minister and Granville continued Clarendon's idea of an entente. Gladstone was always interested in clean, accountable government, tax cuts, and retrenchment in colonial defense and domestic military spending. He made large cuts in colonial defense in 1869, withdrew the last troops from Canada in 1871, and cut military spending by 15 percent. He introduced civil service reform to reduce special patronage by requiring competitive examinations. He abolished the system of purchasing army commissions in 1871 to improve the public service.[10]

To enact these reforms, Gladstone brought into his cabinet all of the rapprochement-minded ministers, which included John Bright. Russell was excluded and forced into retirement. He understandably could not get over his responsibility for the *Alabama* claims, and he might have been a hindrance to treaty making on resolving this issue had he been in the cabinet. With Lord Russell out, Clarendon was an obvious choice for the Foreign Office and served until his death in late June 1870. Under his successor, Lord Granville, who had played a central role in dissolving the intervention dispute in the fall of 1862, private discussions for a comprehensive treaty began almost immediately. Granville wasted no time representing the wishes of the Liberal cabinet to work with Thornton, Fish, and Rose. They were the chief actors in the private rounds of diplomacy that brought about the comprehensive Treaty of Washington, which was negotiated privately and signed on 8 May 1871. The treaty resolved all of the outstanding issues that had plagued relations since 1815 and even before. In that way, it expressed the rapprochement more clearly than any previous pact. Gladstone saved the negotiations by agreeing to a "near-apology" about the *Alabama* claims in the preamble. His moral sense enabled him to distinguish between the intangible indirect claims and the fact that no one could deny that the Confederate cruisers were constructed and escaped from Britain.[11] His willingness to negotiate resulted from the dependable private relations that transcended the Civil War, and from European upheaval, which left Britain more isolated than at any time since 1815. Under these conditions the treaty was the paramount diplomatic effort in the relationship. But it was not a watershed so much as the latest and finest example of managing national interests to maintain the peaceful tradition.

In these negotiations and reforms, Gladstonians no longer had to worry about what the erstwhile opportunist Napoleon III might try next. In 1870, Napoleon's defeat by Prussia brought his abdication, the siege of Paris, and the Third Republic. The emperor's fall validated the nonintervention of Palmerston, Lincoln, Russell, Stanley, and Gladstone. The emperor had not done anything positive for the relations of the Anglo-Saxon cousins except to support Britain during the *Trent* affair. In a negative sense, however, he represented a potential second front for Britain if it ever got into a conflict with North America. Otherwise, Napoleon III had created massive distrust with all of the powers, and it had finally caught up with him.

Napoleon's defeat confirmed the Liberals' perception that intervention in Europe or North America was detrimental to the national self-interest. Palmerston's distrust of the emperor was imparted to his successors and coincided with the post–Civil War period when Britain, as it had discovered in the Polish Rebellion of 1863, Schleswig-Holstein's war with Prussia in 1864, the Austro-Prussian War of 1866, and the Franco-Prussian War of 1870–71, could no longer sway continental rivalries. In isolation from Europe, Britain needed the United States as a dependable friend more than ever before, and the recovering republic needed British investments on an unprecedented scale. In parallel, Lincoln and his successors contributed to mutual goodwill by refusing to act against Britain in Canada and France in Mexico. Indeed, the United States was acting in isolation just as Britain was forced to do in Europe. Gladstone's cabinet realized that it could not control Europe, and for this reason, and because of Gladstone's need for moral order, the time was right to settle all disputes with the United States.

Moreover, in early 1871, the *Alabama* claims and the Russian abrogation of the Black Sea clauses of the Treaty of Paris of 1856 created stress for Gladstone's government after two years of a relatively calm administration. The British people once more worried about invasion threats, this time by Germans, the nemesis of continental autocracy. When the Treaty of Washington was negotiated in the spring, Gladstone's domestic and foreign policies seemed to backfire on the government. The treaty was the only bright spot for a now rapidly failing administration. Gladstone failed to maintain British interests toward Russia in the state that Palmerston had left them. Yet Gladstone refused to surrender to the tensions. He had been a free trader since the mid-1840s and focused on economy to continue prosperity. Along with his free trade ministry was abhorrence of militarism, which personified a British civil tradition.[12] It is ironic that the government deteriorated when the rapprochement was embodied in the Treaty of Washington, which upheld the Liberals' noninterventionism and antimilitarism. Almost a year after the treaty was signed, Disraeli taunted on 3 April 1872 that the Liberal ministry reminded him "of one of those marine landscapes not very uncommon on the coasts of South America. You behold a range of exhausted volcanoes. Not a flame flickers on a single pallid crest. But the situation is still dangerous. There are occasional earthquakes, and ever and anon the dark rumbling of the sea."[13]

But the work the Liberals had done was irreversible and certainly supported by Disraeli and his Conservatives. Disraeli and Gladstone gained from the antebellum rapprochement and the persistent cooperation on the disputes that the American war raised for relations. Taken with the accommodations since the 1840s, the Civil

War created additional pillars of stability. First and most basic was the early pro-nouncement of British neutrality, which favored the Union as the war progressed. Second, Britain recognized the blockade before it was effective. The governments arranged the peaceful compromise of the San Juan water boundary conflict that easily outlasted the Civil War. Third, they refused to allow their agents or naval of-ficers to do anything to breach neutrality during the critical months from April to November 1861. Traditional private diplomacy quickly resolved the *Trent* affair.[14] That affair stands as an aberration in the Civil War relationship for a number of reasons. Diplomatic and naval relations returned to normal after the *Trent* affair and contributed greatly to the stability. Fourth, Lincoln refused to act against the tripartite alliance in Mexico or to block Spain's reconquest of Santo Domingo. Cooperation over Federal seizures of British ships on the high seas continued throughout the war. Fifth, the British intervention movement lasted only several months (like the *Trent* issue) and never came close to gaining cabinet support. Sixth, American rage at the depredations of the Confederate raiders floundered while diplomats pursued settlement, and the Laird rams dispute was managed by Russell's arbitrary seizures, which headed off Adams's protest. Finally, the Eman-cipation Proclamation enabled the British to understand why Lincoln fought the South. Most of these examples of British-American cooperation neutralized Con-federate diplomacy. The Confederates failed to drive a wedge between Britain and the Unites States by the middle of 1862. The cotton embargo and slavery ruined Confederate attempts to obtain recognition of independence. As Duncan Andrew Campbell points out, "By withholding cotton, the Confederate states blockaded themselves before Lincoln's embargo even began, much less became effective, and by the time they realized their error, it was too late. . . . King Cotton alienated the very nation the South needed on its side. . . . Before the war, Southerners were fond of affirming that a strand of cotton could hang the world. King Cotton did not hang the world—he hanged his subjects."[15]

Slavery was just as important in keeping the British people from support-ing the South. Steeped in their antislavery history, the British never supported the South evenly throughout the war or in large groups because, as Campbell points out, "despite historians' constant minimisation of its significance, slavery was unquestionably the great millstone about the neck of the South."[16] Indeed, the British antislavery stance coupled with the nonintervention policy was much more consistent over the course of the war than was Lincoln's stand on slavery. As shown earlier, Lincoln vacillated on emancipation until he was assured that he had support in the North, in the Border States, and among pro-Northerners in the South. From the preliminary emancipation proclamation just after Antietam, British-American relations improved as measured by the two governments' work to keep each other in power and the accumulation of examples of cooperation in 1863 until the end of the war.

Moreover, the bipartisan British political opposition to the Confederate lobby in 1862 and 1863 ended a weak and awkward attempt at turning the House of Commons against the Union. The Union government noted the regular opposition of Palmerston, Russell, and other Liberal leaders to the Confederate lobby. It prevailed whether the Confederates were winning battles or not. Palmerston's position to wait until a decisive Confederate victory lacked force when weighed against his anti-Rebel position in the Commons and the longer list of reasons not to intervene led by Lincoln's policy stating that intervention meant war. Like Lincoln had delayed his proclamation of emancipation, Palmerston delayed his decision until he sensed that public opinion had turned against the North, and it never pivoted in the Rebels' favor with enough force for action. But this waffling might have been a dodge not to intervene at all. Palmerston refused to risk his power and fame in a region that he did not understand, that had always troubled him, and that he could not let himself admire. There were too many possible outcomes of fighting the Union, and he could not envisage any that were conducive to Britain's national interest. Moreover, his antislavery vendetta during his public career of more than sixty years may have stopped him no matter what the public said. Beyond that, his dependence on the pacifist Quakers as a barometer may have kept him from fighting and ruining his power and Britain's economic prosperity. Although a direct connection cannot be made, Richard Carwardine's award-winning work divulges the American evangelicals' influence on Lincoln's conduct of the war.[17]

Palmerston was also protected by the Lincoln administration. Lincoln and Seward reined in offensive commanders such as Wilkes to help Palmerston keep his slim majority. Under Admiralty direction, Milne reciprocated and even fraternized with the Union navy, Seward, and Welles. Lincoln and Seward overcame Welles in ordering that suspected blockade-runners in Mexican waters should not be seized and that royal mail taken from prize ships should be returned. Conversely, Lincoln supported Welles in prohibiting Seward from using privateers in early 1863. And Seward and his successor, Hamilton Fish, protected the frontier to defend Canada from Fenians, and in conjunction with Britain, the North Atlantic fisheries as well.

Furthermore, the rapprochement was expressed in an unprecedented series of British-American international arbitrations concerning neutral and belligerent maritime rights and the San Juan Island water boundary dispute. Private diplomacy was critical leading up to the arbitrations. Clarendon's work during the *Alabama* dispute just after the Civil War kept that charged issue from boiling over. Not until his last days in office in 1866 did his friendly American policy promise results. He suggested arbitration to resolve the dispute, which suited Seward's postwar politics, although he had to wait to avoid public antipathy. Early in the succeeding Conservative ministry, Seward proposed negotiations to Clarendon's successor, the liberal-minded Conservative foreign secretary Lord Stanley. In January

1869, Clarendon was back in the Foreign Office under Gladstone and quickly concluded a comprehensive convention with Reverdy Johnson, the American minister to Britain. The Senate refused to approve it because Sumnerites considered it too soft on the *Alabama* claims, and Minister Johnson made himself unpopular back home by breaching confidentiality in British society. But as this convention indicated, the times favored talks. As shown earlier, Seward began negotiations for a naturalization treaty to enable British subjects to become citizens, and Fish and Granville confirmed Seward's Protocol of 1868 with the signing of a treaty in 1870, thus removing an age-old sore in relations.[18]

Meanwhile, President Grant ordered Fish to remove Sumner as chairman of the Senate Foreign Relations Committee for opposing the president's desire to annex Cuba, which muted the radical senator's cries for annexing Canada as payment for the *Alabama* depredations. Sumner became less attuned to the temperament of American foreign policy, and his idea to annex Canada was thoroughly out of step with the times and was the final blow to his career. Sumner's removal enabled private talks for the comprehensive treaty. Rose quietly returned to Washington to prepare preliminaries for formal negotiations with Fish in early January 1871. Again, these conversations were held in the utmost secrecy. But the time was right for a comprehensive treaty. The American debt, Liberal politics, and the situation in Europe took turns for the worse during 1870, and from their respective cockpits Fish and Granville, both of whom were new to their offices, saw the merits of negotiations to maintain national interests. Within a month, the handpicked British High Commission steamed to Washington to negotiate with Fish's American commission. In keeping with the tradition of private talks since the 1840s, the negotiations focused on the private discussions between Fish and one of Gladstone's cabinet members, Palmerston's minister of war from 1863 to 1866, and now Lord President of the Council Lord de Grey, the chairman of the British High Commission. Prime Minister John A. Macdonald, the Canadian commissioner, lent credence to the cooperative direction in which the triangular relations tended, even though he threatened his political career by agreeing to a reciprocal fisheries arrangement that enabled New Englanders free access to colonial inshore waters once more. Yet the fact that Canada was invited to sit on the Joint High Commission was a British-American cooperative gesture, exhibited that the United States accepted Canadian dominionhood, and illustrated that annexation, never a strong force, was spent.

The resulting Treaty of Washington established international arbitrations of the *Alabama* claims, the San Juan water boundary, and the North Atlantic fisheries. This treaty included British-American rules that in 1872 dominated the Geneva Arbitration over the escape and depredations of the *Alabama* and its sister cruisers. Over the summer and fall of 1871, Gladstone and Granville continued negotiations with Fish to create the parameters for the upcoming arbitration at

Geneva. Gladstone kept the informal argument to the treaty's wording and suppressed the indirect claims, which were agreed on by the respective counsels and by a supplementary article to the treaty. Both parties, and the American public, including Sumner, realized that peace was more important than the arbitration itself, and Gladstone, Granville, and Charles Francis Adams, the chief American negotiator, ensured the success of the arbitration. The arbitrators determined that Confederate acts in Britain did not relieve the ministry from stopping the warships, although the ministry had applied due and like diligence to the *Nashville* and the *Florida* and had promoted stricter neutrality rules after the *Alabama* escaped. As a further indication of cooperation, Britain agreed to reimburse Canada for expenses and damages resulting from the Fenian raids.[19]

Gladstone accepted the arbitrators' judgment and paid the United States an indemnity of $15.5 million to settle the claims. In 1880, he said that he regarded the award as "dust in the balance compared with the moral value of the example set when these two great nations of England and America went in peace and concord before a judicial tribunal rather than resort to the arbitrament of the sword." Adrian Cook summarizes: "Anglo-American friendship gained in strength and depth from the testing time of the indirect claims." Norman Ferris writes in the same vein: "Never before had Great Britain been so thoroughly vanquished by peaceful diplomacy. Yet the settlement left behind no residue of rancor; indeed, the Geneva arbitration of 1872 may have been the key event in changing the Anglo-American relationship from one of traditional enmity to one of friendly, if informal, alliance."[20]

The "friendly, if informal" tradition had become the way of British-American relations long before the Civil War. The cost Britain paid for the *Alabama* claims was a fair price when compared to the cost of a British-American war. Most important for the future of relations was that international arbitration rather than arms settled the issue. This was the Christian way to settle disputes in Gladstone's lexicon of how to manage foreign relations.[21]

Most Americans were tired of the dispute and applauded the arbitration and those that followed. Historians sometimes overlook that the Americans had to pay also as a result of other arbitrations associated with the Treaty of Washington. A joint commission determined that the United States pay $2 million in indemnity to British subjects who lost personal property in the war. In addition, the United States paid $5.5 million to Canada for American inshore fishing rights to settle that century-long controversy. Conversely, the San Juan Island water boundary controversy was handed over to international arbitrators headed by the German emperor. He ruled for U.S. possession of the archipelago in 1872, thus settling that quarter-century-long dispute and completing the Canadian-American water boundary on a course bisecting Haro Strait between Vancouver Island and the archipelago in a mutual spirit of cooperation. Left unsaid in this settlement was the fact that the

Haro Strait was no longer regarded as strategic because of dependable relations, which had outdistanced naval strategy. These arbitrations were timed perfectly for the best interests of both nations. The Americans needed peace to recover from the Civil War debt. American credit could not afford a foreign war, and the Navy was reduced back to its antebellum status. Finally, the Union victory ended British bluster that the Republic could not survive. The victory instilled a strong pride that removed "the anti-British overtones of revolutionary lore." Moreover, by 1872, Gladstone's first ministry was faltering from the failure of its reform programs, and the arbitrations gave the Liberals a badly needed foreign policy victory.[22] It did not hurt British-German relations either when the German emperor was asked to head the international arbitral commission on the San Juan water boundary.

Baron Stoeckl perhaps best showed the gradual realization of the British-American rapprochement at war's end. Stoeckl and his colleagues were slow to see the long-standing traditions of caution and cooperation in British-American relations. This oversight was because so much of the diplomatic intercourse was private, time tested, and true. In focusing on each dispute of the moment, the envoys lost track of the overall course of relations and the will to settle that characterized them. This dependable infrastructure was actually strengthened during the Civil War by Palmerston's realism and Lincoln's realism and humility, which continued to pervade diplomacy. The victorious Americans never made the foreign powers "eat crow" over their alleged support for the South. Instead it was Stoeckl and his ilk that had always doubted the North. Stoeckl disliked democracy and believed in Union defeat almost until Lee surrendered, and he "ate humble pie" in a private letter to Prince Gorchakov. Sounding somewhat like Gladstone, Stoeckl wrote on the day Lincoln was assassinated, "by an irresistible strength of the nation at large this exceptional people has given the lie to all predictions and calculations. They have passed through one of the greatest revolutions of a century . . . and they have come out of it with their resources unexhausted, their energy renewed . . . and the prestige of their power greater than ever."[23]

Stoeckl still did not see the full picture of what had transpired, however. He failed to see that in employing a mutual cautious and cooperative policy the two governments had saved each other during a time of unprecedented challenges. Straining and struggling as they might, Civil War diplomats determined not to throw off the sheer weight of antebellum ways of defusing hard problems. Palmerston and Lincoln, assisted by their cabinets and pro-North groups in Britain, maintained and strengthened the antebellum rapprochement. Their work was carried on after the Civil War. Since American Independence, their quest for peace

Facing page: The Citadel and Quebec City, 1870. Along with Montreal and Halifax, Nova Scotia, the Citadel was a site for the last defense of British North America in case of an American invasion. By permission of the Syndics of Cambridge University Library

was aided by a history of peaceful treaties and agreements to alleviate times of stress to the relationship. These methods continued to dominate so that the Civil War was contained within the traditions of relations and led instead to new arbitral methods of settlement. Summarized another way, Civil War diplomacy depended more on past methods and outcomes and less on new ones erupting from the war itself. Simply put, diplomacy dominated the Civil War: the Civil War did not dominate diplomacy. In this way, the worst bloodbath in American history was prevented from expanding into an international war so that Anglo-American relations became more stable for the remainder of the century and beyond.

Notes

ABBREVIATIONS

Add. Mss.	Additional Manuscripts, British Library, London
BDFA	*British Documents on Foreign Affairs: Reports and Papers from the Foreign Office Confidential Print,* pt. 1, ser. C., vols. 5–8, ed. Kenneth Bourne. Frederick, Md.: University Publications of America, 1986
BL	British Library, London
CO	Colonial Office
CWL	Roy P. Basler, ed., *Collected Works of Abraham Lincoln*
FO	Foreign Office
FO 5	General Correspondence, America, United States, ser. II. Public Record Office, London
FO 115	United States of America (Embassy and Consular), Correspondence. Public Record Office, London
Lincoln Papers	Abraham Lincoln Papers, Library of Congress, Manuscript Division, Washington, D.C.: American Memory Project, 2000–2002, ser. 1–3.
LC	Library of Congress, Washington, D.C.
LRO	Liverpool Record Office, William Brown Library, Liverpool
MG	Public Archives of Canada, Manuscript Group
NA	National Archives, Washington, D.C.
NMM	National Maritime Museum, Greenwich, England
ORN	*Official Records of the Union and Confederate Navies in the War of the Rebellion,* ser. II.
PAC	Public Archives of Canada, Ottawa
PAC, RG 7, G10	Public Archives of Canada, Record Group 7, Group 10, Drafts of Secret and Confidential Despatches to the Colonial Office, 1856–1913
PAC, RG 7, G12	Letterbooks of Confidential Despatches from the Governor-General of Canada to the Colonial Office, 1799–1902
PRO	Public Record Office, Kew, England

INTRODUCTION

1. D. P. Crook, *The North, the South, and the Powers, 1861–1865* (New York: John Wiley & Sons, 1974); Brian Jenkins, *Britain and the War for the Union,* 2 vols. (Montreal: McGill-Queens Univ. Press, 1974–80); Howard Jones, *Abraham Lincoln and a New Birth of Freedom: The Union and Slavery in the Diplomacy of the Civil War* (Lincoln: Univ. of Nebraska Press, 1999), and especially his *Union in Peril: The Crisis over British Intervention in the Civil War* (Chapel Hill: Univ. of North Carolina Press, 1992); Dean B. Mahin, *One War at a Time: The International Dimensions of the American Civil War* (Washington, D.C.: Brassey's, 1999).

2. Works that argue for the significance of prewar contingencies to best analyze wartime Anglo-American relations are Ephraim D. Adams, *Great Britain and the American Civil War,* 2 vols. (New York: Longmans, Green, 1925); Duncan Andrew Campbell, *English Public Opinion and the American Civil War* (Woodbridge, UK: Royal Historical Society, 2003); Adrian Cook, *The* Alabama *Claims: American Politics and Anglo-American Relations, 1865–1872* (Ithaca, N.Y.: Cornell Univ. Press, 1974); Martin Crawford, *The Anglo-American Crisis of the Mid-Nineteenth Century:* The Times *and America, 1850–1862* (Athens: Univ. of Georgia Press, 1987); James W. Daddysman, *The Matamoros Trade: Confederate Commerce, Diplomacy, and Intrigue* (Newark: Univ. of Delaware Press, 1984); Reginald C. Stuart, *United States Expansionism and British North America, 1775–1871* (Chapel Hill: Univ. of North Carolina Press, 1988); also see a perceptive article, George L. Bernstein, "Special Relationship and Appeasement: Liberal Policy towards America in the Age of Palmerston," *Historical Journal* 41, no. 3 (1998): 725–50; and two dissertations, my "Mask of Indifference: Great Britain's North American Policy and the Path to the Treaty of Washington, 1815–1871" (Ph.D. diss., University of Iowa, 1978); and Joseph M. Schweninger, "'A lingering war must be prevented': The Defense of the Northern Frontier, 1812–1871" (Ph.D. diss., Ohio State University, 1998). One work that does not consider prewar or postwar relations in any detail but that argues that British-American cooperation prevented a flash point in relations is Frank J. Merli, *Great Britain and the Confederate Navy, 1861–1865* (Bloomington: Indiana Univ. Press, 1970). Two books that take the long view but repeat the traditional view that an identifiable rapprochement did not occur until the late 1890s are Kenneth Bourne, *Britain and the Balance of Power in North America, 1815–1908* (Berkeley: Univ. of California Press, 1967), in which he sees better relations coming out of the 1850s that were threatened by the Civil War and failed to recover until the 1890s; and a survey by Charles S. Campbell, *From Revolution to Rapprochement: The United States and Great Britain, 1783–1900.* America and the World Series (New York: John Wiley & Sons, 1974).

3. David Hepburn Milton, *Lincoln's Spymaster: Thomas Haines Dudley and the Liverpool Network* (Mechanicsburg, Pa.: Stackpole Books, 2003), 114.

1. THE ANTEBELLUM RAPPROCHEMENT

1. Fred Anderson and Andrew Clayton, *The Dominion of War: Empire and Liberty in North America, 1500–2000* (New York: Viking, 2005), xvii. Pierre-Henri Laurent writes about the "ripening of the Anglo-American friendship in the first half of the nineteenth century" as "truly an evolutionary process, but most observers agree that in the diplomatic sphere the significant aspects of that early rapprochement took place about the time of the

Webster-Ashburton agreement." See Laurent's "Anglo-American Diplomacy and the Belgian Indemnities Controversy, 1836–42," *Historical Journal* 10, no. 2 (1967): 197. H. C. Allen argues that a smoother relationship was detectable after George Canning died in 1827 and agrees that, although a follower of Canning, Palmerston's foreign secretaryship from 1830 to 1841 was indicative of "new warmth" in relations. See Allen, *Great Britain and the United States: A History of Anglo-American Relations, 1783–1952* (Watford, Herts.: Odhams Press, 1954; repr., New York: Archon Books, 1969), 388–404. Most recently, see Jay Sexton, *Debtor Diplomacy: Finance and American Foreign Relations in the Civil War Era, 1837–1873*, Oxford Historical Monographs (New York: Oxford Univ. Press, 2005), 4, 7. Sexton argues that finance, as well as trade, served as "peace factors" and shaped the foreign policy of the American Whig and Republican parties in Anglo-American relations in the Civil War era.

2. Hubert Dubrulle, "'A War of Wonders': The Battle in Britain over Americanization and the American Civil War" (Ph.D. diss., University of California-Santa Barbara, 1999), 99.

3. Brougham Villiers and W. H. Chesson, *Anglo-American Relations, 1861–1865* (New York: Charles Scribner's Sons, 1920).

4. Quoted in Dubrulle, "A War of Wonders," 11.

5. Besides Walter A. McDougall's *Promised Land, Crusader State: The American Encounter with the World Since 1776* (New York: Houghton Mifflin Company, 1997), see Scott Kaufman, *The Pig War: The United States, Britain, and the Balance of Power in the Pacific Northwest, 1846–72* (Lanham, Md.: Lexington Books, 2004), 1; Sexton, *Debtor Diplomacy,* 12, 20–21, 32–33. Webster was a legal and financial consultant for the Barings from 1831 until his death in 1852.

6. Glynn Barratt, *Russian Shadows on the Northwest Coast of North America, 1810–1890: A Study in the Rejection of Defence Responsibilities* (Vancouver: Univ. of British Columbia Press, 1983), vii; Kaufman, *Pig War,* 4–5. The quote about the significance of Rush-Bagot is in Samuel Flagg Bemis, *John Quincy Adams and the Foundations of American Foreign Policy* (New York: W. W. Norton, 1973), 211–12.

7. Sexton, *Debtor Diplomacy,* 23, 45.

8. Ibid., 13–14.

9. On British antislavery legislation and its coordination with American abolitionists, see Betty Fladeland, *Men and Brothers: Anglo-American Antislavery Cooperation* (Urbana: Univ. of Illinois Press, 1972), esp. chap. 9. Sexton, *Debtor Diplomacy,* 46.

10. Laurent, "Anglo-American Diplomacy," 197–98. This controversy stemmed from the loss of American and British goods stored in the entrepôt of Antwerp during Belgian shelling and conquest of the Dutch-held city in October 1830. Belgian independence did not lead to indemnifying the powers for losses. In October 1837 the personal friendship and professional collaboration of the American lawyer Virgil Maxcy and British Minister Resident in Brussels Sir Hamilton Seymour ultimately led to Belgium's paying out indemnities. Ibid., 197–202.

11. Quoted in Sexton, *Debtor Diplomacy,* 31, 35, 37–38.

12. Ibid., 38.

13. Alexander H. Everett to James K. Polk, Boston, 8 Dec. 1845, *Correspondence of James K. Polk,* vol. 10: *July–December 1945,* ed. Wayne Cutler (Knoxville: Univ. of Tennessee Press, 2004), 410.

14. Sexton, *Debtor Diplomacy,* 50–51.

15. Ibid., 48, 52.

16. J. B. Conacher, "British Policy in the Anglo-American Enlistment Crisis of 1855–1856," *Proceedings of the American Philosophical Society* 136, no. 4 (1992): 538.

17. Franklin William Hill, "The Anglo-American Recruitment Crisis, 1854–1856: Origins, Events, and Outcomes" (Ph.D. diss., Washington State University, 1996), chap. 3; Bernstein, "Special Relationship and Appeasement," 735.

18. The paragraphs on the Crampton affair were informed by Bernstein's argument from the primary correspondence in "Special Relationship and Appeasement," 735–38; J. B. Conacher, *Britain and the Crimea, 1855–56* (New York: St. Martin's Press, 1987), 213; Dallas to Marcy, London, 7 Apr. 1856, George Mifflin Dallas, *A Series of Letters from London Written during the Years, 1856, '57, '58, '59, and '60,* ed. Julia Dallas, 2 vols. in 1 (Philadelphia: J. B. Lippincott & Co., 1869), 16–17. See also *Gladstone to his Wife,* British Museum, Sat. 5 Apr. 1856, Arthur Tilney Bassett, ed., *Gladstone to His Wife* (London: Methuen & Co., 1936), 113, in which he wrote: "If you have the [London] 'Times' you will see that Palmerston last night replied with extraordinary asperity to an innocent little speech enough of mine." Dallas to Marcy, London, 7 Apr. 1856, in Dallas, *Letters from London,* 15–16. Gladstone's speech in the Commons, according to Dallas, was evoked "with considerable animation;—so much so as to cause Lord Palmerston to lose his temper, a thing he very rarely does, and to occasion quite a general surprise." Indeed, Dallas believed the situation would force Palmerston out and Gladstone to become premier. Gladstone's speech called for a friendly settlement with the United States over Central America, but he was not thinking seriously about replacing Palmerston. See H. C. G. Matthew, ed., *The Gladstone Diaries,* vol. 5, *1855–1860* (Oxford: Clarendon Press, 1978), 120 and n6. Ultimately, the restraint of Palmerston and Clarendon is shown in J. B. Conacher, "Lessons in Twisting the Lion's Tail: Two Sidelights of the Crimean War," in *Policy by Other Means: Essays in Honour of C. P. Stacey,* ed. Michael Cross and Robert Bothwell (Toronto: Clarke, Irwin & Company, 1972), 91. The quote about Roebuck is from Don Alan Smith, "Cabinet and Constitution in the Age of Peel and Palmerston" (Ph.D. diss., Yale University, 1966), 130.

19. Allan Nevins, *The War for the Union,* vol. 3: *The Organized War, 1863–1864* (New York: Charles Scribner's Sons, 1971), 145.

20. Merli, *Great Britain and the Confederate Navy,* 8.

21. Jenkins, *Britain and the War for the Union,* 2:61; M. S. Partridge, "The Russell Cabinet and National Defense, 1846–1852," *History* 72, no. 235 (1987): 244–45, 247, 249–50; Conacher, *Britain and the Crimea,* esp. chaps. 4 and 5, 227–29; Eugenio F. Biagini, *Gladstone,* British History in Perspective series (New York: St. Martin's, 2000), 32; Paul Sweetman, *War and Administration: The Significance of the Crimean War for the British Army* (Edinburgh: Scottish Academic Press, 1984), 5–20, 28–33, 42. Gladstone, Cobden, and Bright "deplored the immoral nature of armies, which brutalized and degraded their soldiery." Support for pacifism by merchants searching for markets, the short-lived peace society, and the general excitement about the Great Exhibition of 1850 distracted attention from military reforms.

22. Howard Temperley, *Britain and America since Independence* (New York: Palgrave, 2002), 65; Muriel E. Chamberlain, *"Pax Britannica?": British Foreign Policy, 1789–1914,* Studies in Modern History series (New York: Longman, 1988), 9; Brian R. Dirck, *Lincoln & Davis: Imagining America, 1809–1865* (Lawrence: Univ. Press of Kansas, 2001), 92. The statement about consistency in British foreign policy is in John William McCleary, "Anglo-French Naval Strategy, 1815–1848" (Ph.D. diss., Johns Hopkins University, 1947), 88. Finan-

cial pressures are quoted in Jay Winik, *April 1865: The Month That Saved America* (New York: HarperCollins, 2001), 274; Brian Holden Reid, "Civil-Military Relations and the Legacy of the Civil War," in *Legacy of Disunion: The Enduring Significance of the American Civil War*, ed. Susan-Mary Grant and Peter J. Parish (Baton Rouge: Louisiana State Univ. Press, 2003), 152. The small British and American standing armies and navies along the Canadian-American frontier, and the remote possibility of war throughout the century, is described in detail in Schweninger, "A lingering war," 64–65, 80–82, 107, 118, 121, 123–24, 146–47, 183–84, 186, 239, 245–46, 248, 274–75, 284, 379 and n68, and 380.

23. Dubrulle, "War of Wonders," 246.

24. Max Beloff, "Historical Revision No. CXVIII: Great Britain and the American Civil War," *History* 37 (February 1952): 41–44.

25. Castlereagh to Liverpool, private and confidential, 1 Mar. 1821, Liverpool Papers, BL, Loan 72/25, fol. 39; Aberdeen to Princess Lieven, 21 Dec. 1847, in Lady F. Balfour, *Life of George Fourth Earl of Aberdeen*, 2 vols. (London: n.p., 1923), 2:136–37; R. A. J. Walling, *The Diaries of John Bright* (London: Cassell & Co., 1930), 138–39 (4 June 1859). All are in M. S. Partridge, *Military Planning for the Defense of the United Kingdom, 1814–1870*, Contributions in Military Studies, no. 91 (Westport, Conn.: Greenwood Press, 1989), 18–19. On the rivalry in the 1840s, see Roger Bullen, "Peel, Aberdeen and the *Entente Cordiale*," *Bulletin of the Institute of Historical Research* 30 (1957): 204–6.

26. Melbourne to Russell, 27 Nov. 1838, in L. C. Sanders, ed., *Lord Melbourne's Papers* (London: Longman's, Green, and Sons, 1889), 387; Aberdeen to Peel, 31 Dec. 1844, in C. S. Parker, *Sir Robert Peel from His Private Papers*, 3 vols. (London: n.p., 1891–99), 3:396; and Peel to Haddington, 13 Sept. 1845, Peel Papers, BL, Add. Mss. 40460, fols. 191–92. All are quoted in Partridge, *Military Planning*, 13.

27. Sexton, *Debtor Diplomacy*, 48.

28. Burgoyne quoted in Partridge, *Military Planning*, 11–13, 21, 45, 65–67. In 1852, for instance, Disraeli was Derby's chancellor of the exchequer and expressed his frustration at the pressure for defense expenditures to John Bright. He decried "these damned defences, and said he had cut and slashed them to trim the estimates for them to a more moderate sum." Gladstone could have said the same at any time when he was chancellor. Robert Blake, *Disraeli* (New York: St. Martin's, 1967), 428.

29. John Charmley, "Palmerston: 'Artful Old Dodger' or 'Babe of Grace'?" in *The Makers of British Foreign Policy from Pitt to Thatcher*, ed. T. G. Otte (New York: Palgrave, 2002), 75.

30. Roger Bullen, *Palmerston, Guizot and the Collapse of the* Entente Cordiale (London: Athlone Press, 1974), 209; C. J. Bartlett, *Great Britain and Sea Power, 1815–1853* (Oxford: Clarendon Press, 1963), viii, 332.

31. Bullen, *Palmerston, Guizot and the Collapse of the* Entente Cordiale, 201; Bartlett, *Great Britain and Sea Power*, 188.

32. Bullen, *Palmerston, Guizot and the Collapse of the Entente Cordiale*, 205; Bartlett, *Great Britain and Sea Power*, 189–92.

33. Sexton, *Debtor Diplomacy*, 57–61.

34. Ibid., 62–63, and n163 for the quote on Clayton's cooperation.

35. Ibid., 64–66.

36. Crampton to Clarendon, private, 6 Mar. 1854, fourth Earl of Clarendon Papers, Bodleian Library, Oxford University, Oxford, England, Ms Clar. dep. c. 24, fol. 170 (hereafter cited as Clarendon Papers).

37. Crampton to Clarendon, 12 June 1854, Clarendon Papers, c. 24, cited in Kinley Brauer, "The United States and British Imperial Expansion, 1815–1860," *Diplomatic History* 12, no. 1 (Winter 1988): 34; Donald F. Warner, *The Idea of Continental Union: Agitation for the Annexation of Canada to the United Sates, 1849–1893* (Lexington: Univ. Press of Kentucky, 1960); Bernstein, "Special Relationship and Appeasement," 733.

38. Democracies are not precluded from fighting each other, but they are reluctant to fight, especially when one party quits empire in a mutually contested world region, argues Joel Blank, "The Decline of Democratic Imperialism and the Rise of Democratic Peace: Case Studies in Anglo-American Relations, 1800 to the Present" (Ph.D. diss., University of California, Los Angeles, 2000), 7, 11–14, 19, 289, 292, 294–95. I hope to show my opposition to Blank's argument that British-American relations in the Civil War showed a conflict rather than a cooperative worldview. See ibid., 22–23. Kenneth E. Shewmaker, "Daniel Webster and American Conservatism," in *Tradition and Values: American Diplomacy, 1790–1865,* ed. Norman Graebner (Lanham, Md.: Univ. Press of America, 1985), 134–38; and Emory M. Thomas, *The Confederate Nation, 1861–1865,* New American Nation series (New York: Harper & Row, 1979), 171.

39. Quoted in David Brown, *Palmerston and the Politics of Foreign Policy, 1846–55* (New York: Manchester Univ. Press, 2002), 3.

40. Chamberlain, *"Pax Britannica?"* 9, 14; Bernstein, "Special Relationship and Appeasement," 725–28, 730–34. Paul Kennedy, *The Rise and Fall of the Great Powers: Economic Change and Military Conflict from 1500 to 2000* (New York: Random House, 1987), 178, remarks that the growing economic relationship and the Royal Navy's protection of the Western Hemisphere after 1815 brought closer understandings about the various disputes of the post-1815 era and that "an Anglo-American war was unlikely." On Palmerston's realism, see Paul R. Ziegler, *Palmerston* (New York: Palgrave Macmillan, 2003), 2–3; and Smith, "Cabinet and Constitution," 206. Palmerston's ability to sense the public mind and play to it in the media to maintain his power, his "media premiership," is discussed in Simon Peaple and John Vincent, "Gladstone and the Working Man," in *Gladstone,* ed. Peter J. Jagger (London: Hambledon Press, 1998), 71.

41. Anna A. W. Ramsay, *Idealism and Foreign Policy: A Study in the Relations of Great Britain with Germany and France, 1850–1878* (London: John Murray, 1925), 99. David Krein, *The Last Palmerston Government: Foreign Policy, Domestic Politics, and the Genesis of "Splendid Isolation"* (Ames: Iowa State Univ. Press, 1978), 7; and T. A. Jenkins, *The Liberal Ascendancy, 1830–1886* (New York: St. Martin's Press, 1994), 78–79, 86, 90–92, 120 (on Liberal progress). For Palmerston's aloofness abroad, see Ziegler, *Palmerston,* 4–5. For the Conservatives, see Blake, *Disraeli,* 428–29; and Kennedy, *Rise and Fall of the Great Powers,* 182; and Angus Hawkins, *Parliament, Party and the Art of Politics in Britain, 1855–59* (Stanford, Calif.: Stanford Univ. Press, 1987), 2–3, 26–29. The term *Radicals* is not used to denote a political party like the Whig Party, Liberal Party, and Conservative Party. Instead, the Radicals wanted legislative control over the cabinet. Most Radicals refused cabinet office because they believed that the cabinet should await the guidance of the Commons for policy making, and if they joined a cabinet their views would be compromised. See Smith, "Cabinet and Constitution," 148–59.

42. Partridge, *Military Planning,* 76–77.

43. Ibid., 16.

44. Ibid., 25. Britain's ardent desire to compromise with the United States in the *Trent* affair will be emphasized in chapter 3.

45. Russell F. Weigley, *A Great Civil War: A Military and Policy History, 1861–1865* (Bloomington: Indiana Univ. Press, 2000), 80–81.

46. Palmerston to Russell, 20, 26 July 1860, Russell Papers, PRO 30/22/21, in Michael Gary Poulton, "Great Britain and Intervention in Mexico, 1861–1865" (Ph.D. diss., Miami University of Ohio, 1976), 5, 10–11, 53–55; Anne Pottinger Saab, *Reluctant Icon: Gladstone, Bulgaria, and the Working Classes, 1856–1878,* Harvard Historical Studies, 109 (Cambridge, Mass.: Harvard Univ. Press, 1991), 36–40; C. I. Hamilton, *Anglo-French Naval Rivalry, 1840–1870* (Oxford: Clarendon Press, 1993), 80; William E. Echard, *Napoleon III and Concert of Europe* (Baton Rouge: Louisiana State Univ. Press, 1983), 129, 131–33, 136–40; Jasper Ridley, *Lord Palmerston* (London: Constable & Co., 1970; repr., London: Granada, 1972), 717–22; Herbert C. F. Bell, *Lord Palmerston,* 2 vols. in one (London: Longmans, Green and Co., 1936; repr., Hamden, Conn.: Archon Books, 1966), 2:356–60; Chamberlain, *"Pax Britannica?"* 138; Michael Stephen Partridge, *Gladstone* (New York: Routledge, 2003), 88. The Suez Canal was internationalized in 1888. For Palmerston's early opposition to the Canal, see McCleary, "Anglo-French Naval Rivalry," 78, 81–84; Krein, *Last Palmerston Government,* 57–58.

47. *The Times* (London), 15 Oct. 1852, 17 Mar. 1853, quoted in Martin Crawford, "The Anglo-American Crisis of the Early 1860s: A Framework for Revision," *The South Atlantic Quarterly* 82, no. 4 (Autumn 1983): 412, and 39–40, respectively. Crawford's "Framework for Revision" excludes the period before the 1850s, the Anglo-French rivalry, Britain's withdrawal from North America, and the proven success of private diplomacy by 1861. He ignores the policies of the two governments in the 1983 article and focuses on newspapers that governments ignored repeatedly. For his conception of good relations before 1861, see his "Anglo-American Perspectives: J. C. Bancroft Davis, New York Correspondent of *The Times,* 1854–1861," *New York Historical Society Quarterly* 62, no. 3 (1978): 191, 195–96; and for the deeper positive substance of relations, see Charles R. Ritcheson, "The British Role in American Life, 1800–1850," *History Teacher* 7, no. 4 (1974): 574–96.

48. Campbell, *English Public Opinion and the American Civil War,* 12, 20–22, 31; Richard D. Fulton, "The London *Times* and the Anglo-American Boarding Dispute of 1858," *Nineteenth-Century Contexts* 17, no. 2 (1993): 134, 137–39, 142.

49. Kenneth Bourne, *The Foreign Policy of Victorian England, 1830–1902* (Oxford: Clarendon Press, 1970), 92–93.

50. Ibid., 91; T. Harry Williams, "Canada and the Civil War," in *Heard Round the World: The Impact Abroad of the Civil War,* ed. Harold Hyman (New York: Alfred A. Knopf, 1969), 296; Sexton, *Debtor Diplomacy,* 70–76; Bernstein, "Special Relationship and Appeasement," 749.

51. Charles P. Cullop, *Confederate Propaganda in Europe, 1861–1865* (Coral Gables, Fla.: Univ. of Miami Press, 1969), 11. Quotes are from Dubrulle, "War of Wonders," 44.

52. Temperley, *Britain and America,* 35; Villiers and Chesson, *Anglo-American Relations,* 61–62; quotes on the prince's visit are from Fred M. Leventhal and Roland Quinault, eds., *Anglo-American Attitudes: From Revolution to Partnership* (Burlington, Vt.: Ashgate, 2000), 96; William J. Baker, "Anglo-American Relations in Miniature: The Prince of Wales in Portland, Maine, 1860," *New England Quarterly* 45, no. 4 (1972): 559–68. The newest study is: Ian Radforth, *Royal Spectacle: The 1860 Visit of the Prince of Wales to Canada and the United States* (Buffalo: University of Toronto Press, 2004).

53. This wish may have been the concoction of Pickett's wife who glorified her husband after the Civil War. See Lesley J. Gordon, *General George E. Pickett in Life and Legend,* Civil War America series (Chapel Hill: Univ. of North Carolina Press, 1998), 63.

54. The Hon. Mrs. Hardcastle, ed., *Life of John, Lord Campbell, Lord High Chancellor of Great Britain: Consisting of a Selection from His Autobiography, Diary, and Letters,* 2d ed., 2 vols. (London: John Murray, 1881), 2: (15 Oct. 1859) 380, (27 Oct. 1859) 383. On Esquimalt, see Bourne, *Britain and the Balance of Power,* 208–9.

55. For neutrality doctrine at work in the San Juan affair before and during the early Civil War years, see Myers, "Mask of Indifference," 117–30. De Courcey to Baynes, 5 Aug. 1859, enclosure 2 in Baynes to Admiralty, 3 Oct. 1859, PRO, FO 5/730.

56. Barry M. Gough, *The Royal Navy and the Northwest Coast of North America, 1810–1914: A Study of British Maritime Ascendancy* (Vancouver: Univ. of British Columbia Press, 1971), 160.

57. In 1838 General Scott had been sent on a similar mission to Niagara to maintain peace after the *Caroline* affair when British-led Canadian militiamen burned the American-owned transport *Caroline,* which was assisting Canadian rebels. He performed the same service along the Maine-New Brunswick boundary a few years later. Gladstone to Russell, 22 Aug. 1859, private, copy, Gladstone Papers, BL, Add. Mss. 44304, fols. 13–14 (hereafter cited as Gladstone Papers); Somerset to Gladstone, Oct. 1859, in ibid., fols,. 17–18. For Gladstone's conviction that the British case might not be superior, see Gladstone to Lord Aberdeen, 20 Oct. 1859, Aberdeen Papers, and John Duke, Lord Coleridge to Ellis Yarnall, 1 Oct. 1859, both cited in Crawford, *Anglo-American Crisis of the Mid-Nineteenth Century,* 8. James O. McCabe backs Gough's view in *The San Juan Water Boundary Question,* Canadian Studies in History and Government, no. 5 (Toronto: Univ. of Toronto Press, 1964), esp. 48–49. For Scott's diplomacy, see George Rollie Adams, *General William S. Harney: Prince of Dragoons* (Lincoln: Univ. of Nebraska Press, 2001), 202–12; and David M. Kennedy, "San Juan Island, Washington: The 'Pig War' and the Vagaries of Identity and History," in *American Places: Encounters with History; A Celebration of Sheldon Meyer,* ed. William E. Leuchtenberg (New York: Oxford Univ. Press, 2000), 227.

58. Robin Winks, *Canada and the United States: The Civil War Years* (Montreal: McGill-Queen's Univ. Press, 1998), 34–36; Bourne, *Britain and the Balance of Power,* 211.

59. Gordon, *Pickett,* 62–65.

60. Adams, *Harney,* 212–14. Harney was reassigned to command the Department of the West headquartered in St. Louis. This assignment covered the territory west of the Mississippi to the Rocky Mountains, excluding Texas. His experience with Indian affairs and previous service in Kansas, then torn by the sectional crisis, meant he was being relieved from the tinderbox that he had created to a readily awaiting tinderbox. Ibid., 216. Kennedy, "San Juan Island," 229.

61. David M. Pletcher, *The Diplomacy of Involvement: American Economic Expansion across the Pacific, 1784–1900* (Columbia: Univ. of Missouri Press, 2001), 46. For the British-French-American diplomacy over Hawaii, which resulted in a British victory and a defeat for the annexationist aspirations of the pro-South Franklin Pierce administration by 1855, see Richard W. Van Alstyne, "Great Britain, the United States, and Hawaiian Independence, 1850–1855," *Pacific Historical Review* 4 (1935): 15–24.

62. Somerset to Russell, 19, 26 July 1861, Russell Papers, PRO 30/22/24, in Colin F. Baxter, "Admiralty Problems during the Second Palmerston Administration, 1859–1865" (Ph.D.

diss., University of Georgia, 1965), 106–7. Argyll is important as a conscience of this study because of his pro-North proclivities. He had been loosely associated with the Peelites served as Lord Privy Seal, 1853–55, 1859–66, and 1880–81. He was postmaster general from 1855 to 1858 and secretary for India, 1868–74. His son married Queen Victoria's daughter. Jonathan Parry, *The Rise and Fall of Liberal Government in Victorian Britain* (New Haven, Conn.: Yale Univ. Press, 1993), 319.

63. Sexton, *Debtor Diplomacy,* 78; Amos Khasigian, "Economic Factors and British Neutrality, 1861–1865," *Historian* 25 (August 1963): 463, 465.

2. CAUTION, COOPERATION, AND MUTUAL UNDERSTANDING, 1860–1864

1. Palmerston memorandum, 11 Dec. 1860, Russell Papers, PRO 30/22/21, and Russell to Baring, 21 Dec. 1860, Russell Papers, PRO 30/22/97, in Wilbur D. Jones, *The American Problem in British Diplomacy, 1841–1861* (London: Macmillan, 1974), 198; Ziegler, *Palmerston,* 116. The Barings thought that the British government should have intervened for the North. The financiers helped the North purchase ironclads in Britain, and American purchasing agents praised them for their liberal terms of credit. In August 1861 the Barings advanced $500,000 to help Northern agents buy arms without authorization from the Federal government. See Philip Ziegler, *The Sixth Great Power: A History of One of the Greatest of All Banking Families, the House of Barings, 1762–1929* (New York: Alfred A. Knopf, 1988), 213–14. See Russell to Lyons, 26 Dec. 1860, *BDFA* 5:169, and Russell to Lyons, 5 Jan. 1861, *BDFA* 5:173, for Russell's approval of the cautious foreign affairs perspective implied in Lincoln's message about his desire to placate the Southern states. Russell instructed Lyons to tell British consuls to remain neutral if asked for advice by the Southern states and speak only for continued peace. Lyons to Russell, 4 Feb. 1861, and Russell to Lyons, 20 Feb., 22 Mar. 1961, *BDFA* 5:180–81, 183.

2. Weigley, *Great Civil War,* 179.

3. Sexton, *Debtor Diplomacy,* 87–88.

4. Seward's utterance is quoted in Doris Kearns Goodwin, *Team of Rivals: The Political Genius of Abraham Lincoln* (New York: Simon & Schuster, 2005), 299.

5. Lyons to Russell, 26 Mar. 1861, Russell Papers, PRO 30/22/35, fols. 24–35; Lyons to Russell, 15 Apr. 1861, ibid., PRO 30/22/35, fols. 50–54, in James J. Barnes and Patience P. Barnes, *Private and Confidential: Letters from British Ministers in Washington to the Foreign Secretaries in London, 1844–67* (Selinsgrove, Pa.: Susquehanna Univ. Press, 1993), 246. Kaufman, *Pig War,* 98, on Seward's nonpunitive attitude toward Britain early in the Civil War. Lyons's 15 April letter is also cited in Mahin, *One War at a Time,* 45–46. Lyons's advice to Russell of 18 March 1861 not to form a coherent policy is cited in Crawford, *Anglo-American Crisis of the Mid-Nineteenth Century,* 88. This letter is not included in the Barnes's work. For the description of Lyons, see Jay Monaghan, *Diplomat in Carpet Slippers: Abraham Lincoln Deals with Foreign Affairs* (New York: Charter Books/Bobbs-Merrill, 1945), 35.

6. Temperley, *Britain and America,* 96; Campbell, *English Public Opinion,* 31–32, and n82, 32; Ben Ames Williams, ed., *A Diary from Dixie by Mary Boykin Chesnut* (New York: Houghton Mifflin, 1949; repr., Cambridge, Mass.: Harvard Univ. Press, 1980), 11. For the ascendancy of the Anglo-French ironclad race and France's ambitions in interpreting Britain's role in the American Civil War, see Andrew D. Lambert, "Politics, Technology and Policy-Making, 1859–1865: Palmerston, Gladstone and the Management of the Naval Arms Race," *Northern Mariner* 8, no. 3 (July 1998): 9–15.

7. Andrew Lambert, "Winning without Fighting: British Grand Strategy and Its Application to the United States, 1815–1865," in *Strategic Logic and Political Rationality: Essays in Honor of Michael I. Handel,* ed. Bradford A. Lee and Michael I. Handel (Portland, Ore.: Frank Cass, 2003), 179. I wish to thank Duncan Andrew Campbell for calling this source to my attention.

8. Myers, "Mask of Indifference," 123–24; Kaufman, *Pig War,* 99.

9. Campbell, *English Public Opinion,* 32.

10. D. P. Crook, *Diplomacy during the American Civil War* (New York: John Wiley & Sons, 1975), 35; D. G. Wright, "Bradford and the American Civil War," *Journal of British Studies* 8, no. 2 (May 1969): 77.

11. David G. Surdam, *Northern Naval Superiority and the Economics of the American Civil War* (Columbia: Univ. of South Carolina Press, 2001), 6 (emphasis in original).

12. Williams, ed., *Diary from Dixie,* 235 (2 June 1862).

13. Monaghan, *Diplomat in Carpet Slippers,* 40–42, 73, for Russell's view of Seward and the first Confederate emissaries to Britain; Philip Van Doren Stern, *When the Guns Roared: World Aspects of the American Civil War* (Garden City, N.Y.: Doubleday & Company, 1965), 43–44; Krein, *Last Palmerston Government,* 10. Russell was elevated to the House of Lords as an earl on 30 July 1861. Henry Adams, *The Education of Henry Adams: An Autobiography* (Boston: Houghton Mifflin, 1918; repr., Sentry ed. of the 1918 Massachusetts Historical Society ed., 1961), 135.

14. Jones, *American Problem,* 199; Jenkins, *Britain and the War for the Union,* 2:59. Another American reviler was the veteran and powerful British Foreign Office permanent undersecretary, Edmund Hammond.

15. E. D. Steele, *Palmerston and Liberalism, 1855–65* (Cambridge: Cambridge Univ. Press, 1991), 293.

16. Shelby Foote, *The Civil War: A Narrative,* vol. 1, *From Fort Sumter to Perryville* (New York: Random House, 1958; repr., New York: Vintage Books, 1986), 136–37; Stern, *When the Guns Roared,* 112; on the Southern belief in cotton as a coercive force see Surdam, *Northern Naval Supremacy,* 7. James Morton Callahan, *Diplomatic History of the Southern Confederacy* (1901; repr., New York: Frederick Ungar, 1964), 127–28. James Morton Callahan, "Diplomatic Relations of the Confederate States with England (1861–1865)," *Annual Report of the American Historical Association,* 1898, 270.

17. Sexton, *Debtor Diplomacy,* 89–91.

18. Quoted in Glyndon G. Van Deusen, *William Henry Seward* (New York: Oxford Univ. Press, 1967), 301. He made the same point in 1863 by calling the impression that he had wanted war with Britain an "injurious error" that Adams had done much to correct. Ibid., 301–2.

19. Norman B. Ferris, *Desperate Diplomacy: William H. Seward's Foreign Policy, 1861* (Knoxville: Univ. of Tennessee Press, 1976), 75–79, 83–86.

20. Wilbur D. Jones, *The Confederate Rams at Birkenhead: A Chapter in Anglo-American Relations,* Confederate Centennial Studies, no. 19 (Tuscaloosa, Ala.: Confederate, 1961), 32; Lyons to Milne, private, 8 July 1861, Milne Papers, MLN/116/1a [1–2], NMM (hereafter cited as Milne Papers).

21. Sumner to Richard Henry Dana Jr., Washington, 29 Mar., 14, 16 Apr., 30 June 1861; Sumner to John Andrew, Washington, 24 May 1861. All cited in *The Selected Letters of Charles Sumner,* ed. Beverly Wilson Palmer, 2 vols. (Boston: Northeastern Univ. Press, 1990), 2:62, 64–65, 68, 72.

22. Seward to Adams, 21 July 1861; and Lyons to Russell, 30 July 1861, in Ferris, *Desperate Diplomacy*, 89–92; Lyons to Milne, private, 22 July, 5 Aug. 1861, Milne Papers, MLN/116/1a[1–2].

23. Lyons to Milne, private, 22 July, 19 Aug. 1861, 2, 29 Sept. Milne Papers, MLN/116/1a[1–2].

24. Ferris, *Desperate Diplomacy*, 92–93; Lyons to Milne, private, 12 Oct. 1861, Milne Papers, MLN/116/1a[1–2]; Milne to Lyons, private, Admiralty House, Halifax, 14 Oct., in ibid.; Lyons to Bunch, Confidential, Copy, 23 Oct., in ibid., in which Lyons crisply scolds Bunch for wanting to breach Britain's neutrality and involve Britain in a war with the Union.

25. Henry Adams to Horace Gray Jr., [Confidential], London, 17 June 1861, in *Henry Adams: Selected Letters*, ed. Ernest Samuels (Cambridge, Mass.: Belknap Press of Harvard Univ. Press, 1992), 38–39. See Stern, *When the Guns Roared*, 45–47, 51, on the Russell-Adams relationship.

26. Quoted by Frank L. Owsley, *King Cotton Diplomacy: Foreign Relations of the Confederate State of America*, 2d ed., rev. Harriet Chappell Owsley (Chicago: Univ. of Chicago Press, 1959), chap. 7 and p. 267; Stephen R. Wise, *Lifeline of the Confederacy: Blockade Running during the Civil War* (Columbia: Univ. of South Carolina Press, 1988), 24.

27. Seward's placatory actions early on are noted in Norman B. Ferris, "Seward and the Faith of a Nation," in *Tradition and Values: American Diplomacy, 1790–1865*, ed. Norman A. Graebner (Lanham, Md.: Univ. Press of America, 1985), 164–65. Motley is quoted by John Hay, *Lincoln and the Civil War in the Diaries and Letters of John Hay*, selected and introduced by Tyler Dennett (New York: Dodd, Mead & Company, 1939), 28. See also Russell to Cowley (British ambassador to France), 13 July, 9 Sept. 1861; Russell to the queen, 27 Sept. 1861, both in *The Later Correspondence of Lord John Russell, 1840–1878*, ed. G. P. Gooch, 2 vols. (London: Longmans, Green and Co., 1925), 2:320–21. Owsley, *King Cotton Diplomacy*, 334; and Sumner to Seward, Boston, 12 June 1861, in Palmer, *Selected Letters of Charles Sumner*, 2:70–71.

28. Palmerston to Somerset, 26 May 1861, Somerset Papers; Somerset to Palmerston, 25 June 1861, Palmerston Papers; Palmerston to Somerset, 27 June 1861, Somerset Papers; and Palmerston to Somerset, 1 July 1861, all cited in Baxter, "Admiralty Problems," 105–6.

29. In Regis A. Courtemanche, *No Need of Glory: The British Navy in American Waters, 1860–1864* (Annapolis, Md.: Naval Institute Press, 1977), 23–24. Russell's 15 Feb. 1862 statement was written for publication. See Owsley, *King Cotton Diplomacy*, 222–23. See chapters 3 and 4 herein for the stronger cooperation resulting from the *Trent* affair.

30. Courtemanche, *No Need of Glory*, 32–37, 40; Andrew Lambert, *Battleships in Transition: The Creation of the Steam Battlefleet, 1815–1860* (Annapolis, Md.: Naval Institute Press, 1984), 84–85.

31. Quoted in Stuart W. Bernath, "British Neutrality and the Civil War Prize Cases," *Civil War History* 15, no. 1 (1969): 330; James Daddysman, "British Neutrality and the Matamoros Trade: A Step Toward Anglo-American Rapprochement," *Journal of the West Virginia Historical Association* 9, no. 1 (1985): 7.

32. Somerset to Palmerston, 19 Aug. 1861, Palmerston Papers, quoted in Baxter, "Admiralty Problems," 107–8. See Paul Scherer, *Lord John Russell: A Biography* (Selinsgrove, Pa.: Susquehanna Univ. Press, 1999), 296, on Russell's tolerance.

33. Daddysman, *Matamoros Trade*, 153. The *Times* of 30 June 1863 is quoted in Daddysman, "British Neutrality and Matamoros Trade," 1.

34. Daddysman, *Matamoros Trade*, 38, 155, 158, 160. Daddysman takes his statistics from Somerset and Grey to Rodney, 3 Feb. 1864, Admiralty Papers, PRO Adm. 13/5. According to

these statistics, 100,000–150,000 bales reached New York and other Northern ports. Daddysman, "British Neutrality and the Matamoros Trade," 3; Wise, *Lifeline of the Confederacy,* 169.

35. Surdam, *Northern Naval Superiority,* 8, 89. New Orleans was the "focal point of the world's cotton trade" in 1860. See Wise, *Lifeline of the Confederacy,* 21.

36. Daniel B. Carroll, *Henri Mercier and the American Civil War* (Princeton, N.J.: Princeton Univ. Press, 1971), 123. See David Donald, ed., *Why the North Won the Civil War* (1960; repr., New York: Simon & Schuster, 1996), 16, on the difficulties facing the blockade. The dwindling efficacy of running the blockade is in Surdam, *Northern Naval Supremacy,* 90, 92–95, 97, 103–6. For the view that the blockade was critical for keeping the Confederate military effort alive, see Wise, *Lifeline of the Confederacy,* 7–8.

37. Crook, *North, South, and Powers,* 173–75.

38. Williams, ed., *A Diary from Dixie,* 103.

39. Daddysman, *Matamoros Trade,* 24–25; Owsley, *King Cotton Diplomacy,* 40–41, 46–49; Wise, *Lifeline of the Confederacy,* 167.

40. Daddysman, *Matamoros Trade,* 161–63.

41. Norman B. Ferris, "Lincoln and Seward in Civil War Diplomacy," in *"For a Vast Future Also": Essays from the Journal of the Abraham Lincoln Association,* ed. Thomas F. Swartz (New York: Fordham Univ. Press, 1999), 178.

42. Daddysman, *Matamoros Trade,* 163.

43. Ibid., 166–67.

44. Ibid., 167.

45. Quoted in Surdam, *Northern Naval Superiority,* 109, 112–13, 133, 198–99.

46. Frank J. Merli and Theodore A. Wilson, "The British Cabinet and the Confederacy: Autumn, 1862," *Maryland Historical Magazine* 65 (Fall 1970): 244; Callahan, "Diplomatic Relations," 271.

47. Crook, *North, South, and Powers,* 175–77.

48. James A. McPherson, *Crossroads of Freedom: Antietam,* Pivotal Moments in American History series (New York: Oxford Univ. Press, 2002), 35.

49. Quoted in Owsley, *King Cotton Diplomacy,* 226.

50. Ibid., 225.

51. Crook, *North, South, and Powers,* 177–80. See Henry Adams's descriptions of Forster and Milnes in *Education of Henry Adams,* 124–25. Milnes, according to Adams, was a political and social power to be reckoned with and led the pro-Union charge in Britain along with Bright and Cobden, who were less powerful socially than Milnes. Owsley, *King Cotton Diplomacy,* 224–25. Lynn M. Case and Warren F. Spencer, *The United States and France: Civil War Diplomacy* (Philadelphia: Univ. of Pennsylvania Press, 1970), 269. On Forster, see Wright, "Bradford and the American Civil War," 77.

52. Owsley, *King Cotton Diplomacy,* 226.

53. Ibid., 227.

54. McPherson, *Crossroads of Freedom,* 39.

55. Case and Spencer, *U.S. and France,* 269–70. Gen. Count Auguste Charles Flahault de la Billarderie had been a close advisor to the Bonaparte family for years. See A. R. Tyrner-Tyrnauer, *Lincoln and the Emperors* (New York: Harcourt Brace and World, 1962), 71–72.

56. Owsley, *King Cotton Diplomacy,* 275, 277; Case and Spencer, *U.S. and France,* 270–71.

57. Owsley, *King Cotton Diplomacy, 278;* Case and Spencer, *U.S. and France,* 271.

58. Owsley, *King Cotton Diplomacy,* 278–81; Cowley to Russell, Paris, 13 May 1862, quoted in Case and Spencer, *U.S. and France,* 272–75.

59. Dayton to Seward, 17 Apr. 1862, *FRUS,* 1862, pt. 1, 333, quoted in McPherson, *Crossroads of Freedom,* 39–40, as is Palmerston's missive to Layard. For Adams's remarks, see Adams to Henry Adams, London, 21 Mar., 4 Apr., 16 May 1862, in *The Cycle of Adams Letters, 1861–1865,* ed. Worthington Chauncey Ford, 2 vols. (Boston: Houghton Mifflin, 1920), 1:122–24, 145; Charles M. Hubbard, "James Mason, the 'Confederate Lobby' and the Blockade Debate of March 1862," *Civil War History* 45, no. 3 (Sept. 1999): 226, 229–31, 233–36; Wise, *Lifeline of the Confederacy,* 172–90.

60. Quoted in Khasigian, "Economic Factors and British Neutrality," 457–59.

61. Courtemanche, *No Need of Glory,* 95–98 (emphasis in Milne's quote in original).

62. Ibid., 100.

63. Owsley, *King Cotton Diplomacy,* 211–12.

64. Quoted in Owsley, *King Cotton Diplomacy,* 215; Thouvenel to Mercier, 13 Mar. 1862, quoted in Case and Spencer, *U.S. and France,* 276–77.

65. Flahault to Thouvenel, 5 May 1862, in Case and Spencer, *U.S. and France,* 283–84.

66. Mercier to Thouvenel, Washington, 11 Feb. 1862, in Carroll, *Henri Mercier,* 41 (on Mercier and Seward), 85 (on Seward's satisfaction with European recognition of the blockade's effectiveness), 133; on Mercier, see Monaghan, *Diplomat in Carpet Slippers,* 35. For his journey see Owsley, *King Cotton Diplomacy,* 282–93; and Case and Spencer, *U.S. and France,* 275–81. Thouvenel to Mercier, 1 May 1862, and to Flahault, 2 May, both in Case and Spencer, *U.S. and France,* 283–84.

67. Weigley, *Great Civil War,* 71; Krein, *Last Palmerston Government,* 62–63. Lyons to Russell, 31 Mar. 1862, Russell Papers, PRO 30/22/36; Russell to Lyons, 17 May 1862, Russell Papers, PRO 30/22/96.

3. The *Trent* Affair and Its Aftermath in the Rapprochement

1. Campbell, *English Public Opinion,* 14, 78–79.

2. Kaufman, *Pig War,* 98–99; Jones, *Union in Peril,* 88; Van Deusen, *Seward,* 301–2.

3. Campbell, *English Public Opinion,* 85; Andrew D. Lambert, "Winning without Fighting; British Grand Strategy and Its Application to the United States, 1815–1865," in *Strategic Logic and Political Rationality: Essays in Honor of Michael I. Handel,* ed. Bradford Lee and Michael I. Handel (Portland, Ore.: Frank Cass, 2003), 179–80; Lambert, "Politics, Technology and Policy-Making," 9–15.

4. Quoted in Sexton, *Debtor Diplomacy,* 98–99.

5. Campbell, *English Public Opinion,* 64n10, 71; Russell to Palmerston, 16 Dec. 1861, Palmerston Papers, GC/RU/685, quoted in Campbell, *English Public Opinion,* 85; Campbell, *English Public Opinion,* 86, 94–95; Nathaniel Philbrick, *Sea of Glory: America's Voyage of Discovery, The U.S. Exploring Expedition* (New York: Penguin Books, 2003), 353–56.

6. Winks, *Canada and the United States,* 103; Campbell, *English Public Opinion,* 66–67, 67n17, 68.

7. Gordon H. Warren, *Fountain of Discontent: The* Trent *Affair and Freedom of the Seas* (Boston: Northeastern Univ. Press, 1981), esp. 222–23; Crook, *North, South, and Powers.*

8. Krein, *Last Palmerston Government,* 54; Campbell, *English Public Opinion,* 61, 90, 94–95.

9. Stuart, *United States Expansionism;* Mahin, *One War at a Time,* chap. 5, especially his emphasis that the economic factor was ultimately an important obstacle to conflict: see 73. Norman B. Ferris, *The Trent Affair: A Diplomatic Crisis* (Knoxville: Univ. of Tennessee Press, 1977), vii, 215n22, announces that he will emphasize the "cooling down" process rather than the traditional escalation as a crisis. He makes the point that Palmerston saw the affair as one more in a long list of issues rather than as an emergency. Jones, *Union in Peril,* 87, makes the point that Russell remained confident that strife could be avoided. Scherer, *Russell,* 291–92, finds Russell "peaceably inclined" throughout the event.

10. Weigley, *Great Civil War,* 80.

11. Milton, *Lincoln's Spymaster,* 30–31. On Dudley and the Trent affair, see also Coy F. Cross, III, *Lincoln's Men in Liverpool: Consul Dudley and the Legal Battle to Stop Confederate Warships* (Dekalb: Northern Illinois Univ. Press, 2007), 39.

12. Russell to Lyons, FO, copy, 30 Nov. 1861, Lincoln Papers, ser. 1, General Correspondence, 1833–1916, LC (hereafter cited as Lincoln Papers); Campbell, *English Public Opinion,* 72, for Campbell's interpretation that "it is too much of a simplification to state that commentators saw a Machiavellian Seward forcing conflict upon Britain."

13. Ferris, "Seward and Faith of a Nation," 165–66.

14. Lambert, "Winning without Fighting," 164, 178. Lambert argues that "British planning was essentially defensive and deterrent" because the British knew that they could not "overthrow any of their great power rivals." Moreover, he believes that good sense always prevailed about Anglo-American disputes before 1861, that "Britain did not want to fight the United States," and that its war planning was "reactive." Britain, he continues, was interested in how to "'win' without fighting."

15. Scherer, *Russell,* 291; David Paull Nickles, *Under the Wire: How the Telegraph Changed Diplomacy,* Harvard Historical Series 144 (Cambridge, Mass.: Harvard Univ. Press, 2003), 77. Nickles argues that a functioning telegraph would have increased the pressure and impaired the traditional diplomatic institutions from managing the affair.

16. Quoted in Owsley, *King Cotton Diplomacy,* 84–85. The *Spectator, Saturday Review,* and *Times* are quoted in John Malloy Owen, "Testing the Democratic Peace: American Diplomatic Crises, 1794–1917" (Ph.D. diss., Harvard University, 1993), 238. Seward is quoted in Ferris, "Seward and Faith of a Nation," 164.

17. Magazines are quoted in Campbell, *English Public Opinion,* 73–75.

18. Milton, *Lincoln's Spymaster,* 24–25.

19. Sir John Wheeler-Bennett, "The *Trent* Affair: How the Prince Consort Saved the United States," *History Today* 11, no. 2 (1961): 813–14. See Colonel the Hon. F. A. Wellesley, ed., *The Paris Embassy during the Second Empire: Selections from the Papers of Henry Richard Charles Wellesley, 1st Earl Cowley, Ambassador at Paris, 1852–1867* (London: Thornton Butterworth, 1928), 228–29, on Palmerston's illness during the *Trent* Affair; Russell to Somerset, 28 Dec. 1861, Somerset Papers, in Baxter, "Admiralty Problems," 113; Tyrner-Tyrnauer, *Lincoln and the Emperors,* 39; Campbell, *English Public Opinion,* 87.

20. Sumner's influence on the president is stressed in Norman B. Ferris, "*Trent* Affair," *Lincoln Herald* 49, no. 2 (1967): 132–33; John Niven, ed., *The Salmon P. Chase Papers,* vol. 1, *Journals, 1829–1872* (Kent, Ohio: Kent State Univ. Press, 1993), 314–20.

21. David Donald, *Lincoln* (New York: Simon and Schuster, 1995), 331–33; Ferris, *Trent Affair,* 134.

22. The previous two paragraphs were informed by Victor H. Cohen, "Charles Sumner and the *Trent* Affair," *Journal of Southern History* 12 (1956): 215–19. See also Sumner to Cobden, Senate Chamber, 13 Jan. 1862, in Palmer, *Selected Letters of Charles Sumner*, 2:97, where he wrote that as a result of his speech, "Our people are tranquil, &, I think, that my speech has satisfied the country as to the surrender [of Mason and Slidell]."

23. Owsley, *King Cotton Diplomacy*, 82.

24. Stoeckl to the Russian FO, no. 68, 18 Nov. 1861, in Albert A. Woldman, *Lincoln and the Russians* (Cleveland: World, 1952), 92. Stoeckl thought that Seward ordered the arrests.

25. Thomas, *Confederate Nation*, 174.

26. Foote, *Civil War*, 1:159–60.

27. Pletcher, *Diplomacy of Involvement*, 26–27; William W. Jeffries, "The Civil War Career of Charles Wilkes," *Journal of Southern History* 11 (1945): 324.

28. Howard K. Beale, ed., *The Diary of Edward Bates, 1859–1866*, vol. 4, *Annual Report of the American Historical Association for the Year 1930* (Washington, D.C.: GPO, 1933), 213 (25 Dec. 1861); Philbrick, *Sea of Glory*, 354.

29. Mahin, *One War at a Time*, 62–63.

30. Ibid., 62; Philbrick, *Sea of Glory*, 354.

31. Mahin, *One War at a Time*, 63–64; Wheeler-Bennett, "*Trent* Affair," 814. Sumner to Cobden, private and confidential, Washington, 31 Dec. 1861, in Palmer, *Selected Letters of Charles Sumner*, 2:92–93; Sumner to Bright, Washington, 23 Dec. 1861, in ibid., 2:87.

32. Owsley, *King Cotton Diplomacy*, 86.

33. Donaldson Jordan and Edwin J. Pratt, *Europe and the American Civil War* (New York: Houghton Mifflin, 1931), 206–7; David Pinkney, "France and the Civil War," in Hyman, ed., *Heard Round the World*, 101 (on the attitude of the French workers).

34. Seward knew of Napoleon's schemes since at least the previous February. See A. O'Reilly to James Watson Webb, Paris, 1 Feb. 1861, enclosed in James Watson Webb to Seward, private, 13 Feb. 1861, William Henry Seward Papers, Rush Rhees Memorial Library, Department of Rare Books and Special Collections, University of Rochester, Microfilm Reel 61 (hereafter cited as Seward Papers).

35. Palmerston to Russell, Piccadilly, 30 Dec. 1861, in Wellesley, *Paris Embassy*, 233–34. Cowley refused to believe that Napoleon III had a war plan. He thought that Napoleon would never put himself in a position that might bring Britain into a war against him. Cowley to Russell, memorandum, 10 Jan. 1862, in Wellesley, *Paris Embassy*, 234–40. The British cabinet and Clarendon agreed with Cowley's assessment. Clarendon to Cowley, 17 Jan. 1861, in ibid., 240–41.

36. Jordan and Pratt, *Europe and the American Civil War*, 197–98; Warren, *Fountain of Discontent*, 139, 173; Campbell, *English Public Opinion*, 87.

37. Mahin, *One War at a Time*, 57; Callahan, *Diplomatic History of the Southern Confederacy*, 85.

38. Herman Hattaway and Richard E. Beringer, *Jefferson Davis: Confederate President* (Lawrence: Univ. Press of Kansas, 2002), 50.

39. Foote, *Civil War*, 1:135; Callahan, *Diplomatic History of the Southern Confederacy*, 86.

40. Mahin, *One War at a Time*, 81–82. Commager wrote that Lee might have thought the South would lose, in Donald, *Why the North Won the Civil War*, 16–17.

41. Crook, *Diplomacy during the American Civil War,* 49; Warren, *Fountain of Discontent,* 40; Ferris, Trent *Affair,* 32–35 and n2; Norman B. Ferris, "The Prince Consort, *The Times,* and the *Trent* Affair," *Civil War History* 6 (1960): 154–56.

42. Fillmore to Lincoln, Buffalo, 16 Dec. 1861, Lincoln Papers, ser. 1.

43. Ferris, Trent *Affair,* 36.

44. Ibid.

45. Ibid., 47; Jordan and Pratt, *Europe and the American Civil War,* 30–32, and quote at end of 35. Wright, "Bradford and the American Civil War," 72.

46. Winks, *Canada and the United States,* 206–7. Winks made his point clear: "A daring cavalry raid by J. E. B. Stuart was exciting; what one chancery clerk said to another chancery clerk was not."

47. Jordan and Pratt, *Europe and the American Civil War,* 29, 33. On Acton, see C. Collyer, "Gladstone and the American Civil War," *Proceedings of the Leeds Philosophical Society* 6, no. 8 (1951): 587. Gladstone's theory of why the South seceded was not this elaborate, and he did not share Acton's distrust of Federal power.

48. Ferris, Trent *Affair,* 45–46; Alfred E. Gathorne-Hardy, ed., *Gathorne Hardy, First Earl of Cranbrook: A Memoir, with Extracts from his Diary and Correspondence,* 2 vols. (London: Longman's, Green and Co., 1910), 1:153–54.

49. Ferris, Trent *Affair,* 51–52; and Mahin, *One War at a Time,* 72. On Lewis, see Duchess of Argyll, ed., *Douglas, Eighth Duke of Argyll, K.G., K.T., Autobiography and Memoirs,* 2 vols. (London: John Murray, 1902), 1:540. Lewis had great knowledge and integrity, but he was grave and quiet. He once said, "Life would be very pleasant if it were not for its amusements."

50. Mahin, *One War at a Time,* 68. Matthew, *Gladstone Diaries,* 6:77. Gladstone disapproved of a Canadian proposal for Britain to finance an intercolonial railway. He refused to let the *Trent* incident change his mind that Canada needed to assume more of the cost. See Matthew, *Gladstone Diaries,* 6:80–83.

51. Stern, *When the Guns Roared,* 91.

52. Ferris, Trent *Affair,* 52–53; Wheeler-Bennett, "*Trent* Affair," 815; Ferris, "Seward and the Faith of a Nation," 166.

53. Ferris, "Prince Consort, *The Times,* and the *Trent* Affair," 154.

54. See, for instance, Lyons to Russell, 8 May 1860, in Crawford, *Anglo-American Crisis,* 78; Ferris, Trent *Affair,* 57. Lord Stanley of Alderley to Lady Stanley, Dover Street, 4, 19, 22, 28, 29, 30, Nov., 3 Dec., in Nancy Mitford, ed., *The Stanleys of Alderley: Their Letters between the Years 1851–1865* (London: Hamish Hamilton, 1939; repr., 1968), ix, 269–79. The rapid economic recovery is in Wright, "Bradford and the American Civil War," 80.

55. Monaghan, *Diplomat in Carpet Slippers,* 178–80; Stern, *When the Guns Roared,* 92; Weed to Lincoln, London, 6 P.M., 4 Dec. 1861, Lincoln Papers, ser. 1; Weed to ?, London, 5 Dec. 1861, Thurlow Weed Papers, Rush Rhees Library Rare Books and Special Collections, University of Rochester, BP.C64, box I, (hereafter cited as Weed Papers) wherein Weed recounts, "The Queen, alone, it is said, shows friendly feeling for us."

56. Queen Victoria to Russell, Osborne, 25 Dec. 1861, in Gooch, *Later Correspondence of Lord John Russell,* 2:322–23. The queen wrote: "The Queen is very weak—very much shattered and feels dreadfully worn and exhausted. Business of a public kind she can hardly yet attend to."

57. Cullop, *Confederate Propaganda*, 26–27; Jordan and Pratt, *Europe and the American Civil War*, 36–37.

58. Ferris, Trent *Affair*, 141, 172; Crook, *Diplomacy during the American Civil War*, 47.

59. Ferris, "Trent *Affair*," 133–34; Theodore Calvin Pease and James G. Randall, eds., *The Diary of Orville Hickman Browning*, vol. 1, *1850–1864*, Collections of the Illinois State Historical Library, 2 vols., Lincoln series, vol. 2 (Springfield: Illinois State Historical Library), 514.

60. Jordan and Pratt, *Europe and the American Civil War*, 37–41; Monaghan, *Diplomat in Carpet Slippers*, 185–86; Angus Hawkins, *British Party Politics, 1852–1886* (New York: St. Martin's Press, 1998), 85, on the nonconformists' strength in public opinion.

61. Ferris, Trent *Affair*, 62–63.

62. Ferris, "Prince Consort, *The Times*, and the *Trent* Affair," 154.

63. Ferris, Trent *Affair*, 64; Stern, *When the Guns Roared*, 93.

64. Ferris, Trent *Affair*, 65–66.

65. Ibid., 71.

66. Sarah Agnes Wallace and Frances Elma Gillespie, eds., *The Journal of Benjamin Moran, 1857–1865*, 2 vols. (Chicago: Univ. of Illinois Press, 1948), 2:916–17, 922, 924–30.

67. For the preceding three paragraphs, see Ferris, Trent *Affair*, 78–81.

68. Weigley, *Great Civil War*, 79–80.

69. Frederick W. Seward, *Reminiscences of a War-Time Statesman and Diplomat* (New York: G. P. Putnam's Sons, 1916), 189–90 (emphasis in original).

70. Warren, *Fountain of Discontent*, 181–85, 217. Gladstone read the U.S. Financial Report on 3 January 1862 and wrote to Russell his "amazement" that expenditures for 1861–62 were to be £109 million while U.S. revenues in hand were "seven millions!!" Matthew, *Gladstone Diaries*, 6:87 and n4. On Lincoln's secret draft, see Stern, *When the Guns Roared*, 94.

71. Seward, *Reminiscences*, 190–91.

72. Warren, *Fountain of Discontent*, 208–13; Lincoln quote is in Nevins, *War for the Union*, 2:1. For the *Times*' barbs, see Monaghan, *Diplomat in Carpet Slippers*, 204; and Foote, *Civil War*, 1:162, 220 for the longer quote. Stern, *When the Guns Roared*, 94, for Lincoln's solutions and financial recovery after the prisoners were sent on their way. Seward and Lyons planned the quiet removal of the Confederates by tug from Fort Warren and their passage to out-of-the-way Provincetown on the tip of Cape Cod for pickup by the *Rinaldo* to save either government, but particularly the United States, from any embarrassments that "disloyalists" might have caused over the release. See Seward, *Reminiscences*, 191–93.

73. Weigley, *Great Civil War*, 80; Warren F. Spencer, *The Confederate Navy in Europe* (Tuscaloosa, Ala.: Univ. of Alabama Press, 1983); Wheeler-Bennett, "*Trent* Affair," 816; Wallace and Gillespie, *Journal of Moran*, 2:939–40.

74. Palmerston to George Hamilton, Lord Haddo (fourth Earl of Aberdeen), 26 Jan. 1862, in Kenneth Bourne, ed., *The Letters of the Third Viscount Palmerston to Laurence and Elizabeth Sulivan, 1804–1863*, Camden 4th ser., vol. 23 (London: Offices of the Royal Historical Society, 1979), 4. Lyons to Milne, private and confidential, Washington, 27 Feb. 1862, Milne Papers, NMM (microfilm), MLN/116/1a[1–2]; Lyons to Milne, private, 12 May 1862, Milne Papers.

75. Wallace and Gillespie, *Journal of Moran*, 2:941; Crawford, *Anglo-American Crisis*, 135; Russell's comment cited in Jones, *Union in Peril*, 87.

76. Sexton, *Debtor Diplomacy*, 102–4.

77. Russell to Lyons, 2 Mar. 1862, Russell Papers, PRO 30/22/96, in Wilbur D. Jones, "The British Conservatives and the Civil War," *American Historical Review* 58 (Apr. 1953): 527, 530–31; Adams, *Education of Henry Adams*, 121, 126; Jones, *Union in Peril*, 96–97; Owsley, *King Cotton Diplomacy*, 82; Seward, *Reminiscences*, 192; Scherer, *Russell*, 292; Williams, ed., *Diary from Dixie*, 195 (5 Mar. 1862).

78. Williams, ed., *Diary from Dixie*, 187 (11 Feb. 1862).

4. Averting Crisis in 1862

1. Sexton, *Debtor Diplomacy*, 104–5. For the Russell-Mason and Thouvenel-Slidell encounters, see Monaghan, *Diplomat in Carpet Slippers*, 205–6; Jones, *Union in Peril*, 102; Mahin, *One War at a Time*, 123.

2. Foote, *Civil War*, 1:231, 395, 416. For Captain Hewitt's visit with Seward at Norfolk, see Seward, *Reminiscences*, 199–200. Hewitt had just returned from escorting Mason and Slidell to England.

3. Cullop, *Confederate Propaganda*, 33; Hotze to R. M. T. Hunter (Confederate Secretary of State), 1 Feb. 1862, ORN, vol. 3: *Proclamations, Appointments, etc. of President Davis; State Department Correspondence with Diplomatic Agents, etc.* [hereafter ORN II:3] 325–26; Mason to Hunter, 7 Feb. 1862, in ibid., 331–32; Mason to Hunter, no. 4, 22 Feb. 1861, in ibid., 343–45.

4. Matthew, *Gladstone Diaries*, 6:93, and n6; Somerset to Palmerston, 6 Feb. 1862, Palmerston Papers, GC/SO/78, in Lambert, "Winning without Fighting," 186–87. It cost £234,338 to transport troops to Canada.

5. Wheeler-Bennett, *"Trent* Affair," 816; Nevins, *War for Union*, 2:3–4.

6. Russell to the Lords Commissioners of the Admiralty, 4 Apr. 1862, *BDFA* 6:45–46; Lyons to Russell, confidential, 25 Apr. 1862, in ibid., 46; Baxter, "Admiralty Problems," 119. Seward's cooperation immediately after the affair is summarized in Ferris, "Seward and Faith of a Nation," 168–69; Lyons to Milne, private, Washington, 24 Apr. 1862, Letters from Lord Lyons, 1861–62, Milne Papers, MLN/116/1a[1–2].

7. Lyons to Russell, 3 June 1862, *BDFA* 6:49.

8. Jordan and Pratt, *Europe and the American Civil War*, 98–99.

9. Ibid., 98–101; Jones, *Union in Peril*, 105–6; Wallace and Gillespie, eds., *Journal of Moran*, 2:962–64 (Saturday, 8 Mar. 1862). Moran recorded that he had assisted Forster with compiling evidence of the blockade's effectiveness and had visited Forster and his wife for breakfast before the debate to go over the facts he had uncovered. See Wallace and Gillespie, eds., *Journal of Moran*, 2:961 (Thursday, 6 Mar.)

10. Adams, *Great Britain and the American Civil War*, 1:261–62; Charles M. Bullard, *The Burden of Confederate Diplomacy* (Knoxville: Univ. of Tennessee Press, 1998), 54–56, 64, 66, 70–75, 78–79; Jones, *Union in Peril*, 106; Lyons to Milne, Washington, private and confidential, 23 June 1862, Letters from Lord Lyons, 1861–62, Milne Papers MLN/116/1a[1–2].

11. Matthew, *Gladstone Diaries*, 6:114.

12. Russell to Palmerston, 31 Mar. 1862, Broadlands Mss., GC/RU/708; Palmerston to Russell, 25 Apr. 1862, Russell Papers, PRO 30/22/22; Palmerston to Gladstone, 29 Apr. 1862, Gladstone Papers, Add. Mss. 44272, fol. 126; same to same, 7 May 1862, Palmerston Letter Book, Add. Mss. 48582, fol. 113. All are in Krein, *Last Palmerston Government*, 22, 58–59. With penetrating insight, Cobden held that Gladstone's conscience made a strong impression but that when it became entangled with his intellect it affected his reason. See William

Harbutt Dawson, *Richard Cobden and Foreign Policy: A Critical Exposition, With Special Reference to Our Day and Its Problems* (London: George Allen & Unwin, 1926), 79.

13. Nevins, *War for the Union,* 2:52–55. Palmerston to Somerset, 22 Oct. and 16 Dec. 1860, Somerset Papers, Devon Record Office, Box 15, in Partridge, *Military Planning,* 8–9, 25; Lambert, *Battleships in Transition,* 51, 77; Colin F. Baxter, "The Duke of Somerset and Creation of the British Ironclad Navy, 1859–66" *Mariner's Mirror* 63, no. 3 (1977): 282, Palmerston likened French naval building at Cherbourg as pointing at Britain's "jugular." Hamilton, *Anglo-French Naval Rivalry,* 84, 92.

14. Partridge, *Military Planning,* 13, 16–17.

15. Gideon Welles, *Diary of Gideon Welles: Secretary of the Navy under Lincoln and Johnson* (Boston and New York: Houghton Mifflin, 1909), 1:79 (Mon., 11 Aug. 1862).

16. Ridley, *Palmerston,* 738.

17. Jenkins, *Britain and the War for the Union,* 2:115–16; Allen, *Great Britain and the United States,* 454, on Stuart's "unrealistically sanguine view of the prospects of the South."

18. Sexton, *Debtor Diplomacy,* 106–7.

19. Monaghan, *Diplomat in Carpet Slippers,* 234; quote is from Edward W. Ellsworth, "Anglo-American Affairs in October of 1862," *Lincoln Herald* 66, no. 2 (1964): 89.

20. Weigley, *Great Civil War,* 309–10; Nevins, *War for the Union,* 2:266–67.

21. Baxter, "Admiralty Problems," 123; Nevins, *War for the Union,* 2:264.

22. Baxter, "Admiralty Problems," 123–24.

23. Palmer to Russell, 13 Nov. 1865, Russell Papers, PRO 30/22/15, in Jones, *Confederate Rams at Birkenhead,* 32.

24. Jones, *Confederate Rams at Birkenhead,* 33.

25. Welles, *Diary,* 1:74 (Sunday, 10 Aug. 1862). Welles was critical of Britain for allowing this and for British officials in ports such as Nassau treating American naval officers with disregard while lavishing attention on Confederate sailors. Welles was also critical of Seward for not pressuring the British ministry into not cooperating with the Confederates at ports such as Nassau.

26. Russell to Adams, 2 Aug. 1862, PRO, FO 5/1313, in Jones, *Confederate Rams at Birkenhead,* 39.

27. Russell to Lyons, 1 Mar. 1862, Russell Papers, PRO 30/22/96, in Jones, *Confederate Rams at Birkenhead,* 42.

28. Welles, *Diary,* 1:165 (Friday, 10 Oct. 1862), 497 (Saturday, 26 Dec. 1863).

29. Bulloch to Mallory, 14 Mar. and 11 Apr. 1862, *Official Records of the Union and Confederate Navies in the War of the Rebellion,* 30 vols. (Washington, D.C.: GPO, 1894–1922), ser. 2, vol. 2:151, in Spencer, *Confederate Navy in Europe,* 67–68. David F. Krein, "Russell's Decision to Detain the Laird Rams," *Civil War History* 22, no. 2 (June 1976): 158–59.

30. Jones, *Confederate Rams at Birkenhead,* 47–48; Weigley, *Great Civil War,* xxvii, 10, 217–18, 315, 456; T. Harry Williams, "Two War Leaders: Lincoln and Davis," in *"For a Vast Future Also": Essays from the Journal of the Abraham Lincoln Association,* ed. Thomas F. Swartz (New York: Fordham Univ. Press, 1999), 220. Davis's poor judgment about the causes that he selected stirred up trouble for him from the beginning of the war. His misery can be followed in Hattaway and Beringer, *Davis,* 99–103, 184. They see Davis with the active-negative presidential style after James Barber's model in *The Presidential Character: Predicting Performance in the White House,* 4th ed. (Englewood Cliffs, N.J.: Prentice Hall, 1992). Barber's work is helpful for seeing Davis as a perfectionist who became frustrated and introverted

as he transgressed his abilities. Barber's Davis is afflicted with a sense of failure and pride when provoked. Barber believes that such a specimen retreats inwardly when reality becomes too complex to handle. He tries to neutralize conflicts (so Hattaway and Beringer interpret Barber's model) "by *invoking abstract principles*" when practical solutions were needed to prosecute the war. Barber believes that "the most persuasive feelings in the active-negative's makeup is '*I must.*'" Davis was engrossed in an eternal conflict between virtue and power and helplessness. Hattaway and Beringer write that at the outset of an event the active-negative seems capable, but as the event wears on he grows, in Barber's words, "extraordinarily rigid, becoming more and more closed to experience, including the advice of his ardent allies." His critics do not understand this transition and question his goals. But they point out that Davis rode "the tiger to the end." Hattaway and Beringer drew from Barber that, to quote Barber, "in failing [, an active-negative president such as Davis, will have] found proofs that he had been right all along in seeing the world as he saw it and in acting as he had to act." Hattaway and Beringer continue that "[Davis's] own quirky personality was just as malignant an enemy. . . . He wasted his time resenting and revenging personal affronts that larger-minded men would have ignored" (103). By early 1862, Davis helped cement closer British-American relations because he angered the British just as he did his own people with his unrelenting, prideful style and his frustration at diplomacy from which he retreated as he had retreated from so much else he found distasteful (ibid., 438–39).

31. Jones, *Confederate Rams at Birkenhead*, 33–34.

5. DISSOLVING INTERVENTION IN 1862

1. Frank J. Merli, *The* Alabama, *British Neutrality, and the American Civil War*, ed. David M. Fahey (Bloomington: Indiana Univ. Press, 2004), 20. See Crook, *North, South, and Powers*, 4, 374.

2. Merli, Alabama, *British Neutrality, and the American Civil War*, 22.

3. William Stuart (British chargé d'affaires in Washington—Lyons was on leave in Britain) to Russell, No. 100, 25 July 1862, *BDFA* 6:74–75; and Russell to Stuart, No. 55, 7 Aug. 1862, FO, in ibid., 74. On the issue of increasing cotton shipments from New Orleans, Russell and Seward engaged in a long correspondence over the summer and into the fall. Seward approved of Russell's plan to directly compensate the planters for their crops. However, the plan fell through because the planters refused to support it. Russell to Stuart, No. 164, FO, 23 Oct. 1862, in ibid., 6:108–9.

4. Stuart to Russell, No. 87, Confidential, 21 July 1862, *BDFA* 6:73.

5. Merli, Alabama, *British Neutrality, and the American Civil War*, ix, xv, xvi, 9, 39, 49, 52–54, 58–61, 64, 66–67, 71–72, and esp. 72 for the primary conclusion that Adams and Dudley, the American officials in Britain, were dilatory and not the British. This conclusion fits with Russell's patient cooperation throughout the Civil War and helps explain why he was reluctant to involve Britain's honor in arbitrating the *Alabama* dispute after the war. Professor Merli passed away in 2000 after devoting more than two decades to research on this problem. His book goes far to show that British-American relations were more cooperative during the Civil War than any other study to date that I know about.

6. Ferris, *Desperate Diplomacy*, 42, 132.

7. See, for instance, Gathorne-Hardy, *Gathorne Hardy*, 1:156. Russell to Mason, 2 Aug. 1862, and Russell to Victoria, 24, 25 Aug 1962, in Merli and Wilson, "British Cabinet and

Confederacy," 245; Russell to Lewis, 26 Oct. 1862, in Gooch, *Later Correspondence of Lord John Russell,* 2:329.

8. Nevins, *War for the Union,* 2:273.

9. Bourne, *Britain and the Balance of Power,* 253.

10. Owen, "Testing the Democratic Peace," 212; Ridley, *Palmerston,* 750. The quote is from Richard Shannon, *Gladstone, 1865–1898* (Chapel Hill: Univ. of North Carolina Press, 1999), 2:87.

11. Palmerston to the Queen, 18 July 1862, cited in Merli and Wilson, "British Cabinet and Confederacy," 245.

12. Merli and Wilson, "British Cabinet and Confederacy," 246.

13. Wallace and Gillespie, eds., *Journal of Moran,* 2:965 (Friday, 14 Mar. 1862).

14. Hattaway and Beringer, *Davis,* 179. Antietam statistics are in McPherson, *Crossroads of Freedom,* 3, 133, the best brief analysis of the battle in all of its ramifications. See also Murfin's analysis of the outcome of the daylong battle in James V. Murfin, *The Gleam of Bayonets: The Battle of Antietam and the Maryland Campaign of 1862* (New York: Thomas Yoseloff, 1965), chap. 11, esp. 297–98. Stephen W. Sears, *Landscape Turned Red: The Battle of Antietam* (Boston: Houghton Mifflin, 1983; repr., Mariner Books, 2003), 234–97, 310, for a cogent narrative of the battle. On the morning of 18 Sept., McClellan had nearly 25,000 fresh troops, and at least 6,000 more came overnight. He outnumbered Lee two to one but believed Lee had more troops.

15. Michael C. C. Adams, *Our Masters the Rebels: A Speculation on Union Military Failure in the East, 1861–1865* (Cambridge, Mass.: Harvard Univ. Press, 1978), 105.

16. Ellsworth, "Anglo-American Affairs," 91.

17. Owsley, *King Cotton Diplomacy,* 348.

18. Russell to Lyons, 16 June 1862, cited in Owsley, *King Cotton Diplomacy,* 321–22, 324.

19. Russell to Mason, 2 Aug. 1862, cited in Owsley, *King Cotton Diplomacy,* 321.

20. Brauer, "Slavery Problem," 466; Ellsworth, "Anglo-American Affairs," 90–91; Slidell to Benjamin, Sept. 13, 1862, cited in Owsley, *King Cotton Diplomacy,* 326–27; Tyrner-Tyrnauer, *Lincoln and the Emperors,* 80.

21. Ridley, *Palmerston,* 736; Cook, Alabama *Claims,* 25.

22. Maxwell, *Clarendon,* 2:263–64. On Somerset see Campbell, *English Public Opinion,* 136. In a speech at Exeter in early November 1862, Somerset called for "calm with respect to the North and argued that allowance had to be made for the position in which both sides—but especially the Union—were placed." He opposed intervention and mediation, causing Campbell to conclude: "The Union could hardly have asked for more from this member of the aristocracy." This example is part of Campbell's evidence to debunk the myth of aristocratic support for the South. See especially 134–39.

23. Nevins, *War for the Union,* 2:289.

24. Welles, *Diary,* 1:89–90 (Friday, 22 Aug. 1862).

25. Bunch to Russell, 16 Mar. 1862, PRO, FO 5/843, in Jenkins, *Britain and the War for Union,* 2:13.

26. Jenkins, *Britain and the War for Union,* 2:3–4.

27. Ibid., 2:17–18; Gladstone to Russell, 30 Aug. 1862, and to William Stuart, 8 Sept. 1862, quoted in McPherson, *Crossroads of Freedom,* 93–94.

28. Ellsworth, "Anglo-American Affairs," 94; Peter Parish, "Gladstone and America," in *Gladstone,* ed. Peter J. Jagger (London: Hambledon Press, 1998), 90–95.

29. Gladstone to Denison, 16 Aug. 1861, Gladstone Papers, Add. Mss. 44532, in Ferris, Trent *Affair*, 222n14; Ellsworth, "Anglo-American Affairs in October of 1862," 92–93; Palmerston to Gladstone, 24 Sept. 1862, Gladstone Papers, Add. Mss. 44272, cited in Merli and Wilson, "British Cabinet and Confederacy," 247–48.

30. Merli and Wilson, "British Cabinet and Confederacy," 248; Gladstone to (Arthur Hamilton) Gordon, Hawarden, 22 Sept. 1862, in Paul Knaplund, ed., *Gladstone-Gordon Correspondence, 1851–1896: Selections from the Private Correspondence of a British Prime Minister and a Colonial Governor*, Transactions of the American Philosophical Society, n.s., vol. 51, pt. 4 (Philadelphia: American Philosophical Society, 1961), 41.

31. Russell to Gladstone, 26 Sept. 1862, Gladstone Papers, Add. Mss. 44292, and n16; Russell to Cowley, 26 Sept. 1862, Cowley Papers, PRO, FO 519/199, both cited in Merli and Wilson, "British Cabinet and Confederacy," 247.

32. Jones, *Lincoln and a New Birth of Freedom*, 16, 41–43, 93, 103–4, 107, 121; Bunch to Russell, 21 June 1862, FO 5/780, and same to same, 21 Oct. 1862, FO 5/844, for instance, in Berwanger, *British Foreign Service*, 21; Ridley, *Palmerston, 737*, on the slave revolt fear. Gladstone to Argyll, 29 Sept. 1862, Gladstone Papers, Add. Mss. 44533, vol. 448, in Jones, *Union in Peril*, 168.

33. Merli and Wilson, "British Cabinet and Confederacy," 248n18.

34. Ridley, *Palmerston, 737–38.*

35. Donald, *Charles Sumner and Rights of Man*, 112–14.

36. Jones, *Lincoln and a New Birth of Freedom*, 48, 92, 107.

37. Ibid., 93, 129; Jones, *Union in Peril*, 154, 170–71; Hubbard, *Burden of Confederate Diplomacy,* 120–21; *Times* (London), 13 Nov., 1862, in Merli, *Great Britain and the Confederate Navy,* 255; Ellsworth, "Anglo-American Affairs," 94.

38. Granville to Russell, 27 Oct. 1862, Granville Papers, PRO 30/29/18, Bundle 7, fols. 14–15. See also Lord Edmond Fitzmaurice, *The Life of Granville George Leveson Gower: Second Earl Granville, K.G., 1815–1891,* 2 vols. (New York: Longmans, Green, and Co., 1905), 1:442; Duberman, *Charles Francis Adams,* 294; Owsley, *King Cotton Diplomacy,* 346–47; and Thomas, *Confederate Nation,* 180–81, for an excellent synopsis of Granville's "stream-of-consciousness" memorandum.

39. Granville to Russell, 27 Oct. 1862, Granville Papers, PRO 30/29/18, Bundle 7, fols. 16–17; Granville to Lord Stanley of Alderley, 1 Oct. 1862, cited in Fitzmaurice, *Granville,* 1:442.

40. Owsley, *King Cotton Diplomacy,* 348; Fitzmaurice, *Granville,* 1:442; Krein, *Last Palmerston Government,* 71–72.

41. Fitzmaurice, *Granville,* 1:442–44; Case and Spencer, *U.S. and France,* 344.

42. McPherson, *Crossroads of Freedom,* 137, 141, 155–56.

43. The *Times* (London), 2 Oct. 1862, and Charles Francis Adams to Charles Francis Adams, Jr., 17 Oct. 1862, both quoted in McPherson, *Crossroads of Freedom,* 141–42.

44. Palmerston to Russell, 22 Oct. 1862, quoted in McPherson, *Crossroads of Freedom,* 142 (emphasis in original); Owsley, *King Cotton Diplomacy,* 347.

45. Crook, *North, South, and Powers,* 224–25.

46. Gladstone to the Duchess of Sutherland, 29 May 1861, Gladstone Papers, Add. Mss. 44531, in Ferris, *Desperate Diplomacy,* 35.

47. Parish, "Gladstone and America," 97; Matthew, *Gladstone Diaries,* 6:117; Jenkins, *Britain and the War for the Union,* 2:22–23; Michael J. Winstanley, *Gladstone and the Liberal Party* (New York: Routledge, 1990), 40.

48. Parish, "Gladstone and America," 97; McPherson, *Battle Cry of Freedom,* 548.

49. Crook, *North, South, and Powers,* 230; Owsley, *King Cotton Diplomacy,* 340.

50. Krein, *Last Palmerston Government,* 26–27.

51. Matthew, *Gladstone Diaries,* 6:152; Cook, Alabama *Claims,* 25; Crook, *North, South, and Powers,* 227–28; Nevins, *War for the Union,* 2:168; Monaghan, *Diplomat in Carpet Slippers,* 255. Dubrulle discusses the Neville-Gladstone correspondence of June and July 1862 in "War of Wonders," 97. Lt. Col. Neville to Gladstone, Washington, 4 July 1862, Gladstone Papers, Add. Mss. 44399, fols. 5–9, in Collyer, "Gladstone and the American Civil War," 588.

52. Gladstone to A. C. Coxe, 5 June 1861, Gladstone Papers, Add. Mss. 44396, fols. 107, 109–10; Gladstone to Cornewall Lewis, 4 Sept. 1861, Gladstone Papers, Add. Mss. 44532, fol. 42; Gladstone to Cobden, 27 Jan. 1862, Gladstone Papers, Add. Mss. 44136, fol. 168, (emphasis in original) all in Collyer, "Gladstone and the American Civil War," 588–89.

53. Crook, *North, South, and Powers,* 228–29; Foote, *Civil War,* 1:791, for quote from Gladstone's speech. Adams, *Education of Henry Adams,* 157. On Bagehot, see Allen, "Civil War, Reconstruction, and Great Britain," in Hyman, ed., *Heard Round the World,* 43.

54. Joseph M. Hernon, Jr., "British Sympathies in the American Civil War: A Reconsideration," *Journal of Southern History* 33 (Aug. 1967): 366; Collyer, "Gladstone and the American Civil War," 590.

55. Russell to Gladstone, 20 Oct. 1862, Gladstone Papers, Add. Mss. 44292; Palmerston to Russell, 12 Oct. 1862, Russell Papers, PRO 30/22/22; Palmerston to Russell, 17 Oct. 1862, Russell Papers, PRO 3022/14D; *Saturday Review,* 25 Oct. 1862, vol. 14, no. 365, 494, all quoted in Dubrulle, "War of Wonders," 171n4. Merli and Wilson, "British Cabinet and Confederacy," 248n18. Gladstone's earlier use of the phrase that the time had come to recognize the independence of the South is noted by Matthew, *Gladstone Diaries* 6:133 (7 July 1862), where Gladstone recorded: "In a box of Lord P[almerston]'s with an anon. letter recommending intervention of Europe in U.S. I put a mem. with my opinion that the time for something of the kind is coming."

56. Cowley to Russell, 3 Oct. 1862, in Sir Victor Wellesley and Robert Sencourt, eds., *Conversations with Napoleon III: A Collection of Documents, Mostly Unpublished and Almost Entirely Diplomatic, Selected and Arranged with Introductions* (London: Ernest Benn Limited, 1934), 212. Merli and Wilson, "British Cabinet and Confederacy," 248–50, and n18, wherein the authors point out that historians have agreed that the speech was one of the biggest blunders of Gladstone's career for which he apologized much later. The apology is quoted from Parish, "Gladstone and America," 99. Collyer, "Gladstone and the American Civil War," 590–92.

57. On Bright's words, see Winstanley, *Gladstone and the Liberal Party,* 40. Russell to Palmerston, Pembroke Lodge, 2 Oct. 1862, University of Southampton Library, Broadlands Mss. GC/RU/691–758, 1862 (hereafter Broadlands Mss.); same to same, Woburn Abbey, 9 Oct. 1862, in ibid. On Napoleon III, see Collyer, "Gladstone and the American Civil War," 591.

58. Keith Robbins, *John Bright* (Boston: Routledge & Kegan Paul, 1979), 163–64; Jones, *Lincoln and a New Birth of Freedom,* 124–25; Morley, *Gladstone,* 2:80, n2, 83; Jones, *Union in Peril,* 186; Merli and Wilson, "British Cabinet and Confederacy," 251.

59. Nevins, *War for the Union,* 2:269.

60. Merli and Wilson, "British Cabinet and Confederacy," 251. Russell's memorandum of 13 October is printed in *BDFA* 6:91–96. Russell's major points for a friendly and conciliatory mediation were his fear of emancipation leading to a slave revolt, the inability of the

Union to open up the cotton trade after taking New Orleans, the punishment of the North on the South because Southerners rued Federal conquest, the loss of half of McClellan's army in the Richmond campaign, and the human costs of the war in general while neither army gained a decisive military advantage.

61. Ibid., 251–52.

62. Russell to Palmerston, 18 Oct. 1862, cited in Merli and Wilson, "British Cabinet and Confederacy," 252–53 and n25.

63. Adams, *Great Britain and the American Civil War*, 2:49–54; Jones, *Lincoln and a New Birth of Freedom*, 126, 128–29; Case and Spencer, *U.S. and France*, 344–45; Crook, *North, South, and Powers*, 232–33; Nevins, *War for the Union*, 2:269; Monaghan, *Diplomat in Carpet Slippers*, 257, 262. Monaghan cites John Bigelow's *Retrospections* that Palmerston arranged for Lewis's speech. Morley, *Gladstone*, 2:80, writes: "A week after the [Gladstone] deliverance at Newcastle, Lewis at Lord Palmerston's request *as I have heard*, [emphasis mine] put things right in a speech at Hereford." Howard Jones believes that the rumors of Palmerston's duplicity were unfounded. See *Union in Peril*, 191n16. More recently, Parish seems to accept Morley, despite using Jones as a reference also. Parish writes that "Palmerston put up . . . Lewis to make a speech," in his article "Gladstone and America," 98. For Grey's remarks, see Owsley, *King Cotton Diplomacy*, 353. For the workers, see ibid., 183. For Palmerston's sticking to neutrality, see Palmerston to Russell, October 22, 24, 1862, in Merli and Wilson, "British Cabinet and Confederacy," 254.

64. Crook, *North, South, and Powers*, 241; Merli and Wilson, "British Cabinet and Confederacy," 252.

65. Russell to Palmerston, 20 Oct. 1862, cited in Merli and Wilson, "British Cabinet and Confederacy," 257 and n33.

66. Cowley to Russell, 28, 31 Oct. 1862, Layard to Russell, 13 Nov. 1862, cited in Merli and Wilson, "British Cabinet and Confederacy, 257 and n34; Parish, "Gladstone and America," 98.

67. Stuart to Russell, No. 336, 7 Nov. 1862 (received 20 Nov.), *BDFA* 6:112–13.

68. Crook, *North, South, and Powers*, 253.

69. Bullard, *Burden of Confederate Diplomacy*, 121–22; Jones, *Union in Peril*, 206–11, 214. Harcourt was a barrister, a leading journalist, and the Whewell Professor of International Law at Cambridge from 1869 to 1887. He was a "tireless critic" of Gladstone, who bought him off with the office of solicitor general in 1873, and he was a strong critic of Disraeli. See Parry, *Rise and Fall of the Liberal Government*, 325–26. The fifteenth Earl of Derby wrote in 1872, "Harcourt is clever, though unpopular from the general arrogance of his manner: radical as far as he has any convictions, but mainly bent on making a great personal name for himself," in John Vincent, ed., *A Selection from the Diaries of Edward Henry Stanley, 15th Earl of Derby (1826–93) between September 1869 and March 1878*, Camden Fifth series, vol. 4 (London: Offices of the Royal Historical Society, 1994), 106–7 (10 May 1872).

70. Russell to Cowley, FO, 13 Nov. 1862, *BDFA* 6:111–12.

71. Lyons to Russell, 14 Nov. 1862, Russell Papers, PRO 30/22/36, fols. 291–300, cited in Barnes and Barnes, *Private and Confidential*, 308–9.

72. Lyons to Russell, 24 Nov. 1862, Russell Papers, PRO 30/22/36, fols. 306–9, cited in Barnes and Barnes, *Private and Confidential*, 310; Lyons to Russell, No. 466, 28 Nov. 1862, *BDFA* 6:121; Lyons to Russell, No. 467, Confidential, in ibid., 121–22; Lyons to Russell, No. 477, 2 Dec. 1862, in ibid., 127. Howard Jones writes that Seward's remarks to Lyons were

heated, that he lauded Russia's refusal, and that he then "focused his wrath on France and England." *Union in Peril,* 220–21.

73. Lyons to Russell, No. 494, Confidential, 8 Dec. 1862, *BDFA* 6:129–30.

74. Clarendon to Lewis, The Grove, 24 Oct. 1962, in Maxwell, *Clarendon,* 2:265–67; Case and Spencer, *U.S. and France,* 345–46, who cite Clarendon's 24 Oct. letter to Lewis; Adams, *Great Britain and the American Civil War,* 2:58; Nevins, *War for the Union,* 2:270. Palmerston's letter to Leopold is summarized in McPherson, *Crossroads of Freedom,* 142 (Palmerston's emphasis). See Merli and Wilson, "British Cabinet and Confederacy," 254, 261–62, for quotes from Palmerston's message to Leopold. Gladstone to Catherine Gladstone, Downing Street, 12 Nov. 1862, Bassett, *Gladstone to His Wife,* 140. But Gladstone was beginning to repent his misdeed of 7 October. A year later he was writing his wife about his "incautious speech" at Newcastle while criticizing Russell for being too "incautious" in his speech about the Laird rams. Gladstone to Catherine Gladstone, Balmoral, 29 Sept. 1863, in ibid., 150.

75. Quoted in Stern, *When the Guns Roared,* 188–89.

76. Quoted in McPherson, *Crossroads of Freedom,* 143.

77. Callahan, *Diplomatic History of the Southern Confederacy,* 94–97; Cullop, *Confederate Propaganda,* 85.

78. Dayton, Stuart, and Russell letters are in McPherson, *Crossroads of Freedom,* 143.

79. Quoted in ibid., 145.

80. Quoted in ibid.

81. Weigley, *Great Civil War,* 191–92; Stern, *When the Guns Roared,* 191–92; quotes are in McPherson, *Crossroads of Freedom,* 146. The quote by Henry Adams is in Temperley, *Britain and America,* 4.

82. Quoted in McPherson, *Crossroads of Freedom,* 146.

83. Weigley, *Great Civil War,* 192; Callahan, *Diplomatic History of the Southern Confederacy,* 184–86.

84. M. F. Maury to B. Franklin Minor, 14 Jan. 1863, Maury Papers, vol. 17, in Spencer, *Confederate Navy in Europe,* 136, and n18 (emphasis in original); Cullop, *Confederate Propaganda,* 86.

6. Lincoln's Cabinet Crisis of December 1862 in the Rapprochement

1. Even pro-South British chargé d'affaires Stuart wrote to Russell, "I should not be acting fairly towards Mr. Seward did I not express to your Lordship my belief that he has been most anxious to do all in his power to facilitate the export of cotton to Europe." Stuart to Russell, No. 125, 3 Aug. 1862, *BDFA* 6:76. Russell informed Stuart on 21 Aug. that Seward was making progress on facilitating cotton exports at New Orleans. Russell made it clear that Seward's government could not be responsible for obstacles to cotton exports put up by the South. Ibid., 78.

2. *CWL,* 5:518 (1 Dec. 1862).

3. Stuart to Russell, No. 136, 8 Aug. 1862, *BDFA* 6:77–78.

4. Stoeckl to the Russian FO, No. 82, 1 Dec. 1862, in Woldman, *Lincoln and the Russians,* 135; Lyons to Russell, 19 Dec. 1862, Russell Papers, PRO 30/22/36, fols. 324–26, in Barnes and Barnes, *Private and Confidential,* 312; J. W. Schulte Nordholt, "The Civil War Letters of the

Dutch Ambassador," *Journal of the Illinois State Historical Society* 54 (Winter 1961): 341–373. Roest, the Dutch minister, was critical of Lincoln personally and of Lincoln's government and the Americans in general. He disliked his posting much as Lyons did. For the roots of the Republican Party's being the first American political party to completely repudiate the South as part of its original reason for formation, see William J. Cooper, Jr., *Jefferson Davis, American* (New York: Alfred A. Knopf, 2000), 274–75. The Radicals' distrust of Lincoln is discussed by David Donald, *Lincoln* (New York: Simon & Schuster, 1995), 423–24. Lincoln is quoted in James A. Rawley, *Lincoln and a Nation Worth Fighting For* (Wheeling, Ill: Harlan Davidson, 1996; repr., Lincoln: Univ. of Nebraska Press, 2003), 119.

5. Donald, *Lincoln*, 282.

6. Van Deusen, *Seward*, 339, 341–44; Welles, *Diary*, 104 (Tuesday, 2 Sept. 1862), 124 (Friday, 12 Sept. 1863); Donald, *Lincoln*, 400–401.

7. Van Deusen, *Seward*, 339–41; Donald, *Lincoln*, 281, on Seward's relationship with Lincoln and Lincoln's penchant to follow Seward "docilely" early in the administration.

8. Welles, *Diary*, 131–39 (16 Sept. 1862); David Donald, ed., *Inside Lincoln's Cabinet: The Civil War Diaries of Salmon P. Chase* (New York: Longman's, Green and Co., 1954); Niven, *Chase Papers*.

9. Welles, *Diary*, 141 (Saturday, 30 Sept. 1862), 198–200 (Saturday, 20 Dec. 1862). Hamilton Fish, a patrician Republican from New York, who succeeded Seward in 1869, thought Seward was a failure in 1862.

10. Quoted in Bruce Tap, *Over Lincoln's Shoulder: The Committee on the Conduct of the War* (Lawrence: Univ. Press of Kansas, 1998), 45.

11. Donald, *Charles Sumner and Rights of Man*, 317.

12. The previous two paragraphs are from Nevins, *War for the Union*, 2:200–203, and the caning incident is from David Potter, *The Impending Crisis: 1848–1861*, completed and edited by Don E. Fehrenbacher (New York: Harper & Row, 1976), 209–11; Donald, *Charles Sumner and Rights of Man*, 7–8, for Adams and Sumner and for Brooks's assault on Sumner. For Cornewall Lewis, see Crawford, *Anglo-American Crisis of the Mid-Nineteenth Century*, 68. Woldman, *Lincoln and the Russians*, 44, shows that Stoeckl and other foreign ministers in Washington knew of the cabinet's disunity. Welles, *Diary*, 1:502–3 (Saturday, 2 Jan. 1864).

13. Donald, *Charles Sumner and Rights of Man*, 87–90; Donald, *Lincoln*, 398–99, on the defeat at Fredericksburg. Adams, *Our Masters the Rebels*, 136.

14. Quoted in Tap, *Over Lincoln's Shoulder*, 18, 25, 141–42, 144.

15. Lincoln had appointed Stanton the previous January, and Stanton, a Democrat and a "political enigma" with strong antislavery proclivities, "got along well" with Wade's Committee on the Conduct of the War. The words are Tap's, in *Over Lincoln's Shoulder*, 67.

16. Nevins, *War for the Union*, 2:352–53; Donald, *Lincoln*, 399–406, on the Radicals' attempts to oust Seward.

17. Pease and Randall, ed., *Diary of Browning*, 1:596–98.

18. Nevins, *War for the Union*, 2:353–54; Van Deusen, *Seward*, 344; Monaghan, *Diplomat in Carpet Slippers*, 27, for Browning's mixed feelings about Lincoln; Pease and Randall, ed., *Diary of Browning*, 1:598–99 (Wednesday, Dec. 17, 1862).

19. Pease and Randall, ed., *Diary of Browning*, 1:600–601.

20. Tap, *Over Lincoln's Shoulder*, 148.

21. Nevins, *War for the Union*, 2:354; Weigley, *Great Civil War*, 197–98; Lincoln's retort is quoted in Van Deusen, *Seward*, 345.

22. Tap, *Over Lincoln's Shoulder*, 148.

23. Nevins, *War for the Union*, 2:356–57; Van Deusen, *Seward*, 345–46.

24. Nevins, *War for the Union*, 2:357–58; Weigley, *Great Civil War*, 198; Van Deusen, *Seward*, 346.

25. Tap, *Over Lincoln's Shoulder*, 146, 148.

26. Weigley, *Great Civil War*, 198; Nevins, *War for the Union*, 2:358–59.

27. Nevins, *War for the Union*, 2:359; Van Deusen, *Seward*, 346.

28. Tap, *Over Lincoln's Shoulder*, 148.

29. Weigley, *Great Civil War*, 199; Nevins, *War for the Union*, 2:362–63; Van Deusen, *Seward*, 347; Tap, *Over Lincoln's Shoulder*, 148.

30. William E. Gienapp, *Abraham Lincoln and Civil War America: A Biography* (New York: Oxford Univ. Press, 2002), 122. Chase's resignation letter is in Chase to Lincoln, 20 Dec. 1862, Lincoln Papers, ser. 1. Thomas T. Davis to Lincoln, 20 Dec. 1862, Lincoln Papers, ser. 1.

31. Weigley, *Great Civil War*, 200; Seward to Lincoln, Sunday morning, 21 Dec. 1862, Lincoln Papers, ser. 1.

32. Mahin, *One War at a Time*, 11. Quote is from Gienapp, *Lincoln and Civil War America*, 123 (emphasis in original).

33. Lyons to Russell, 19 Dec. 1862, Russell Papers, PRO 30/22/36, fols. 324–26, in Barnes and Barnes, *Private and Confidential*, 312.

34. Lyons to Russell, 22 December 1862, Russell Papers, PRO 30/22/36, fols. 327–30 in ibid. 312; Mahin, *One War at a Time*, 43; Adams, *Great Britain and the American Civil War*, 2:72; Tyrner-Tyrnauer, *Lincoln and the Emperors*, 85.

35. Donald, *Inside Lincoln's Cabinet*, 16.

36. Nevins, *War for the Union*, 2:362; Donald, *Inside Lincoln's Cabinet*, 174–75; Donald, *Lincoln*, chap. 14, "A Pumpkin in Each End of My Bag," 377–406.

37. Nevins, *War for the Union*, 2:362, and 3:151 for the quote.

38. Ibid., 3:153.

39. Quoted in Gienapp, *Lincoln and Civil War America*, 147.

40. Jones, *Lincoln and a New Birth of Freedom*, 155; Stern, *When the Guns Roared*, 177.

41. Chase to James Watson Webb, 7 Nov. 1863, Chase Collection, Historical Society of Pennsylvania, in Nevins, *War for the Union*, 3:149–51.

7. Mutual Support in 1863

1. Annual Message to Congress, 8 Dec. 1863, *CWL*, 7:36, 46.

2. Sumner to Bright, private, 25 May 1863, Bright Papers, BL, Add. Mss. 43390, fol. 159.

3. Nevins, *War for the Union*, 3:77; Dennett, ed., *Lincoln and the Civil War*, 75.

4. Lincoln to Grant, 8 Dec. 1863, *CWL*, 7:53.

5. Campbell, *English Public Opinion*, 240–41.

6. Ibid., 96–97 and n2; Jones, *Union in Peril*, 167–72.

7. Quoted in Owsley, *King Cotton Diplomacy*, 440.

8. Ibid., 441.

9. Adams, *Great Britain and the American Civil War*, 2:66–67, 77–78; Russell to Lyons, FO, 28 Mar. 1863, copy, Russell Papers, PRO 30/22/97, fols. 15–16; Stern, *When the Guns Roared*, 199–200.

10. Quoted in Owsley, *King Cotton Diplomacy*, 443–45.

11. Quoted in ibid., 453; Case and Spencer, *U.S. and France,* 413.

12. Owsley, *King Cotton Diplomacy,* 453.

13. Callahan, *Diplomatic History of the Southern Confederacy,* 187–93; Owsley, *King Cotton Diplomacy,* 455–56; Robert Eadon Leader, ed., *Life and Letters of John Arthur Roebuck, P.C., Q.C., M.P.: With Chapters of Autobiography* (New York: Edward Arnold, 1897), 299.

14. McPherson, *Battle Cry of Freedom,* 664; Weigley, *Great Civil War,* 309–12; the quote is by Callahan, *Diplomatic History of the Southern Confederacy,* 195.

15. Russell to Mason, FO, 25 Sept. 1863, enclosed in Mason to Benjamin, 19 Oct. 1863, James D. Richardson, ed. and comp., *The Messages and Papers of Jefferson Davis and the Confederacy: Including Diplomatic Correspondence, 1861–1865* (New York: Chelsea House-Robert Hector in association with R. R. Bowker, 1966), 2:588; Nevins, *War for the Union,* 3:75–76; Callahan, *Diplomatic History of the Southern Confederacy,* 198–99; Owsley, *King Cotton Diplomacy,* 465–66. Mason went to Paris to live with Slidell and was appointed "Commissioner on the Continent" on 13 November 1863.

16. J. R. Vincent, ed., *Disraeli, Derby and Conservative Party: The Political Journals of Lord Stanley, 1849–1869* (New York: Barnes & Noble, 1978), 199.

17. Quoted in Owsley, *King Cotton Diplomacy,* 447–49. On Drouyn de Lhuys, see Case and Spencer, *U.S. and France,* 350–52. Despite his loyalty to Napoleon III, Drouyn de Lhuys had resigned from the Foreign Office in 1855 and had refused the emperor's pleas that he resume office in 1859 because of a policy difference, and he continued to maintain independence in foreign policy.

18. Adams, *Great Britain and the American Civil War,* 2:38–39, 45; Jones, *Lincoln and a New Birth of Freedom,* 164, 169.

19. Quote is from McPherson, *Crossroads of Freedom,* 155.

20. Stuart L. Bernath, *Squall across the Atlantic,* 63.

21. Somerset to Milne, private, Admiralty, Monday, 2 Feb. 1863, Milne Papers, NMM, MLN/116/1c, Letters from the Duke of Somerset, 1860–64.

22. Bernath, *Squall across the Atlantic,* 64; Carroll, *Henri Mercier,* 293; Daddysman, *Matamoros Trade,* 168; Philbrick, *Sea of Glory,* 355.

23. The opinion about Palmerston is George Joachim Goschen's in Hon. Arthur D. Elliot, *The Life of George Joachim Goschen First Viscount Goschen, 1831–1907* (New York: Longmans, Green, and Co., 1911), 1:60. Russell to Lyons, 7 Mar. 1863, Lyons Papers, in Jenkins, *Britain and the War for the Union,* 2:257–58; Wilkes to Welles, 2 Feb. 1863, *ORN,* 1st ser., 2:71; Daddysman, *Matamoros Trade,* 168; Scherer, *Russell,* 296.

24. Daddysman, *Matamoros Trade,* 168.

25. Wilkes to Welles, 4 Nov. 1862, Welles Papers; Lyons to Russell, 30 Dec. 1862, Russell Papers, PRO 30/22/36; Russell to Lyons, 16 Jan. 1863, PRO 30/22/36, all in Jenkins, *Britain and the War for Union,* 2:259; Milne to Somerset, HMS *Nile,* 25 Feb. 1863, Milne Papers, NMM, MLN/116/1c.

26. Daddysman, *Matamoros Trade,* 168–69.

27. Milne to Somerset, Bermuda, HMS *Nile,* 18 Apr. 1863, Milne Papers, NMM, MLN/116/1c; Somerset to Milne, private, Admiralty, Saturday, 25 Apr. 1863, in ibid.

28. Callahan, *Diplomatic History of the Southern Confederacy,* 174–75.

29. Milne to Somerset, HMS *Nile,* Bermuda, 6 May 1863, Milne Papers, NMM, MLN/116/1c.

30. Callahan, *Diplomatic History of the Southern Confederacy,* 175–76.

31. Milne to Somerset, HMS *Nile,* Bermuda, 21 May 1863, Milne Papers, NMM, MLN116/1c.

32. Bernath, *Squall across the Atlantic,* 65–67; Courtemanche, *No Need of Glory,* 98; Daddysman, *Matamoros Trade,* 169–70; Thomas, *Confederate Nation,* 184.

33. Baxter, "Admiralty Problems," 120.

34. FO to Admiralty, 8 Mar. 1864, ADM 1/5901, in ibid., 120.

35. Lyons to Russell, 12 Jan. 1864; Russell to Lyons, 5 Feb. 1864, PRO, 5/1181, in Daddysman, *Matamoros Trade,* 171.

36. Mahin, *One War at a Time,* 187–88; Donald, *Charles Sumner and Rights of Man,* 108; Carroll, *Henri Mercier,* 293; Bernath, *Squall across the Atlantic,* 64–65, where he explains that neither government knew that mail from the Confederate emissaries was thrown overboard during the seizure. Had the British known, Lyons would have had no grounds for protesting to Seward. Seizure and condemnation of ships carrying enemy dispatches was standard practice. Welles's feelings about Seward's arbitrariness to keep the peace, and the quotation about Sumner's visit with Lincoln are in Welles, *Diary,* 1:287 (Tuesday, 28 Apr. 1863). The situation unfolds from Welles's pen in ibid., 266–89 (Saturday, 11 Apr.; Sunday, 12 Apr.; Monday, 13 Apr.; Thursday, 16 Apr.; Friday, 17 Apr.; Saturday, 18 Apr.; Tuesday, 21 Apr.,; Wednesday, 22 Apr.; Thursday, 23 Apr.; Tuesday, 28 Apr.). Welles thought that Seward was keeping Lincoln ignorant, but the president seemed uninterested, with his focus on peace. See Donald, *Lincoln,* 413–14.

37. Lyons to Russell, private and confidential, 10 May 1863, in Barnes and Barnes, *Private and Confidential,* 323; Courtemanche, *No Need of Glory,* 107–12; Clarendon to Cowley, 6 May 1862, in Wellesley, *Paris Embassy,* 252.

38. Bigelow to Seward, 17 Apr. 1863, Seward Papers; Bigelow to Bright, 30 Apr. 1863, Bright Papers, Add. Mss. 43390; Adams, *Diary,* 15 Apr. 1863, Adams Papers, reel 77; Wallace and Gillespie, *Journal of Moran,* 2:250, all in Jenkins, *Britain and the War for Union,* 2:261.

39. Welles, *Diary,* 1:291, 298–99 (Friday, 1 May; Tuesday, 12 May 1863). Welles also recalled that Wilkes was posted to the West Indies at Seward's "special request" and reflected that perhaps war with England was not the "worst alternative, she behaves so badly." Monaghan, *Diplomat in Carpet Slippers,* 309–10; Philbrick, *Sea of Glory,* 355. Welles was upset about the time Wilkes had taken commandeering the *Vanderbilt,* a "plushly appointed" warship, as his flagship, instead of chasing the raiders. "This is the vessel for me," he wrote to his wife. "She has speed and appliances for comforts I am entitled to." His court-martial in 1864 found him guilty on every count, and he was suspended for three years, which, as he was prone to do in such cases, Lincoln commuted to a year. Yet Wilkes never saw active duty again. Wilkes's fate is discussed in Philbrick, *Sea of Glory,* 355–56.

40. Courtemanche, *No Need of Glory,* 112–19.

41. Lyons to Russell, 5 May 1863, Russell Papers, PRO 30/22/37, fols. 57–60, in Barnes and Barnes, *Private and Confidential,* 322–23; same to same, 8 May 1863, fols. 61–62, in ibid.

42. Russell to Lyons, 22 April 1864, in Bernath, *Squall across the Atlantic,* 78.

43. Russell to Lyons, 25 Apr., 13, 20 June 1863, Russell Papers, PRO 30/22/97, in Daddysman, *Matamoros Trade,* 171–72; Somerset to Milne, private, Admiralty, Saturday, 17 Apr. 1863, Milne Papers, NMM, MLN116/1c.

44. Somerset to Grey and Rodney, 3 Feb. 1864, PRO Adm. 13/5, in Daddysman, *Matamoros Trade,* 172. "At all costs" are Daddysman's words.

45. Quoted in Bernath, *Squall across the Atlantic,* 73–74; Carroll, *Henri Mercier,* 293–94.

46. Bernath, *Squall across the Atlantic,* 74–75.

47. Weigley, *Great Civil War,* 311; Crook, *Diplomacy during the American Civil War,* 136; Russell to Cowley, FO, 20 Apr. 1863, Cowley Papers, PRO, fol. 519/200, part I, fol. 96; Russell to Sir George Grey, 19 Sept. 1863, in Gooch, *Later Correspondence of Lord John Russell,* 2:335. Desmond MacCarthy and Agatha Russell, eds., *Lady John Russell: A Memoir with Selections from Her Diaries and Correspondence* (New York: John Lane Company, 1911), 197; Bruce to his wife, home office, 8 Oct. 1863, in Henry Austin Bruce, *Letters of the Rt. Hon. H. A. Bruce, Lord Aberdare of Duffryn,* (Oxford: Printed for private circulation, 1902), 1:203. The following April, Palmerston made Bruce vice president of the Privy Council. This was not a cabinet seat, however, but a promotion nonetheless. Bruce to his father, 17 Apr. 1864, in Bruce, *Letters of Bruce,* 207.

48. Mahin, *One War at a Time,* 188–89, 193; Lincoln to Welles, Executive Mansion, Washington, 25 July 1863, *ORN II* 2:411.

49. Lyons to Russell, 14 Aug. 1863, Russell Papers, PRO 30/22/37, fols. 143–46, quoted in Barnes and Barnes, *Private and Confidential,* 332.

50. Mahin, *One War at a Time,* 193; Carroll, *Henri Mercier,* 340–42.

51. Mahin, *One War at a Time,* 193–94.

52. Quoted in ibid., 194.

53. Quoted in ibid., 194–95.

54. Lyons to Russell, 3 Nov. 1863, quoted in ibid., 195.

55. Donald, *Charles Sumner and Rights of Man,* 126, 129, 132–35, including the quotes from Russell and Adams on 135.

56. See, for instance, Gladstone to Duchess of Argyll (a primary Sumner correspondent), 18 May 1869, in Donald, *Charles Sumner and Rights of Man,* 385. Gladstone catches the irony of Sumner's anti-British speeches, which resulted in closer relations between the governments.

57. Lyons to Russell, 6 Nov. 1863, private and confidential, Russell Papers, PRO 30/22/37, fols. 327–30, in Barnes and Barnes, *Private and Confidential,* 337; Donald, *Charles Sumner and Rights of Man,* 142. A succinct summary of the Hudson's Bay treaty is in Winks, *Canada and the United States,* 160–61. Disputes over the Puget Sound Company's legal rights to the territory held up settlement until 1865. Winks points out that Sir John Rose, who later helped to arrange the Treaty of Washington negotiations, was appointed British commissioner. He first met with his American counterpart in Washington in January 1865.

58. Kaufman, *Pig War,* 93–94.

59. Ibid., 97; Lincoln to the Senate, 16 Mar. 1861, *CWL,* 4:287–88 and n1.

60. Kaufman, *Pig War,* 99–100.

61. Ibid., 100–101.

62. Quoted in Mahin, *One War at a Time,* 195–96.

63. Welles, *Diary,* 1:493 (Tuesday, 22 Dec. 1863), 495 (Saturday, 25 Dec. 1863); Alfred Jackson Hanna and Kathryn Abbey Hanna, *Napoleon III and Mexico: American Triumph over Monarchy* (Chapel Hill: Univ. of North Carolina Press, 1971), 121–22; Mahin, *One War at a Time,* 120–21; Van Deusen, *Seward,* 368–69.

64. Krein, "Russell's Decision," 59.

65. Spencer, *Confederate Navy in Europe,* 97–98.

66. Ibid., 98–99; Jenkins, *Britain and the War for the Union,* 2:250–51. For his attempt at a refugee act, Palmerston was exculpated for being the dupe of Napoleon III.

67. Adams to Seward, 2 Apr. 1863, in Jenkins, *Britain and the War for the Union*, 2:251.

68. Welles, *Diary*, 1:250–63 (31 Mar.; 2 Apr.; Friday, 3 Apr.; Monday, 6 Apr. 1863). Welles's letter to Seward of 31 March 1863 against privateering, which Sumner urged him to send Lincoln, is printed in full at 252–56; Owen, "Testing the Democratic Peace," 213.

69. Thomas, *Confederate Nation*, 183; Spencer, *Confederate Navy in Europe*, 100–101; on Hotze's feeling, see Stern, *When the Guns Roared*, 201.

70. Spencer, *Confederate Navy in Europe*, 100–103; Jenkins, *Britain and the War for the Union*, 2:252–54. For Russell's actions on the *Alexandra*, see *Papers Relating to the Treaty of Washington*, vol. 6, *The Geneva Arbitration* (Washington, D.C.: GPO, 1872), 275. Available at http://books.google.com/books?vid=LCCN10016558&id=1Mlpyjkfy5cC&pg=PP3&printsec=8&dq=Lord+Tenterden (accessed 20 May 2006).

71. Jenkins, *Britain and the War for the Union*, 2:185–86.

72. See Bernath, *Squall across the Atlantic*, 11–13. The cooperation was amazing as blockade-runners were reputed by Bernath to have made 8,250 violations.

73. Stern, *When the Guns Roared*, 201–6.

74. Lyons to Russell, 17, 20 July 1863, PRO 30/22/37, fols. 114–15, in Van Deusen, *Seward*, 355; Barnes and Barnes, *Private and Confidential*, 330. Lyons said that Lincoln's entire cabinet except Seward did not want to make examples of potential British blockade-runners whose captains felt they had the neutral right to run contraband from the West Indies to neutral ports such as Matamoros. Either Seward was posturing, as he was known to do, or his loyalty to the British-American peace was far greater in the long run, and Lyons and Russell's query offered a way out for him, with the president making the decision to be more careful about seizures. Hattaway and Beringer, *Davis*, 211.

75. Lincoln to Welles, Executive Mansion, 25 July 1863, 10 Aug. 1863, *CWL*, 6: 348–50, 378–80; Welles, *Diary*, 1:451–52.

76. Welles to Lincoln, 30 Sept. 1863, Welles, *Diary*, 1:452–53.

77. Russell memorandum, 21 Aug. 1863, Russell Papers, PRO 30/22/27, in Krein, "Russell's Decision," 160.

78. For Newcastle's, Palmerston's, and Westbury's comments on the Russell memorandum, 23 Aug. 1863, Russell Papers, PRO 30/22/27, in Krein, "Russell's Decision," 160–61.

79. Krein, "Russell's Decision," 161.

80. Russell to Adams, 1 Sept. 1963, PRO, fol. 5/1000; Russell to Layard, 1 Sept. 1863, Layard Papers, BL, Add. Mss. 38989, fol. 293, in Krein, "Russell's Decision," 162.

81. Russell to Layard, 2 Sept. 1863, Layard Papers, BL, Add. Mss. 38959, fol. 299; same to same, 3 Sept. 1863, in ibid., fol. 303; Russell to Palmerston, Sept. 3, 1863, Broadlands Manuscripts, GC/RU/802; Russell to Layard, 3 Sept. 1863, Layard Papers, BL, Add. Mss. 38989, fol. 307; all in Krein, "Russell's Decision," 162–63. The newspapers are quoted in Owen, "Testing the Democratic Peace," 241.

82. Somerset to Palmerston, 19 Sept. 1863, Palmerston Papers, quoted in Baxter, "Admiralty Problems," 124–25.

83. Beloff, "Historical Revision No. CXVIII," 47.

84. Jones, *Confederate Rams at Birkenhead*, 15.

85. Merli, *Great Britain and the Confederate Navy*, 201–2; Spencer, *Confederate Navy in Europe*, 110–11.

86. Somerset to Gladstone, 13 June 1864, Gladstone Papers, Add. Mss. 44304, in Spencer, *Confederate Navy in Europe*, 112–16; Scherer, *Russell*, 297.

87. Quoted in Owsley, *King Cotton Diplomacy,* 402, 413–14.

88. Palmerston to Russell, 7 Sept. 1863, Russell Papers, PRO 30/22/14, and Palmerston to de Grey, 9 Sept. 1863, Ripon Papers, BL, Add. Mss. 43512, in Jones, *Confederate Rams at Birkenhead,* 113.

89. Cobden to Bright, 8, 12 Oct. 1863, Cobden Papers, BL, Add. Mss. 43652, in Jones, *Confederate Rams at Birkenhead,* 114–17, and n13. Even so, Welles was not as certain of his monitors' defensive abilities as Cobden.

90. Somerset to Russell, 28 May 1864, Russell Papers, PRO 30/22/26; same to same, 18 Feb. 1864, ibid.; and Palmerston to Russell, 13 Sept. 1863, ibid., PRO 30/22/14, in Jones, *Confederate Rams at Birkenhead,* 118–19.

91. Quoted in Owsley, *King Cotton Diplomacy,* 412.

92. Wallace and Gillespie, eds., *Journal of Moran,* 2:1212.

93. Stuart to Russell, private and confidential, 28 Sept. 1863, Russell Papers, PRO 30/22/37, fols. 183–87, in Barnes and Barnes, *Private and Confidential,* 334–35.

94. Welles, *Diary,* 1:436–38 (Friday, 18 Sept. 1863); Donald, *Lincoln,* 468.

95. Spencer, *Confederate Navy in Europe,* 119–20.

96. Ibid., 120–22.

97. Courtemanche, *No Need of Glory,* 119–20.

98. Welles, *Diary,* 1:467–69 (Saturday, 10 Oct. 1863); Courtmanche, *No Need of Glory,* 122–23.

99. Courtmanche, *No Need of Glory,* 124.

100. Lyons to Russell, 16 Oct. 1863; Welles, *Diary,* 1:468, Milne Memo, 9 Sept. 1862, Adm. 128/56, (emphasis in original) Supplemental Instructions for Cruisers employed on the Coast of America, 12 Nov. 1861; Milne to Watson, 8 Aug. 1862, Adm. 128/56, 58, in Daddysman, *Matamoros Trade,* 172–73.

101. Bernath, *Squall Across the Atlantic,* 83–84.

102. Rawley, *Lincoln and a Nation Worth Fighting For,* 162.

8. MUTUAL DEPENDENCE IN 1864

1. Scherer, *Russell,* 108; Schweninger, "A lingering war," 292.

2. Newcastle to Manners Sutton, 8 Mar. 1861, Newcastle Papers, PAC, A 307/B2, fols. 41–45; Sir Edmund Head (outgoing governor-general) to Newcastle, private, 10 May 1861, ibid., fol. 144; same to same, 5 June 1861. The second and third letters are also cited in James A. Gibson, "The Duke of Newcastle and British North American Affairs, 1859–64," *Canadian Historical Review* 44, no. 2 (1963): 145; Beloff, "Historical Revision No. CXVIII," 43.

3. Blank, "Decline of Democratic Imperialism," 100.

4. Bourne, *Britain and the Balance of Power,* 156–57, 172–75.

5. Beloff, "Historical Revision No. CXVIII," 43.

6. Bourne, *Britain and the Balance of Power,* 259.

7. Callahan, *Diplomacy of the Southern Confederacy,* 222; Jenkins, *Britain and the War for the Union,* 2:357–58, 360–62.

8. Baxter, "Admiralty Problems," 127; Winks, *Canada and the United States,* 314–15. Winks shows cooperation and understanding and how the Confederates lost out on the St. Albans

raid. In 1872, a claims commission authorized by the Treaty of Washington turned down American claims on behalf of the St. Albanites, and the United States did not press the decision.

9. Winks, *Canada and the United States,* 330.

10. Baxter, "Admiralty Problems," 127–28.

11. Williams, "Canada and the Civil War," 282–83.

12. Winks, *Canada and the United States,* 336; Gordon T. Stewart, *The American Response to Canada since 1776* (East Lansing: Michigan State Univ. Press, 1992), 62–70, for a good analysis of why the United States refused to renew the treaty.

13. Williams, "Canada and the Civil War," 273–82.

14. Donald Kelley, *The Transatlantic Persuasion: The Liberal-Democratic Mind in the Age of Gladstone* (New York: Alfred A. Knopf, 1969), 168.

15. Ibid., 145–46; P. B. Waite, "Cardwell and Confederation," *Canadian Historical Review* 43, no. 1 (1962): 20, and his *Life and Times of Confederation, 1864–1867: Politics, Newspapers, and the Union of British North America* (Toronto: Univ. of Toronto Press, 1962; repr., Toronto: Univ. of Toronto Press, 1977), 20–21; Arvel B. Erickson, *Edward T. Cardwell: Peelite* (Philadelphia: American Philosophical Society, 1959), 13.

16. Erickson, *Cardwell,* 40.

17. Waite, *Life and Times of Confederation,* 20; Erickson, *Cardwell,* 32.

18. Waite, *Life and Times of Confederation,* 20; Russell to Newcastle, 12 June 1862, copy, confidential, Russell Papers, PRO 30/22/31, fols. 97–98; Russell to Lyons, 4 July 1863, in ibid., PRO 30/22/97, fol. 33. Russell closed: "I should like to see some federal tie uniting the whole of British America in a semi-independent connexion with Great Britain." Monck to Sir George Cornewall Lewis, Minister of War, 22 Aug. 1962, private, Broadlands Mss., MM/CA/1–3.

19. Winks, *Canada and the United States,* 115–16.

20. Ged Martin, *The Durham Report and British Policy: A Critical Essay* (Cambridge: Cambridge Univ. Press, 1972), 109; de Grey to Monck, 23 Mar. 1863, private, Monck Papers, PAC, Microfilm Reel A-756; same to same, 28 Aug. 1863, ibid.; de Grey to Cardwell, [14 Apr.] 1864, copy, Ripon Papers, BL, Add. Mss. 43551, fols. 19–20; Cardwell to de Grey, 19 Apr. 1864, copy, ibid., fols. 21–22; de Grey to Cardwell, 28 June 1864, copy, ibid., fol. 40; Cardwell to de Grey, 28 June 1864, copy, private, ibid, fol. 43; de Grey to Cardwell, 28 June 1864, copy, private, ibid., fol. 44; Cardwell to Monck, 7 July 1864, private, Monck Papers, Microfilm Reel A-755. W. L. Morton, ed., *Monck Letters and Journal: Canada from Government House to Confederation,* The Carleton Library No. 52 (Toronto: McClelland and Stewart Ltd., 1970), 45, and nn. 39–40.

21. Erickson, *Cardwell,* 34; C. C. Eldridge notes in *England's Mission: The Imperial Idea in the Age of Gladstone and Disraeli, 1868–1880* (Chapel Hill: Univ. of North Carolina Press, 1973), 45, that Adderley was close to Gladstone's idea of colonial self-reliance. Elisabeth Batt, *Monck: Governor General of Canada, 1861–68* (Toronto: McClelland and Stewart, 1976), 21.

22. J. Mackay Hitsman, *Safeguarding Canada, 1763–1871* (Toronto: Univ. of Toronto Press, 1968), 190. There was no American annexationist plan either, although Gladstone did not know it. See Ernest N. Paolino, *The Foundations of American Empire: William Henry Seward and U.S. Foreign Policy* (Ithaca, N.Y.: Cornell Univ. Press, 1973), 14–16.

23. Erickson, *Cardwell,* 35; Hitsman, *Safeguarding Canada,* 190–91.

24. "Report on the Defence of Canada and of the British Naval Stations in the Atlantic, by Lt. Col. Jervois . . . Pt. I, Defence of Canada," War Office, Feb. 1864, Confidential W. O. Print, PAC, RG 8, ser. 2, vol. 20, quoted in Bourne, *Britain and the Balance of Power,* 263.

25. Bourne, *Britain and the Balance of Power,* 264; Cardwell to Monck, 16 July 1864, private, Monck Papers, Microfilm Reel A-755. Russell approved Cardwell's policy but for a Palmerstonian reason: a sudden American attack might overrun Quebec and Montreal if these citadels went unstrengthened. See Russell to Lyons, 23 July 1864, copy, Russell Papers, PRO 30/22/97, fol. 85; Gladstone to Cardwell, 25 July 1864, Gladstone Papers, Add. Mss. 44118. Erickson, *Cardwell,* 35; Donald Creighton, *John A. Macdonald: The Young Politician* (Toronto: Macmillan, 1952), 361.

26. Waite, "Cardwell and Confederation," 23; Bourne, *Britain and the Balance of Power,* 267–68. Bourne shows that the cabinet was divided, but Cardwell was on Gladstone's side. His opinion is shown in his letters to Monck, which Bourne did not use. See, for instance, Cardwell to Monck, 30 July 1864, private and confidential, Monck Papers, Microfilm Reel A-755.

27. Cardwell to Monck, 6 Aug. 1864, private, Monck Papers, Microfilm Reel A-755; Batt, *Monck,* 92; Lyons to Russell, 9 Aug. 1864, Russell Papers, PRO 30/22/38, fols. 85–90, in Barnes and Barnes, *Private and Confidential,* 346.

28. Bourne, *Britain and the Balance of Power,* 267–69. Cardwell's minutes of 28 Sept. 1864 on Macdonald to Cardwell, 15 Sept. 1864, PRO, CO 217, in Waite, "Cardwell and Confederation," 24–25; Waite, *Life and Times of Confederation,* 18; Creighton, *Macdonald,* 372, 380.

29. Morton, *Monck Letters and Journal,* 183–85, 362.

30. Macdonald to Thomas Swinyard, 1 Jan. 1865, in Creighton, *Macdonald,* 394.

31. Creighton, *Macdonald,* 388.

32. William Lewis Morton, *The Critical Years: The Union of British North America, 1857–1873* (Toronto: McClelland and Stewart, 1964), 168–69; Cardwell to Monck, 2 Dec. 1864, private, Monck Papers, Microfilm Reel A-755.

33. Erickson, *Cardwell,* 37. The idea for a joint conference had been Russell's.

34. Russell to Palmerston, 15 Dec. 1864, Broadlands Mss., GC/RU/884.

35. Burnley to Russell, 27 Dec. 1864, Russell Papers, 30/22/38, in Creighton, *Macdonald,* 393.

36. Gladstone to Cardwell, 21 Dec. 1864, copy, Gladstone Papers, Add. Mss. 44118, fols. 181–82. Cardwell had mistakenly allowed Gladstone to see a report on the topic. It was titled *Report on the Defences of the Northeastern Frontier,* of 20 June 1864, House Reports, No. 119, 38th Cong. 1st sess., vol. 2. Gladstone thought that it showed the futility of the defense question, but he did not get his way because of the alarm felt by Palmerston and Russell about the rumored plot to reconcile North and South. See Bourne, *Britain and the Balance of Power,* 283. Gladstone did not see the Admiralty papers on the feasibility of sending more gunboats to the Great Lakes prepared by W. G. Romaine, the permanent undersecretary. Romaine concluded that no matter how many were sent out, American naval superiority would remain. See ibid., 280–84, 405. Gladstone note: "Defence of B. N. A., 19–20 Jan. 1865," Gladstone Papers, Add. Mss 44754, fols. 3–5.

37. Russell to Palmerston, 10 Jan. 1865, Broadlands Mss., GC/RU/891.

38. Cardwell to Monck, 21 Jan. 1865, private, Monck Papers, Microfilm Reel A-755; Creighton, *Macdonald,* 405–6; Gladstone to Cardwell, 2 Feb. 1865, Gladstone Papers, Add. Mss. 44118, fol. 183.

39. Palmerston to the queen, 20 Jan. 1865, in George Earle Buckle, ed., *The Letters of Queen Victoria: A Selection from Her Majesty's Correspondence and Journal between the Years 1862 and 1878,* 2d ser. (London: John Murray, 1901), 1:248–49.

40. Russell to Palmerston, 27 Feb. 1865, Broadlands Mss., GC/RU/892.

41. Palmerston to the queen, 13 Mar. 1865, in Buckle, *Letters of Queen Victoria,* 1:262–63.

42. Charles Perry Stacey, *Canada and the British Army, 1846–1871: A Study in the Practice of Responsible Government,* rev. ed. (Toronto: Univ. of Toronto Press, 1963), 171; *Hansard Parliamentary Debates,* Commons, 3d ser., 177 (1865): 1577, 1614, 1617–18, 1635.

43. *Hansard,* 3d ser., 177 (1965): 1556, 1562, 1567–70; Duberman, *Charles Francis Adams,* 320, 332.

44. Cardwell to Monck, 1 Apr. 1865, private, Monck Papers, Microfilm Reel A-755. See also James Winter, *Robert Lowe* (Toronto: Univ. of Toronto Press, 1976), 133–34. Cardwell to Monck, 8 Apr. 1865, private, Monck Papers, Microfilm Reel A-755.

45. De Grey to Cardwell, 13 Apr. 1865, copy, Ripon Papers, Add. Mss. 43551, fols. 161–62; Gladstone to Cardwell, 23 May 1865, private, copy, Gladstone Papers, Add. Mss. 44118, fols. 187–90.

46. Gladstone to H. H. Gordon, 11 July 1865, Gladstone Papers, Add. Mss. 44320, also quoted by Creighton, *Macdonald,* 412; Gladstone to Argyll, 2 June 1865, Gladstone Papers, Add. Mss. 44100, also quoted in Morton, *Critical Years,* 180; Bell, *Palmerston,* 2:387–88.

47. Cardwell to Monck, 17 June 1865, private, Monck Papers, Microfilm Reel, A-755; Cardwell to Macdonnell, 24 June 1865, PRO, CO 281/37, fols. 33–37, in Erickson, *Cardwell,* 38; Gladstone to Cardwell, 28 Aug. 1865, copy, Gladstone Papers, Add. Mss. 44118, fol. 193; Cardwell to Monck, 1 Sept. 1865, private, Monck Papers, Microfilm Reel, A-755; Batt, *Monck,* 110.

48. Gladstone to Russell, 6 Sept. 1865, Russell Papers, PRO 30/22/15E, fols. 31–32, in Morton, *Critical Years,* 182; Russell to Cardwell, 4 Sept. 1865, copy, Russell Papers, PRO 30/22/31, fol. 1; Cardwell to Russell, 22 July 1865, ibid., PRO 30/22/26. Creighton, *Macdonald,* 423; Williams to Cardwell, 27 Sept. 1865, in Morton, *Critical Years,* 182.

49. Russell to Gladstone, 20 Oct. 1865, Gladstone Papers, Add. Mss. 44292, fols. 190–91; Clarendon to Hammond, 4 Sept. 1865, Hammond Papers, PRO, FO 391/4; Russell to Burnley, 24 Feb. 1865, No. 69, draft, PRO, FO 5/1099; FO to Admiralty, 27 Mar. 1865, No. 69, draft, PRO, FO 5/1099. On 24 March Russell suggested four boats each on the Great Lakes, or some other limited number. But the peaceful atmosphere left this in the draft stage. Russell to Bruce, who was embarking for Washington, 24 Mar. 1865, No. 112, PRO, FO 115/432; Seward to Bruce, 16 June 1865, PRO, FO 115/440, fol. 346; Same to Same, 22 Aug. 1865, PRO, FO 115/440, fol. 386; same to same, 4 Nov. 1865, PRO, FO 115/440, fol. 406.

50. Bythesea to Russell, 11 Sept. 1865, PRO, FO 5/1099, fols. 386–88; FO to Admiralty, 29 Sept. 1865, draft, PRO, FO 5/1099, fol. 381; Russell minute on Romaine to Hammond, Admiralty, 7 Oct. 1865, Confidential, PRO, FO 5/1099, fols. 399–400; Admiralty Report No. 3958, 4 Oct. 1865, signed by W. D. Eden for the Controller, PRO, FO 5/1099, fol. 400; Sir Frederick Rogers, permanent undersecretary at the Colonial Office, to Hammond, 25 Oct. 1865, PRO, FO 5/1099, fol. 403; Russell to Admiralty, 30 Oct. 1865, draft, PRO, FO 5/1099, fol. 405.

51. James Morton Callahan, *The Neutrality of the American Lakes and Anglo-American Relations,* Johns Hopkins University Studies in Historical and Political Science, ser. 16, nos. 1–4 (Baltimore: Johns Hopkins Univ. Press, 1898), 166–67; Bruce to Clarendon, 30 Nov. 1865, Clarendon Papers, c. 90, fol. 3, in Barnes and Barnes, *Private and Confidential,* 352.

Bruce had aided Ashburton in Washington in 1842 during the Northeastern Boundary negotiations and served as lieutenant governor of Newfoundland from 1846 to 1848. The Radical Republicans wanted a harsh Reconstruction policy with strong central controls. President Andrew Johnson, Seward, and the Democrats, in general, wanted a moderate policy, with the states having a significant role. The Reconstruction debate would influence the timing of the settlement of British-American disputes for the next five years. Politicians on both sides of the issue were sensitive to political futures if they moved for settlement on any foreign policy issue lest their detractors make use of their desire. For a succinct summary, see Robert Kagan, *Dangerous Nation: America's Place in the World from Its Earliest Days to the Dawn of the Twentieth Century* (New York: Alfred A. Knopf, 2006), 270–73.

52. Bruce to Clarendon, 4 Dec. 1865, private and confidential, Clarendon Papers, c. 90, fols. 14–17; Clarendon to Bruce, 9 Dec. 1865, copy, ibid., c. 142, fols. 19–20; Bruce to Clarendon, 31 Dec. 1865, ibid., c. 90, fols. 44–50; Clarendon to Bruce, 16 Jan. 1866, No. 14, PRO, FO 115/449, fols. 52–55; FO to Admiralty, 16 Jan. 1866, draft, PRO, FO 115/449, fol. 428.

53. Bythesea to Bruce, 20 Jan. 1866, PRO, FO 5/1099, fol. 435.

9. THE FAILURE OF CONFEDERATE DIPLOMACY AND BRITISH PRO-SOUTH IMPOTENCE

1. Cooper, *Jefferson Davis,* 292. Davis made these remarks during a trip to Maine in the late summer and fall of 1858 at a time when he believed there would be no secession and spoke for the Union. His speeches in the Northeast were well received, although he did not mention slavery or abolitionism, giving credence to the higher cause of union.

2. Dirck, *Lincoln & Davis,* 68.

3. Monaghan, *Diplomat in Carpet Slippers,* 83–91.

4. Donald, ed., *Why the North Won the Civil War,* 15.

5. Ibid., 19, 23–24.

6. Quoted in Surdam, *Northern Naval Superiority,* 198.

7. Richardson, *Message and Papers of Jefferson Davis and the Confederacy,* 1:xxvi, xxix (emphasis in original); Dirck, *Lincoln & Davis,* 183.

8. Crawford, *Anglo-American Crisis of the Mid-Nineteenth Century,* 126–27, and n48 for Russell to Layard, 17 Sept. 1861, Layard Papers, BL, and the *Times,* 20 June, 17 Aug., 24, 29 Oct., 16 Nov. 1861.

9. Hanna and Hanna, *Napoleon III and Mexico,* 52–53; Hubbard, *Burden of Confederate Diplomacy,* 46–47; Stern, *When the Guns Roared,* 58.

10. Surdam, *Northern Naval Superiority,* 6.

11. Crook, *North, the South, and the Powers,* 211.

12. Hanna and Hanna, *Napoleon III and Mexico,* 118–19; Hubbard, *Burden of Confederate Diplomacy,* 178.

13. Richard N. Current, "God and the Strongest Battalions," in *Why the North Won the Civil War,* ed. Donald, 27, on the cotton embargo; Richardson, *Messages and Papers of Jefferson Davis and the Confederacy,* 1:xxiii; the quote is by Dirck, *Lincoln & Davis,* 188.

14. R. J. M. Blackett, *Divided Hearts: Britain and the American Civil War* (Baton Rouge: Louisiana State Univ. Press, 2001), 129.

15. Mahin, *One War at a Time,* 19–20.

16. Ibid., 22.

17. Spencer, *Confederate Navy in Europe*, 13.

18. Blackett, *Divided Hearts*, 129–30.

19. Ibid., 131.

20. Crook, *North, the South, and Powers*, 284.

21. Cook, Alabama *Claims*, 24–25; Crook, *North, the South and the Powers*, 297–98.

22. Berwanger, *British Foreign Service*, 117; Hubbard, *Burden of Confederate Diplomacy*, 21–26, 38.

23. Spencer, *Confederate Navy in Europe*, 13.

24. McPherson, *Battle Cry of Freedom*, 386.

25. Monaghan, *Diplomat in Carpet Slippers*, 398–400.

26. Weigley, *Great Civil War*, 399, who erroneously uses "Kerner"; Crook, *North, the South, and Powers*, 356–58; Hubbard, *Burden of Confederate Diplomacy*, 168–71; Cooper, *Jefferson Davis*, 514–15 (for the statement that the Europeans would never have accepted an offer to help in return for gradual emancipation).

27. Spencer, *Confederate Navy in Europe*, 14.

28. Berwanger, *British Foreign Service*, 123–24; Hubbard, *Burden of Confederate Diplomacy*, 177–78; Crook, *North, South, and Powers*, 358, on American neutrality in Mexico and Palmerston's discussion with Mason; Weigley, *Great Civil War*, 400–401, and Cooper, *Jefferson Davis*, 511–12, on the Hampton Roads conference.

29. Allen, "Civil War, Reconstruction, and Great Britain," 74.

30. Bell, *Palmerston*, 2:337–38, 353–54.

31. Ibid., 2:354–55.

32. Allen, *Great Britain and the United States*, 457–58; Wilbur Devereux Jones, "British Conservatives and Civil War," 527–43; Howard Jones, *Union in Peril*, 233–34, n12, upheld Jones's evidence nearly thirty years later.

33. Roy Jenkins, *Gladstone: A Biography* (New York: Random House, 1995), 241.

34. Bell, *Palmerston*, 2:341.

35. Ibid., 2:342–43.

36. Adams to Seward, 9 July 1863, in Mahin, *One War at a Time*, 189.

37. In Mahin, *One War at a Time*, 189.

38. Spencer, *Confederate Navy in Europe*, 72; Mahin, *One War at a Time*, 189–90; Jones, "British Conservatives and Civil War," 533.

39. Russell to Lyons, 30 May 1863, Russell Papers, PRO 30/22/97, in Jones, "British Conservatives and Civil War," 535.

40. Weigley, *Great Civil War*, 310–11; Blackett, *Divided Hearts*, 161; Mahin, *One War at a Time*, 190–91; Carroll, *Henri Mercier*, 321; Stern, *When the Guns Roared*, 208. For Bright's handling of Roebuck and Hotze's admission of the end of the Southern cause in England, see Monaghan, *Diplomat in Carpet Slippers*, 317–18, and Adams, *Education of Henry Adams*, 186–87.

41. Blackett, *Divided Hearts*, 160.

42. Palmerston to Russell, 27 Apr. 1861, Russell Papers, PRO 30/22/21, in Ferris, *Desperate Diplomacy*, 36–37.

43. Adams to Seward, 26 Feb. 1863, no. 334, in Adams, *Great Britain and the American Civil War*, 2:288–292; Cook, Alabama *Claims*, 25–26, on the aristocracy's attitude.

44. Welles, *Diary*, 1:385 (Monday, 27 July 1863).

45. Adams, *Great Britain and the American Civil War*, 2:294–96; Adams to Seward, 29 Jan. 1864, quoted in ibid., 2:298–300; Blackett, *Divided Hearts*, 164–65; Carroll, *Henri Mercier*, 326.

46. Adams, *Great Britain and the American Civil War*, 2:291; Monaghan, *Diplomat in Carpet Slippers*, 319.

47. Adams, *Great Britain and the American Civil War*, 2:302; W. A. Williams, *The Rise of Gladstone to the Leadership of the Liberal Party, 1859–1868* (Cambridge: Cambridge Univ. Press, 1934), chap. 6.

10. Cooperation to End the Slave Trade and for Commercial Expansion

1. Jones, *Lincoln and a New Birth of Freedom*, 62.

2. Ibid., 63–64.

3. Donald, *Lincoln*, 344–45. For the realist school of thought about the place of slavery in Civil War international relations, see Brauer, "Slavery Problem," 439–40. In addition to David Donald, advocates of the realist school are Howard Jones, Norman A. Graebner, Robert Huhn Jones, Frank L. Owsley, Frank J. Merli, Robin W. Winks, and Brian Jenkins. These historians are cited to support my argument that national self-interest, commerce, peaceful international relations, and Union military victories, especially after Antietam in mid-September 1862, kept the Europeans from intervening. The realist view supports the platform offered here for British-American rapprochement during the war because larger issues than slavery kept the powers out. Slavery became most important as a preventive after the fall of 1862, when Lincoln implemented emancipation.

4. Temperley's *Britain and America*, 40; Conway W. Henderson, "The Anglo-American Treaty of 1862 in Civil War Diplomacy," *Civil War History* 15, no. 1 (1969): 309; David L. Dykstra, *Shifting Balance of Power: American-British Diplomacy in North America, 1842–1848* (Lanham, Md.: Univ. Press of America, Inc., 1999), 177–78; Francis M. Carroll, *A Good and Wise Measure: The Search for the Canadian-American Boundary, 1783–1842* (Toronto: Univ. of Toronto Press, 2001), chap. 12.

5. Henderson, "Anglo-American Treaty of 1862," 309.

6. Somerset to Russell, 29 Aug. 1860, Russell Papers, 30/22/24, in Baxter, "Admiralty Problems," 162–64. Regis Courtemanche writes that from September 1859 to September 1860, 30,473 slaves were landed in Cuba. *No Need of Glory*, 89.

7. Baxter, "Admiralty Problems," 166–71; Jenkins, *Britain and the War for the Union*, 1:249.

8. Baxter, "Admiralty Problems," 171–72; Donald, *Lincoln*, 342, on Lincoln's antislavery; Jenkins, *Britain and the War for the Union*, 1:249.

9. Jenkins, *Britain and the War for the Union*, 1:250; Stern, *When the Guns Roared*, 120–21, points out that the American public knew nothing about the anti–slave trade treaty negotiations; Baxter, "Admiralty Problems," 172.

10. On Gordon, see Stern, *When the Guns Roared*, 119; Courtemanche, *No Need of Glory*, 88; Jenkins, *Britain and the War for the Union*, 1:250–51; Donald, *Lincoln*, 342.

11. Jenkins, *Britain and the War for the Union*, 1:251–52; see Donald, *Lincoln*, 346–48, for the speech. None of the Border States adopted the resolution. The only concrete outcome was compensated emancipation in the District of Columbia. Courtemanche, *No Need of Glory*, 89–90.

12. Jenkins, *Britain and the War for Union*, 1:252; Adams, *Great Britain and the American Civil War*, 1:275–76; Wallace and Gillespie, eds., *Journal of Moran*, 1:xxvi; Case and Spencer, *U.S. and France*, 318; Berwanger, *British Foreign Service*, 34–35; Weigley, *Great Civil War*, 170; Courtemanche, *No Need of Glory*, 90.

13. Seward to Lincoln, Department of State, 24 Apr. 1862, Lincoln Papers, ser. 1.

14. Baxter, "Admiralty Problems," 173.

15. Jones, *Union in Peril*, 118 and n32; Adams, *Great Britain and the American Civil War*, 2:90–91. Rawley, *Lincoln and a Nation Worth Fighting For*, 97.

16. Van Deusen, *Seward*, 320; Jenkins, *Britain and the War for the Union*, 1:266; Sumner to Francis Lieber, Senate Chamber, Friday, 25 Apr. 1862, Executive Session, in Palmer, *Selected Letters of Charles Sumner*, 2:111.

17. Somerset to Palmerston, 3 Feb. 1864, in Baxter, "Admiralty Problems," 173.

18. Welles, *Diary*, 1:156 (Monday, 29 Sept. 1862), 171 (Tuesday, 14 Oct. 1862), where Welles argues that Seward lost his nerve after first "taking the high ground" early in the *Trent* incident and now "has lost heart and courage." Courtemanche, *No Need of Glory*, 90–92; Stern, *When the Guns Roared*, 121; Baxter, "Admiralty Problems," 174–76.

19. In Hubbard, *Burden of Confederate Diplomacy*, 105.

20. In Weigley, *Great Civil War*, 174.

21. Ibid., 176.

22. Allen, *Great Britain and the United States*, 454.

23. Welles, *Diary*, 1:166–67 (Friday, 10 Oct. 1862).

24. Ibid., 1:192–93 (Sunday, 14 Dec. 1862).

25. Berwanger, *British Foreign Service*, 24, 35.

26. Ibid., 17, 19–20, 29–30; Ferris, *Desperate Diplomacy*, 148. See Frank L. Owsley's treatment of the South's conviction that the embargo would bring European interference in *King Cotton Diplomacy*, 24–39.

27. Ferris, *Desperate Diplomacy*, 149–50.

28. Adams, *Great Britain and the American Civil War*, 1:244–66.

29. Te-kong Tong, *United States Diplomacy in China, 1844–60* (Seattle: Univ. of Washington Press, 1964), 146–47.

30. Baxter, "Admiralty Problems," 129–30.

31. Somerset to Russell, 19 Sept. 1859, and Somerset to Palmerston, 14 Feb. 1860, in Baxter, "Admiralty Problems," 131–36. Key debates in the Commons were in July 1860.

32. Baxter, "Admiralty Problems," 132–38.

33. Brauer, "Slavery Problem," 442–43.

34. Pletcher, *Diplomacy of Involvement*, 106–8; David L. Anderson, "Anson Burlingame, American Architect of the Cooperative Policy in China, 1861–71," *Diplomatic History* 1 (Summer 1977): 242–43.

35. Pletcher, *Diplomacy of Involvement*, 109–13; Anderson, "Burlingame," 246–48.

36. Brauer, "Slavery Problem," 441.

37. Blake, *Disraeli*, 429–30; Michael Bentley, *Politics without Democracy, 1815–1914: Perception and Preoccupation in British Government*, 2d ed., Blackwell Classic Histories of England (Oxford: Blackwell, 1999), 120.

38. Jenkins, *Britain and the War for the Union*, 2:358–59; Donald, *Charles Sumner and the Rights of Man*, 142–43, 101–2 (for a similar earlier attempt by McDougall in 1863); Thomas D. Schoonover, ed. and trans., *Mexican Lobby: Matias Romero in Washington, 1861–1867* (Lexington: Univ. Press of Kentucky, 1986), 28–29 (18 Jan. 1863), 31.

39. Paolino, *Foundations of American Empire*, 19–23, 32–35, Henry Blumenthal, *A Reappraisal of Franco-American Relations, 1830–1871* (Chapel Hill: Univ. of North Carolina Press, 1959), 172.

40. Blumenthal, *Reappraisal of Franco-American Relations,* 173–77 n32 and n42. France had 30,000 troops in Mexico and 80,000 in Algeria, which were liabilities with new European events threatening the shattered balance of power.

41. James L. Crouthamel, *James Watson Webb: A Biography* (Middletown, Conn.: Wesleyan Univ. Press, 1969), 183. Webb told the emperor, an old friend, not to intervene in Mexico in October 1863 but was not heeded.

42. Blumenthal, *Reappraisal of Franco-American Relations,* 178–82, and n69, 182 is the quote from L. A. Garnier-Pagès, *Discours sur la politique extérieure* (Versailles, 1868), 12; Thomas Schoonover, *Mexican Lobby,* 167. The tragedy of Carlotta quote is by James M. McPherson, *Drawn with the Sword: Reflections on the American Civil War* (New York: Oxford Univ. Press, 1996), 226.

43. Paolino, *Foundations of American Empire,* 28–29, 34–40. For the Russo-American conflict over the Northwest, see Howard I. Kushner, *Conflict on the Northwest Coast: American-Russian Rivalry in the Pacific Northwest, 1790–1867,* Contributions in American History ser., no. 41 (Westport, Conn.: Greenwood Press, 1975), 93–142.

44. Kushner, *Conflict on the Northwest Coast,* 107–8.

45. Quoted in ibid., 109–10 (emphasis in original).

46. Charles Vevier, "The Collins Overland Line and American Continentalism," *Pacific Historical Review* 28 (August 1959): 238–39.

47. Paolino, *Foundations of American Empire,* 48–51, 59, 68–69; Pletcher, *Diplomacy of Involvement,* 2, 36; Kushner, *Conflict on the Northwest Coast,* 110–15, 126; Vevier, "Collins Overland Line," 245.

48. Ferris, Trent *Affair,* 97–98.

49. H. W. Brands, *What America Owes the World: The Struggle for the Soul of Foreign Policy* (New York: Cambridge Univ. Press, 1998), 14.

50. Quoted in Pletcher, *Diplomacy of Involvement,* 154–55; also in William G. Beasley, *Great Britain and the Opening of Japan, 1834–58* (London: Luzac & Company, 1951), 93.

51. Beasley, *Great Britain and the Opening of Japan,* 87–94.

52. Ibid., 96–101.

53. Clarendon to Bowring, 8 Dec. 1855, Clarendon Papers, c. 134, fols. 415–20, quoted in Beasley, *Great Britain and the Opening of Japan,* 157n48.

54. Beasley, *Great Britain and the Opening of Japan,* 157–59, 171–72.

55. Ibid., 102, 168.

56. Pletcher, *Diplomacy of Involvement,* 97–98, 100–106. British-American cooperation in China benefited both countries through the end of the century, with the United States gaining on British leadership in the trade. See ibid. Britain's move into China with the implicit consent of the United States is recounted in Peter Ward Fay, *The Opium War, 1840–1842: Barbarians in the Celestial Empire in the Early Part of the Nineteenth Century and the War by which They Forced Her Gates Ajar* (Chapel Hill: Univ. of North Carolina Press, 1975). Anglo-American attempts to gain stronger footholds in Chinese culture is the subject of Karen Elizabeth Vanlandingham's, "Anglo-American Relations with the Chinese in Shanghai, 1860–1875: A Study of Cultural Conflict" (Ph.D. diss., University of Tennessee, 1993).

57. Beasley, *Great Britain and the Opening of Japan,* 199–200.

58. Ibid., 180–81.

59. Van Deusen, *Seward,* 518–19; Pletcher, *Diplomacy of Involvement,* 165.

60. Van Deusen, *Seward,* 519.

61. Ibid., 520.

62. Stern, *When the Guns Roared,* 313–14.

63. Ibid., 314.

64. Van Deusen, *Seward,* 520; Welles, *Diary,* 2:188–89 (30 Nov. 1864).

11. War's End: Retrenchment and Commerce Ascendant

1. Leventhal and Quinault, *Anglo-American Attitudes,* 98.

2. For examples of British policy in the making on the disputes, see Bruce to Russell, private, copies, 20 Apr. 1865, 5 May, 26 May, 13 June, 24 July, 8 Aug.; Bruce to Clarendon, private, copies, 26 Mar. 1866, 3 Apr., private and confidential, 12 Apr., 17 Apr., Sir Frederick William Adolphus Bruce Papers, Correspondence, Copies, April 1865–August 1867, D34, Box 1, Rush Rhees Library Rarebooks and Special Collections, University of Rochester. Bruce's letters home show time and again that he never faltered in his trust of Seward on these issues and that the cabinets, whether Liberal or Conservative, followed his recommendations for patience and indifference.

3. William C. Davis, *An Honorable Defeat: The Last Days of the Confederate Government* (New York: Harcourt, 2001).

4. Jenkins, *Britain and the War for the Union,* 2:382–83. Quotes from the London *Times* are from Stern, *When the Guns Roared,* 340–41; Hyman, *Heard Round the World,* 12.

5. Seward to Reverdy Johnson (Adams' successor as minister to Britain), 20 July 1868, quoted in David E. Shi, "Seward's Attempt to Annex British Columbia, 1865–1869," *Pacific Historical Review* 47, no. 2 (1978): 222, 227, 235, 237–38.

6. Donald, *Charles Sumner and the Rights of Man,* 232–33; Bruce to Russell, 13 June 1865, private, Russell Papers, PRO 30/22/18, fol. 269; Sumner to Bright, 8 Aug. 1865, private, Bright Papers, Add. Mss. 43390; Donald, *Lincoln,* 508; Blank, "Decline of Democratic Imperialism," 113.

7. Bruce to Russell, 19 May 1865, Russell Papers, PRO 30/22/38, cited in Dubrulle, "War of Wonders," 200; Bruce to Clarendon, 20 Nov. 1865, private, Clarendon Papers, c. 90, fol. 3; Jenkins, *Britain and the War for the Union,* 2:397. The destruction of the South is from Winik, *April 1865,* 287, 301.

8. Ziegler, *Sixth Great Power,* 216.

9. Jenkins, *Britain and the War for the Union,* 2:383–84, 386; Campbell, *From Revolution to Rapprochement,* 163, 245; Hamilton, *Anglo-French Naval Rivalry,* 309; Ziegler, *Sixth Great Power,* 215.

10. Allen Nevins, *The War for the Union,* vol. 4, *The Organized War to Victory, 1864–1865* (New York: Charles Scribner's Sons, 1971), 400–401.

11. Owsley, *King Cotton Diplomacy,* 554–56.

12. Sumner to Bright, Boston, 22 Sept. 1863, Bright Papers, Add. Mss. 43390, fol. 172.

13. Crook, *North, South, and Powers,* 269–72.

14. Campbell, *From Revolution to Rapprochement,* 241–42; Steele, *Palmerston and Liberalism,* 331; Crook, *Diplomacy during the American Civil War,* 11–13.

15. Steele, *Palmerston and Liberalism,* 281; Bruce to Russell, 26 May 1865, Russell Papers, PRO 30/22/18, fol. 251.

16. Steele, *Palmerston and Liberalism,* 305.

17. John Beeler, *British Naval Policy in the Gladstone-Disraeli Era, 1866–1889* (Stanford,

Calif.: Stanford Univ. Press, 1997), 60, 64, 83–84; Somerset to Gladstone, n.d., 1865, Gladstone Papers, Add. Mss. 44304; Courtmanche, *No Need of Glory,* 172.

18. Nevins, *War for the Union,* 4:367.

19. Ibid.; McPherson, *Battle Cry of Freedom,* 853.

20. Nevins, *War for the Union,* 4:367.

21. Ibid., 4:368.

22. Courtmanche, *No Need of Glory,* 172.

23. Nevins, *War for the Union,* 4:368.

24. Adams, *Education of Henry Adams,* 239.

25. Quoted in Nevins, *War for the Union,* 4:372, 383–85, Peto was a Unionist during the late conflict. See Campbell, *English Public Opinion,* 247.

26. Matthew, ed., *Gladstone Diaries,* 6:431.

27. Nevins, *War for the Union,* 4:388, 390–91.

Conclusion

1. The treaty also shows Seward's cooperation because much of it was done before he left office in early 1869. See Stanley to Delane, 20 May 1868, private, copy, Derby Papers, William Brown Library, Liverpool, 920 DER 13/1/18; Brian Jenkins, *Fenians and Anglo-American Relations During Reconstruction* (Ithaca, N.Y.: Cornell Univ. Press, 1969), 278–80; Cook, Alabama *Claims,* 51–52.

2. Clarendon to Thornton, The Grove, 26 Dec. 1868, private, copy, Clarendon Papers, c. 476, fols. 25–30. Bruce had passed away suddenly in Boston in September 1867.

3. Clarendon to Thornton, 16 Apr. 1869, confidential, no. 93, PRO, FO 115/486, fol. 94.

4. Clarendon to Thornton, 16 Apr. 1869, private, copy, Clarendon Papers, c. 476, fol. 152.

5. Rose to Macdonald, July 1869, private, Macdonald Papers, PAC, MG 26 A(1a), vol. 258.

6. Jay Sexton, "The Funded Loan and the *Alabama* Claims," *Diplomatic History* 27, no. 4 (2003): 449, 458, 476–78.

7. Sumner to Bright, private, Boston, 8 Aug. 1865, in Palmer, *Selected Letters of Charles Sumner,* 2:322–23 and n5. Grant was in Boston on a public visit. Sumner also congratulated Gladstone on his electoral victory and believed he was moving closer to Bright.

8. These notes informed the previous several paragraphs also: Owen, "Testing the Democratic Peace," 247; Schweninger, "A lingering war," 365–70, and 379n68, where numerous examples are cited of the decay of fortifications. Forster's antiwar speech is in Patrick Jackson, *Education Act Forster: A Political Biography of W. E. Forster (1818–1886)* (Madison, N.J.: Fairleigh Dickinson Univ., 1997), 93; and Angus Hawkins, *British Political Parties, 1852–1886* (New York: St. Martin's Press, 1998), 156–57. On Gladstone's turnabout to see the war as a positive force for reform, and for his admiration of the United States by war's end, see Parish, "Gladstone and America," 100–101.

9. Parish, "Gladstone and America," 102–3; Parry, "Gladstone and Cobden," in Bebbington and Swift, eds., *Gladstone Centenary Essays,* 123.

10. Parry, "Gladstone and Liberalism," 97.

11. Agatha Ramm, *William Ewart Gladstone* (Cardiff: GPC Books, 1989), 65–66.

12. Parry, "Gladstone and Liberalism," 102, 109, 115.

13. Quoted in Bentley, *Politics without Democracy,* 144.

14. Francis M. Carroll, "Review Article: The Perils of Mid-Nineteenth-Century Anglo-American Relations," *International History Review* 16, no. 2 (1994): 306. For Lincoln's refusal to allow sabotage of Confederate efforts to build ships and gain military supplies in Britain, or to stop Spain's reconquest of Santo Domingo, see Neill F. Sanders, "Henry Shelton Sanford in England, April–November, 1861: A Reappraisal," *Lincoln Herald* 77, no. 2 (1975): 87–95; Clifford L. Egan, "The Monroe Doctrine and Santo Domingo in Spanish-American Diplomacy, 1861–1865," *Lincoln Herald* 71, no. 2 (1969): 55–66.

15. Quoted in Campbell, *English Public Opinion,* 239.

16. Quoted in ibid.

17. Richard Carwardine, *Lincoln: A Life of Purpose and Power* (New York: Alfred A. Knopf 2006), 274–82.

18. Ferris, "Seward and Faith of a Nation," 171.

19. Spencer, *Confederate Navy in Europe,* 61–62. For cooperation in 1864 over a new raider, see Mary Elizabeth Thomas, "The CSS *Tallahassee:* A Factor in Anglo-American Relations, 1864–1866," *Civil War History* 21, no. 2 (1975): 148–59.

20. Bassett, *Gladstone to His Wife,* 140; Ramm, *Gladstone,* 65–66; Cook, Alabama *Claims,* 243–44; Ferris, "Seward and Faith of a Nation," 170.

21. Biagini, *Gladstone,* 82.

22. Cook, Alabama *Claims,* 245–46; Ferris, "Seward and Faith of a Nation," 170.

23. Quoted in McPherson, *Drawn with the Sword,* 225.

Bibliography

PRIMARY SOURCES

UNPUBLISHED MANUSCRIPT SOURCES

Adams, Charles Francis. Diary. Adams Family Papers. Part I: 79, 1 July 1865–31 July 1866. Microfilm. University of Iowa Libraries, Iowa City, Iowa.

Archibald, Edward Mortimer. Papers. Public Archives of Canada, Ottawa.

Bright, John. Papers. British Library, London.

Bruce, Sir Frederick William Augustus. Papers. Rush Rhees Library, Department of Rare Books and Special Collections, University of Rochester, New York.

Clarendon, Fourth Earl of (George William Frederick Villiers). Papers. Bodleian Library, Oxford University, Oxford, England.

Cobden, Richard. Papers. British Library, London.

Cowley, Lord (Henry Richard Charles Wellesley, First Earl Cowley. Papers. FO 146. Public Record Office. Kew, England.

Fifteenth Earl of Derby (Edward Henry, Lord Stanley). Papers. William Brown Library, Liverpool.

First Earl of Iddesleigh (Sir Stafford Northcote). Papers. British Library. London.

Fish, Hamilton. Papers. Library of Congress Manuscripts Division, Washington, D.C.

Gladstone, William Ewart. Papers. British Library, London.

Granville, Lord (George Leveson Gower, second Earl Granville). Papers. Public Record Office, Kew, England.

Hammond, Sir Edmund. Papers. FO 391. Public Record Office, Kew, England.

Layard, Sir Austen Henry. Papers. British Library, London.

Lincoln, Abraham. Papers. Library of Congress, Manuscript Division. Washington D.C.: American Memory Project, (2000–2002), ser. 1–3, General Correspondence. Available at http://memory.loc.gov/ammem/alhtml/alhome.html (accessed 2003–7).

Macdonald, Sir John A. Papers. Public Archives of Canada, Ottawa.

Milne, Alexander. Papers. National Maritime Museum, Greenwich, London. (Microfilm courtesy of Dr. John Beeler):

———. Admiralty Letterbook (Letters from Admiralty) no. 1–14 January 1860 to 31 December 1860; MLN/104/1.

———. Admiralty Letterbook (Letters from Admiralty) no. 2–1 January 1861—MLN/104/2.

———. Letters From Lord Lyons, 1861–62, MLN/116/1a[1–2].

———. Letters from Lord Lyons, 1864, MLN/116/1a[Part 4].

Monck, Baron. Papers. Public Archives of Canada, Ottawa (Microfilm).

Newcastle, Fifth Duke of (Henry Pelham Finnes Pelham-Clinton, Twelfth Earl of Lincoln). Papers. Public Archives of Canada, Ottawa (Microfilm).

Palmerston, Lord (Henry John Temple). Letterbooks. British Library, London.

———. Papers. University of Southampton, England.

Ripon, First Marquis of (Earl de Grey, George Frederick Samuel Robinson). Papers. British Library, London.

Russell, Lord John (First Earl Russell). Papers. Public Record Office, Kew, England.

Seward, William Henry. Papers. Rush Rhees Memorial Library, Department of Rarebooks and Special Collections, University of Rochester (Microfilm, courtesy of Middle Tennessee State University and William and Mary College).

Weed, Thurlow. Papers. Department of Rarebooks and Special Collections, Rush Rhees Library, University of Rochester.

UNPUBLISHED OFFICIAL SERIES

United Kingdom. Foreign Office 5, General Correspondence, America, United States, ser. II. Public Record Office, Kew, England.

United Kingdom. Foreign Office 115. United States of America (Embassy and Consular), Correspondence. Public Record Office, Kew, England.

United States. National Archives. RG 59. Diplomatic Dispatches, vol. 20, 1 Jan. 1865–24 Aug. 1866, Microfilm 77/79, Washington, D.C.

PRINTED PRIMARY SOURCES

Argyll, The Dowager Duchess, ed. *George Douglas, Eighth Duke of Argyll, K.G., K.T., Autobiography and Memoirs.* 2 vols. London: John Murray, 1902.

Barnes, James J., and Patience P. Barnes, eds. *The American Civil War through British Eyes: Dispatches from British Diplomats.* Vol. 1, *November 1860–April 1862.* Kent, Ohio: Kent State Univ. Press, 2003.

———. *Private and Confidential: Letters from British Ministers in Washington to the Foreign Secretaries in London, 1844–67.* Selinsgrove, Pa.: Susquehanna Univ. Press, 1993.

Basler, Roy P., ed. *The Collected Works of Abraham Lincoln.* 8 vols. and index. New Brunswick: Rutgers Univ. Press, 1953–55.

Basoco, Richard, William E. Geoghegan, and Frank J. Merli, eds. "A British View of the Union Navy, 1864: A Report Addressed to Her Majesty's Minister at Washington." *American Neptune* 27, no. 1 (1967): 30–45.

Bassett, Arthur Tilney. *Gladstone's Speeches: Descriptive Index and Bibliography.* London: Methuen & Co., Ltd., 1916.

———, ed. *Gladstone to His Wife.* London: Methuen & Co. Ltd., 1936.

Beale, Howard K., ed. *The Diary of Edward Bates, 1859–1866.* Vol. 4 of the Annual Report of the American Historical Association for the Year 1930; 71st Cong., 3rd sess.; House Document, no. 818. Washington, D.C.: GPO, 1933.

Bourne, Kenneth, ed. *The Letters of the Third Viscount Palmerston to Laurence and Elizabeth Sulivan, 1804–1863.* Camden 4th ser., vol. 23. London: Offices of the Royal Historical Society, 1979.

British Documents on Foreign Affairs: Reports and Papers from the Foreign Office Confidential Print, pt. 1, ser C., vols. 5–8. Ed. Kenneth Bourne. Frederick, Md.: University Publications of America, 1986.

Bruce, Henry Austin. *Letters of the Rt. Hon. Henry Austin Bruce G.C.B., Lord Aberdare of Duffryn.* 2 vols. Oxford: Privately printed, 1902.

Buckle, George Earle, ed. *The Letters of Queen Victoria: A Selection from Her Majesty's Correspondence and Journal between the Year 1862 and 1878.* 2d ser., 3 vols. London: John Murray, 1901.

Cartwright, Julia, ed. *The Journals of Lady Knightley of Fawsley, 1856–1884.* New York: E. P. Dutton and Company, 1916.

Cavendish, Francis. *Society, Politics and Diplomacy, 1820–1864: Passages from the Journal of Francis W. H. Cavendish.* London: T. Fisher Unwin, 1913.

Connell, Brian, ed. *Regina vs. Palmerston: The Correspondence between Queen Victoria and Her Foreign and Prime Minister, 1837–1865.* Garden City, N.Y.: Doubleday & Company, 1961.

Cutler, Wayne, ed. *Correspondence of James K. Polk.* Vol. 10, *July–December 1845.* Knoxville: Univ. of Tennessee Press, 2004.

Dallas, George Mifflin. *A Series of Letters from London Written during the Years, 1856, '57, '58, '59, and '60.* Ed. Julia Dallas. 2 vols. in 1. Philadelphia: J. B. Lippincott & Co., 1869.

De Leon, Edwin. *Secret History of Confederate Diplomacy Abroad.* Ed. William C. Davis. Lawrence: Univ. Press of Kansas, 2005.

Dennett, Tyler, ed. *Lincoln and the Civil War in the Diaries and Letters of John Hay.* New York: Dodd, Mead, 1939.

Donald, David, ed. *Inside Lincoln's Cabinet: The Civil War Diaries of Salmon P. Chase.* New York: Longman's, Green and Co., 1954.

———. *Charles Sumner and the Rights of Man.* New York: Alfred A. Knopf, 1970.

Douglas, Sir George, and Sir George Dalhousie Ramsay, eds. *The Panmure Papers: Being a Selection from the Correspondence of Fox Maule, Second Baron Panmure, Afterwards Eleventh Earl Dalhousie, K. T. G. C. B.* 2 vols. London: Hodder and Stoughton, 1908.

Ford, Worthington Chauncey, ed. *A Cycle of Adams Letters, 1861–1865.* 2 vols. New York: Houghton Mifflin Company, 1920.

Gathorne-Hardy, Alfred E., ed. *Gathorne Hardy, First Earl of Cranbrook: A Memoir with Extracts from His Diary and Correspondence.* 2 vols. London: Longmans, Green, and Co., 1910.

Gooch, George Peabody, ed. *The Later Correspondence of Lord John Russell, 1840–1878.* 2 vols. London: Longmans, Green and Co., 1925.

Guedalla, Philip, ed. *Gladstone and Palmerston: Being the Correspondence of Lord Palmerston and Mr. Gladstone, 1851–1865.* Covent Garden: Victor Gollancz, 1928; repr., Freeport, N.Y.: Books for Libraries Press, 1971.

Hansard Parliamentary Debates. Commons, 3d ser., vol. 177 (1865).

Hardcastle, The Hon. Mrs., ed. *Life of John, Lord Campbell, Lord High Chancellor of Great Britain: Consisting of a Selection from His Autobiography, Diary, and Letters.* 2d ed., 2 vols. London: John Murray, 1881.

Hawkins, Angus, and John Powell, eds. *The Journal of John Wodehouse, First Earl of Kimberley for 1862–1902.* Camden Fifth series, vol. 9. London: Royal Historical Society, 1997.

Hay, John. *Letters of John Hay and Extracts from Diary.* Vol. 1. 1908; repr., New York: Gordian Press, 1969.

———. *Lincoln and the Civil War in the Diaries and Letters of John Hay.* Selected and introduced by Tyler Dennett. New York: Dodd, Mead & Company, 1939.

Jenkins, T. A., ed. *The Parliamentary Diaries of Sir John Trelawny, 1858–1865.* Camden Fourth series, vol. 40. London: Offices of the Royal Historical Society, 1990.

Johnson, A. H., ed. *The Letters of Charles Greville and Henry Reeve, 1836–1865.* London: T. Fisher Unwin, Ltd., 1924.

Knaplund, Paul, ed. *Gladstone-Gordon Correspondence, 1851–1896: Selections from the Private Correspondence of a British Prime Minister and a Colonial Governor.* Transactions of the American Philosophical Society, n.s., vol. 51, pt. 4. Philadelphia: American Philosophical Society, 1961.

Leader, Robert Eadon, ed. *Life and Letters of John Arthur Roebuck, P.C., Q.C., M.P: With Chapters of Autobiography.* New York: Edward Arnold, 1897.

Lever, Tresham, ed. *The Letters of Lady Palmerston: Selected and Edited from the Originals at Broadlands and Elsewhere.* London: John Murray, 1957.

MacCarthy, Desmond, and Agatha Russell, eds. *Lady John Russell: A Memoir with Selections from Her Diaries and Correspondence.* New York: John Lane Company, 1911.

Mallock, W. D., and Lady Gwendolen Ramsden, eds. *Letters, Remains, and Memoirs of Edward Adolphus Seymour Twelfth Duke of Somerset, K. G.* London: Richard Bentley and Son, 1893.

Manning, William R., ed. *Diplomatic Correspondence of the United States: Canadian Relations, 1784–1860.* 4 vols. Washington, D.C.: Carnegie Endowment for Peace, 1940–45.

Matthew, H. C. G., ed. *The Gladstone Diaries.* Vol. 5, *1855–1860.* Oxford: Clarendon Press, 1978.

———. *The Gladstone Diaries.* Vol. 6, *1861–1868.* Oxford: Clarendon Press, 1978.

Mitford, Nancy, ed. *The Stanleys of Alderley: Their Letters between the Years, 1851–1865.* London: Hamish Hamilton, 1939; repr., 1968.

Morton, W. L., ed. *Monck Letters and Journal, 1863–1868: Canada from Government House to Confederation.* The Carleton Library, no. 52. Toronto: McClelland and Stewart Ltd., 1970.

Niven, John, ed. *The Salmon P. Chase* Vol. 1, *Journals, 1829–1872.* Kent, Ohio: Kent State Univ. Press, 1993.

O'Brien, D. P., ed. *The Correspondence of Lord Overstone.* 3 vols. Cambridge: Cambridge Univ. Press, 1971.

Official Records of the Union and Confederate Navies in the War of the Rebellion. 30 vols., ser. 2. Washington, D.C.: GPO, 1894–1922.

Palmer, Beverly Wilson, ed. *The Selected Letters of Charles Sumner.* 2 vols. Boston: Northeastern Univ. Press, 1990.

Papers Relating to the Treaty of Washington. Vol. 6, *The Geneva Arbitration.* Washington, D.C.: GPO, 1872. Available from http://books.google.com/books?id=Tv7mja5WrqMC& pg=PA534&lpg=PA534&dq=papers+relating+to+the+treaty+of+washington+vol+6&s ource=web&ots=md3wv1AVB7&sig=wThbXo9Q2ZlBWuElJLGYV4QAk58#PPA8,M1

Parry, E. Jones, ed. *The Correspondence of Lord Aberdeen and Princess Lieven, 1832–1854.* Vol. 1, *1832–1848.* Camden Third ser., vol. 60. London: Offices of the Royal Historical Society, 1938.

Pease, Theodore Calvin, and James G. Randall, eds. *The Diary of Orville Hickman Browning,* 2 vols. Springfield: Illinois State Historical Library, 1925.

Powell, John, ed. *Liberal by Principle: The Politics of John Wodehouse 1st Earl of Kimberley, 1843–1902*. London: Historians' Press, 1996.

Ramm, Agatha, ed. *The Gladstone-Granville Correspondence*. Camden 3d ser., vols. 81 and 82. London: Royal Historical Society, 1952; repr., Cambridge: Cambridge Univ. Press, 1998.

Richardson, James D., ed. and comp. *The Messages and Papers of Jefferson Davis and the Confederacy: Including Diplomatic Correspondence, 1861–1865*. 2 vols. New York: Chelsea House-Robert Hector Publishers in Association with R. R. Bowker, 1966.

Russell, William Howard. *My Diary North and South*. Ed. Eugene H. Berwanger. Introduction by William E. Gienapp. Baton Rouge: Louisiana State Univ. Press, 2001.

Samuels, Ernest, ed. *Henry Adams: Selected Letters*. Cambridge, Mass.: Belknap Press of Harvard Univ. Press, 1992.

Schoonover, Thomas D., ed. and trans. *Mexican Lobby: Matias Romero in Washington, 1861–1867.* Lexington: Univ. Press of Kentucky, 1986.

Seward, Frederick W. *Reminiscences of a War-Time Statesman and Diplomat, 1830–1915*. New York: Putnam's, 1916.

Seward, William Henry. *The Works of William Henry Seward*. Vol. 5, *Diplomatic History of the War for the Union*. Ed. George K. Baker. New ed. Boston: Houghton-Mifflin, 1884.

Shewmaker, Kenneth E., Kenneth Stevens, and Alan R. Berolzheimer, eds. *The Papers of Daniel Webster: Diplomatic Papers*. Vol. 2, *1850–1852*. Hanover, N.H.: Univ. Press of New England, 1987.

U.S. Department of State. *Papers Relating to Foreign Affairs, Accompanying the Annual Message of the President to the Two Houses of Congress at the Commencement of the Third Session of the Thirty-Seventh Congress*. Vol. 1, *1862*. Washington, D.C.: GPO, 1862. Available from the University of Wisconsin Digital Collections. http://digital.library.wisc.edu/1711.dl/FRUS.FRUS1862v01 (accessed 20 May 2006).

Vincent, J. R., ed. *Disraeli, Derby and Conservative Party: The Political Journals of Lord Stanley, 1849–1869*. New York: Barnes & Noble, 1978.

———, ed. *A Selection from the Diaries of Edward Henry Stanley, 15th Earl of Derby (1826–93): Between September 1869 and March 1878*. Camden Fifth ser., vol. 4. London: Offices of the Royal Historical Society, 1994.

Wallace, Sarah Agnes, and Frances Elma Gillespie, eds. *The Journal of Benjamin Moran, 1857–1865*. 2 vols. Chicago: Univ. of Illinois Press, 1948.

Walling, R. A. J., ed. *The Diaries of John Bright*. London: Cassell & Co. Ltd., 1930.

Welles, Gideon. *Diary of Gideon Welles: Secretary of the Navy under Lincoln and Johnson*. 3 vols. Boston: Houghton Mifflin, 1909.

Wellesley, Colonel the Hon. F. A. (ed.). *The Paris Embassy during the Second Empire: Selections from the Papers of Henry Richard Charles Wellesley, 1st Earl Cowley, Ambassador at Paris, 1852–1867.* London: Thornton Butterworth, Ltd., 1928.

Wellesley, Sir Victor, and Robert Sencourt, eds. *Conversations with Napoleon III: A Collection of Documents, mostly unpublished and almost entirely Diplomatic, Selected and arranged with Introductions*. London: Ernest Benn Ltd., 1934.

Williams, Ben Ames, ed. *A Diary from Dixie*. New York: Houghton Mifflin, 1949; repr., Cambridge, Mass.: Harvard Univ. Press, 1980.

PUBLISHED SOURCES

BOOKS

Adams, Ephraim D. *Great Britain and the American Civil War.* 2 vols. New York: Longmans, Green, 1925.

Adams, George Rollie. *General William S. Harney: Prince of Dragoons.* Lincoln: Univ. of Nebraska Press, 2001.

Adams, Henry. *The Education of Henry Adams: An Autobiography.* Boston: Houghton Mifflin, 1918; repr., Sentry ed. of the 1918 Massachusetts Historical Society ed., 1961.

Adams, Michael C. C. *Our Masters the Rebels: A Speculation on Union Military Failure in the East, 1861–1865.* Cambridge, Mass.: Harvard Univ. Press, 1978.

Allen, H. C. *Great Britain and the United States: A History of Anglo-American relations (1783–1952)* Watford Herts. Adams Press, Ltd, 1954; repr. New York: Archon Books, 1969.

Anderson, Fred, and Andrew Clayton. *The Dominion of War: Empire and Liberty in North America, 1500–2000.* New York: Viking, 2005.

Bailey, Thomas A. *A Diplomatic History of the American People.* 10th ed. Englewood Cliffs, N.J.: Prentice Hall, 1980.

Baldelli, Pia Celozzi. *Power Politics, Diplomacy, and the Avoidance of Hostilities between England and the United States in the Wake of the Civil War.* Trans. from the Italian by Elena Bertozzi, note translation by Cynthia DeNardi Ipsen. Studies in American History, vol. 21. Lewiston, N.Y.: Edward Mellen Press, 1998.

Bancroft, Frederic. *The Life of William H. Seward.* 2 vols. New York: Harper and Brothers, 1900.

Barber, James. *The Presidential Character: Predicting Performance in the White House.* Englewood Cliffs, N.J.: Prentice-Hall, 1992.

Barratt, Glynn. *Russian Shadows on the British Northwest Coast of North America, 1810–1890: A Study in the Rejection of Defence Responsibilities.* Vancouver: Univ. of British Columbia Press, 1983.

Bartlett, C. J. *Great Britain and Sea Power, 1815–1853.* Oxford: Clarendon Press, 1963.

Batt, Elisabeth. *Monck: Governor General of Canada, 1861–68.* Toronto: McClelland and Stewart, 1976.

Beales, Derek. *England and Italy, 1859–60.* London: Thomas Nelson and Sons, Ltd., 1961.

Beasley, William G. *Great Britain and the Opening of Japan, 1834–58.* London: Luzac & Company, 1951.

Bebbington, David, and Roger Swift, eds. *Gladstone Centenary Essays.* Liverpool: Liverpool Univ. Press, 2000.

Beeler, John F. *British Naval Policy in Gladstone-Disraeli Era, 1866–1880.* Palo Alto, Calif.: Stanford Univ. Press, 1997.

Bell, Herbert C. F. *Lord Palmerston.* 2 vols. in 1. London: Longmans, Green and Co., Ltd., 1936; repr., Hamden, Conn.: Archon Books, 1966.

Bemis, Samuel Flagg. *John Quincy Adams and the Foundations of American Foreign Policy.* New York: W. W. Norton, 1973.

Bentley, Michael. *Politics without Democracy, 1815–1914: Perception and Preoccupation in British Government.* 2d ed. Blackwell Classic Histories of England. Oxford: Blackwell Ltd., 1999.

Bernath, Stuart L. *Squall Across the Atlantic: American Civil War Prize Cases and Diplomacy*. Berkeley: Univ. of California Press, 1970.

Berwanger, Eugene H. *The British Foreign Service and the American Civil War*. Lexington: Univ. Press of Kentucky, 1994.

Biagini, Eugenio F. *Gladstone*. British History in Perspective series. New York: St. Martin's, 2000.

———. *Liberty, Retrenchment and Reform: Popular Liberalism in the Age of Gladstone, 1860–1880*. New York: Cambridge Univ. Press, 1992.

Blackburn, George M. *French Newspaper Opinion on the American Civil War*. Contributions in American History, no. 171. Westport, Conn.: Greenwood Press, 1997.

Blackett, R. J. M. *Divided Hearts: Britain and the American Civil War*. Baton Rouge: Louisiana State Univ. Press, 2001.

Blake, Robert. *Disraeli*. New York: St. Martin's Press, 1967.

Blumenthal, Henry. *France and the United States: Their Diplomatic Relations, 1789–1914*. Chapel Hill: Univ. of North Carolina Press, 1970.

———. *A Reappraisal of Franco-American Relations, 1830–1871*. Chapel Hill: Univ. of North Carolina Press, 1959.

Boritt, Gabor S., ed. *Why the Confederacy Lost*. New York: Oxford Univ. Press, 1992.

Bourne, Kenneth. *Britain and the Balance of Power in North America, 1815–1908*. Berkeley: Univ. of California Press, 1967.

———. *The Foreign Policy of Victorian England, 1830–1902*. Oxford: Clarendon Press, 1970.

Brands, H. W. *What America Owes the World: The Struggle for the Soul of Foreign Policy*. New York: Cambridge Univ. Press, 1998.

Brooke, John, and Mary Sorensen, eds. *The Prime Ministers' Papers: W. E. Gladstone, I: Autobiographica*. London: Her Majesty's Stationery Office, 1971.

Brown, David. *Palmerston and the Politics of Foreign Policy, 1846–55*. New York: Manchester Univ. Press, 2002.

Browning, Robert M., Jr. *From Cape Charles to Cape Fear: The North Atlantic Blockading Squadron during the Civil War*. Tuscaloosa: Univ. of Alabama Press, 1993.

Bullen, Roger. *Palmerston, Guizot and the Collapse of the Entente Cordiale*. London: Athlone Press, 1974.

Callahan, James Morton. *Diplomatic History of the Southern Confederacy*. 1901; repr., New York: Frederick Ungar, 1964.

———. *The Neutrality of the Great Lakes and Anglo-American Relations*. Johns Hopkins Studies in Historical and Political Science 16, nos. 1–4. Baltimore: Johns Hopkins Univ. Press, 1898.

Campbell, Charles S. *From Revolution to Rapprochement: The United States and Great Britain, 1783–1900*. America and the World series. New York: John Wiley & Sons, Inc., 1974.

Campbell, Duncan Andrew. *English Public Opinion and the American Civil War*. Woodbridge, UK: Royal Historical Society, 2003.

Carroll, Daniel B. *Henri Mercier and the American Civil War*. Princeton, N.J.: Princeton Univ. Press, 1971.

Carroll, Francis M. *A Good and Wise Measure: The Search for the Canadian-American Boundary, 1783–1842*. Toronto: Univ. of Toronto Press, 2001.

Carwardine, Richard. *Lincoln: A Life of Purpose and Power*. New York: Alfred A. Knopf, 2006.

Case, Lynn M., and Warren F. Spencer. *The United States and France: Civil War Diplomacy.* Philadelphia: Univ. of Pennsylvania Press, 1970.

Chamberlain, Muriel E. *Lord Palmerston.* Washington, D.C.: Catholic Univ. of America Press, 1987.

———. *'Pax Britannica'?: British Foreign Policy, 1789–1914.* Studies in Modern History series. New York: Longman, 1988.

Charmly, John. "Palmerston: 'Artful Old Dodger' or 'Babe of Grace'?", in *The Makers of British Foreign Policy from Pitt to Thatcher,* ed. T. G. Otte. New York: Palgrave, 2002.

Conacher, J. B. *Britain and the Crimea, 1855–56.* New York: St. Martin's Press, 1987.

———. "Lessons in Twisting the Lion's Tale: Two Sidelights of the Crimean War." In *Policy by Other Means: Essays in Honour of C. P. Stacey,* ed. Michael Cross and Robert Bothwell, 77–94 Toronto: Clarke, Irwin & Company Ltd., 1972.

Cook, Adrian. *The Alabama Claims: American Politics and Anglo-American Relations, 1865–1872.* Ithaca, N.Y.: Cornell Univ. Press, 1974.

Cooper, William J., Jr. *Jefferson Davis, American.* New York: Alfred A. Knopf, 2000.

Courtemanche, Regis A. *No Need of Glory: The British Navy in American Waters, 1860–1864.* Annapolis, Md.: Naval Institute Press, 1977.

Crawford, Martin. *The Anglo-American Crisis of the Mid-Nineteenth Century: The Times and America, 1850–1862.* Athens: Univ. of Georgia Press, 1987.

Creighton, Donald. *John A. Macdonald: The Old Chieftan.* Toronto: Macmillan, 1955.

———. *John A. Macdonald: The Young Politician.* Toronto: Macmillan, 1952.

Crook, D. P. *Diplomacy during the American Civil War.* New York: John Wiley & Sons, 1975.

———. *The North, the South, and the Powers, 1861–1865.* New York: John Wiley & Sons, 1974.

Crosby, Travis L. *The Two Mr. Gladstones: A Study in Psychology and History.* New Haven, Conn.: Yale Univ. Press, 1997.

Cross, Coy F., III. *Lincoln's Man in Liverpool: Consul Dudley and the Legal Battle to Stop Confederate Warships.* Dekalb: Northern Illinois Univ. Press, 2007.

Crouthamel, James L. *James Watson Webb: A Biography.* Middletown, Conn.: Wesleyan Univ. Press, 1969.

Cullop, Charles P. *Confederate Propaganda in Europe, 1861–1865.* Coral Gables, Fla.: Univ. of Miami Press, 1969.

Cunningham, Michele. *Mexico and the Foreign Policy of Napoleon III.* New York: Palgrave, 2001.

Current, Richard N. "God and the Strongest Battalions," in David Herbert Donald, ed.: *Why the North Won the Civil War.* New York: A Touchtone Book; Simon & Schuster, 1960.

Daddysman, James W. *The Matamoros Trade: Confederate Commerce, Diplomacy, and Intrigue.* Newark: Univ. of Delaware Press, 1984.

Davies, William Watkin. *Gladstone and the Unification of Italy.* Oxford: B. H. Blackwell, 1918.

Davis, William C. *An Honorable Defeat: The Last Days of the Confederate Government.* New York: Harcourt, 2001.

———. *Look Away! A History of the Confederate States of America.* New York: Free Press, 2002.

Dawson, William Harbutt. *Richard Cobden and Foreign Policy: A Critical Exposition, With Special Reference to Our Day and Its Problems.* London: George Allen & Unwin, 1926.

Denholm, Anthony. *Lord Ripon, 1827–1909: A Political Biography.* London: Croom Helm, 1982.

Dirck, Brian R. *Lincoln and Davis: Imagining America, 1809–1865.* Lawrence: Univ. Press of Kansas, 2001.

Donald, David. *Lincoln.* New York: Simon & Schuster, 1995.

———, ed. *Why the North Won the Civil War.* Touchstone ed. 1960; repr., New York: Simon & Schuster, 1996.

Dowty, Alan. *The Limits of American Isolation: The United States and the Crimean War.* New York: New York Univ. Press, 1971.

Duberman, Martin. *Charles Francis Adams, 1807–1886.* Stanford, Cal.: Stanford Univ. Press, 1960.

Dudley, Wade G. *Splintering the Wooden Walls: The British Blockade of the United States, 1812–1815.* Annapolis, Md.: Naval Institute Press, 2003.

Dunham, Arthur Louis. *The Anglo-French Treaty of Commerce of 1860 and the Progress of the Industrial Revolution in France.* Ann Arbor: Univ. of Michigan Press, 1930; repr., New York: Octagon Books, 1971.

Dykstra, David L. *The Shifting Balance of Power: American-British Diplomacy in North America, 1842–1848.* Lanham, Md.: Univ. Press of America, 1999.

Echard, William E. *Napoleon III and the Concert of Europe.* Baton Rouge: Louisiana State Univ. Press, 1983.

Edwards, Ruth Dudley. *The Pursuit of Reason:* The Economist, *1843–1993.* Boston: Harvard Business School Press, 1993.

Eldridge, C. C. *England's Mission: The Imperial Idea in the Age of Gladstone and Disraeli, 1868–1880.* Chapel Hill: Univ. of North Carolina Press, 1973.

Elliot, Hon. Arthur D. *The Life of George Joachim Goschen, First Viscount Goschen, 1831–1907.* 2 vols. New York: Longmans, Green, and Co., 1911.

Erickson, Arvel B. *Edward T. Cardwell: Peelite.* Vol. 49. Philadelphia: American Philosophical Society, 1959.

Farnsworth, Susan H. *The Evolution of British Imperial Policy during the Mid-Nineteenth Century: A Study of the Peelite Contribution, 1846–1874.* New York: Garland, 1992.

Fay, Peter Ward. *The Opium War, 1840–1842: Barbarians in the Celestial Empire in the Early Part of the Nineteenth Century and the War by Which They Forced Her Gates Ajar.* Chapel Hill: Univ. of North Carolina Press, 1975.

Ferris, Norman B. *Desperate Diplomacy: William H. Seward's Foreign Policy, 1861.* Knoxville: Univ. of Tennessee Press, 1976.

———. *The* Trent *Affair: A Diplomatic Crisis.* Knoxville: Univ. of Tennessee Press, 1977.

———. "William H. Seward and the Faith of a Nation." In *Traditions and Values: American Diplomacy, 1790–1865* Lanham, Md.: Univ. Press of America, 1985, 153–77

———. "Lincoln and Seward in Civil War Diplomacy," in *"For a Vast Future Also": Essays from the Journal of the Abraham Lincoln Association,* ed. Thomas F. Swartz. New York: Fordham Univ. Press, 1999, 21–42.

Fitzmaurice, Lord Edmund. *The Life of Granville George Leveson Gower: Second Earl Granville, K.G., 1815–1891.* 2 vols. New York: Longman's, Green, and Co., 1905.

Fladeland, Betty Lorraine. *Men and Brothers: Anglo-American Antislavery Cooperation.* Urbana: Univ. of Illinois Press, 1972.

Foner, Eric. *Reconstruction: America's Unfinished Revolution, 1863–1877.* New American Nation series. New York: Harper and Row, 1988.

Foote, Shelby. *The Civil War: A Narrative*. Vol. 1, *From Fort Sumter to Perryville*. New York: Random House, 1958; repr., New York: Vintage Books, 1986.

———. *The Civil War: A Narrative*. Vol. 2, *From Fredericksburg to Meridian*. New York: Random House, 1963; repr., New York: Vintage Books, 1986.

———. *The Civil War: A Narrative*. Vol. 3, *Red River to Appomattox*. New York: Vintage Books, 1974.

Förster, Stig, and Jörg Nagler, eds. *On the Road to Total War: The American Civil War and the German Wars of Unification, 1861–1871*. German Historical Institute. Washington, D.C.: Cambridge Univ. Press, 1997.

Gavronsky, Serge. *The French Liberal Opposition and the American Civil War*. New York: Humanities Press, 1968.

Gienapp, William E. *Abraham Lincoln and Civil War America: A Biography*. New York: Oxford Univ. Press, 2002.

Goodwin, Doris Kearns. *Team of Rivals: The Political Genius of Abraham Lincoln*. New York: Simon & Schuster, 2005.

Gordon, Lesley J. *General George E. Pickett in Life and Legend*. Civil War America series. Chapel Hill: Univ. of North Carolina Press, 1998.

Gough, Barry M. *The Royal Navy and the Northwest Coast of North America, 1810–1914: A Study in British Maritime Ascendancy*. Vancouver: Univ. of British Columbia Press, 1971.

Graebner, Norman A., ed. *Tradition and Values: American Diplomacy, 1790–1865*. Lanham, Md.: Univ. Press of America, 1985.

Grant, Alfred. *The American Civil War and the British Press*. Jefferson, N.C.: McFarland & Company, 2000.

Grant, Susan-Mary, and Peter J. Parish, eds. *Legacy of Disunion: The Enduring Significance of the American Civil War*. Baton Rouge: Louisiana State Univ. Press, 2003.

Hamilton, C. I. *Anglo-French Naval Rivalry, 1840–1870*. Oxford: Clarendon Press, 1993.

Hanna, Alfred Jackson, and Kathryn Abbey Hanna. *Napoleon III and Mexico: American Triumph over Monarchy*. Chapel Hill: Univ. of North Carolina Press, 1971.

Hattaway, Herman, and Richard E. Beringer. *Jefferson Davis, Confederate President*. Lawrence: Univ. Press of Kansas, 2002.

Hawkins, Angus. *British Party Politics, 1852–1886*. New York: St. Martin's Press, 1998.

———. *Parliament, Party and the Art of Politics in Britain, 1855–59*. Stanford, Calif.: Stanford Univ. Press, 1987.

Hitsman, J. Mackay. *Safeguarding Canada, 1763–1871*. Toronto: Univ. of Toronto Press, 1968.

Hoppen, K. Theodore. *The Mid-Victorian Generation, 1846–1886*. Oxford: Clarendon Press, 1998.

Howard, Christopher. *Britain and the Casus Belli, 1822–1902*. London: Athlone Press, 1974.

Howe, Anthony. *Free Trade and Liberal England, 1846–1946*. Oxford: Clarendon Press, 1997.

Hubbard, Charles M. *The Burden of Confederate Diplomacy*. Knoxville: The Univ. of Tennessee Press, 1998.

Hyman, Harold, ed. *Heard Round the World: The Impact Abroad of the Civil War*. New York: Alfred A. Knopf, 1969.

Jackson, Patrick. *Education Act Forster: A Political Biography of W. E. Forster (1818–1886)*. Madison, N.J.: Fairleigh Dickinson University Press, 1997.

———. *The Last of the Whigs: A Political Biography of Lord Hartington, Later Eighth Duke of Devonshire (1833–1908)*. Rutherford, N.J.: Fairleigh Dickinson Univ. Press, 1994.

Jenkins, Brian. *Britain and the War for the Union.* 2 vols. Montreal: McGill-Queens Univ. Press, 1974–80.

———. *Fenians and Anglo-American Relations during Reconstruction.* Ithaca, N.Y.: Cornell Univ. Press, 1969.

Jenkins, Roy. *Gladstone: A Biography.* New York: Random House, 1995.

Jenkins, T. A. *The Liberal Ascendancy, 1830–1886.* New York: St. Martin's Press, 1994.

Jones, Howard. *Abraham Lincoln and a New Birth of Freedom: The Union and Slavery in the Diplomacy of the Civil War.* Lincoln: Univ. of Nebraska Press, 1999.

———. *To the Webster-Ashburton Treaty: A Study in Anglo-American Relations, 1783–1843.* Chapel Hill: Univ. of North Carolina Press, 1977.

———. *Union in Peril: The Crisis over British Intervention in the Civil War.* Chapel Hill: Univ. of North Carolina Press, 1992.

Jones, Howard, and Donald A. Rakestraw. *Prologue to Manifest Destiny: Anglo-American Relations in the 1840s,* Wilmington, Del.: Scholarly Resources, 1995.

Jones, Wilbur Devereux. *The American Problem in British Diplomacy, 1841–1861.* London: Macmillan, 1974.

———. *The Confederate Rams at Birkenhead: A Chapter in Anglo-American Relations.* Confederate Centennial Studies, no. 19. Tuscaloosa, Ala.: Confederate, 1961.

Jordan, Donaldson, and Edwin J. Pratt. *Europe and the American Civil War.* Boston: Houghton Mifflin, 1931.

Kagan, Robert. *Dangerous Nation: America's Place in the World from Its Earliest Days to the Dawn of the Twentieth Century.* New York: Alfred A. Knopf, 2006.

Kaplan, Lawrence S. *Colonies into Nation: American Diplomacy, 1763–1801.* American Diplomatic History series. New York: Macmillan, 1972.

Kaufman, Scott. *The Pig War: The United States, Britain, and the Balance of Power in the Pacific Northwest, 1846–72.* Lanham, Md.: Lexington Books, 2004.

Kelley, Robert. *The Transatlantic Persuasion: The Liberal-Democratic Mind in the Age of Gladstone.* New York: Alfred A. Knopf, 1969.

Kennedy, David M. "San Juan Island, Washington: The 'Pig War' and the Vagaries of Identity and History," in *American Places: Encounters with History. A Celebration of Sheldon Meyer,* ed. William E. Leuchtenberg. New York: Oxford Univ. Press, 2000.

Kennedy, Paul. *The Rise and Fall of the Great Powers: Economic Change and Military Conflict from 1500 to 2000.* New York: Random House, 1987.

Kinzer, Bruce L. *The Gladstonian Turn of Mind: Essays Presented to J. B. Conacher.* Toronto: Univ. of Toronto Press, 1985.

Krein, David F. *The Last Palmerston Government: Foreign Policy, Domestic Politics, and the Genesis of "Splendid Isolation."* Ames: Iowa State Univ. Press, 1978.

Kushner, Howard I. *Conflict on the Northwest Coast: American-Russian Rivalry in the Pacific Northwest, 1790–1867.* Contributions in American History series, no. 41. Westport, Conn.: Greenwood Press, 1975.

Lambert, Andrew. *Battleships in Transition: The Creation of the Steam Battlefleet, 1815–1860.* Annapolis, Md.: Naval Institute Press, 1984.

———. *The Crimean War: British Grand Strategy, 1853–56.* New York: Manchester Univ. Press, 1990.

———. "Winning without Fighting: British Grand Strategy and its Application to the United States, 1815–1865," in *Strategic Logic and Political Rationality: Essays in Honor of Michael I. Handel,* ed. Bradford A. Lee and Michael I. Handel. Portland, Ore.: Frank Cass, 2003.

Leventhal, Fred M., and Roland Quinault, eds. *Anglo-American Attitudes: From Revolution to Partnership.* Burlington, Vt.: Ashgate, 2000.

Lillibridge, G. D. *Beacon of Freedom: The Impact of American Democracy upon Great Britain, 1830–1870.* Philadelphia: Univ. of Pennsylvania Press, 1955.

Mahin, Dean B. *One War at a Time: The International Dimensions of the American Civil War.* Washington, D.C.: Brassey's, 1999.

Marquis, Greg. *In Armageddon's Shadow: The Civil War and Canada's Maritime Provinces.* Montreal: McGill-Queen's Univ. Press, 1998.

Martin, Ged. *The Durham Report and British Policy: A Critical Essay.* Cambridge: Cambridge Univ. Press, 1972.

Martineau, J. *Life of Henry Pelham, Fifth Duke of Newcastle.* London: John Murray, 1908.

Maxwell, Herbert Eustace. *The Life and Letters of George William Frederick Fourth Earl of Clarendon.* 2 vols. London: Edward Arnold, 1913; repr. Ann Arbor: University Microfilms International, 2003

May, Robert E., ed. *The Union, the Confederacy, and the Atlantic Rim.* West Lafayette, Ind.: Purdue Univ. Press, 1995.

McCabe, James O. *The San Juan Water Boundary Question.* Canadian Studies in History and Government, no 5. Toronto: Univ. of Toronto Press, 1964.

McDougall, Walter A. *Promised Land Crusader State: The American Encounter with the World Since 1776.* New York: Houghton Mifflin Company, 1997.

McPherson, James M. *Battle Cry of Freedom: The Civil War Era.* New York: Ballantine Books, 1988.

———. *Crossroads of Freedom: Antietam.* Pivotal Moments in American History series. New York: Oxford Univ. Press, 2002.

———. *Drawn with the Sword: Reflections on the American Civil War.* New York: Oxford Univ. Press, 1996.

———. *Lincoln and the Second American Revolution.* New York: Oxford Univ. Press, 1990.

Merli, Frank J. *The Alabama, British Neutrality, and the American Civil War.* Ed. David M. Fahey. Bloomington: Indiana Univ. Press, 2004.

———. *Great Britain and the Confederate Navy, 1861–1865.* Bloomington: Indiana Univ. Press, 1970.

Milton, David Hepburn. *Lincoln's Spymaster: Thomas Haines Dudley and the Liverpool Network.* Mechanicsburg, Pa.: Stackpole Books, 2003.

Monaghan, Jay. *Diplomat in Carpet Slippers: Abraham Lincoln Deals with Foreign Affairs.* New York: Charter Books/Bobbs-Merrill, 1945.

Morley, John. *The Life of William Evart Gladstone.* 3 vols. New York: The Macmillan Company, 1903.

Morton, William Lewis. *The Critical Years: The Union of British North America, 1857–1873.* Toronto: McClelland and Stewart, 1964.

Munsell, F. Darrell. *The Unfortunate Duke: Henry Pelham, Fifth Duke of Newcastle, 1811–1864.* Columbia: Univ. of Missouri Press, 1985.

Murfin, James V. *The Gleam of Bayonets: The Battle of Antietam and the Maryland Campaign of 1862.* New York: Thomas Yoseloff, 1965.

Neidhardt, William S. *Fenianism in North America.* University Park: Pennsylvania State Univ. Press, 1975.

Nevins, Allan. *The War for the Union.* Vol. 2, *War Becomes a Revolution.* New York: Charles Scribner's Sons, 1960.

———. *The War for the Union.* Vol. 3, *The Organized War, 1863–1864.* New York: Charles Scribner's Sons, 1971.

———. *The War for the Union.* Vol. 4, *The Organized War to Victory, 1864–1865.* New York: Charles Scribner's Sons, 1971.

Newton, Lord. *Lord Lyons: A Record of British Diplomacy.* 2 vols. London: Arnold, 1913.

Nickles, David Paull. *Under the Wire: How the Telegraph Changed Diplomacy,* Harvard Historical Series 144. Cambridge, Mass.: Harvard Univ. Press, 2003.

Otte, T. G., ed. *The Makers of British Foreign Policy from Pitt to Thatcher.* New York: Palgrave, 2002.

Owsley, Frank Lawrence. *King Cotton Diplomacy: Foreign Relations of the Confederate States of America.* 2d rev. ed., Chicago: Univ. of Chicago Press, 1959.

Palm, Franklin Charles. *England and Napoleon III: A Study in the Rise of a Utopian Dictator.* Durham: Duke Univ. Press, 1948.

Paolino, Ernest N. *The Foundations of the American Empire: William Henry Seward and U. S. Foreign Policy.* Ithaca, N.Y.: Cornell Univ. Press, 1973.

Parry, Jonathan P. "Gladstone and Cobden." In David Bebbington and Roger Swift, ed. *Gladstone Centenary Essays.* Liverpool: Liverpool Univ. Press, 2000.

———. *The Rise and Fall of Liberal Government in Victorian Britain.* New Haven, Conn.: Yale Univ. Press, 1993.

Partridge, Michael Stephen. *Gladstone.* New York: Routledge, 2003.

———. *Military Planning for the Defense of the United Kingdom, 1814–1870.* Contributions in Military Studies, no. 91. Westport, Conn.: Greenwood Press, 1989.

Partridge, Michael Stephen, and Karen E. Partridge, eds. *Lord Palmerston, 1784–1865: A Bibliography.* Bibliographies of British Statesmen, no. 16. Westport, Conn.: Greenwood Press, 1994.

Philbrick, Nathaniel. *Sea of Glory: America's Voyage of Discovery, The U.S. Exploring Expedition, 1838–1842.* New York: Penguin Books, 2003.

Phillips, Kevin. *The Cousins' Wars: Religion, Politics, and the Triumph of Anglo-America.* New York: Basic Books, 1999.

Platt, D. C. M. *Finance, Trade and Politics: British Foreign Policy, 1815–1914.* Oxford: Clarendon Press, 1968.

Pletcher, David M. *The Diplomacy of Annexation: Texas, Oregon, and the Mexican War.* Columbia: Univ. of Missouri Press, 1973.

———. *The Diplomacy of Involvement: American Economic Expansion across the Pacific, 1784–1900.* Columbia: Univ. of Missouri Press, 2001.

Potter, David. *The Impending Crisis 1848–1861.* Edited by Don E. Fehrenbacher. New York: Harper & Row, 1976.

Pottinger, E. Ann. *Napoleon III and the German Crisis, 1865–1866.* Harvard Historical Studies, vol. 75. Cambridge, Mass.: Harvard Univ. Press, 1966.

Prest, John M. *Lord John Russell.* Columbia: Univ. of South Carolina Press, 1972.

Preston, Richard A. *Canada and "Imperial Defense": A Study of the Origins of the British Commonwealth's Defense Organization, 1867–1919.* Publication no. 29. Duke University Commonwealth-Studies Center. Durham, N.C.: Duke Univ. Press, 1967.

———. *The Defence of an Undefended Border: Planning for War in North America, 1867–1939.* Montreal: McGill-Queen's Univ. Press, 1977.

Price, Roger. *The Second French Empire: An Anatomy of Political Power.* New York: Cambridge Univ. Press, 2001.

Radforth, Ian. *Royal Spectacle: The 1860 Visit of the Prince of Wales to Canada and the United States.* Toronto: Univ. of Toronto Press, 2004.

Rakestraw, Donald. *For Honor or Destiny: The Anglo-American Crisis over the Oregon Territory.* American University Studies, ser. 9, History, vol. 160. New York: Peter Lang, 1995.

Ramm, Agatha. *William Ewart Gladstone.* Cardiff: GPC Books, 1989.

Ramsay, A. A. W. *Idealism and Foreign Policy: A Study of the Relations of Great Britain with Germany and France, 1850–1878.* London: John Murray, 1925.

Rawley, James A. *Abraham Lincoln and a Nation Worth Fighting For.* Wheeling, Ill.: Harlan Davidson, 1996; repr., Lincoln: Univ. of Nebraska Press, 2003.

Raymond, Dora Neill. *British Policy and Opinion during the Franco-Prussian War.* Studies in History, Economics and Public Law, vol. C, no 1. New York: AMS Press, 1967.

Reid, Brian Holden. "Civil–Military relations and the Legacy of the Civil War," in *Legacy of Disunion: The Enduring Significance of the Civil War.*, ed. Susan-Mary Grant and Peter J. Parrish. Baton Rouge: Louisiana State Univ. Press, 2003; 151–70.

Renwick, Sir Robin. *Fighting with Allies: America and Britain in Peace and War.* New York: Random House, 1996.

Rich, Norman. *Why the Crimean War? A Cautionary Tale.* Hanover, N.H.: Univ. Press of New England, 1985.

Ridley, Jasper. *Lord Palmerston.* London: Constable & Co., 1970; repr., London: Panther Books, 1972.

Robbins, Keith. *John Bright.* Boston: Routledge and Kegan Paul, 1979.

Rock, Stephen R. *Why Peace Breaks Out: Great Power Rapprochement in Historical Perspective.* Chapel Hill: Univ. of North Carolina Press, 1989.

Saab, Anne Pottinger. *Reluctant Icon: Gladstone, Bulgaria and the Working Classes.* Harvard Historical Studies 109. Cambridge, Mass.: Harvard Univ. Press, 1991.

Saul, Norman E. *Distant Friends: The United States and Russia, 1763–1867.* Lawrence: Univ. Press of Kansas, 1991.

Scherer, Paul. *Lord John Russell: A Biography.* Selinsgrove, Pa.: Susquehanna Univ. Press, 1999.

Schroeder, John H. *Shaping a Maritime Empire: The Commercial and Diplomatic Role of the American Navy, 1829–1861.* Contributions in Military Studies, no. 48. Westport, Conn.: Greenwood Press, 1985.

Searle, G. R. *Entrepreneurial Politics in Mid-Victorian Britain.* New York: Oxford Univ. Press, 1993.

Sears, Stephen W. *Landscape Turned Red: The Battle of Antietam.* Boston: Houghton Mifflin Company, 1983; repr., Mariner Books, 2003.

Sedgwick, Jeffrey Leigh. "Abraham Lincoln and the Character of Liberal Statesmanship." In *Legacy of Disunion: The Enduring Significance of the American Civil War,* ed. Susan-Mary Grant and Peter J. Parish. Baton Rouge: Louisiana State Univ. Press, 2003; 100–115.

Senior, Hereward. *The Fenians and Canada.* Toronto: Macmillan, 1978.

Sexton, Jay. *Debtor Diplomacy: Finance and American Foreign Relations in the Civil War Era, 1837–1873.* Oxford Historical Monographs. Oxford: Clarendon Press, 2005.

Shannon, Richard. *Gladstone, 1865–1898.* Vol. 2. Chapel Hill: Univ. of North Carolina Press, 1999.

Shewmaker, Kenneth L. "Daniel Webster and American Conservatism" in *Traditions and Values: American Diplomacy, 1790–1865*. Lanham, Md.: Univ. Press of America, 1985; 129–51.

Sideman, Belle Becker, and Lillian Friedman, eds. *Europe Looks at the Civil War*. New York: Orion Press, 1960.

Skelton, William B. *An American Profession of Arms: The Army Officer Corps, 1784–1861*. Lawrence: Univ. Press of Kansas, 1992.

Smith, Paul, ed. *Lord Salisbury on Politics: A Selection from His Articles in the* Quarterly Review, *1860–1883*. Cambridge: Cambridge Univ. Press, 1972.

Smith, William H. C. *Napoleon III: The Pursuit of Prestige*. London: Collins & Brown, 1991.

Southgate, Donald. *"The Most English Minister": The Policies and Politics of Palmerston*. New York: St. Martin's Press, 1966.

Spencer, Warren F. *The Confederate Navy in Europe*. Tuscaloosa: Univ. of Alabama Press, 1983.

Stacey, Charles Perry. *Canada and the British Army, 1846–1871: A Study in the Practice of Responsible Government*. Rev. ed. Toronto: Univ. of Toronto Press, 1963.

Steele, E. D. *Palmerston and Liberalism, 1855–1865*. Cambridge: Cambridge Univ. Press, 1991.

Stern, Philip Van Doren. *When the Guns Roared: World Aspects of the American Civil War*. Garden City, N.Y.: Doubleday & Company, 1965.

Stewart, Gordon T. *The American Response to Canada since 1776*. East Lansing: Michigan State Univ. Press, 1992.

Stuart, Reginald C. *United States Expansionism and British North America, 1775–1871*. Chapel Hill: Univ. of North Carolina Press, 1988.

Surdam, David G. *Northern Naval Superiority and the Economics of the American Civil War*. Columbia: Univ. of South Carolina Press, 2001.

Swartz, Marvin. *The Politics of British Foreign Policy in the Era of Disraeli and Gladstone*. New York: St. Martin's Press, 1985.

Swartz, Thomas F., ed. *"For a Vast Future Also": Essays from the Journal of the Abraham Lincoln Association*. New York: Fordham Univ. Press, 1999.

Sweetman, Paul. *War and Administration: The Significance of the Crimean War to the British Army*. Edinburgh: Scottish Academic Press, 1984.

Tap, Bruce. *Over Lincoln's Shoulder: The Committee on the Conduct of the War*. Lawrence: Univ. Press of Kansas, 1998.

Taylor, John M. *Confederate Raider: Raphael Semmes of the* Alabama. Washington, D.C.: Brassey's, 1994.

Temperley, Howard. *Britain and America since Independence*. New York: Palgrave, 2002.
———. *British Antislavery, 1933–1870*. Columbia: Univ. of South Carolina Press, 1972.

Thomas, Benjamin Platt. *Russo-American Relations, 1815–1867*. Baltimore: Johns Hopkins Univ. Press, 1930.

Thomas, Emory M. *The Confederate Nation, 1861–1865*. New American Nation series. New York: Harper & Row, 1979.

de Tocqueville, Alexis. *Democracy in America*. 2 vols. 1835; repr., New York: Alfred A. Knopf, 1980.

Tong, Te-kong. *United States Diplomacy in China, 1844–60*. Seattle: Univ. of Washington Press, 1964.

Tuchman, Barbara W. *The Proud Tower: A Portrait of the World before the War, 1890–1914*. New York: Macmillan, 1962; repr., New York: Macmillan, 1966.

Tulloch, Hugh. *The Debate on the American Civil War Era*. Issues in Historiography. New York: Manchester Univ. Press, 1999.

Tyrner-Tyrnauer, A. R. *Lincoln and the Emperors*. New York: Harcourt Brace & World, 1962.

Vanauken, Sheldon. *The Glittering Illusion: English Sympathy for the South Confederacy*. Washington, D.C.: Regnery Gateway, 1989.

Van Deusen, Glyndon G. *William Henry Seward*. New York: Oxford Univ. Press, 1967.

Villiers, Brougham, and W. H. Chesson. *Anglo-American Relations, 1861–1865*. New York: Charles Scribner's Sons, 1920.

Waite, P. B. *The Life and Times of Confederation, 1864–1867: Politics, Newspapers, and the Union of British North America*. Toronto: Univ. of Toronto Press, 1962; repr., Toronto: Univ. of Toronto Press, 1977.

Ward, J. T. *Sir James Graham*. New York: St. Martin's Press, 1967.

Warner, Donald F. *The Idea of Continental Union: Agitation for the Annexation of Canada to the United States, 1849–1893*. Lexington: Univ. Press of Kentucky, 1960.

Warren, Gordon H. *Fountain of Discontent: The Trent Affair and Freedom of the Seas*. Boston: Northeastern Univ. Press, 1981.

Wawro, Geoffrey. *The Austro-Prussian War: Austria's War with Prussia and Italy in 1866*. New York: Cambridge Univ. Press, 1996.

Weigley, Russell F. *A Great Civil War: A Military and Political History, 1861–1865*. Bloomington: Indiana Univ. Press, 2000.

Weinberg, Adelaide. *John Eliot Cairnes and the American Civil War: A Study in Anglo-American Relations*. London: Kingswood Press, 1968.

Wetzel, David. *The Crimean War: A Diplomatic History*. New York: Columbia Univ. Press, 1985.

Williams, T. Harry. "Canada and the Civil War," in Harold Hyman, ed. *Heard Round the World: The Impact Abroad of the Civil War*. New York: Alfred A. Knopf, 1969.

Williams, W. A. *The Rise of Gladstone to the Leadership of the Liberal Party, 1859–1868*. Cambridge: Cambridge Univ. Press, 1934.

Willson, Beckles. *Friendly Relations: A Narrative of Britain's Ministers and Ambassadors to America (1791–1930)*. Freeport, N.Y.: Books for Libraries Press, 1934; repr., Freeport, N.Y.: Books for Libraries Press, 1969.

Winik, Jay. *April 1865: The Month That Saved America*. New York: HarperCollins, 2001.

Winks, Robin W. *Canada and the United States: The Civil War Years*. 4th ed. Montreal: McGill-Queen's Univ. Press, 1998.

Winstanley, Michael J. *Gladstone and the Liberal Party*. New York: Routledge, 1990.

Winter, James. *Robert Lowe*. Toronto: Univ. of Toronto Press, 1976.

Wise, Stephen R. *Lifeline of the Confederacy: Blockade Running during the Civil War*. Columbia: Univ. of South Carolina Press, 1988.

Woldman, Albert A. *Lincoln and the Russians*. Cleveland, Oh.: World, 1952.

Ziegler, Paul R. *Palmerston*. New York: Palgrave Macmillan, 2003.

Ziegler, Philip. *The Sixth Great Power: A History of One of the Greatest of All Banking Families, the House of Barings, 1762–1929*. New York: Alfred A. Knopf, 1988.

ARTICLES

Adams, Charles Francis. "The *Trent* Affair." *The American Historical Review* 17, no. 3 (1912): 540–62.

Allen, H. C. "Two Hundred Years: Anglo-American Relations." *Encounter* 46, no. 1 (1976): 66–70.

Anderson, David L. "Anson Burlingame, American Architect of the Cooperative Policy in China, 1861–71." *Diplomatic History* 1 (summer 1977): 239–55.

Antony, Robert J. "China and William Seward's Vision of Empire." *Sino-American Relations* 10, no. 3 (1984): 34–43.

Ashcroft, Neil. "British Trade with the Confederacy and the Effectiveness of Union Maritime Strategy during the Civil War." *International Journal of Maritime History* 10, no. 2 (1998): 155–76.

Baker, William J. "Anglo-American Relations in Miniature: The Prince of Wales in Portland, Maine, 1860." *New England Quarterly* 45, no. 4 (1972): 559–68.

Baxter, Colin F. "The Duke of Somerset and the Creation of the British Ironclad Navy, 1859–66." *Mariner's Mirror* 63, no. 3 (1977): 279–84.

Bell, K. "British Policy towards the Construction of the Suez Canal, 1859–65." *Transactions of the Royal Historical Society* 15 (1965): 121–43.

Bellows, Donald. "A Study of British Conservative Reaction to the American Civil War." *Journal of Southern History* 51, no. 4 (1985): 505–26.

Beloff, Max. "Historical Revision No. CXVII: Great Britain and the American Civil War." *History* 37 (Feb. 1952): 40–48.

Bernath, Stuart W. "British Neutrality and the Civil War Prize Cases." *Civil War History* 15, no. 1 (1969): 320–31.

Bernstein, George L. "Special Relationship and Appeasement: Liberal Policy towards America in the Age of Palmerston." *Historical Journal* 41, no. 3 (1998): 725–50.

Binder, Frederick Moore. "James Buchanan and the Earl of Clarendon: An Uncertain Relationship." *Diplomacy and Statecraft* 6, no. 2 (1995): 323–441.

Blanco, Richard L. "Reform and Wellington's Post Waterloo Army, 1815–1854." *Military Affairs* 29 (Fall 1965): 123–31.

Blinn, Harold E. "Seward and the Polish Rebellion of 1863." *American Historical Review* 45 (1939–40): 828–33.

Brady, Eugene A. "A Reconsideration of the Lancashire 'Cotton Famine.'" *Agriculture History* 37 (1963): 156–62.

Brauer, Kinley J. "Seward's 'Foreign War Panacea': An Interpretation." *New York History* 55 (Apr. 1974): 133–57.

———. "The Slavery Problem in the Diplomacy of the American Civil War." *Pacific Historical Review* 46 (Aug. 1977): 439–69.

———. "The United States and British Imperial Expansion, 1815–1860." *Diplomatic History* 12, no. 1 (1988): 19–37.

Braun, Lindsay Frederick. "The Roebuck Motion and the Issue of British Recognition of the Confederate States of America." *UCLA Historical Journal* 17 (1997): 1–19.

Bullen, Roger. "Peel, Aberdeen and the *Entente Cordiale*," *Bulletin of the Institute of Historical Research* 30, (1957): 204–206.

Callahan, James Morton. "Diplomatic Relations of the Confederate States with England (1861–1865)." *Annual Report of the American Historical Association* (1898): 265–83.

Carroll, Daniel B. "Abraham Lincoln and the Minister of France, 1860–1863." *Lincoln Herald* 70, no. 3 (1968): 142–53.

Carroll, Francis M. "British North America and American Expansionism." *Canadian Review of American Studies* 23, no. 1 (1992): 157–64.

———. "Review Article: The Perils of Mid-Nineteenth-Century Anglo-American Relations." *International History Review* 16, no. 2 (1994): 304–16.

Claussen, Martin P. "Peace Factors in Anglo-American Relations, 1861–1865." *Mississippi Valley Historical Review* 26 (Mar. 1940): 511–15.

Cohen, Victor H. "Charles Sumner and the *Trent* Affair." *Journal of Southern History* 12 (1956): 205–19.

Collyer, C. "Gladstone and the American Civil War." *Proceedings of the Leeds Philosophical Society* 6, no. 8 (1951): 583–94.

Conacher, J. B. "British Policy in the Anglo-American Enlistment Crisis of 1855–1856." *Proceedings of the American Philosophical Society* 136, no. 4 (1992): 531–76.

Cook, Adrian. "A Lost Opportunity in Anglo-American Relations: The *Alabama* Claims, 1865–1867." *Australian Journal of Politics and History* 12, no. 1 (1966), 54–65.

Crawford, Martin. "The Anglo-American Crisis of the Early 1860s: A Framework for Revision." *South Atlantic Quarterly* 82, no. 4 (1983): 406–23.

———. "Anglo-American Perspectives: J. C. Bancroft Davis, New York Correspondent of *The Times*, 1854–1861." *New York Historical Society Quarterly* 63, no. 3 (1978): 190–217.

Crook, D. P. "Portents of War: English Opinion on Secession." *American Studies* 4, no. 2 (1970): 163–79.

Cunningham, A. B. "Peel, Aberdeen and the *Entente Cordiale*." *Bulletin of the Institute for Historical Research* 30 (1957): 189–206.

Daddysman, Jim, "British Neutrality and the Matamoros Trade: A Step toward Anglo-American Rapprochement." *The Journal of the West Virginia Historical Association* 9, no. 1 (1985): 1–12.

Dashew, Doris W. "The Story of an Illusion: The Plan to Trade the *Alabama* Claims for Canada." *Civil War History* 15, no. 1 (1969): 332–48.

Egan, Clifford L. "The Monroe Doctrine and Santo Domingo in Spanish-American Diplomacy, 1861–1865." *Lincoln Herald* 71, no. 2 (1969): 55–66.

Ellsworth, Edward W. "America's Gideon in 'the Scepter'd Isle,' The British Tour of Henry War Beecher in 1863." *Lincoln Herald,* 73, no. 3 (1971): 138–49.

———. "Anglo-American Affairs in October 1862." *Lincoln Herald* 66, no. 2 (1964): 89–96.

———. "British Consuls in the Confederacy during 1862." *Lincoln Herald* 66, no. 2 (1964): 149–54.

———. "British Parliamentary Reaction to Lincoln's Assassination." *Lincoln Herald* 60, no. 2 (1958): 47–57.

———. "Lord John Russell and British Consuls in America in 1861." *Lincoln Herald* 66, no. 1 (1964): 34–40.

Ferris, Norman B. "The Prince Consort, *The Times*, and the *Trent* Affair." *Civil War History* 6 (1960): 152–56.

———. "*Trent* Affair." *Lincoln Herald* 49, no. 2 (1967): 131–35.

Fulton, Richard D. "The London *Times* and the Anglo-American Boarding Dispute of 1858." *Nineteenth-Century Contexts* 17, no. 2 (1993): 134–45.

Gelfand, Lawrence E. "Strains in a Special Relationship." *Reviews in American History* 22 (1994): 691–97.

Gibson, James A. "The Duke of Newcastle and British North American Affairs, 1859–64." *Canadian Historical Review* 44, no. 2 (1963): 142–56.

Golder, Frank A. "Russian-American Relations during the Crimean War." *American Historical Review* 31, no. 3 (1925): 462–76.

Graebner, Norman A. "European Interventionism and the Crisis of 1862." *Journal of the Illinois State Historical Society* 69, no. 1 (1976): 36–46.

Gurowich, P. M. "The Continuation of War by Other Means: Party and Politics, 1855–1865." *Historical Journal* 27, no. 3 (1984): 603–31.

Hanna, Kathryn Abbey. "The Roles of the South in French Intervention in Mexico." *Journal of Southern History* 20 (1954): 3–21.

Harcourt, Freda. "Gladstone, Monarchism and the 'New' Imperialism, 1868–74." *Journal of Imperial and Commonwealth History* 14 (1985): 20–51.

Hawkins, Angus. "'Parliamentary Government' and Victorian Political Parties, c. 1830–c. 1880." *English Historical Review* 104 (1989): 638–69.

Heckman, Richard Allen. "British Press Reaction to the Emancipation Proclamation." *Lincoln Herald* 71, no. 4 (1969): 150–53.

Henderson, Conway W. "The Anglo-American Treaty of 1862 in Civil War Diplomacy." *Civil War History* 15, no. 1 (1969): 308–19.

Hernon, Joseph M., Jr. "British Sympathies in the American Civil War: A Reconsideration." *Journal of Southern History* 33 (Aug. 1967): 356–67.

Hitsman, J. Mackay. "Had Britain Intervened." *Canadian Army Journal* 17, no. 1 (1963): 34–37.

Hubbard, Charles M. "James Mason, the 'Confederate Lobby' and the Blockade Debate of March 1862." *Civil War History* 45, no. 3 (1999): 223–37.

———. "Lincoln's Choice of Foreign Ministers." *Lincoln Herald* 96, no. 2 (1994): 52–55.

Jeffries, William W. "The Civil War Career of Charles Wilkes." *Journal of Southern History* 11 (1945): 324–48.

Jenkins, T. A. "Gladstone, the Whigs and the Leadership of the Liberal Party." *Historical Journal* 28, no. 2 (1984): 337–60.

Jones, Wilbur D. "The British Conservatives and the American Civil War." *American Historical Review* 58 (Apr. 1953): 527–43.

Kaufman, Scott, and John A. Soares Jr. "'Sagacious Beyond Praise'? Winfield Scott and Anglo-American-Canadian Border Diplomacy, 1837–1860." *Diplomatic History* 30, no. 1 (2006): 57–82.

Khasigian, Amos. "Economic Factors and British Neutrality, 1861–1865." *Historian* 25 (Aug. 1963): 451–65.

Krein, David F. "Russell's Decision to Detain the Laird Rams." *Civil War History* 22, no. 2 (1976): 158–63.

———. "War and Reform: Russell, Palmerston, and the Struggle for Power in the Aberdeen Cabinet, 1853–1854." *Maryland Historian* 7, no. 2 (1976): 67–84.

Lambert, Andrew D. "Politics, Technology and Policy-Making, 1859–1865: Palmerston, Gladstone and the Management of the Naval Arms Race." *Northern Mariner* 8, no. 3 (July 1998): 9–38.

Laurent, Pierre-Henri. "Anglo-American Diplomacy and the Belgian Indemnities Controversy, 1836–42." *Historical Journal* 10, no. 2 (1967): 197–217.

Lester, Richard I. "Construction and Purchase of Confederate Cruisers in Great Britain during the American Civil War." *Mariner's Mirror* 63 (Feb. 1977): 71–92.

Libby, Justin. "Hamilton Fish and the Origins of Anglo-American Solidarity." *Mid-America: A Historical Review* 76, no. 1 (1994): 205–26.

Lorimer, Douglas A. "The Role of Anti-Slavery Sentiment in English Reactions to the American Civil War." *Historical Journal* 19, no. 2 (1976): 405–20.

Matzke, Rebecca Berens. "Britain Gets Its Way: Power and Peace in Anglo-American Relations, 1838–1846." *War in History* 8, no. 1 (2001): 19–46.

Merli, Frank J., and Theodore A. Wilson. "The British Cabinet and the Confederacy: Autumn, 1862." *Maryland Historical Magazine* 65 (Fall 1970): 239–62.

Messamore, Barbara J. "Diplomacy or Duplicity? Lord Lisgar, John A. Macdonald, and the Treaty of Washington, 1871." *Journal of Imperial and Commonwealth History* 32, no. 2 (May 2004): 29–53.

Milne, A. Taylor. "The Lyons-Seward Treaty of 1862." *American Historical Review* 38 (Apr. 1933): 511–25.

Mosse, W. E. "The Crown and Foreign Policy. Queen Victoria and the Austro-Prussian Conflict, March–May, 1866." *Cambridge Historical Journal* 10 (1951): 205–23.

Nordholt, J. W. Schulte. "The Civil War Letters of the Dutch Ambassador." *Journal of the Illinois State Historical Society* 54 (Winter 1961): 341–73.

Oates, Stephen B. "Henry Hotze: Confederate Agent Abroad." *Historian* 27 (1965): 131–54.

Officer, Lawrence H., and Lawrence B. Smith. "The Canadian-American Reciprocity Treaty of 1855 to 1866." *Journal of Economic History* 28 (Dec. 1968): 598–623.

O'Rourke, Alice. "The Law Officers of the Crown and the *Trent* Affair." *Mid-America* 54, no. 3 (1972): 157–71.

Owsley, Harriet Chappell. "Henry Shelton Sanford and Federal Surveillance Abroad, 1861–1865." *Mississippi Valley Historical Review* 48 (1961): 211–28.

Parish, Peter J. "Gladstone and America." In *Gladstone,* ed. Peter J. Jagger. London: Hambledon Press, 1998: 85–104.

Parry, J. R. "The Impact of Napoleon III on British Politics, 1851–1880." *Transactions of the Royal Historical Society.* Sixth ser. (2001): 147–75.

Partridge, M. S. "The Russell Cabinet and National Defense, 1846–1852." *History* 72, no. 235 (1987): 231–50.

Peaple, Simon, and John Vincent. "Gladstone and the Working Man." London: Hambledon Press, 1998. 71–84.

Pratt, Julius W. "James K. Polk and John Bull." *Canadian Historical Review* 25, no. 1 (1943): 341–49.

Prucha, Francis Paul. "Distribution of Regular Army Troops before the Civil War." *Military Affairs* 16 (1952): 169–73.

———. "The United States Army as Viewed by British Travelers, 1825–1860." *Military Affairs* 17 (Fall 1953): 113–24.

Reid, Robert L., ed. "William E. Gladstone's 'Insincere Neutrality' during the Civil War." *Civil War History* 15, no. 1 (1969): 293–307.

Reuter, William C. "The Anatomy of Political Anglophobia in the United States, 1865–1900." *Mid-America: An Historical Review* 61, no. 2 (1980): 117–32.

Reynolds, David. "Rethinking Anglo-American Relations." *International Affairs* 65 (1988–89): 89–111.

Ritcheson, Charles R. "The British Role in American Life, 1800–1850." *History Teacher* 7, no. 4 (1974): 574–96.

Robson, Maureen M. "The *Alabama* Claims and the Anglo-American Reconciliation, 1865–71." *Canadian Historical Review* 42, no. 1 (1961): 1–22.

Rodgers, Bradley A. "The Northern Theater in the Civil War: The USS *Michigan* and Confederate Intrigue on the Great Lakes." *American Neptune* 48 (Spring 1988): 96–105.

Sanders, Neill F. "Henry Shelton Sanford in England, April–November, 1861: A Reappraisal." *Lincoln Herald* 77, no. 2 (1975): 87–95.

Scherer, Paul H. "Partner or Puppet? Lord John Russell at the Foreign Office, 1859–1862." *Albion* 19, no. 3 (1987): 347–71.

Sears, Louis Martin. "A Confederate Diplomat at the Court of Napoleon III." *American Historical Review* 26, no. 2 (1921): 255–81.

Sexton, Jay. "Transatlantic Financiers and the Civil War." *American Nineteenth Century History* 2, no. 3 (autumn 2001): 29–46.

———. Sexton, Jay. "The Funded Loan and the *Alabama* Claims." *Diplomatic History* 17, no. 4 (2003): 449–78.

———. "Toward a Synthesis of Foreign Relations in the Civil War Era, 1848–77." *American Nineteenth Century History* 5, no. 3 (2004): 50–73.

———. "Transatlantic Financiers and the Civil War." *American Nineteenth Century History* 2, no. 3 (2001): 29–46.

Shi, David E. "Seward's Attempt to Annex British Columbia, 1865–1869." *Pacific Historical Review* 47, no. 2 (1978): 217–38.

Stacey, C. P. "Britain's Withdrawal from North America, 1864–1871." *Canadian Historical Review* 36, no. 3 (1955): 69–85.

Thomas, Mary Elizabeth. "The CSS *Tallahassee:* A Factor in Anglo-American Relations, 1864–1866." *Civil War History* 21, no. 2 (1975): 148–59.

———. "Jamaica and the U.S. Civil War." *Americas* 24, no. 1 (1972): 25–32.

Topik, Steven C. "When Mexico Had the Blues: A Transatlantic Tale of Bonds, Bankers, and Nationalists, 1862–1910." *American Historical Review* 105, no. 3 (2000): 714–38.

Van Alstyne, Richard W. "Great Britain, the United States, and Hawaiian Independence, 1850–1855." *Pacific Historical Review* 4 (1935): 15–24.

Vevier, Charles. "The Collins Overland Line and American Continentalism." *Pacific Historical Review* 28 (Aug. 1959): 237–53.

Waite, P. B. "Cardwell and Confederation." *Canadian Historical Review* 43, no. 1 (1962): 17–41.

Wheeler-Bennett, Sir John. "The *Trent* Affair: How the Prince Consort Saved the United States." *History Today* 11, no. 2 (1961): 811–16.

Wright, D. G. "Bradford and the American Civil War." *Journal of British Studies* 8, no. 2 (1969): 69–85.

Wright, Richard J. "Green Flags and Red-Coated Gunboats: Naval Activities on the Great Lakes during the Fenian Scares, 1866–1870." *Inland Seas* 22 (Summer 1966): 91–110.

DISSERTATIONS AND THESES

Baxter, Colin F. "Admiralty Problems during the Second Palmerston Administration, 1859–1865." Ph.D. diss., University of Georgia, 1965.

Blank, Joel Harold. "The Decline of Democratic Imperialism and the Rise of Democratic Peace: Case Studies in Anglo-American Relations, 1800 to the Present." Ph.D. diss., University of California-Los Angeles, 2000.

Casper, Henry W. "American Attitudes toward the Rise of Napoleon III: A Cross Section of Public Opinion." Ph.D. diss., Catholic University of America Press, Washington, D.C., 1947.

Dubrulle, Hubert F. "'A War of Wonders': The Battle in Britain over Americanization and the American Civil War." Ph.D. diss., University of California-Santa Barbara, 1999.

Gallas, Stanley. "Lord Lyons and the Civil War, 1859–1864." Ph.D. diss., University of Illinois at Chicago Circle, 1982.

Hill, Franklin William. "The Anglo-American Recruitment Crisis, 1854–1856: Origins, Events, and Outcomes." Ph.D. diss., Washington State University, 1996.

Kortge, Dean. "Then Central American Policy of Lord Palmerston, 1855–1865" Ph.D. diss., University of Kansas, 1973.

McCleary, John William. "Anglo-French Naval Rivalry, 1815–1848." Ph.D. diss., Johns-Hopkins University, 1947.

Myers, Phillip E. "Mask of Indifference: Great Britain's North American Policy and the Path to the Treaty of Washington, 1815–1871." Ph.D. diss., University of Iowa, 1978.

Owen, John Malloy, IV. "Testing the Democratic Peace: American Diplomatic Crises, 1794–1917." Ph.D. diss., Harvard University, 1993.

Poulton, Gary Michael. "Great Britain and the Intervention in Mexico, 1861–1865." Ph.D. diss., Miami University of Ohio, 1976.

Schweninger, Joseph M. "'A lingering war must be prevented': The Defense of the Northern Frontier, 1812–1871." Ph.D. diss., Ohio State University, 1998.

Silverstein, Mary Poindexter. "Diplomacy and Politics: A British View of the Reciprocity-Fisheries Negotiations, 1853–1854." Master's thesis, University of Chicago, 1961.

Smith, Don Alan. "Cabinet and Constitution in the Age of Peel and Palmerston." Ph.D. diss., Yale University, 1966.

Tallman, Ronald D. "Warships and Mackerel: The North Atlantic Fisheries in Canadian-American Relations, 1867–1877." Ph.D. diss., University of Maine, 1971.

Vanlandingham, Karen Elizabeth. "Anglo-American Relations with the Chinese in Shanghai, 1860–1875: A Study of Cultural Conflict." Ph.D. diss., University of Tennessee, 1993.

Weise, Selene Harding Curd. "Negotiating the Treaty of Washington, 1871." Ph.D. diss., Syracuse University, 1971.

Index

Aberdeen, 4th Earl of (George Hamilton-Gordon), 11, 16, 18, 21, 28, 173
abolition, 11
Acton, Lord (John Emerich Edward): view on Civil War and friend of Gladstone, 77, 115
Adams, Charles Francis: advises Seward on aristocracy, 205; amicable relations with Russell, 47–48, 50, 102 117, 123, 182; on Antietam, 111; blockade debate, 59; and British Columbia, 222; British intervention debate, 118, 202; Confederate emancipation plan, 208; and Confederate shipbuilding in Britain, 96, 99, 197; and Geneva Arbitration, 253; imprudent act, 153–54; postwar popularity, 231; relations with Palmerston, 104; on Roebuck, 202; Seward and annexation, 231; and Sumner, 62, 131; and *Trent* affair, 66, 74, 86; Union memorialists, 204; view of Mason, 90; works to avert foreign war, 45
Adams, Ephraim Douglas, 8–9
Adams, Henry: on anti-slave trade treaty, 212; on blockade debate in House of Commons, 93; and fall of New Orleans, 60; and intervention debate, 59, 61, 125; on Laird rams, 167; postwar comment, 237; on Roebuck, 203; Russell's support for Union, 47; on Sumner, 131
Adams, John Quincy, 221
Adderley, Charles Bowyer, 177–78; defense of Canada, 182
Africa, West, 209
Alderley, Lord Stanley of: and *Trent* affair, 77, 80, 111
Admiralty, 18, 30; and blockade, 47–48, 61; cautious policy, 175, 186; cooperation with

Union navy, 50, 89, 91, 123, 153, 251; court and slave trade, 209; and Japan, 223; and seizure of Laird rams, 154
Alabama: Britain's policy, 229; claims, 7, 96, 185, 187, 222, 228; Grant wants to drop, 245; indirect claims, 228, 248; influence of trade, 233; international arbitration, 251, 252; and rapprochement, 229; Russell's shibboleth, 248; settlement, 243; stress on Gladstone's first ministry, 249; Sumner, 231, 252; and U.S. debt, 232. *See also* Johnson-Clarendon Convention
Alabama, CSS, 97; British disdain at, 165, 167, 196–97; British tried to detain, 101; depredations, 123, 127, 132, 144, 147, 153, 155, 159, 162–63; and reason for intervention, 103
Alaska, 221
Alcock, Rutherford, 226
Albert, Prince: death of, 81; Pro-North, 43, 49; Russell's memorandum to Seward on *Trent* affair, 70, 77–78
Alexandra: British-American cooperation, 161, 163–65; case; 161; Charles Francis Adams, 161; Confederacy, 161; Foreign Enlistment Act, 161; Palmerston's support for Russell, 161; Russell's arbitrary action, 161–64; Thomas Dudley, 161
Amur River, 221–22
Anglo-American Treaty of 1862 (Anti-Slave Trade Treaty), 106; Lincoln and Radical Republicans, 212; making of, 209–13; private diplomacy, 211–12, 215–16, 240; provisions, 211–12
Annual Register (British), 201
Anthony, Henry B., 133
Antietam, Battle of (1862): historians and

proclamation, 107; pro-South, 144; Radical Liberals, 98, 107, 114–15; read Peto, 237; reforms, 241; supports Union, 156–57; tax program, 201, 231; *Trent* affair, 77–79, 83; U.S. debt, 247. *See also* Geneva Arbitration; Gladstone, William Ewart, cabinet intervention debate

Gladstone, William Ewart, cabinet intervention debate: cabinet opposed, 107–8; cabinets, 119, 123; continues, 113, 115–16; death of intervention, 138–39; lack of justification, 95; national self-interest, 100; North, 104

Glasgow, Scotland, 168, 205
Gorchakov, Alexander Mikhailovich, 122, 254
Gordon, Nathaniel, 211
Graham, James Robert George, 15
Grant, Ulysses S.: 5, 143, 181, 193, 235–36, 246; as president, 252
Granville, 2nd earl of, 17, 23; and foreign policy, 248; as a Liberal, 206; noninterventionist, 33, 95, 103, 115, 109–110, 112, 117. *See also* Geneva Arbitration
Great Eastern, 38
Great Lakes, 174–80, 185–86
Gregory, William H., 57, 93, 143, 204
Grey, Frederick William, 213
Grey, George, 14, 17, 118, 144, 154, 166
de Grey, Lord. *See* Ripon, Earl de Grey
Grimes, James W., 131, 133, 137
Guardian (Manchester), 58
Guizot, François, 19
Gwin, William McKendree, 221

Halifax (Nova Scotia), 169, 180–81, 245
Hamilton-Gordon, Arthur, 116
Hamlin, Hannibal, 133
Hammond, Edmund, 30, 109, 185, 223
Hampton Roads Conference, 189, 198
Hancock, George, 50
Harcourt, William Vernon (Historicus), 72, 120, 154, 164–65
Harding, John, 83, 96
Hardy, Gathorne: opinion on *Trent* affair, 77
Harney, William S., 29–32
Haro Strait. *See* San Juan Island water boundary dispute
Harris, Ira, 137
Harris, Townsend, 224–25
Hautefeuille, Laurent-Basile, 57
Hawaii, 221
Hay, John, 138, 142
Henry, Fort, 90

Hensken, Henry, 225
Herald (London), 145
Holland, Henry: visit with Mercier in 1863, 205
Hong Kong, 166
Hope, James, 217
Hornby, Geoffrey Phipps. *See* San Juan Island water boundary dispute
Hotze, Henry, 58–59, 91, 161, 203
House of Commons. *See* Parliament
Howard, Jacob M., 137
Hudson's Bay Company, 29–30, 32, 38; and American expansion, 222; treaty, 157–58, 241
Hume, David, 17

Immortalité, HMS, 168
Index (London), 202
Indian Mutiny, 15
informal empire, 30, 174, 237, 241
Inland Sea (Japan), 226
intervention: antebellum policy, 104; British cabinet 3, 5, 33, 89, 95, 202; British public opinion, 100, 102–3, 116; cabinet opposition, 105, 109–11, 113; in Civil War, 25, 35; Confederate foreign policy, 6; cotton embargo, 53; and the North, 104. *See also* Gladstone, William Ewart
Ionian Islands, 107

Jackson, Andrew, 11
James Adger, 67
Jamestown, USS, 226
Japan, 2, 15, 96, 217, 222–27
Jervois, W. F. D., 178–80
Johnson, Andrew, 220, 229, 240
Johnson-Clarendon Convention, 229
Johnson, Reverdy, 252
Johnston, Joseph E., 230
Juàrez, Benito Pablo, 192, 220

Kansas, 24
Kearsarge, 96
Kenner, Duncan, 197–98
Kentucky, 90, 111
Kincardine, 12th Earl of. *See* Bruce, James
"King Corn," 197
King, Preston, 133–34
Knoxville (Tenn.), 105

Labuan: seizure of, 54–56, 89, 91
Laird rams, 96; cooperation, 165–68, 205; seizure of, 155, 159–60, 163–65, 250
Lairds, of Liverpool, 96, 144